SHINTO, NATURE AND IDEOLOGY
IN CONTEMPORARY JAPAN

Bloomsbury Shinto Studies
Series editor: Fabio Rambelli

The Shinto tradition is an essential component of Japanese religious culture. In addition to indigenous elements, it contains aspects mediated from Buddhism, Daoism, Confucianism and, in more recent times, Western religious culture as well – plus, various forms of hybridization among all of these different traditions. Despite its cultural and historical importance, Shinto studies have failed to attract wide attention also because of the lingering effects of uses of aspects of Shinto for the ultranationalistic propaganda of Japan during the Second World War. The series makes available to a broad audience a number of important texts that help to dispel the widespread misconception that Shinto is intrinsically related to Japanese nationalism, and at the same time promote further research and understanding of what is still an underdeveloped field.

Mountain Mandalas: Shugendo in Kyushu, Allan G. Grapard
The Origin of Modern Shinto in Japan:
The Vanquished Gods of Izumo, Yijiang Zhong
A Social History of the Ise Shrines, Mark Teeuwen and John Breen

SHINTO, NATURE AND IDEOLOGY IN CONTEMPORARY JAPAN

Making Sacred Forests

Aike P. Rots

BLOOMSBURY ACADEMIC
LONDON • NEW YORK • OXFORD • NEW DELHI • SYDNEY

BLOOMSBURY ACADEMIC
Bloomsbury Publishing Plc
50 Bedford Square, London, WC1B 3DP, UK
1385 Broadway, New York, NY 10018, USA

BLOOMSBURY, BLOOMSBURY ACADEMIC and the Diana logo are trademarks of
Bloomsbury Publishing Plc

First published 2017
Paperback edition first published 2019

Series design by Dani Leigh

Cover image: "Shin-to Shrine in the Woods", c.1889 (oil on panel), East, Alfred (1849–1913)/
Private Collection/Photo © The Fine Art Society, London, UK/Bridgeman Images

Bloomsbury Publishing Plc does not have any control over, or responsibility for, any
third-party websites referred to or in this book. All internet addresses given in this book
were correct at the time of going to press. The author and publisher regret
any inconvenience caused if addresses have changed or sites have ceased to exist,
but can accept no responsibility for any such changes.

A catalogue record for this book is available from the British Library.

Library of Congress Cataloging-in-Publication Data
Names: Rots, Aike P., author.
Title: Shinto, nature, and ideology in contemporary Japan:
making sacred forests / Aike P Rots.
Description: New York : Bloomsbury Academic, 2017. | Series: Bloomsbury
Shinto studies | Includes bibliographical references and index.
Identifiers: LCCN 2017005667| ISBN 9781474289931 (hh) |
ISBN 9781474289955 (epdf)
Subjects: LCSH: Shinto–Japan. | Sacred groves–Japan. | Trees–Religious
aspects–Shinto.| Shinto shrines–Japan. | Environmentalism.
Classification: LCC BL2211.G76 R68 2017 | DDC299.5/61095209051–dc23 LC record
available at https://lccn.loc.gov/2017005667

ISBN: HB: 978-1-4742-8993-1
PB: 978-1-3501-0591-1
ePDF: 978-1-4742-8995-5
ePub: 978-1-4742-8994-8

Series: Bloomsbury Shinto Studies

Typeset by Integra Software Services Pvt. Ltd.

To find out more about our authors and books visit
www.bloomsbury.com and sign up for our newsletters.

CONTENTS

LIST OF FIGURES

PREFACE

This book is the result of a long journey. My love for forests goes back to my childhood, when I spent many Sunday afternoons in the forest with my family, searching for beechnuts and blackberries. One of the first short stories I wrote was set in a deep forest. It was about a small community, isolated from the rest of the world, which had banned all weapons and polluting industries and lived in harmony with nature. Considering these early precedents, it was perhaps inevitable that one day I would write an entire book about forests. My love for Japan came a bit later: it goes back to the time when I was a teenager and spent my first weeks in the country, living with a host family, going to Japanese high school and seeing my first *matsuri*.

At some point during my stay, my friends invited me to go the cinema and watch the newest movie of a famous anime director, a certain Miyazaki Hayao. I happily joined them, and even though I could not understand most of the conversations, I was mesmerized by the story of a young girl who somehow ends up in a world inhabited by spirits, demons and deities, and has to work at a bathhouse in order to be able to rescue her parents and find her way home. One scene in particular drew my attention: a stinking demon enters the bathhouse, and the girl is given the task of washing him, which seems nearly impossible. However, with some luck and a little help from her friends, she succeeds. The demon turns out to be an ancient river god whose river is heavily polluted, and the god is trapped in the waste produced by humans until little Chihiro saves him. The scene raised many questions, and I resolved to find out more about Shinto, pollution and its relationship to environmental issues.

Spirited Away is a fictional text, inhabited by imaginary characters that are not necessarily representative of Shinto. Nevertheless, my interest had been captured. At university, I studied a wide range of topics in Japanese and religious studies, not limited to Shinto or the environment. Yet the questions remained: how does Shinto conceive of the natural environment? Can Shinto notions of pollution and purification play a part in raising environmental awareness? What is the meaning of *kami* in this respect? And how do popular images of Shinto as an ancient tradition of nature worship relate to its modern associations with nationalism and imperialism? During my MA, I wanted to write a paper about this topic. I came across many texts claiming that Shinto is a nature religion that has an important role to play in solving the environmental crisis. To my surprise, however, I could hardly find any secondary sources that engaged critically with these questions, let alone a comprehensive overview or analysis of contemporary discourse and practices. It was then that I came up with the idea to conduct this research myself.

This book is the result of several years of research on contemporary Shinto. The bulk of the ethnographic research was conducted between 2011 and 2013. During this time, I spent a total of five months in Japan in order to conduct interviews and engage in participant observation; in addition, I studied relevant texts, both academic and popular. I have continued to follow developments in Shinto since, and revisited the country twice for short periods in order to do follow-up research, in 2015 and 2016. In the meantime, some of my findings were published elsewhere (Rots 2013a,b, 2014a,b, 2015a,b,c, 2017). This book brings together and complements the different observations and arguments made in these various publications, in order to present a comprehensive overview and analysis of the reconceptualization of Shinto as a nature religion, the significance of sacred shrine forests in this discourse, and the ways in which such ideas are manifested and adapted in local shrine forest conservation projects.

There are many people who have contributed to this book. I am grateful to Mark Teeuwen, my former PhD supervisor and colleague, for his support, feedback and friendship. Working with Mark has been a pleasure, and I look forward to more collaboration in the future. I also wish to thank Reiko Abe Auestad, for all her moral and practical support during the past years; Terje Stordalen, my former second PhD supervisor, for his encouragement and helpful feedback on various theoretical topics; and John Breen, for his important suggestions and support during my time in Kyoto. In addition, I am very grateful to Satō Hiroo, for his great hospitality and practical support during my visits to Tohoku; to Nitta Hitoshi and Sakurai Haruo, who were very kind and helpful when I visited Ise; to Michael Shackleton, for sharing his experiences and visiting *chinju no mori* with me; to Nakao Isako, who kindly invited me on a shrine trip with some green activists and entrepreneurs; and to Patricia Ormsby, who introduced me to nature-related worship traditions near Mount Fuji. I am also indebted to Arne Kalland, who has given me useful advice during the early stages of my project. Sadly, he passed away in 2012, but his scholarship has been a great source of inspiration for me.

During my research, I have had the opportunity to interview and learn from a great number of people. I am particularly grateful to Araki Sōko, John Dougill, Fujinami Shōko, Fujioka Iku, Hasegawa Yasuhiro, Imaizumi Yoshiko, Iume Emi, Iwahashi Katsuji, Kamata Tōji, Kurata Katsuhiko, Paul de Leeuw, Muramatsu Teruo, Nakanishi Yoshitsugu, Sagai Tatsuru, Sakurai Takashi, Sonoda Minoru, Takahashi Tomoaki, Takeda Naoki and Ueda Masaaki for their important contributions. In addition, I wish to thank all the other shrine priests, volunteers, scientists, scholars, foresters, activists, worshippers, public relations officers and students who have kindly and patiently answered my many questions. I do not have the space to name each of them, but their contributions have been invaluable. And many thanks to Rianne Hidding and Iida Yūya, Inō Kinuko and Inō Minoru, Kurokawa Takahiro and Margarite Westra, and Yaguchi Katsuo, for their hospitality and practical support.

In the course of the past years, many people have given me helpful feedback. I am grateful to Brian Bocking and Scott Schnell, the opponents during my PhD defence in February 2014, for their inspiring questions and comments. I would also like to thank Ioannis Gaitanidis, Kim Knott, Hans Martin Krämer, Takashi Miura, Elisabetta Porcu, Arne Røkkum, James Mark Shields, Sueki Fumihiko, Sarah Thal, Notto Thelle, Jolyon Thomas, Christine Walley, Chika Watanabe and David White for reading and commenting on some of my work and/or being a paper discussant at different stages of this project. And I am grateful to my colleagues at the University of Oslo, at the Department of Culture Studies and Oriental Languages as well as in the PhD colloquium of the interfaculty research network PluRel. I have been fortunate to work in an inspiring work environment, with many kind and supportive colleagues. I also wish to thank the anonymous reviewers who have commented on my article manuscripts in recent years – their feedback has been useful for developing my arguments.

I have been able to use various libraries in the course of my research. Most importantly, I am very grateful to Naomi Yabe Magnussen from the Oslo University library, whose help in finding sources has been of great importance. I would also like to thank the staff of the International House of Japan Library and the National Diet Library for inviting me to take part in a workshop on data collection, as well as the helpful staff at other libraries I have used in the course of this research: the Kōgakkan, Kokugakuin, Tohoku and Waseda university libraries, and the library of the International Research Center for Japanese Studies (Nichibunken).

This research would not have been possible without financial support from the Faculty of Humanities, the interfaculty research network PluRel and the Department of Culture Studies and Oriental Languages at the University of Oslo, as well as the Oslo-based Institute for Comparative Research in Human Culture. During the past years, I was given the opportunity to present my research on various occasions. I wish to thank the organizers and sponsors of the IHJ Japan Specialist Workshop (Tokyo, 2011), the EAJS PhD Workshop (Käsmu, Estonia, 2011) and the Nichibunken Overseas Symposium (Copenhagen, 2012) for financing my travel costs and accommodation during these events. I am also grateful to others who have invited me to give lectures or take part in conferences or workshops: Erica Baffelli and Jane Caple (University of Manchester, 2014), Jakub Havlíček (Palacký University, Olomouc, Czech Republic, 2014), Lucia Dolce and Tatsuma Padoan (SOAS, London, 2015), the Belgian Royal Academy for Overseas Sciences (Brussels, 2016) and Shibuya Momoyo and Vladimir Tikhonov (Saitama University, 2016). Last but not least, the workshop and symposium 'What Isn't Shinto' organized by Jolyon Thomas (University of Pennsylvania, 2016) was very inspiring, and most useful for fine-tuning some of the arguments made in this book.

I am most grateful to series editor Fabio Rambelli and the staff at Bloomsbury Academic for their trust in my project. Lucy Carroll and Lalle Pursglove have been very supportive throughout the process, and Manikandan Kuppan and his team have done a great job copyediting this work. I also wish to thank the Alliance of Religions and Conservation and the Brooklyn Botanic Garden, who have kindly given me permission to use their photos. All other pictures used in this book are my own.

Finally, I do not think I could have pursued an academic career and written this book without the support of my family. I am deeply grateful to my parents, who took us to the forest on Sunday afternoons to search for beechnuts and blackberries, who supported my wish to go to Japan as a teenager, and who have always encouraged me to follow my dreams. Most importantly, my heartfelt thanks to Nhung and Anne Xuân, for teaching me what matters most. Your love and support has been truly invaluable.

NOTE ON STYLE

Japanese terms are written according to the common Hepburn transcription method. Long vowels are indicated by a macron, except for common geographical names (Tokyo, Osaka, Kyoto, Tohoku, Ryukyu and so on) and words that have been incorporated into English (e.g. 'Shinto' instead of '*shintō*'). Japanese and other names are written in the standard fashion (i.e. family name followed by given name), with the exception of names that are normally written the opposite way.

I do not use Japanese script in the main text, unless necessary to convey the meaning of a particular argument. Japanese concepts are written in italics. The meaning of most of these concepts will be explained when they are introduced. Japanese script is provided for terms listed in the index.

There are several trees and other species mentioned in the text. To avoid confusion, I have chosen to refer to them mostly by their Japanese names, as the common English translations are not always botanically correct (for instance, *futaba aoi* is commonly translated as hollyhock, but it is actually a species of wild ginger). For clarity's sake, when I first mention a tree or plant species, I also give the scientific name.

JAPANESE HISTORICAL PERIODS

Jōmon period	Ca. 14000 BCE–300 BCE
Yayoi period	Ca. 300 BCE–250 CE
Kofun period	Ca. 250–592
Asuka period	592–710
Nara period	710–794
Heian period	794–1185
Kamakura period	1185–1333
Muromachi period	1336–1573
Azuchi-Momoyama period	1573–1603
Edo period	1603–1868
Meiji period	1868–1912
Taishō period	1912–1926
Shōwa period	1926–1989
Heisei period	1989–present

Chapter 1

INTRODUCTION

The Power of Ise

On 26 May 2016, Ise Jingū welcomed a group of unusual visitors. On this day, the leaders of the G7 visited Ise's Inner Shrine, widely considered as one of the most sacred sites in Japan. The presidents (or, in some cases, prime ministers) of Canada, France, Germany, Italy, Japan, the United Kingdom and the United States, as well as those of the European Council and European Parliament, collectively paid a visit to this famous shrine.[1] In addition to viewing the shrine and enjoying its 'solemn and majestic atmosphere', they all participated in a tree-planting ceremony, together with twenty elementary school students and the governor of Mie Prefecture, where Ise is located (Ministry of Foreign Affairs of Japan 2016). Afterwards, they discussed matters related to international trade, security, foreign policy and climate change at their annual summit, which took place at a nearby resort.

Although they did not engage in worship activities, the visit of the G7 leaders to Ise was of profound symbolic significance. The two shrines of Ise have played a central part in the development of modern Shinto and were deeply embedded in the imperial-national ideology that was developed during the Meiji period (Breen 2015). Ise's Outer Shrine (Gekū) is dedicated to the goddess Toyouke-Ōmikami, who is associated with rice cultivation – which, not coincidentally, became an important marker of national identity during the modern period (Gluck 1985: 178–203; Ohnuki-Tierney 1993). The Inner Shrine (Naikū), meanwhile, is home to Amaterasu-Ōmikami: the sun goddess, believed to be the divine ancestress of the imperial lineage. According to Shinto-nationalist mythology, the modern emperor is a direct descendant of the mythical first emperor, Jinmu, who is believed to have founded Japan in the seventh century BCE. Jinmu was the great-grandson of the god Ninigi-no-Mikoto, who was the grandson of Amaterasu. Thus, the site where the sun goddess is enshrined is intimately connected with notions of the imperial institution as divinely ordained. Today, the Ise shrines are typically framed as essentially apolitical vestiges of ancient Japanese tradition, characterized by harmony with nature and supposedly unchanging ritual practices (Inata 2009; Public Affairs Headquarters for Shikinen-Sengu 2010). In reality, however, they have been closely intertwined with politics throughout their history and are subject to continuous re-signification and change (Breen 2016; Breen & Teeuwen 2017; Rambelli 2014). As a site deeply associated with the nation, imperial power and natural environment of Japan, Ise remains of great ideological significance today.

Prime Minister Abe Shinzō is well aware of the symbolic capital provided by the Ise shrines.[2] For him, Ise is the prime manifestation of Japan's 'traditional culture' (*dentō bunka*), allegedly characterized by social harmony, unique aesthetics and a patriotic love of the country. In reality, much of what today counts as 'traditional' or 'ancient' – including the 'love of nature' supposedly expressed in ritual and (agri)cultural practices at Ise – goes back to nineteenth- and early twentieth-century myth-making and was part of the modern nation-building project. To Abe and his allies, however, Ise is a unique manifestation of 'the ancient Japanese spirit' and of core importance for the continuation of the imperial institution – and, by extension, the well-being of the nation as a whole. Significantly, Abe was the first prime minister since the end of the Second World War who participated in a major ceremony at Ise: he took part in the 2013 *shikinen sengū* ceremony, which consists of the rebuilding of the shrines and ritual removal of the deities to their new homes once every twenty years. Abe's participation constituted a major change in state-religion relations and a profound reinterpretation of post-war Japanese secularism. Since 1945, political patronage of religious institutions has been rare, as the Constitution prohibits state support of religion (Breen 2010a). By taking part in such a major shrine ceremony, however, Abe has successfully contributed to the reshaping of state-religion boundaries and to the reconfiguration of Shinto as a 'public' worship tradition (Breen & Teeuwen 2017; Rots 2017).

Thus, the choice to invite the leaders of the other G7 countries to visit the shrines of Ise was highly political indeed. One of the core symbols of the nation's unity, uniqueness and divine character, Ise plays a central part in Abe's ideology; international recognition of Ise's importance was expected to provide him with legitimacy, domestically as well as internationally. Significantly, Abe is currently involved in a lengthy and controversial political process to change the Japanese Constitution, including Article 9, which denounces Japan's sovereign right to engage in war with other countries. In addition, he is actively trying to recommence Japan's nuclear energy project, while stimulating the export of Japanese nuclear technology to foreign countries (Kingston 2016). As he is pushing forward these controversial projects, Abe seeks to gain legitimacy by advocating romantic-nationalist notions of Japan as a sacred country with a unique traditional culture, as embodied by Ise.

Abe's choice to invite his colleagues on a visit to Ise Jingū illustrates one of the core arguments of this book: Shinto plays a central part in contemporary Japanese politics and ideology, perhaps more so than at any time since the end of the Second World War. In the imagination of Abe and his allies, shrines are intimately connected with the nation as a whole, as well as the physical landscape of the Japanese isles. Correspondingly, as this book demonstrates, they have also come to be associated with notions of 'nature' and 'environmental sustainability'. Ideologically speaking, Abe is very close to the conservative shrine establishment and associated lobby groups, which promote a view of Shinto as the ancient, 'public' worship tradition of Japan, intimately connected with the sacred land and imperial family (Breen 2010b; Rots 2015a, 2017). Influential organizations include Jinja Honchō (Association of Shinto Shrines), with which the majority of shrines in Japan are affiliated and which functions as Shinto's *de facto* central authority; Shintō Seiji Renmei (Shinto Association of Spiritual Leadership), Jinja Honchō's political arm, which maintains close links with a large number of MPs from Abe's party LDP; and Nippon Kaigi (Japan Conference), a right-wing umbrella organization that brings together a number of nationalist groups, both religious and secular, as well as several leading politicians – including Abe and most of his cabinet. As several scholars have demonstrated, these groups maintain close links with each other (Guthmann 2010, 2017; Mizohata 2016; Mullins 2012, 2016; Narusawa 2016).

Abe was not the first to discover the symbolic capital of Ise and invite foreign dignitaries to the shrine as a means to acquire legitimacy and promote Shinto internationally. In June 2014, Jinja Honchō organized a large interreligious conference in Ise, titled 'Tradition for the Future: Culture, Faith and Values for a Sustainable Planet', where various issues related to religion and environmental issues were discussed (Kōshitsu Henshūbu 2014; Rots 2015a). The conference was organized in cooperation with the Alliance of Religions and Conservation (ARC), a UK-based non-profit organization that defines itself as 'a secular body that helps the major religions of the world to develop their own environmental programmes, based on their own core teachings, beliefs and practices' (ARC n.d.-a). It was attended by representatives of various religious organizations from all over the world, affiliated with Buddhism, Confucianism, Daoism, Hinduism, Islam, Roman Catholicism, Sikhism, Shinto and various Protestant denominations. In addition to discussing matters related to religion and environmental sustainability, they collectively paid their respects to the sun goddess.[3] They were accompanied by representatives of the United Nations and international NGOs, as well as approximately 700 Shinto priests from all over the country (Dougill 2014) and a number of carefully selected journalists. One of them, Paul Vallely (a well-known author who has written several books and articles on religion, ethics and development issues) published a report in *The Independent*, in which he described the conference as part of the 'remarkable resurgence of Japan's ancient religion of Shintoism', which, according to him, 'has produced a new Japanese openness to the wider world'. This openness was illustrated by the event's interreligious character, as well as the apparent environmental awareness of the actors involved, which, he suggested, 'could benefit the whole world' (Vallely 2014).

One of the keynote speakers was the assistant secretary general of the United Nations Development Program, Olav Kjørven. His participation is significant for several reasons. Internationally, Shinto has long been associated with Japanese imperialism, as it played a central part in the ideological state apparatus prior to 1945 (Hardacre 1989). After the war, it received little international scholarly attention, and organizations such as Jinja Honchō showed no interest in establishing international connections. In the last two decades or so, this has changed. The organization of a large academic conference on 'Shinto and Ecology' at Harvard University in 1997 was a first step towards the 'internationalization' of Shinto, bringing together some leading scholars in the field and a number of Shinto priests – some of whom would continue to play an important part in the movement to redefine Shinto as a 'green religion', as we shall see (Jinja Honchō 2000). The establishment of the International Shinto Foundation in 1994 was also significant in this respect; even though this organization is not associated with Jinja Honchō and does not represent the majority of shrines in Japan, it did contribute to Shinto's increased visibility abroad, as well as the association between Shinto and environmental issues (e.g. International Shinto Foundation 2000).

    Jinja Honchō's attempts to present Shinto in a positive light internationally are of a more recent date, more or less coinciding with the presidency of Tanaka Tsunekiyo, which started in 2010. It is illustrated by the establishment of a small department for international PR within Jinja Honchō's main office, the development of a professional English-language website and related glossy publications (e.g. Public Affairs Headquarters for Shikinen-Sengu 2013), and the intensification of cooperation with ARC, which led to the organization of the conference of 2014. Although it has been argued that 'internationalization' primarily serves the purpose of acquiring more legitimacy domestically (Isomae & Jang 2012: 1081), these developments have undeniably contributed to changes within religious practices and self-understandings, as well as global perceptions of Shinto.[4]

    In any case, the fact that a leading UN diplomat delivers a keynote speech at a conference in Ise illustrates that, to many at least, Shinto has lost its strong connotations with pre-war imperialism. Instead, today it is widely perceived and promoted as an ancient 'nature religion' offering solutions for living sustainably. Moreover, Kjørven's contribution illustrates another important trend: the UN and related organizations (such as UNESCO and UNDP) have embraced the notion that religions can play a central role in countering environmental degradation and climate change, and they are actively cooperating with religious actors on these issues.[5] Kjørven, for instance, advocates the idea that religion has the potential to play a significant role in sustainable development. In his conference speech, which was later published online, he argued that 'spiritual capital' is of profound importance for achieving sustainable development and that religious institutions are crucial for mobilizing people to live in harmony with the environment (Kjørven 2014).

    Not surprisingly, then, the UNDP is one of ARC's secular partners, as are the World Bank and the World Wildlife Fund, all of which apparently perceive religious organizations as potential allies when it comes to nature conservation and sustainable development. Likewise, organizations such as UNESCO and IUCN (International Union for Conservation of Nature) actively cooperate with religious actors, based on the assumption that 'sacred sites' constitute important natural and cultural resources that are in need of protection (Palmer & Finlay 2003; Schaaf & Lee 2006). Such practices are sanctioned by scientific initiatives to study sacred sites for the purpose of biodiversity conservation, exemplified by research projects at the universities of Oxford and Zürich.[6] As this book illustrates,

Figure 1.1 Representatives of different religions cross the Uji bridge into the Inner Shrine during the interreligious conference 'Tradition for the Future', Ise Jingū, June 2014. Photo: ARC/Alexander Mercer (Valley Foundation).

these developments have provided various religious organizations with new opportunities for acquiring legitimacy, locally, domestically and internationally. They have also provided environmental activists with powerful symbolic resources, which can be employed to serve conservationist agendas.

The Religious Environmentalist Paradigm

Jinja Honchō is by no means the only religious organization that has professed a concern with environmental issues. The Ise conference is illustrative of one of the most significant recent developments in religion worldwide: the association of religious beliefs, practices and places with environmental ethics, nature conservation and the fight against climate change. For instance, Pope Francis' encyclical letter *Laudato Si'*, published in May 2015, contains a passionate plea for a global awakening to the reality of the ecological crises we are facing and calls for corresponding policy changes (Francis 2015).[7] Subsequently, 2015 saw the publication of official statements on climate change by groups of Muslim, Buddhist and Jewish leaders, all of whom called upon world leaders to reach to a meaningful agreement at the UN Climate Change Conference in Paris.[8] In addition, there have been a number of interfaith statements on the issue, likewise urging world leaders to prevent further climate change.[9] Thus, religious leaders are among today's most vocal advocates of implementing sustainable policies. In this respect, 2015 was a particularly significant year, as it saw global collaboration and political outreach by religious leaders on an unprecedented scale.

Although the scale of action was unprecedented, the association of religion with environmental issues is not new. The attribution of sacred qualities to 'nature', however conceptualized, is a defining characteristic in the oeuvre of well-known nineteenth-century American transcendentalists such as Ralph Waldo Emerson (1803–1882) and Henry David Thoreau (1817–1862) and can be traced back to European Romanticism, in particular to the work of Jean-Jacques Rousseau (1712–1778). In twentieth-century Western thought, the development of religious environmentalism is attributed to scholars such as Aldo Leopold (1887–1948), who developed modern ecological notions and environmental ethics; Arne Næss (1912–2009), seen as the founder of the deep ecology movement, a holistic philosophy based on an understanding of all beings as interconnected and interdependent; and James Lovelock (1919–), who is famous for the Gaia hypothesis, which conceives of the entire planet Earth as a single living organism (Gottlieb 2006; Lovelock [1979] 2000; Næss [1973] 1995; Taylor 2010).

Although Romantic and religious notions of nature as sacred predate modern times, environmental issues did not gain widespread attention until the early 1970s. It was around this time that the Club of Rome published its well-known report *The Limits to Growth* (Meadows et al. 1972), the first international Earth Day was organized, and awareness of resource depletion and pollution spread. Correspondingly, 'religion' came to be strongly associated not only with notions of 'nature' and 'wilderness' as sacred but also with 'the environment', which was conceived on a global scale and believed to be in a state of crisis (Macnaghten & Urry 1998). In response, religion was reinterpreted as a possible resource for establishing sustainable environmental ethics and tackling environmental problems. On the other hand, it was also blamed for some of these problems, as in the case of historian Lynn White's famous argument that the contemporary global environmental crisis was partly due to Judeo-Christian notions of man's divinely ordained domination over nature (1967). White's essay is one of the foundational texts of what anthropologist Poul Pedersen has called 'the religious environmentalist paradigm': the 'appeal to traditional, religious ideas and values' (Pedersen 1995: 258) for tackling environmental problems and the association of religion with environmental ethics.

It is no exaggeration to state that the religious environmentalist paradigm has greatly affected some religious organizations' practices and self-definitions. It should be pointed out, however, that this is not merely the result of the incorporation of environmentalist discourse by religious actors. In fact, one of the defining features of this development is the active collaboration between academia, civil society and religious organizations. One reason why the religious environmentalist paradigm has acquired such prominence and legitimatory power is the fact that it has been sanctioned by leading academic institutions. Of profound significance was Harvard University's series of large-scale international conferences on 'Religions of the World and Ecology' in the mid-1990s, which brought together leading scholars in the field as well as religious actors. The series was organized by John

Grim and Mary Evelyn Tucker, scholars of religion specialized in Native American traditions and Confucianism respectively, who would later establish the Forum on Religion and Ecology at Yale University. Most of the edited volumes with conference proceedings have achieved the status of modern classics in the study of religion and the environment. There are volumes on Buddhism, Christianity, Confucianism, Daoism, Hinduism, Islam, Jainism, Judaism and indigenous traditions, all based on the respective conferences. They present a plethora of voices on the topic, including 'etic' as well as 'emic' perspectives (e.g. Girardot, Miller & Liu 2001; Tucker & Berthrong 1998; Tucker & Williams 1997).

The association of religion and environmental issues is not merely ideological, however. While academic practices and religious identity politics are of great significance, they are not the full story. As I have mentioned above, recent years have seen a growing interest not only in religious cosmologies and belief systems as resources for environmental ethics but also in so-called sacred sites as places of ecological importance. Indeed, the proliferation of the religious environmentalist paradigm may have been one of the factors behind the re-appreciation of 'space' in the study of religion and the corresponding focus on topics such as place-making, territoriality and sacralization (e.g. Chidester & Linenthal 1995a; Gill 1998; Knott 2005; Tweed 2006). Moreover, it has provided religious actors and environmental activists throughout the world with significant symbolic capital, which can be employed for protecting or reclaiming certain contested sites for ritual purposes. There are numerous cases of activists who have tactically employed notions of nature as animated, sacred and/or divine in order to prevent the destruction of natural environments, sometimes successfully (e.g. Chidester & Linenthal 1995b: 3–4, 21–22; Darlington 2012; Duara 2015: 40–44; Kent 2013).

Thus, the religious environmentalist paradigm is concerned with physical space as much as it is about ethics and identity. Japan is no exception: as this study will demonstrate, sacred shrine groves (*chinju no mori*) play a central part in contemporary Shinto practices and ideology, not only as symbolic resources but also, importantly, as real-life physical locations, the shapes and uses of which are closely intertwined with both sociocultural practices and natural environments. This study, therefore, is concerned with physicality, place-making and other spatial practices, as much as with more abstract ideological issues related to the formation of the categories 'Shinto' and 'nature'. Accordingly, it draws on a number of theoretical insights on the production of (sacred) space, which I will briefly introduce in the next section.

Rethinking Sacred Space

It has been argued that 'the investigation of spatiality and religion has a long history' (Corrigan 2009: 157). In particular, 'sacred space' has long been a core category in the academic study of religion, occupying a central place in the theories of Émile Durkheim and Mircea Eliade, which long enjoyed paradigmatic status in the field.[10] Until recently, however, most studies of sacred space produced within religious studies focused on the historical and symbolic significance of particular 'religious sites', but did not address other aspects of spatiality such as landscape construction, territoriality, spatial practices and conflicting land claims (Knott 2005: 2; cf. Chidester & Linenthal 1995b; Gill 1998). Despite the abundance of academic and popular discourse on 'sacred places', therefore, there has been little critical reflection on ways in which those places are constructed, contested and transformed, let alone on the territorial and identity politics implicit in sacralization processes – that is, the processes by which certain sites *become* sacred. Thus, until recently, few scholarly discussions of so-called 'sacred places' took into consideration issues related to (competing) territorial claims, land value, property rights and so on – the realization, in brief, that 'sacred space is contested space' (Knott 2005: 99) and that it has economic value.

One of the first studies that approached the topic from this angle was David Chidester and Edward Linenthal's groundbreaking anthology of sacralization and contested space in the United States, which contains a number of important theoretical insights and case studies (1995a). In their introduction, they describe sacred space as follows:

> Sacred space is inevitably contested space, a site of negotiated contests over the legitimate ownership of sacred symbols. (…) Since no sacred space is merely 'given' in the world, its ownership will always be at stake. In this respect, a sacred space is not merely discovered, or founded, or constructed; it is claimed, owned, and operated by people advancing specific interests. (…) Sacred places are arenas in which power relations can be reinforced, in which relations between insiders and outsiders, rulers and subjects, elders and juniors, males and females, and so on, can be adjudicated. But those power relations are always resisted. Sacred places are always highly charged sites for contested negotiations over the ownership of the symbolic capital (or symbolic real estate) that signifies power relations. (1995b: 15–16)

Thanks to the work of scholars such as Chidester and Linenthal, awareness of the spatial dimensions of religious practice, and of the contested nature of sacred space, has spread. In accordance with the increasing focus on materiality and physical embodiment in religion (e.g. Houtman & Meyer 2012), recent years have seen an emerging scholarly interest in spatial issues, not only in the study of religions but also in the humanities more generally. In the words of Edward Soja, 'a growing community of scholars and citizens has, for perhaps the first time, begun to think about the *spatiality* of human life in much the same way that we have persistently approached life's intrinsic and richly revealing historical and social qualities: its *historicality* and *sociality*' (1996: 2, emphasis in original). This new interest in spatiality in the humanities has been referred to by the term 'spatial turn' (Warf & Arias 2009). Arguably, it constitutes a promising intellectual trend: topics such as physical embodiment, spatial terminology and metaphors, globalization and glocalization, the natural environment, maps and other representations of space, landscape construction and so on are of great relevance for the study of culture and religion, far transcending the theories and methods traditionally associated with the academic discipline geography. As such, the spatial turn creates new opportunities for research that has the potential of overcoming disciplinary and other category boundaries:

> Space can serve as a window into different disciplines, a means of shedding light on what separates and what unites them. Because so many lines of thought converge on the topic of spatiality, space is a vehicle for examining what it means to be interdisciplinary or multidisciplinary, to cross the borders and divides that have organized the academic division of labor, to reveal the cultures that pervade different fields of knowledge, and to bring these contrasting lines of thought into a productive engagement with one another. (2009: 2)

Religious place-making is often central to issues related to the division of power and land control, even (or especially) when not recognized as such. Therefore, following Kim Knott (2005), I would like to suggest that we look at sacralization and related place-making practices from the perspective of spatial theory, borrowing from the works of philosophers such as Henri Lefebvre ([1974] 1991) and Michel de Certeau (1984), as well as critical geographers such as Edward Soja (1996), Doreen Massey (1994) and David Harvey (2000). One crucial thing their works teach us is that space is never politically neutral: land is *possessed* and *exploited* by certain people; it represents a certain economic value (dependent upon geographical conditions, production processes and access to natural resources); and it is often contested, with different actors and parties laying claim to it. Mapping territory therefore is more than simply the construction of mental representations and cosmologies, detached from lived space: mapping can be an act of legitimation or appropriation, a strategy for asserting or challenging control over land and resources, which is highly political.

Sacralization, likewise, can be used strategically, in order to establish and preserve the authority of certain regimes of power.[11] After all, 'religions are central to the operations of knowledge and power, having historically been both institutionally and ideologically dominant' (Knott 2005: 27); in modern times, they have been complicit in the capitalist production of space (Lefebvre [1974] 1991: 44). On the other hand, sacralization may also be employed as a tactic for subverting authority; for example, when a place of worship becomes a site of resistance against totalitarianism, exploitation or environmental destruction – a site of protest and creative re-appropriation, or 'thirdspace', in Soja's terminology (1996).

For instance, in an interesting recent study of sacralization and contested space in India, Eliza Kent discusses how environmental activists in Tamil Nadu have joined forces with village communities in order to protect sacred groves, thus preventing their destruction (Kent 2013). Likewise, as we have seen, 'sacred sites' worldwide have captured the attention of conservationists, environmental scientists and indigenous rights activists, which has led to new coalitions of local actors and activists trying to resist construction projects, mining and other types of exploitation, with varying degrees of success (Klein 2014; Pungetti, Oviedo & Hooke 2012). This does not mean that the conservation of sacred natural sites is always tactical and subversive in nature and necessarily opposed to the interests of powerful elites: as this study will demonstrate, Shinto shrine groves have been appropriated as ideological resources by influential conservative and corporate actors in Japan, who advocate small-scale forest conservation at selected sites without seriously engaging with more profound environmental challenges. It does illustrate, however, that sacred sites possess profound symbolic capital, which can be employed for various purposes, and that the sacralization of landscapes continues to be a potentially effective strategy (or tactic) for laying claim to a certain territory.

In my understanding of the sacralization of space, I am particularly informed by the theories of the French Marxist philosopher Henri Lefebvre (1905–1991). Lefebvre's well-known work *La production de l'espace*, translated as *The Production of Space* (Lefebvre [1974] 1991), is arguably one of the most important theoretical reflections upon space in modernity: it has contributed significantly to present-day understandings of space as, first, historically produced and negotiated, and second, politically and ideologically embedded. In this work, Lefebvre is not only concerned with the question 'what *is* space' but also, more important, with the processes by which different kinds of space (have) come into being; that is, the processes by which they are produced and the conditions of their production.

'Space', Lefebvre argued, is a multilayered concept, containing a number of dimensions (or 'fields', as he called them). His purpose was to develop a theory that takes into account and brings together these different types of space: he wanted 'to discover or construct a theoretical unity between "fields" which are apprehended separately (…). The fields we are concerned with are, first, the *physical* – nature, the Cosmos; secondly, the *mental*, including logical and formal abstractions; and, thirdly, the *social*' ([1974] 1991: 11; italics in original). Thus, space is not merely a physical category; it is also mental (i.e. spaces are *imagined* and *conceived of*) and *social* (i.e. spaces are contingent upon, and shape, social relations; social relations, meanwhile, are spatially embedded). Thus, a Lefebvrean approach to space is inherently transdisciplinary, as it attempts to overcome the conventional categorization between the natural, human and social sciences. Its argument is that, while space can be simultaneously physical, mental and social, these different fields are interdependent and mutually constitutive, and any study of space should take all of them into consideration.[12]

The sacralization of space, then, is a multifaceted process, leading to the transformation of 'physical' as well as 'mental' and 'social' space. It has a strong discursive component, yet the discursive construction of sacredness usually goes together with spatial practices, such as physical demarcation, ritualized movement (e.g. pilgrimage), and the construction of buildings designed for worship, by which particular locales are produced and reproduced as 'sacred sites'. Whereas such places may have originally been chosen because of their unusual physical characteristics (e.g. a waterfall, mountain or peculiar tree), they were transformed and integrated into sociopolitical networks by means of sacralization processes.

Indeed, it may be argued that it is exactly *because* they were set apart as 'sacred' that these places are politically relevant. In the words of Lefebvre:

> *Absolute space* [i.e., sacred space] was made up of fragments of nature located at sites which were chosen for their intrinsic qualities (cave, mountaintop, spring, river), but whose very consecration ended up by stripping them of their natural characteristics and uniqueness. Thus natural space was soon populated by political forces. Typically, architecture picked a site in nature and transferred it to the political realm by means of a symbolic mediation; one thinks, for example, of the statues of local gods and goddesses in Greek temples, or of the Shintoist's sanctuary, empty or else containing nothing but a mirror. (...) The absolute space where rites and ceremonies were performed retained a number of aspects of nature, albeit in a form modified by ceremonial requirements: age, sex, genitality (fertility) – all still had a part to play. At once civil and religious, absolute space thus preserved and incorporated bloodlines, family, unmediated relationships – but it transformed them to the city, to the political state. (Lefebvre [1974] 1991: 48)

As Lefebvre points out, the sacralization of 'natural space' leads to its transformation and its appropriation for political purposes. Importantly, then, the sacred is not opposed to politics and society; on the contrary, *it is one of their foundational categories.*[13] Following Lefebvre, we may argue that it was through the rituals enacted at such sacred places that social relations were sanctioned, and that gender and class differences were divinely legitimized. Thus, sacred places are profoundly political, even if they are physically and discursively set apart from everyday life. They constitute an integral part of the wider spatial configurations that shape and condition the ways in which we live, work, consume and reproduce, as well as the power relations embedded in them. This applies to Shinto's sacred forests as much as to other places of worship.

Sacralization and Secularization in Japan

It is important to emphasize that the term 'sacred' should not be seen as the equivalent of 'religious'. This is well illustrated by Chidester and Linenthal in their aforementioned anthology of studies of sacred places in the United States (1995a), which is not only concerned with sites and practices that are commonly classified as 'religious' (e.g. Christian home-making) but also with the sacralization of sites associated with war memory (e.g. Pearl Harbor and the Holocaust Memorial Museum), nation-building (e.g. Mount Rushmore) and the natural environment (e.g. Native American and neo-pagan conceptualizations of natural sites as 'sacred'). Thus, their work demonstrates convincingly that 'sacred' does not equal 'religious', and that secular sites such as memorials may be subjected to sacralization without being associated with particular religious institutions or worship traditions. This observation is of particular significance for Japan as well, where certain sites and symbols may be subjected to sacralization – that is, set apart as special and non-negotiable, by means of discourse, spatial demarcation and ritual practice – without being classified as 'religious'. The imperial institution is a prime example, but similar attempts are made to dissociate Shinto shrines such as Ise and Yasukuni from the category 'religion', while simultaneously increasing their status as 'sacred sites' of public significance (Rots 2017).

Sacralization has been defined as 'the process by which the secular becomes sacred or other new forms of the sacred emerge, whether in matters of personal faith, institutional practice or political power' (Demerath 2007: 66). In other words, it refers to the production and reproduction of 'the sacred' in public. The term 'sacred', then, refers to objects, places and practices that are perceived as non-negotiable; that are set apart from the ordinary, physically as well as discursively; and that are believed to possess certain eternal qualities, that is, that are believed to transcend historical particularities (cf. Anttonen 2000; Chidester & Linenthal 1995b; Knott 2005). Sacredness is neither intrinsic nor permanent: it is produced, maintained, contested and reinvented by means of discursive, spatial and ritual practices (cf. Smith 1987). In this study, 'sacralization' refers primarily to the processes by which 'sacred space' is produced; that is, the practices by which certain places are set apart as non-negotiable.

Thus, importantly, 'sacralization' is not opposed to 'secularization', and does not necessarily imply some sort of religious revival. In fact, the opposite may be the case: sacralization may be a response to secularization processes and can go hand in hand with the decline of particular religious institutions, beliefs and practices. This certainly applies to contemporary Japanese society, which is characterized by multiple processes of secularization, but also by new types of sacralization. As José Casanova has explained, the term 'secularization' refers to three interrelated yet different societal processes: 'the decline of religious beliefs and practices' (which, he adds, 'is the most recent but by now the most widespread usage of the term in contemporary academic debates on secularization'); 'the privatization of religion'; and 'the differentiation of the secular spheres (state, economy, science)' from religion (2006: 7; cf. Casanova 1994). Casanova's conceptual triad was developed further by Charles Taylor, who distinguished between secularization as, first, 'the retreat of religion in public life' (i.e. privatization); second, 'the decline in belief and practice'; and third, 'the change in the conditions of belief' (2007: 423). These are also referred to as, respectively, 'political secularization', 'social secularization' and 'cultural secularization' (2007: 2–3).

The last type of secularization is particularly relevant for Taylor's theory and constitutes his main contribution to earlier theories. For Taylor, the defining feature of secular modernity is not so much the absence or decline of religion, but rather the fact that sociopolitical structures are no longer in need of religious legitimation: our 'secular age' is characterized by an 'immanent frame', that is, an episteme that no longer requires a transcendent point of reference. Religious affiliation and belief, as a consequence, is no longer a pre-given, but has become *optional*. In other words, religion continues to be relevant for numerous individuals and institutions, but it has lost its former self-evidence; in a secular age, religion is but one option among others, including atheism and religious non-affiliation.[14] Although Taylor explicitly limited his historical analysis to 'North Atlantic' or 'Western' civilization, shaped by the legacy of 'Latin Christendom' (2007: 15), his analysis of the formation of this secular age – the 'expansion of cognitive horizons' that has led to a change in the *conditions* of religious belief and practice – arguably also applies to modern Asian societies.

For instance, drawing on Taylor, Richard Madsen has shown convincingly that rapid urbanization, increasing economic diversification and societal differentiation in Asia have created societies in which religion has not disappeared – quite the contrary – but where the *conditions* of religious participation have changed significantly (Madsen 2011). That is, in modern Asian urban centres, participation in a particular worship tradition is no longer a pre-given but becomes a matter of personal choice. In such a plural religious environment, religious revitalization movements that are explicitly anti-plural (i.e. 'fundamentalist') can thrive. Paradoxically, these movements are popular by virtue of the immediate presence of religious and non-religious Others in relation to which they define themselves. While some choose to join such movements, others are opting for religious non-affiliation and/or construct their identity in non-religious terms.

Thus, in Taylorian terms, one could argue that Asian societies have entered a 'secular age' different from, yet comparable to, the Western 'secular age'. This 'secular age' paradoxically is characterized by new types of religious practice, mobilization and identity construction, some of which are strongly politicized and constitute a potential threat to the stability of the secular state and its apparatus. Put differently, in a secular age, new ideologies and practices may emerge, some of which may challenge secular political configurations and reclaim aspects of the public sphere. However, they are but one option among several, including nationalism and non-religious subcultures. This is the situation in Japan as well as many other modern nation-states, in Asia and beyond.

Sacralization, then, can have different shapes: it can be 'religious' (e.g. the return of 'sacred' religious symbols and ideology in the public sphere), or it can be 'secular' (e.g. the sacralization of nationalist symbols or natural environments). It can go hand in hand with the 'deprivatization of religion'; that is, beliefs and practices previously classified as 'religious' (i.e. private) can acquire new significance and be repositioned in the public sphere, becoming some sort of 'sacred secular'. This appears to be the case in India, a politically secular state, which has seen the resurgence of Hindu nationalism and a corresponding 'sacralization' of the public sphere (e.g. Sharma 2012). Likewise, as Mark Mullins has demonstrated (2012), Japan has seen the 'deprivatization' of Shinto sites and symbols, in particular those associated with the imperial institution and war memory (e.g. Yasukuni Jinja), and the increasing interference of Shinto-related lobby organizations such as the aforementioned Shintō Seiji Renmei with political decision-making.

The deprivatization of Shinto, I argue, goes hand in hand with what I have called its 'discursive secularization' (Rots 2017). I use this term to refer to processes by which beliefs, practices and institutions previously classified as 'religion' are redefined and reconfigured (by many of the leading actors involved) as 'culture', 'tradition', 'heritage', 'science' or even 'nature'; in sum, as non-religion. Importantly, discursive secularization does *not* necessarily imply the decline of faith in supernatural beings, ritual activities, or places of worship. Indeed, as this study will demonstrate, gods and rituals remain central to contemporary Shinto practice and ideology, even if they are not conceptualized as 'religious' in emic discourse. It does mean that those gods and rituals acquire new meanings in a changing context, as they are dissociated from the master category 'religion' (*shūkyō*), which in Japan has come to be contaminated quite severely, to the point that few people or institutions are willing to identify with it (Baffelli & Reader 2012).

Thus, discursive secularization does not equal the decline of religion. While it is undeniably true that a number of religious institutions (e.g. Buddhist temples) are experiencing difficulties, and quantitative survey data point to a gradual decline in 'religious belief', scholars disagree on whether these developments should be seen as evidence of nationwide religious decline (e.g. Nelson 2012; Reader 2012). Arguably, the fact that some beliefs and practices (e.g. Buddhist funeral rites) in Japan lose some of their former popularity does not necessarily prove that religion *in general* is disappearing from society.[15] As a matter of fact, new popular devotional practices continue to emerge, such as the so-called 'powerspot boom', which has led to a renewed interest in some places of worship in recent years (Rots 2014b: 41–45; N. Suga 2010). Meanwhile, some religious institutions have successfully redefined themselves in terms of 'heritage' or 'traditional culture', drawing new groups of visitors (Rots 2015b: 134–135).

Importantly, then, discursive secularization may be a strategy for survival employed by religious actors. Simply put, reframing shrine or temple worship as 'traditional culture' instead of 'religion' can be a means to attract more visitors. Significantly, in the Japanese secularist legal system, it is also a strategy to attract corporate and state sponsors. As illustrated by some of the cases discussed in this book, discursive secularization is a common tactic employed by Shinto shrine actors, for instance, for negotiating legal restrictions on receiving public funding or on religious education. Such attempts at institutional redefinition are often combined with claims regarding the essentially 'public' nature of Shinto shrines, as embodied by the *chinju no mori*, which have come to be conceptualized as traditional 'community centres' both physically and metaphorically (e.g. Tanaka 2011; cf. Rots 2015a, 2017). I will return to this topic later.

Notes on Methodology

The main focus of this study are the discursive and spatial practices centred on 'sacred shrine forests' (*chinju no mori*) in contemporary Japan, and the concurrent reconceptualization of Shinto in relation to 'nature' and 'the environment', which will be analysed in its social, historical and ideological context. As I will demonstrate, these shrine forests take centre stage in contemporary Shinto ideology and conservation practices. Therefore, I argue, they can serve as prisms through which to study a wide range of topics, ranging from urban planning and landscape design to shrine ritual and mythology, from education and community-building to nationalism and religious politics, and from forest ecology and botany to environmental history and archaeology. Not surprisingly, the existing Japanese anthologies and journals in the field of 'sacred forest studies' have a strong interdisciplinary character, combining articles that approach their topic matter from completely different disciplinary angles (e.g. Ueda & Ueda 2001; M. Ueda 2004c).[16]

In this context, it is worth recalling Warf and Arias' claim that spatial approaches in the study of culture and society may lead us to 'cross the borders and divides that have organized the academic division of labor' (2009: 2). This reflects Lefebvre's statement that a theory of space should be a 'unitary theory' ([1974] 1991: 11), the purpose of which is 'to expose the actual production of space by bringing the various kinds of space and the modalities of their genesis together within a single theory' ([1974] 1991: 16). Thus, Soja explains, Lefebvre 'called his spatial perspective *transdisciplinary* as a strategy to prevent spatial knowledge and praxis from being fragmented and compartmentalized (again) as a disciplinary specialty' (Soja 1996, 47; emphasis in original). Inspired by Lefebvre's and Soja's attempts to challenge disciplinary fragmentation, the present study constitutes an attempt – however limited – to apply a similar transdisciplinary approach to the study of contemporary Shinto ideology and practices (in particular those pertaining to shrine groves, *chinju no mori*). The term 'transdisciplinarity' here refers to attempts to overcome academic disciplinary boundaries rather than reify and enforce them, by combining different theoretical insights and methodological practices.[17] Instead of approaching the topic of inquiry from a single disciplinary perspective, I will draw upon insights from cultural anthropology and comparative religion as well as history, philosophy, social geography and ecology. Hopefully, my focus on spatial practices – in particular, the production of sacred shrine groves (*chinju no mori*), in physical as well as mental and social space – will help me integrate some of these different insights, as suggested by Warf and Arias, Lefebvre and Soja.

Methodologically speaking, this study is based on a combination of discourse analysis and ethnographic research. First, a significant proportion of this study consists of critical analyses of texts. These texts are selected based on their subject matter: they all address some of the core topics in which I am interested here: Shinto, nature, environmental issues, shrine forests and sacred space. Most of the primary sources on which my discussion is based are in Japanese, some are in English. Several of these texts may be classified as 'academic' or 'scientific', others as 'popular' or 'religious'. It should be noted, however, that in Japan there is often considerable overlap between these different categories, and the distinctions between them are not always clear. For instance, religious institutions may organize 'academic' activities such as seminars or symposia, while scholars and scientists working at universities often produce 'popular-scientific' works and give interviews in mass media, thus contributing to popular discourse. Accordingly, the distinction between 'primary' and 'secondary' sources is by no means clear-cut: as we shall see, some of the main protagonists of this study are Shinto scholars who have an academic background, publish scholarly works on

Shinto history and shrine traditions, and are affiliated with leading universities. Indeed, some of the practices analysed in this book are classified as academic and involve scholarly and scientific contributions, even if they also have a clear ideological component – examples include the aforementioned conference at Harvard University (Jinja Honchō 2000) as well as the activities of the Sacred Forest Research Association, Shasō Gakkai (Ueda & Ueda 2001; M. Ueda 2004c).

Many of these texts are interrelated. In some cases, authors refer explicitly to the texts by which they are informed. More often, they employ similar arguments as others, without referring to them. Thus certain historical narratives, popular etymologies and ontological statements acquire the status of self-evident 'truths' – that is, they become part of a particular religious–academic *doxa*, to use Bourdieu's terminology ([1980] 1990: 68) – and cease to be seen as theories or opinions. Together, these texts come to constitute a particular 'field' or 'network', and operate in a 'discourse': 'a group of statements which provide language for talking about – a way of representing the knowledge about – a particular topic at a particular historical moment' (Hall 2001: 72). Meanings are attributed discursively – 'nothing has any meaning outside of discourse', as Foucault famously stated (Hall 2001: 73) – but no discourse is ever definitive or all-encompassing.

When using the term 'discourse', I am aware of the fact that, as Von Stuckrad has rightly pointed out, it 'is used in many, and often conflicting, ways' (2013: 7). But I am informed by his suggestions with regard to the 'discursive study of religion' (2003, 2013) and follow his lead when he writes (based on his reading of Foucault) that

> Knowledge of the world is not an innate cognitive skill but the cultural response to symbolic systems that are provided by the social environment. These symbolic systems are typically produced, legitimized, communicated, and transformed as discourses. Discourse analysis, from the perspective of the sociology of knowledge, aims at reconstructing the processes of social construction, objectification, communication, and legitimization of meaning structures. (…) Historical analysis of discourse addresses not only the explicitly available forms of knowledge (…) but particularly the 'self-evident knowledge', the truth that is not formalized but generally accepted. (2013: 8–10; emphasis in original)

Von Stuckrad then distinguishes between two types of discourse analysis. The first, 'textually oriented discourse analysis', is used in a philological and linguistic context, associated with speech-act theory, and typically concerned with particular uses of language. The second, 'historical discourse analysis', focuses on context rather than text, on power relations, and on historicity. It is associated with scholars such as Michel Foucault and Roland Barthes, and it 'explores the development of discourses in changing socio-political and historical settings, thus providing means to reconstruct [their] genealogy' (Von Stuckrad 2013: 15; cf. 2003: 266). When I use the term 'discourse analysis', I do so in the latter meaning: the purpose of the analysis is to *contextualize, rehistoricize* and *repoliticize* narratives by looking at historical production processes and political subtexts.

This type of discourse analysis is profoundly historicist in its approach, even if it has a contemporary focus, as it is based on the recognition that what counts as 'truth' in any given society is the outcome of historical processes of knowledge production. All traditions, places and ideologies are subject to change, and all change is socially, politically and spatially embedded. That does not mean such analysis is necessarily *historical* in terms of research methodology, however. Significantly, two of the most famous scholars who applied Foucauldian notions of 'discourse' and 'genealogy' to critical analyses of their own fields are an anthropologist and a literary theorist: Talal Asad has analysed historical knowledge formations such as the construction of 'religion' and 'the secular' (Asad 2003), while Edward Said has deconstructed 'the Orient' in European literature, art and scholarship (Said 1978). Likewise, the present work is not a *historical* study in the narrow sense, as it is not based on archival research and a close reading of historical source materials. It is most certainly *historicist* in orientation, however, as it looks at processes by which ideas, places and practices are shaped and reshaped.

As indicated by the title, this book focuses on 'the contemporary period': a somewhat diffuse category, which can mean different things in different contexts. In the study of Japan, 'contemporary' is often used as a translation of the Japanese term *gendai*, which refers to the entire post-war period. Most of the texts and practices discussed in this study date from the Heisei period (1989–today), even though some of the first 'religious environmentalist' texts to which I refer are older, dating from the 1960s or 1970s (e.g. Earhart 1970; White 1967). The emergence of the shrine forest conservation movement, I will demonstrate, can be traced back to Ueda Atsushi's first attempts to map remaining *chinju no mori* in the late 1970s (Ueda [1984] 2007). Nevertheless, this study is mostly concerned with developments in the last two decades, as this is the period in which the Shinto environmentalist paradigm was established and popularized.

While the focus is on recent developments, I do believe some historical contextualization is necessary in order to comprehend contemporary notions of 'Shinto' and 'nature'. Thus, Chapters 2 and 3 in particular have a strong historical component, providing some necessary background information for later chapters. I will also engage with some of the historical narratives provided by the authors whose works are central to this study, as such narratives are central to their ideologies. Therefore, this book contains a section on the alleged worship practices of the Jōmon-period inhabitants of the Japanese isles, even though I am not an archaeologist or historian of ancient Japan myself. The point of this analysis is not to confirm or falsify these narratives but to analyse their contemporary significance. After all, idealized notions of prehistoric Japanese society and worship traditions are central to much present-day discourse on Shinto and *chinju no mori*.

In addition to historical discourse analysis, this study is based on ethnographic data. As Scott Schnell has pointed out, 'Textual analysis is obviously a very important aspect of religious studies. Exclusive reliance on written documents, however, is insufficient for addressing certain problems involving the actual practice and experience of religion' (2006: 381). I fully agree. Therefore, when studying contemporary understandings and conceptualizations of Shinto and the environment, I did not want to limit myself to texts only, no matter how important. Fujimura Ken'ichi (2010) has rightly criticized the fact that most academic texts on 'religion' and 'the environment' are concerned with doctrines, ethics and abstract theory, rather than 'lived religion': the practices carried out by 'religious' actors and their ideas. Importantly, neither abstract academic discourse nor 'local' practices exist in a vacuum. *Chinju no mori* are discursively mediated, but that does not mean they merely exist in texts: they are physical realities, subject to a variety of spatial practices. Theories on Shinto and nature are enacted, materialized and negotiated by local actors; their practices, in turn, reshape theories. In some cases, the theorist and the local actor is one and the same person. Thus, in order to come to an adequate understanding of contemporary Shinto- and nature-related practices, text analysis must be combined with ethnographic data.

Instead of spending an extended period of time in one particular community, I have chosen to visit a number of different shrines, projects and people related to my main research topic. Thus, this is not a single-site ethnography. Instead, this book constitutes an attempt at *mapping* a variety of contemporary practices. Of course, it is not complete – but then, arguably, no map can ever be – and the choice of shrines and projects is, to a certain extent, based on 'chance encounters and random occurrences' (Schnell 2006: 383). However, I do think that there are significant similarities between the different shrine projects I have studied, and that they share an interesting family resemblance. Most important, they all constitute attempts to give shape to the notion of *chinju no mori* as an invaluable resource (cultural, ecological and spiritual) for twenty-first-century Japanese society.

Between 2011 and 2015, I spent a total of six months in Japan, during which I conducted field research. For practical reasons, the research was divided into four shorter periods: February–March 2011, September–December 2011, May–June 2013 and November–December 2015. This meant that I could not follow a single shrine project intensively for a longer period of time. On the other hand, my choice to divide my research into a number of comparatively short periods did have one great advantage: I could revisit some of the sites I had visited previously, and (on several occasions) talk to people I had met two years earlier, which helped me gain a diachronic perspective. It made me become more aware of the fact that social practices as well as physical sites can change significantly in a fairly short period of time, and that individual opinions and attitudes can be subject to quite profound changes as well.

During these research periods, I have conducted approximately forty semi-structured interviews with shrine priests, scholars and project organizers. In addition, I have talked informally to a great number of people, including priests, volunteers, teachers, students, forest scientists and so on. Furthermore, I have participated in a number of shrine forest activities at Shimogamo Jinja, Kamigamo Jinja and Meiji Jingū; attended several relevant meetings and symposia organized by Shasō Gakkai, Jinja Honchō and Shintō Kokusai Gakkai; participated in guided forest walks at Ise Jingū, Meiji Jingū, Atsuta Jingū and Shiroyama Hachimangū; visited a number of shrines associated with the Shinto environmentalist movement, including Chichibu Jinja, Gosho Komataki Jinja and Tsurugaoka Hachimangū;

participated in several local *mori-zukuri* ('forest-making') and *satoyama*-making activities; and visited the worship centres of two so-called Shinto-derived new religions, where I had the opportunity to talk to members. Moreover, I have twice visited the area of Tohoku hit by the 2011 tsunami, where I talked to shrine priests, volunteers, local politicians and environmental activists. This book is the result of all those conversations and activities.

Outline of the Study

The purpose of this book is to provide an analysis of a development that has significantly transformed Shinto in recent decades: its reconceptualization (by scholars, journalists, priests and other institutional actors) as an ancient tradition of nature worship containing important physical, cultural and ethical resources for tackling today's environmental crisis. I refer to this as the Shinto environmentalist paradigm. I will give an overview of the various ideological and academic currents of thought that have contributed to this development and examine some of the institutional responses to it, both on a national (Jinja Honchō, Shasō Gakkai) and local scale (various shrine projects). In particular, I will discuss the different meanings that are attributed to what has become one of the core symbols of Shinto in the present age: *chinju no mori* (sacred shrine forests). I hope to answer the question how these sacred forests are presently conceptualized by leading actors in the shrine world, and how such abstract notions are given shape locally, by means of various spatial practices. Although some scholars have noticed Shinto's 'green turn' and briefly discussed some of its features (Breen & Teeuwen 2010: 207–210; Dessì 2016: 71–73), this is the first systematic study of the Shinto environmentalist paradigm, and the first analysis of *chinju no mori*-related ideas and practices within this context.

This book is divided into nine chapters, including this introduction. Chapter 2 gives a concise overview of different conceptions of 'Shinto' in modern and contemporary Japan (1868–today). In the process, it provides some important historical context, showing how this tradition was reconceptualized and reshaped at various moments in modern history. I will briefly introduce the historical-constructivist approach in Shinto studies, the insights of which are here applied to more contemporary developments. It is not easy to provide a neutral and historically accurate definition of Shinto, as the tradition has been defined in various ways, depending upon ideological differences and changing historical circumstances. Therefore, the chapter does not present a new definition of Shinto; instead, it lists and compares existing definitions of the tradition. As outlined in this chapter, in modern times Shinto has been conceptualized and imagined according to five different paradigms, each of which will be briefly introduced and discussed: the imperial paradigm, the ethnic paradigm, the local paradigm, the universal paradigm and the spiritual paradigm. The Shinto environmentalist paradigm, I argue, combines elements from these earlier paradigms, reinterpreting them in the light of the global discourse on religion and the environment.

The third chapter complements the second, providing some important historical and ideological context for the rest of the book. I elaborate further upon the significance of the religious environmentalist paradigm, showing how the global proliferation of this paradigm has fuelled new interpretations of East Asian religions such as Buddhism, Daoism and Hinduism as ecologically sustainable. I then proceed to discuss the ideological significance of the category 'nature', before tracing the genealogy of the so-called love of nature myth in Japan: the persistent idea that 'the Japanese' have a unique symbiotic relationship to 'nature', and that Japanese culture has been shaped in constant harmonious interaction with the natural environment of the Japanese archipelago. Some of these notions go back to Edo-period *kokugaku* thought, especially the work of Motoori Norinaga (1730–1801). They became a core aspect of the modern national narrative in the early twentieth century. Of particular significance for the Shinto environmentalist paradigm was the work of Watsuji Tetsurō (1889–1960), whose theory of *fūdo* ('milieu') I introduce here. Finally, I move on to discuss more recent expressions of the 'love of nature myth' in scholarly literature, especially in relation to environmental issues, as well as some of the critique offered on these ideas.

After exploring the various ideological influences on the Shinto environmentalist paradigm in Chapters 2 and 3, in Chapter 4 I provide an in-depth overview of the development and defining characteristics of this paradigm. There are two Japanese academic trends that have contributed to the popularization of the Shinto environmentalist paradigm since the 1980s. The first of these is the proliferation of pseudo-academic writings on 'Japanese culture' in relation to 'spirituality'. The second trend consists of the emerging scientific interest in shrine forest conservation and the corresponding collaboration between scientists and Shinto priests. As I argue, one of the defining features of the Shinto environmentalist paradigm is its inherently transdisciplinary character, bringing together a diversity of academic and religious actors. I then proceed to discuss some academic events that have contributed to the spread of this paradigm, organized by the International Shinto Foundation/Shintō Kokusai Gakkai and the Shintō Bunka Kai. Next, I will look at the international dimension, showing how these ideas gradually achieved mainstream status in Anglophone academia, partly thanks to the 'Shinto and Ecology' conference at Harvard University in 1997. Finally, I will briefly discuss some of the works of Miyazaki Hayao, which have probably had a considerable impact on popular understandings of Shinto, *kami* and nature, not only in Japan but also abroad.

Chapter 5 zooms in on one of contemporary Shinto's core concepts, *chinju no mori*, which may be translated as 'forest of the protector deity' and which is central to most discourse on Shinto and the environment today. I begin by outlining four different meanings of the term and give examples of how they are used. I then provide a brief genealogy of the concept, before looking more closely at its rediscovery in the post-war period. The association of these shrine groves with environmental conservation is largely thanks to the work of Ueda Atsushi (1930–) and Miyawaki Akira (1928–), two scientists who started mapping remaining *chinju no mori* – which they defined as remaining areas of primary or secondary forest, often surrounding shrines, made up of indigenous broad-leaved trees – in the 1980s. After a while, they began cooperating with Shinto scholars and priests who likewise considered shrine forest preservation and research an important task, such as Ueda Masaaki (1927–2016) and Sonoda Minoru (1936–). *Chinju no mori* are not merely significant for ecological reasons, I argue: in contemporary Shinto texts, the term no longer refers to a certain kind of forest but to a particular type of *sacred space* said to be central to 'traditional' Japanese community life. Thus, the term has acquired significant ideological potential, as illustrated by the fact that Jinja Honchō president Tanaka Tsunekiyo (1944–) uses it to justify his claims that Shinto is a public tradition that should not be subjected to the same legal limitations as other religions. Finally, I briefly discuss the work of the Sacred Forest Research Association (Shasō Gakkai), which has contributed to sacred forest research and conservation since its foundation in 2002.

The second part of the book looks more closely at specific themes related to shrine forests, as well as specific shrines and projects. Chapter 6 begins with a discussion of the significance of Ōmiwa Jinja and its adjacent mountain, Mount Miwa, for the discourse on Shinto as an ancient nature religion. Reportedly constituting the body of the deity (*shintaizan*), this mountain and its shrine are often presented (anachronistically, I argue) as models of ancient environmental awareness. Following this example, I analyse popular notions of Japan as a unique 'forest civilization' diametrically opposed to the Western 'civilization of deforestation'. I discuss the idealization of the Jōmon period as Japan's primordial golden age, supposedly characterized by social, ecological and spiritual harmony, in the works of public intellectuals such as Umehara Takeshi (1925–) and Yasuda Yoshinori (1946–). Central to this discourse is the notion of 'animism', which has seen a revival in scholarship in recent years but is not devoid of ideological subtexts. Particularly problematic, I argue, is the association of Ainu and Ryukyu worship traditions with 'original' Shinto, which reflects social-evolutionist models of history that have played an important role in legitimizing colonial exploitation. Finally, I show that notions of primordial forest worship are not merely abstract ideological constructs; they also influence place-making practices such as *chinju no mori* reconstruction activities. In the last section of the chapter, I explore one such project in depth: the reconstruction of World Heritage Site Tadasu no Mori (Shimogamo Jinja) in Kyoto. As I argue, the purpose of this project extends beyond forest conservation proper: concerned with restoring the urban forest to its 'original shape', it seeks to reconstruct a utopian 'traditional' social and physical space.

Not everybody takes claims about Shinto's sustainable character and its social and ecological significance at face value. Some scholars have expressed scepticism towards Shinto expressions of environmentalism and questioned the motives behind them, especially with regards to Jinja Honchō. In Chapter 7, I address the question whether shrines can become centres of environmental advocacy. Although there are some examples of shrine-based activism, most shrine priests would be reluctant to protest construction projects, as shrines are dependent upon corporate sponsors and community support. On the other hand, not all shrine forests are under immediate threat, and several of these forests are now home to conservation and educational practices. After a brief discussion of forest ecology and biodiversity, with special reference to the theories of Miyawaki Akira, I discuss two *mori-zukuri* projects in more detail: the Sennen no Mori no Kai at Gosho Komataki Jinja in Ibaraki Prefecture and Mori-zukuri Kaigi at Shiroyama Hachimangū in the city of Nagoya. These cases illustrate that forest-making activities often go together with educational practices, drawing on ideological notions of the cultivation of morally upright patriotic citizens, and focus on 'community-building' (*komyuniti-zukuri*) as much as ideas of ecological sustainability. There is an important difference between the two projects, however: the former is set up by a shrine priest and represents an attempt at sacralization, whereas the latter is run by non-clergy volunteers who are not particularly interested in Shinto, and who are struggling to convince shrine priests and the neighbouring community of the importance of their work.

In Chapter 8, I look at academic, social and religious responses to the disasters in Tohoku in 2011. I first provide a brief overview of some of the projects that have been developed at shrines in the affected area, including Imaizumi Hachimangū in Rikuzentakata (Iwate Prefecture) and Yaegaki Jinja in Yamamoto (Miyagi Prefecture). I then proceed to discuss two shrine forest projects where educational activities have been combined with fundraising and symbolic support for Tohoku: Afuhi Project at Kamigamo Jinja (Kyoto) and NPO Hibiki at Meiji Jingū (Tokyo). Afuhi Project has been set up for the purpose of educating school children in Shinto and 'traditional culture', as well as for cultivating the plant that is the shrine's core symbol, *futaba aoi* (*Asarum caulescens*), and reintroducing it into the shrine forest ecosystem. Meanwhile, at Meiji Jingū, volunteers are active in cultivating rice, guiding visitors and collecting acorns (*donguri*). These acorns are planted and sent to other shrines in the country for reforestation purposes. In recent years, most seedlings have gone to Tohoku in order to become part of the 'Great Forest Wall', a post-tsunami reforestation project. These activities mirror the foundation history of Meiji Jingū's forest, when seedlings from all over the empire were sent to Tokyo in order to become part of the shrine's 'man-made natural forest'. Such practices can serve to symbolically unite different parts of country, I argue, establishing a sense of national solidarity and shared symbolic capital.

Chapter 9 explores a rather unique shrine forest: the forest of Ise. In the course of history, the meanings attributed to the shrines of Ise have been subject to continuous change. Considering the proliferation of the Shinto environmentalist paradigm, it should come as no surprise that today Ise is redefined as the quintessential example of the ancient 'Shinto' spirit of harmonious coexistence with nature. In the publicity surrounding the 2013 *shikinen sengū*, the building techniques, (agri)cultural traditions and ritual practices of Ise were framed as examples of 'ancient sustainability'. I explore different attitudes and uses of Ise's forest (*kyūikirin*), which consists of different parts, and show how these have changed over time. Following this, I look more closely at Jinja Honchō's appropriation of the *chinju no mori* trope for PR purposes, in particular in relation to Ise, and analyse its collaboration with ARC. The Shinto environmentalist paradigm, I argue, functions differently on different levels: locally, it serves to mobilize community members around the shared ecological and cultural capital of a particular shrine forest; nationally, it is employed to substantiate claims concerning Shinto's public character; and internationally, it provides Shinto with new legitimacy, is used to dissociate it from its imperial past and even draws new worshippers. Indeed, as this chapter shows, the environmental turn has contributed to the popularization of Shinto internationally: for instance, Jinja Honchō has donated a *mikoshi* (portable shrine) to the Brooklyn Botanic Garden in New York and supported the construction of a shrine in San Marino. Other Shinto shrines have been established in the Netherlands and the United States, and there are also online communities of non-Japanese Shinto practitioners, who embrace the notion of Shinto as nature spirituality.

Chapter 2

DEFINING SHINTO

Competing Perspectives

It is not easy to provide a neutral and historically accurate definition of Shinto. In popular discourse – travel guidebooks, popular-scientific introductions, online encyclopaedias and depictions in mass media – Shinto is usually described as Japan's 'indigenous' religion, and contrasted to Buddhism and Christianity, which are supposedly 'foreign.' In such texts, Shinto is portrayed as an ancient tradition, closely related to Japanese culture and society, which has successfully adapted itself to changing historical circumstances, while its essence has remained more or less unchanged since prehistoric times. Such conceptualizations are anachronistic, as they project modern notions of 'Shinto' and 'Japan' as singular, unified and transhistorical categories upon a diversity of historical practices and places. Moreover, the notion of Shinto as 'indigenous Japanese' is problematic, not only because the nation-state 'Japan' is a modern construct (Morris-Suzuki 1998), but also because Shinto took shape in a ritual-ideological system that was predominantly Buddhist (Kuroda 1981; Teeuwen 2007).

In the last three decades or so, popular essentialist notions of Shinto as Japan's indigenous religion have been convincingly challenged by a number of critical historians, who have looked at the processes by which 'Shinto' was constructed out of existing elements in late medieval and early modern times (e.g. Breen & Teeuwen 2000b, 2010, 2017; Grapard 1993; Kuroda 1981; Teeuwen & Scheid 2002; Thal 2005; Zhong 2016). Nevertheless, definitions of Shinto as the 'indigenous', 'ancient' worship tradition of Japan, closely intertwined with 'Japanese culture' and the physical territories where it developed, remain dominant – not in Anglophone academic texts, perhaps, but certainly in Shinto circles and non-academic public discourse, in Japan and elsewhere. A representative example of this approach is the lavishly illustrated booklet *Soul of Japan*, published by Jinja Honchō in the context of the 2013 *shikinen sengū* for the purpose of explaining Shinto to foreign audiences. Here, Shinto is presented as

> the indigenous faith of the Japanese. It is a way of life and a way of thinking that has been an integral part of Japanese culture since ancient times. (…) Shinto places great value in the virtues of purity and honesty, yet as a faith, Shinto

has no dogma, doctrine, or founder. Its origins can be seen in the relationship between the ancient Japanese and the power they found in the natural world. (Public Affairs Headquarters for Shikinen-Sengu 2013: 11–12)

Shinto priests are often quick to assert that Shinto has no dogma – which, paradoxically, has become a dogma of sorts – and that, therefore, there is place for considerable regional, ritual and theological variety. Few of them, however, would deny the underlying assumption that there is unity in this diversity and disagree with the claim that Shinto is *the* indigenous 'way of life' of 'the Japanese people', which has taken shape in close interaction with the culture and natural environment of Japan. That does not mean, however, that they all agree on what exactly this 'way of life' entails. Despite Jinja Honchō's conscious efforts to influence popular perceptions of Shinto and create consensus among shrine priests (by means of priestly education, shrine newspapers and other publications), 'Shinto' remains a contested concept, the category boundaries of which are as fluid as ever. In the course of (modern) history, the term has been employed in a number of different ways, at times contradictory. In academic debates on Shinto, various historical narratives coexist, reflecting a number of ideological and normative positions regarding the essence of the Japanese nation, the position of the emperor and the role of 'religion' and ritual ceremonies in the public sphere.

Thus, the meanings and boundaries of the category 'Shinto' are subject to ongoing negotiation. Competing definitions of the tradition represent different ideological positions or political agendas. Accordingly, it is practically impossible to give a neutral, empirically adequate definition of Shinto, as the very term is ideologically charged. In 1981, Michael Pye noted that 'there is a political factor to be taken into account in any understanding of Shinto' (1981: 61); this observation remains valid today. Hence, the question 'what is Shinto' is not as simple as it may seem at first sight, for any attempt at definition is inevitably bound up with ideology (Bocking 2004: 263–266; Havens 2006: 14–19). It has been argued that 'Shinto' is an ideal typical construction that may be based on actual ritual practices and shrine traditions but does not equal them. In Mark Teeuwen's formulation, it 'is not something that has "existed" in Japanese society in some concrete and definable form during different historical periods; rather, it appears as a conceptualization, an abstraction that has had to be produced actively every time it has been used' (2002: 233).

In other words, Shinto is a historical construct, subject to continuous negotiation and redefinition, instead of a natural given (Breen & Teeuwen 2010; Rambelli 2014). That does not mean, however, that the term is merely an empty signifier which can be projected onto any belief or practice whatsoever. In discursive constructions and definitions of Shinto, there are a limited number of recurring themes, tropes and assumptions, as we shall see later in the text. Most important, in today's Japan, the term serves an important function as a generic category covering a variety of institutions usually called *jinja* (conventionally referred to as 'shrines' in English),[1] as well as associated ritual and discursive practices. In the modern period especially (i.e. from 1868 onwards), Shinto stands out as a very real presence in Japanese society, even though its category boundaries have never been clearly defined, and the societal and political positions of institutions and practices referred to by this term have gone through some significant transformations.

When looking at the premodern and medieval periods, however, the picture gets more complicated. Until the 1980s, the concept of 'Shinto' was generally considered to refer to 'the' indigenous religious/ritual tradition of 'the' Japanese people, which throughout history has existed alongside Buddhism, its essence more or less unchanged since prehistoric times. The historicity of the concept itself was not usually studied, let alone processes of Shintoization. The historian Kuroda Toshio (1926–1993) is usually credited for being the first to question this notion of Shinto as 'the indigenous religion of Japan, continuing in an unbroken line from prehistoric times down to the present', arguing that 'before modern times Shinto did not exist as an independent religion' (Kuroda 1981: 1–3). Kuroda's work has been groundbreaking for a number of reasons, and it has influenced a generation of historians. Although some of his claims have been rejected (e.g. Breen & Teeuwen 2000a: 4–5), his basic argument, that 'Shinto' is the outcome of historical construction and negotiation processes, remains highly significant. As Teeuwen and Scheid write, 'By stripping away the myth of a single, independent Shinto tradition, [Kuroda's] work has led to an emphasis on aspects of discontinuity in kami worship, both diachronically, between various periods of Japanese history, and synchronically, between center and periphery, between different locations and historical contexts' (2002: 197).

Constructions of 'Shinto' as an independent, pre-Buddhist, indigenous Japanese tradition were developed by *kokugaku* scholars such as Motoori Norinaga (1730–1801) and Hirata Atsutane (1776–1843) (Breen & Teeuwen 2010: 60–65), drawing upon the inventions of Yoshida Kanetomo (1435–1511) and others (Breen & Teeuwen 2010: 47–52), as well as the *kami* worship traditions of Ise (Breen & Teeuwen 2017) and, to a certain extent, Izumo (Zhong 2016). Before the Meiji period, however, shrines were not usually independent from Buddhist temples, neither institutionally nor theologically. It may be argued, then, that modern Shinto is largely an invented tradition, which developed out of Buddhism and incorporated elements from a variety of sources – including existing shrine traditions, imperial rites and Confucian ideology (Teeuwen 2002, 2007; cf. Kuroda 1981). Hence, imaginations of 'Shinto' as a tradition going back to primordial times often lead to the anachronistic projection of modern notions onto earlier shrine practices. While some shrines do indeed go back many centuries, in some cases predating the introduction of Buddhism to the Japanese isles, they have been subject to continuous processes of transformation and reinvention (e.g. Breen & Teeuwen 2010: 66–128; Breen & Teeuwen 2017; Grapard 1993; Thal 2005). By no means does the variety of practices concerned with the worship of local deities in ancient times equal the singular, 'indigenous' tradition 'Shinto' as it was imagined in the Edo and Meiji periods. Significantly, then, as Breen and Teeuwen note, there 'have been historical processes of "Shintoization"' (2010: ix): in the course of history, some places and practices were constructed and classified as 'Shinto', while others were excluded.

Although Breen and Teeuwen are primarily concerned with historical processes, their observations are also of profound relevance for the study of contemporary Shinto. 'Shintoization' – the process by which certain practices and beliefs are classified as 'Shinto', and the construction and reconstruction of the category itself – is not only something that happened in the past: it is an ongoing process. As the category 'Shinto' and its relation to the state remain contested, Shinto actors (academic as well as clerical) continue to redefine and rethink their tradition. Importantly, however, 'Shinto' does not equal lived shrine practice, neither today nor in the past. Breen and Teeuwen are right to point out that there is a gap between actual shrine practices on the one hand, and the normative abstraction 'Shinto', on the other (2000a: 3). For the majority of the people participating in shrine rituals, 'Shinto' is a rather irrelevant category: they do not generally conceive of their prayers or rituals as expressions of 'Shinto' (Nelson 2000: 22–52). This is in accordance with my own observations: while shrine priests usually have a more or less clear idea of what 'Shinto' represents, laypeople do not typically identify with the concept, even if they take part in shrine activities and pray to *kami*.

Although 'Shinto' is an abstraction, fraught with ideological connotations, it is not solely the construction of a powerful elite. Other actors have also tried to appropriate and redefine the category. These include scholars, priests and practitioners, as well as representatives of so-called new religions defining themselves as 'Shinto'. As a result, in contemporary academic and popular discourse on Shinto, various ideological positions are represented, leading to some subtle and not-so-subtle differences in perspective. After all, ' "Shinto" is sufficiently vague as a term and loosely organized as an institution to invite any number of interpretations and reinterpretations' (Breen & Teeuwen 2010: 223). Definitions and conceptualizations of Shinto are embedded within, and informed by, wider developments in Japanese society and politics. As such, they are inherently ideological. Accordingly, as Brian Bocking has argued, 'how we approach, understand and most importantly teach about Shintō is not an issue of merely "academic" significance' (2004: 265–266): it can have some real political implications. In recent years, the political dimension of contemporary Shinto has been addressed by a number of scholars, including John Breen (2007, 2010a,b), Thierry Guthmann (2010, 2017) and Mark Mullins (2012, 2016). Nevertheless, apolitical, essentialist accounts of Shinto continue to be prevalent, both inside and outside Japan. In a review article from 2006, Sarah Thal summarized the state of affairs as follows:

> Dangerous traps threaten to ensnare any author writing about Shinto. The 'Way of the Kami' has for so long been touted as 'Japan's indigenous religion' or 'the essence of being Japanese' that essentialism, overgeneralization, and romanticism dominate many discussions of kami-related religious practices in Japan. While most scholars today successfully avoid these problems, others still expound some version of the aesthetic nationalism promoted by nativists

and nationalists since the late eighteenth century. Thus, to read the recent work on Shinto is to be both inspired and dismayed – inspired, because a wealth of solid, innovative work has transformed our understanding of Shinto; dismayed, because old, debilitating ideas about Shinto as 'experientialism' or 'Japaneseness' remain alive. (2006: 145)

This statement arguably remains valid today. In recent years, a number of important historical studies of shrine traditions have been published, which focus on individual actors and processes of historical change, rather than assuming the existence of 'Shinto' as a transhistorical entity (e.g. Ambros 2008; Azegami 2009; Breen & Teeuwen 2010, 2017; Grapard 1993; Imaizumi 2013; Moerman 2005; Thal 2005; Zhong 2016). In addition, there are some important new studies of the historical formation of the category 'religion' in Japan, which developed in tandem with modern notions of Shinto (Hoshino 2012; Isomae 2003; Josephson 2012; Maxey 2014). There have also been some anthropological studies of contemporary shrine practices, which have contributed to our understanding of Shinto today (Ishii 2010; Nelson 1996, 2000; Schnell 1999; Smyers 1999). Nevertheless, as stated, the popular view of Shinto as an ancient, singular worship tradition, the essence of which has supposedly remained unchanged, continues to be influential, both in 'popular' and 'academic' texts – but then, the boundaries between those two categories are not always very clear anyway (e.g. Kamata 2000, 2011; Kasulis 2004; Picken 2002; Rankin 2010; Sonoda 1998; Tanaka 2011; Yamakage [2000] 2006; Yamamura 2011).

In this study, I will not attempt to come up with a new definition of Shinto. Rather, following Breen and Teeuwen's discussions of 'Shintoization', I will adopt a meta-perspective and look at ways in which the category 'Shinto' has been defined and demarcated in recent years, in relation to social, political and environmental developments. Moreover, I will examine some of the ways in which abstract notions of 'Shinto' have been adapted, negotiated and, in some cases, ignored by local actors. As the following section demonstrates, there are some significant differences in perspective, even among people who adhere to 'essentialist' representations of Shinto. These relate to different perceptions of the Japanese nation, the imperial institution, the category 'religion' and, last but not least, the natural environment.

The Imperial Paradigm

Throughout modern history, leading shrine actors have engaged in debates about the nature of Shinto and its position vis-à-vis the nation-state, at times disagreeing with and challenging each other's interpretations. The early post-war period especially was a time of heated debate, as the tradition had to be reinvented after its forced separation from the state apparatus (Breen & Teeuwen 2010: 5–7; Imaizumi 2013: 214–220). And Shinto is by no means unified today: despite Jinja Honchō's best efforts to impose consensus upon the shrine world, there are a number of competing conceptualizations, and Shinto continues to be interpreted and framed differently by different actors. Based on my reading of a variety of primary and secondary sources (both 'academic' and 'popular'),[2] I distinguish between six essentialist paradigms,[3] which have emerged in the course of the modern and contemporary periods for defining, conceptualizing and interpreting 'Shinto'. These paradigms came up in different periods, responding to political and academic developments at the time, and continue to coexist. They are not necessarily incompatible with each other: while some are clearly contradictory, others overlap or can be seen as complementary, and different combinations are possible. I refer to them as the *imperial* paradigm, the *ethnic* paradigm, the *universal* paradigm, the *local* paradigm, the *spiritual* paradigm and the *environmentalist* paradigm.

What these paradigms have in common is that – in sharp contrast to the historical-constructivist understanding of Shinto outlined before – they conceive of Shinto as a unique, singular tradition, the essence of which has remained unchanged since ancient times. They differ, however, in their understanding of that very essence – and, therefore, in their understanding of the defining aspect(s) of the tradition. As their names suggest, they conceive of Shinto as, respectively and essentially, a national, non-religious ritual tradition centred around the imperial institution; the single moral, cultural and religious way of 'the' Japanese people; a religion with global salvific potential; a variety of ancient, rural traditions, best preserved in shrine festivals (*matsuri*) and folklore; a mystical, non-rational tradition which can only be understood intuitively, closely connected to so-called sacred places; and an ancient tradition of nature worship containing valuable ecological knowledge that may help us overcome today's environmental crisis. In this study, I am particularly concerned with the development of the environmentalist paradigm. In order to contextualize this, however, I will first provide a brief overview of the other five, by which it has been influenced.

There are some possible objections to my choice to classify essentialist interpretations of 'Shinto' into these six paradigms. As with any classification, I do not claim that this list is exhaustive or definitive – obviously, alternative conceptualizations of Shinto that do not fit well within any of these six categories may exist. Arguably, however, these have not (yet) received paradigmatic status. Some may argue that what I call the 'local' and the 'spiritual' paradigms are in fact variations of the 'ethnic' paradigm. It is certainly true that these paradigms are not mutually exclusive, and that particular accounts of Shinto may combine elements of two or three different paradigms. However, I do believe that notions of the essence of Shinto as lying in, respectively, the diversity of rural 'folk' traditions (the local paradigm), or in mystical, non-rational experiences of the divine (the spiritual paradigm) are sufficiently different from the understanding of Shinto as the single ritual way of the entire Japanese *minzoku* (the ethnic paradigm) as to justify the choice to classify these as different paradigms. Thus, while acknowledging that the classification model I propose may be a somewhat simplified representation of the entire discourse on 'Shinto' and that the choice of terminology and categories may be subject to further debate, I do believe it captures the main approaches to and understandings of Shinto in modern times.

Of these six, the imperial paradigm is probably the oldest, going back to at least the early Meiji period. It goes beyond the scope of this work to provide a lengthy and in-depth analysis of the processes by which modern Shinto took shape in the Meiji period, in constant interaction with the nation-state, imperial ideology and newly established category 'religion'. Others have written extensively about this topic, which remains controversial today.[4] Here, I will limit myself to describing the main features of the imperial paradigm that was developed during this period, as this continues to be a source of inspiration for some contemporary Shinto ideologues. As the name indicates, the imperial paradigm rests on the assumption that the essence of Shinto lies in its relationship with the divine imperial institution, believed to be of existential importance for the Japanese nation as a whole. These notions were developed by *kokugaku* mythologists such as Motoori Norinaga, Hirata Atsutane and Ōkuni Takamasa (1792–1871) and came to play a central part in Meiji-period *kokutai* thought: the national-organicist ideology that conceives of the nation as an integrated whole akin to a body, headed by the emperor. This was closely intertwined with the notion of *saisei itchi*, 'unity of ritual and government', which played a central part in the development of the ritual-ideological state apparatus that would later be referred to as 'State Shinto' (Teeuwen 2017).

In addition to the importance assigned to the imperial institution, the continuation of which is perceived as crucial for the well-being of the entire nation, the imperial paradigm is characterized by its assertion that Shinto is a public, *non-religious* ritual tradition. Much has been written recently about the applicability and formation of the category 'religion' (*shūkyō*) in the Japanese context. Drawing on the postcolonial critique of non-reflexive uses of 'religion' as a universal, cross-cultural category by Talal Asad (1993), Russell McCutcheon (1997) and Tomoko Masuzawa (2005), some scholars have argued that premodern Japan did not have a differentiated religious realm, that the term was imposed by Western powers in the Meiji period, and that 'Japanese religion' is an academic construct rather than an empirical reality (Fitzgerald 2003; Horii 2016; Isomae 2003, 2012). Others, by contrast, have argued that premodern Japanese society did have notions corresponding to the modern dichotomy between 'religion' and 'the secular', and that it is perfectly possible – even desirable – to use 'religion' as an analytical category, also when describing contemporary beliefs and practices (Kleine 2013; Pye 2003; Reader 2004, 2016). Informed by, yet moving beyond these debates, recent historical studies have convincingly shown that the category *shūkyō* was indeed a Meiji-period product, created in order to translate the European term 'religion' in legal documents and scholarship. Rather than a Western imposition, however, it was the outcome of lengthy negotiations between various stakeholders within Japan, who were actively involved in its formation, and who drew on pre-existing Japanese ideology and institutional practices as much as they were informed by newly imported ideas (Hoshino 2012; Josephson 2012; Krämer 2015; Maxey 2014). As these studies have shown, the definition and demarcation of 'religion' was of great importance for the formation of the modern state apparatus. Not surprisingly, then, it had direct ramifications for the development of Shinto.

The construction of *shūkyō* as a differentiated societal realm in the Meiji period had numerous consequences for existing shrine and temple traditions, whose legal and political status had to be redetermined. Some were configured as 'religions' centred on a particular belief system, which was defined as an essentially private affair; others, by contrast, were categorized as public and, hence, non-religious. During the same period, the sociopolitical functions of the institutions now redefined as 'religion' changed significantly, as did some of the practices associated with these institutions. First, centuries-old temple-shrine complexes were forced to split up into a 'Buddhist' temple and a 'Shinto' shrine in a process called *shinbutsu bunri* ('separation of Shinto and Buddhism'), which took place in 1868 (Hardacre 1989: 27–28). Second, Buddhist temples transformed from semi-public institutions responsible for the registration of all citizens into private religious organizations that had to compete for individual followers. Third, the government reluctantly allowed Christian missionaries to re-enter the country and proselytize. And fourth, popular local devotional movements had to reorganize and register as 'religions'; in the process, many of them adopted elements from Christianity (theological, soteriological and organizational). These movements were classified as 'Sect Shinto' (*shūha shintō*), which was distinguished from regular shrine Shinto; examples include Tenrikyō, Konkōkyō and Kurozumikyō (Hardacre 1986; Inoue 2002).

Until the modern period, then, neither 'Shinto' nor 'religion' existed as independent, differentiated social entities. Hence, it was by no means self-evident that 'Shinto' should be configured as another 'religion' alongside Christianity and Buddhism. The Edo-period *kokugaku* mythologists had reinvented Shinto as the primordial, divinely inspired tradition of the Japanese people, superior to any other ritual traditions and worldviews. Their ideas were incorporated by some of the architects of the Meiji 'restoration', who intended to reshape Shinto as a national ideology surrounding the divine emperor and remodel shrine traditions accordingly. During the first decades of the Meiji period, however, the relations between Shinto, 'religion' and the state were unclear, and subject to continuous negotiation and political experiments. These included debates concerning the nature of Shinto and the question as to whether Shinto should be conceived of as a religion or not (Hardacre 1989: 34–36; cf. Maxey 2014: 154–163). It was in this period that the imperial paradigm was established; that is, the notion that Shinto is the singular, primordial tradition of the Japanese people, which is fundamentally a 'non-religious' collective ritual tradition surrounding the emperor. As such, it was seen as something fundamentally different from traditions concerned with belief, salvation, pastoral care and rituals for personal benefit, which were reconfigured as 'religion'. As Isomae summarizes,

> The argument that Shintō was not a religion was constructed in order to protect Shintō, which was closely connected to the emperor institution, from competition with other religions such as Christianity and Buddhism. In order to overcome its doctrinal weakness, the government had attempted to systematize Shintō doctrine during the early 1870s but did not succeed in creating a unified

system. Following this failure the government recognized the incompatibility between doctrinally-oriented religious concepts and Shintō's own practice-oriented characteristics and, boldly turning the tables, sought to reposition Shintō outside the scope of the Western concept of religion. (2012: 239–240)

By the end of the nineteenth century, 'Shinto' had been established as a non-religious national morality and set of ritual practices, in which all citizens were obliged to take part. 'Religion', by contrast, was seen as a private affair. Contrary to what Isomae suggests in the aforementioned quotation, however, several scholars have demonstrated that the notion of Shinto as a 'non-religion' was not merely a government strategy for protecting Shinto from religious competition. Nor, for that matter, was it actively embraced by all Shinto priests. On the contrary, some of them protested the government's decision to forbid shrine priests from engaging in activities that were considered 'religious' (e.g. individual rituals and pastoral care), which had constituted their main source of income. Significantly, one of the main intellectuals responsible for advocating the notion of Shinto as a non-religious, national ritual system was the Buddhist scholar Shimaji Mokurai (1838–1911) (Krämer 2015; Maxey 2014: 122–139). Thus, Nitta argues, the configuration of Shinto as non-religious was the outcome of what may be called an unholy alliance between *kokugaku*-influenced Shinto ideologues seeking to establish their tradition as *the* national ideology of the modern state Japan, and Buddhist leaders from the powerful Jōdo Shinshū school (Pure Land Buddhism) eager to deny shrine priests access to the newly established religious marketplace (Nitta 2000). In sum, the notion of Shinto as a non-religion, serving the entire nation and surrounding the emperor, is not just an ideological construction made by Shinto actors but was also advocated by some of their rivals – at least in the initial period.

Nevertheless, although Buddhist leaders may have been involved in the establishment of Shinto as a 'non-religion' in the early Meiji period, these notions were subsequently appropriated by powerful members of the ruling oligarchy and prominent Shinto representatives. They used it as a device for the construction of Shinto as a public state cult and morality, participation in which was obligatory for all citizens. As Sarah Thal has argued,

[b]y removing Shinto from the realm of religion, the accumulated rhetoric of decades succeeded in establishing Shinto, in its nineteenth-century form, not as a religious belief but as the fundamental expression of Japanese identity. (…) Using the concept of religion as a political tool, advocates of Shinto confounded the boundaries of church and state, religion and secularism, to shape the very idea of Japaneseness itself. (2002: 112)

Thus, Shinto in its Meiji-period shape – elements derived from shrine worship, which were combined with neo-Confucian notions of ancestor worship, modern nationalism and imperialism – came to be intimately intertwined with normative notions of what it meant to be Japanese. Central to this ritual-ideological system – which Josephson has aptly referred to as the 'Shinto Secular' (2012: 132–163;

cf. Rots 2017) – was the emperor, who served as the embodiment of the divine nation. In this system, those shrines, tombs and ritual ceremonies that were directly associated with the imperial lineage and its ancestral deities acquired special status. This imperial paradigm has never fully disappeared: it continues to influence popular imaginations of what Shinto ought to be, especially in right-wing organizations such as Shintō Seiji Renmei and Nippon Kaigi (Guthmann 2010; Mullins 2016; Shimazono 2007). It did, however, lose much of its former self-evidence after the Japanese surrender in 1945, when the ethnic paradigm became dominant. Although the imperial family continued to play an important part in imaginations of Shinto in relation to the Japanese nation, it ceased to have an explicitly political function.

The Ethnic Paradigm

The legal status of both Shinto and the emperor in post-war Japanese society was a matter of great importance for the Occupation Authorities, which was heavily debated by American policymakers and scholars already during the war (Imaizumi 2013: 200–213). In the end, the decision was made to abolish 'State Shinto', but leave actual shrines intact and the emperor on the throne. In December 1945, the authorities issued the Shinto Directive, which stated that Shinto should be separate from the state. Shinto was now officially reclassified as 'religion', which meant that shrines could no longer receive direct state support and that participation in shrine rituals became voluntary. In 1947, the new, secular Constitution was implemented, which prescribed the strict separation of state and religion. As a consequence, state patronage of Shinto institutions came to be seen as a violation of the Constitution – an issue that has been contested ever since (Breen 2010a). In 1946, Jinja Honchō was founded as the general umbrella organization for Japan's 80,000 or so shrines. Significantly, it was legally defined as a private religious institution instead of, say, a government agency, as the name *honchō* suggests. In sum, Shinto ceased to be state ideology and had to be reinvented as a religion.

There was no consensus, however, on the shape this newly privatized Shinto should take. As Breen and Teeuwen write, during the initial stage, there were three 'camps' within Jinja Honchō:

> The first, led by Ashizu Uzuhiko (1909–1992), stressed Shinto's role in uniting the Japanese people under the spiritual guidance of the emperor. The second, drawing on the work of the ethnologist Yanagita Kunio (1875–1962), rejected the idea that centralist imperial ideology was at the core of Shinto. Instead, this group stressed the spiritual value of local traditions of worshipping local kami, in all their centrifugal variety. The third, fronted by Orikuchi Shinobu (1887–1953), argued that if Shinto was to survive, it should be developed from an ethnic religion into a universal one. These three positions reflected radically different positions to Shinto. (…) Within NAS [Jinja Honchō], Ashizu fought a hard battle to exclude the influence of Yanagita and Orikuchi from

the new shrine organization. (…) Initially, Ashizu prevailed, but over time the alternatives offered by Yanagita and (to a lesser degree) Orikuchi have bounced back. (2010: 6–7)

In these debates concerning the future identity of Shinto, we can distinguish three competing paradigms. I will discuss the views of Yanagita and Orikuchi in more detail later. First, I will focus on what would become the mainstream understanding of Shinto in the post-war period, at least within the shrine establishment and affiliated educational institutions. I refer to this as the *ethnic paradigm*. This paradigm draws upon the imperial paradigm but is less explicitly political. As we have seen, the latter still exists – especially among conservative-nationalist elements within the Shinto establishment and their political allies – but it is not as prominent as before 1945, having given way to the ethnic paradigm as the most dominant 'emic' understanding of Shinto. According to this view, Shinto is *the* indigenous tradition of the Japanese *minzoku* (a concept encompassing yet transcending both 'nation' and 'race', similar to the German notion of *Volk*), which has defined Japanese culture and society since primordial times. While there are significant similarities between the two, one of the main differences between the imperial and ethnic paradigms is that unlike the former, the latter does not deny the religious character of Shinto *per se*. That is, among its various attributes, it is acknowledged that Shinto includes so-called religious elements such as devotion, worship practices and a belief in the existence of deities.

The following definition by Joseph Kitagawa is illustrative for this approach: 'Shinto (…) is the indigenous religion of Japan', which 'may be regarded as the *ensemble* of contradictory and yet peculiarly Japanese types of religious beliefs, sentiments, and approaches, which have been shaped and conditioned by the historical experience of the Japanese people from the prehistoric period to the present' (Kitagawa 1987: 139; italics in original). Needless to say, such a definition is ahistorical: it essentializes 'the Japanese people' as a single entity with a singular historical experience, and denies the diversity of beliefs, practices and experiences of the various people who have lived in the areas that later became the nation-state 'Japan'. But Kitagawa is only one of many advocates of this view, which has long been the dominant perception of Shinto among Shinto scholars and priests alike – and, as I have demonstrated above, continues to be the description of Shinto used in a variety of popular and even academic introductions. Jinja Honchō's English-language booklet, *Soul of Japan*, is a good recent example (Public Affairs Headquarters for Shikinen-Sengu 2013).

In the aforementioned quotation, Kitagawa refers to Shinto as a religion. According to many advocates of the ethnic paradigm, however, Shinto is not *merely* a religion similar to Buddhism, Christianity or Islam. Rather, it is believed to transcend the realm of the religious, encompassing morality, race and national mentality. It is seen as the very essence of Japanese identity, today as much as in the ancient past. For instance, leading post-war Shinto scholars such as Ueda Kenji and Hori Ichirō have described it as 'simply the basic value orientation of the Japanese people' (Ueda 1972: 29) and as 'the underlying will of Japanese culture'

(Hori, quoted in Kuroda 1981: 2). This conceptualization of Shinto is clearly in accordance with *nihonjinron* ideologies concerning Japan's supposed uniqueness and internal homogeneity (Befu 2009).

The ethnic paradigm has long been dominant, influencing scholarly accounts of Shinto in Japan as well as abroad. This is exemplified by the status of Ono Sokyō's classical essentialist introduction to the topic, *Shinto: The Kami Way* (1962), which has been widely quoted and was long considered the main English-language introduction to the topic. The very first sentence of the introduction shows clearly his ahistorical approach: 'From time immemorial the Japanese people have believed in and worshipped kami as an expression of their native racial faith which arose in the mystic days of remote antiquity' (1962: 1). Ono also states that 'Shinto is more than a religious faith', then goes on to define it as 'an amalgam of attitudes, ideas, and ways of doing things that through two millenniums and more have become an integral part of the *way* of the Japanese people' (1962: 3; italics in original). Notions of historical change are largely absent, and Shinto is conceptualized in accordance with nationalist, even racial ideas about 'Japaneseness'. In addition, throughout the book, popular *nihonjinron* myths about 'the Japanese people' (such as their deep-rooted collectivism, their mystical love for nature, and the purity of the nation and its traditions) are employed to strengthen the core argument: the uniqueness and superiority of Shinto and, *ipso facto*, the Japanese nation as such.

Accordingly, in narratives adhering to the ethnic paradigm, the otherness of Shinto vis-à-vis 'ordinary' religions is often stressed, usually by means of the claim that unlike other religions Shinto has no founder, no sacred scripture and no fixed doctrine or dogma (e.g. Ono 1962: 3; Public Affairs Headquarters for Shikinen-Sengu 2013: 11–12). Of course, the same applies to a great variety of so-called indigenous worship traditions worldwide, so such features can hardly be considered special. Moreover, the claim itself can be challenged, not only because modern Shinto is shaped by 'minor founders' (Mullins 1998: 43–47) such as Norinaga and Atsutane, but also because there have been various attempts at canonization and the establishment of some sort of general doctrine, especially in modern times. Nevertheless, in the case of Shinto, this argument is often employed to assert its uniqueness – the standard for 'religion' here is obviously constituted by Shinto's main Others, Christianity and Buddhism, rather than, say, local worship practices in other parts of Asia. This stress on the fundamental otherness of Shinto not only concerns the tradition itself, but also its deities, *kami*, which is often described as a unique category that should not be translated. Indeed, it has become somewhat of a truism in Shinto discourse that *kami* should not be referred to as 'gods' – for 'god', it is often argued, is a 'Western' term not suitable to the Japanese context (e.g. Jinja Honchō n.d.-b; cf. Matsutani 2013).[5]

In sum, the ethnic paradigm is characterized by the following aspects. First, authors and organizations adhering to this paradigm typically assert the transhistorical character of Shinto as a primordial tradition, thus naturalizing it and placing it outside the realm of history. Second, while not denying the existence of religious elements in Shinto *per se*, they usually claim that Shinto is much more than 'merely' a religion: it is the defining essence of the Japanese nation. Thus, this paradigm rests on the assumption that there is an existential correlation between Shinto and 'the' Japanese nation, which is likewise dehistoricized. Third, consequently, the ethnic paradigm reifies that nation as a single, unitary entity, thus denying historical or spatial diversity. And fourth, it asserts the uniqueness of Shinto (and its deities, *kami*) vis-à-vis the other religions in the world, based on some questionable assumptions regarding the basic nature of Shinto. However, while the ethnic paradigm has long been dominant, there are some other conceptualizations of Shinto that challenge, nuance and complement aspects of this view; these may be conceived of as alternative paradigms. I will now move on to discuss them in more detail.

Alternative Paradigms

Although the ethnic paradigm has long been dominant, there are alternative conceptualizations of Shinto which have achieved paradigmatic status – if not in the curricula of the Shinto universities Kokugakuin and Kōgakkan or in the editorial board of *Jinja Shinpō* (the shrine newspaper published by Jinja Honchō), at least among circles of Shinto scholars and within religious movements that likewise define themselves as Shinto. While equally essentialist – that is, their underlying assumption is that Shinto has a core essence not susceptible to historical change – they typically reject the explicit nationalism and emperor-centrism that characterizes the imperial and ethnic paradigms. I have distinguished three alternative paradigms, which I refer to as the local paradigm, the universal paradigm and the spiritual paradigm.

The first two are represented by, respectively, the positions of Yanagita Kunio and Orikuchi Shinobu in the early post-war debates on Shinto's future direction, discussed previously. As Breen and Teeuwen pointed out, while the notion of a unified ethnic tradition has long taken precedence, these alternative conceptualizations have 'bounced back' (2010: 7). Indeed, in contemporary discourse on Shinto, they appear to have gained significant popularity, as illustrated by the fact that in recent popular works on the topic – including some of those discussed in the following chapters – Yanagita and Orikuchi are among the authors that are quoted most often. In addition, the notion that Shinto is a spiritual or mystical tradition which cannot be grasped rationally but only experientially or intuitively has gained significant ground, to the point that it has also taken on paradigmatic status, at least within certain circles not directly connected with the shrine establishment. As these three paradigms continue to coexist and shape popular understandings of Shinto, including contemporary environmentalist conceptualizations, I will briefly discuss each of them.

Yanagita Kunio is well known for being the founder of *minzokugaku*, an academic discipline usually referred to in English as 'folklore studies' – or, alternatively, as 'native/nativist ethnology' (Ivy 1995: 66). In the first half of the twentieth century, he conducted research on rural culture, collecting so-called folktales and studying local dialects. For instance, one of his best-known works, *The Legends of*

Tōno (*Tōno monogatari*), is a compilation of various stories about supernatural creatures (*yōkai*) from Tōno, a rural town in Iwate Prefecture (Yanagita [1910] 2008). His project was not unlike that of the Grimm brothers in Germany: both are characterized by the romantic-nationalist assumption that in rural stories and folk cultural practices the 'original' spirit of the nation is preserved and can be rediscovered (Snyder 1978: 35–54). In addition, Yanagita's work displays a strong concern for the loss of local diversity as a result of modernization, and a corresponding nostalgia for a 'traditional' rural Japan believed to be rapidly disappearing. As Marilyn Ivy (1995) has demonstrated, this nostalgic concern for the loss of 'traditional' culture is a central recurring trope in twentieth-century Japan. The discourse of decay, in which 'rapidly changing' modern urban life is juxtaposed with idealized rural traditions supposedly going back to primordial times yet currently threatened by extinction, has become an integral part of modern imaginations of the nation (cf. Figal 1999). Thus, paradoxically, reified 'folk'/'rural'/'local' culture is very much a product of modernity itself. Idealized notions of a 'disappearing' rural diversity and modern constructions of nationhood are two sides of the same coin.

According to Yanagita, the essence of Shinto is not to be found in ideological abstractions, but rather in rural practices, which have supposedly remained unchanged since ancient times. As one later interpreter has written,

> [Yanagita] distinguishes between Shinto as the indigenous faith (*koyū shinkō*) of Japan, preserved by the common people from prehistoric times to the present, and the Shinto represented by Shinto theologians and historians. The latter, he maintains, is a history of doctrines created by intellectuals; it differs from the history of the indigenous faith that informs the common man. (…) Yanagita's determination to make the popular traditions of the common man the material of his study amounts to a strong criticism against so-called intellectual historians and scholars of religion who rely solely on written materials and neglect the common man. (Mori 1980: 93–94)

While his critique of the textual, intellectual bias in the study of religion (including but not limited to Shinto) continues to be relevant, Yanagita himself subscribed to a particular normative understanding of Shinto, producing another abstract conceptualization alongside those that already existed. Instead of in classical mythology, he asserted that its essence could be found in the ritual practices and beliefs of 'ordinary men'. However, he did not question the assumption that there was such a thing as an underlying transhistorical core essence. In fact, according to Yanagita, paradoxically it was in the diversity of local practices that the essential unitary character of Shinto and the nation could be found. As Schnell and Hashimoto summarize, 'though Yanagita acknowledged cultural diversity within Japan during the early stages of his career, he later turned to the articulation of a unifying essence for the Japanese "mainstream" population. The *jōmin*, or "ordinary folk", as he called them, lived in harmonious rural villages, engaged in irrigated rice cultivation, and venerated their ancestors' (Schnell & Hashimoto

2012: 107). Thus, Yanagita was not opposed to nationalism per se. He was critical, however, of 'State Shinto' as it was developed in pre-war Japan, for it '[exploited] the religious traditions of ordinary people' (Mori 1980: 106). Like his contemporary Minakata Kumagusu (1867–1941), he was especially critical of the 'shrine merger movement' (*jinja gōshi* or *jinja gappei*), a policy imposed in 1906 and implemented in subsequent years, which led to the demolition of a significant number of rural shrines and their groves (Mori 1980: 107; cf. Sakurai 1992).

Yanagita's scholarly yet romantic interest in 'traditional' local practices as remnants of a pure, original, pre-Meiji Shinto may not have been influential enough to set the agenda of Jinja Honchō in the immediate post-war period, it has nonetheless regained significant popularity from the 1970s onwards. Not coincidentally, this resurgence of interest in *minzokugaku* took place around the same time as a new wave of rural nostalgia, which led to the nationwide conservation – or, in some cases, construction – and commodification of 'traditional' rural villages, so-called *furusato* (Moon 1997; Ivy 1995; Robertson 1988, 1998). In recent years, this rural nostalgia has been coupled with environmentalist rhetoric and given rise to a nationwide movement for the conservation and revitalization of *satoyama*: idealized hybrid nature-culture landscapes supposedly characteristic of 'traditional' Japan (Berglund 2008; Brosseau 2013; Takeuchi et al. 2003; Tsing 2015: 179–187; Williams 2010). As we shall see, the notion of *satoyama* has profoundly influenced contemporary Japanese imaginations of the national landscape and corresponding spatial practices. In addition to tourism and conservation practices, the return of the local paradigm has contributed to a new academic interest in local diversity – not only among ethnologists, but also among historians of religion and Shinto scholars, leading to a renewed interest in local shrine histories and *matsuri* (e.g. Azegami 2009; Sakurai 1992, 2010; Schnell 1999; Sonoda 1990; Sonoda & Mogi 2006; Thal 2005). As later chapters will demonstrate, it has also exercised considerable influence upon the development of the Shinto environmentalist paradigm and the *chinju no mori* preservation movement.

Despite all their differences, the imperial, ethnic and local paradigms have one important similarity: the assumption that there is a fundamental connection between Shinto, however conceptualized, and the Japanese nation. This is somewhat different in the case of the universal paradigm. While recognizing that Shinto has emerged and developed in Japan, representatives of this paradigm typically assert that Shinto has (potential) relevance not only for Japanese people but also abroad. According to them, Shinto is, or should become, a 'world religion' – that is, a religion with universal applicability and appeal. This view is perhaps more marginal today than the local or ethnic paradigms, but it constitutes a significant subcurrent in modern Shinto ideology. Besides, there are some indications that this paradigm is currently gaining new popularity and is in the process of being revitalized. This is not necessarily the case for the Japanese shrine world, where the existential intertwinement of the Japanese nation and Shinto continues to be the predominant axiom – although even here we can witness some noteworthy recent attempts at international outreach, as mentioned in the introduction. Yet the universal paradigm is more explicitly advocated by a number of popular authors, priests and self-identifying Shinto practitioners abroad, as well as by followers of a variety of so-called new religions identifying with Shinto.

As we have seen, Breen and Teeuwen associate the idea that Shinto should become a religion with universal appeal and relevance with Orikuchi Shinobu. Like Yanagita, by whom he was influenced, Orikuchi was an ethnologist interested in Japanese 'folklore', rural traditions and stories. Unlike Yanagita, however, he was also strongly interested in classical texts; for instance, he conducted research on the *Man'yōshū*, an eighth-century anthology of classical poetry believed by him and his followers to contain important clues about ancient 'Shinto'. Orikuchi was no less of a cultural essentialist than Yanagita; he believed that both Shinto and the imperial institution were ancient traditions intimately connected with the Japanese nation. However, unlike most of his colleagues, he also believed that in the post-war period Shinto should be reconfigured as a religion open to all humankind (Orikuchi [1949] 2012).

Orikuchi was not the first to suggest that Shinto could be transformed from an ethnic tradition into a world religion. In the pre-war period, a significant number of shrines had been built in overseas occupied areas, in particular Korea and Taiwan. Generally speaking, these were closely associated with imperial rule and ideology. According to historian Nakajima Michio, between the 1890s and 1945 a total of 1640 so-called overseas shrines (*kaigai jinja*) were built outside mainland Japan (2010: 22). Most of these were in Korea (995), followed by Manchuria (243), Taiwan (184) and Sakhalin (128) (2010: 27–28). Although most *kaigai jinja* were incorporated within the imperial system and modelled after shrines in Japan, there were also attempts to develop Shinto into a 'world religion' by accommodating various non-Japanese ritual traditions. This, for example, was the intention of Shinto scholar and missionary Ogasawara Shōzō (1892–1970), whose ideas on the universal applicability of Shinto worldviews echoed contemporaneous notions of Japan's 'civilizing mission' (K. Suga 2010). After the war, however, Shinto virtually disappeared from Japan's former colonies; the vast majority of these shrines were either demolished or converted into temples for other deities, although some traces of Shinto remain (e.g. *torii* gates). Not all *kaigai jinja* were built in the colonies, however. In the Meiji period (1868–1912), sizeable groups of migrants left Japan to settle in Hawaii, North America, and South America. Several shrines were built in those areas, some of which are still used today.

The universal paradigm is particularly popular among members of so-called Sect Shinto organizations, also referred to as 'new religions'. In fact, there is nothing particularly 'new' about the existence of popular charismatic movements that combine healing practices with prophecy, mediumship (the communication of a deity or ancestral spirit's messages to humans), and politically subversive utopian and millenarian promises of world renewal (*yonaoshi*). Such movements existed in the Kamakura period (Nichiren Buddhism is the best-known example) as well as in the Muromachi and Edo periods (e.g. Davis 1992: 45–81). However, in the Meiji period, these movements were institutionalized and developed in hitherto unknown ways, as a result of political transformations, Christian influences and technological developments.[6] Most important, the new legislation concerning 'religion' changed the status of these groups. If they wished to continue their 'religious' activities – proselytization, healing, preaching and so on – they had to be registered as *shūkyō*, private religions, membership of which was a matter of personal choice. Thus, despite their historical connection to particular *kami* and, in some cases, shrine worship traditions, they were not configured as shrine Shinto – which, after all, was redefined as a public 'non-religion' for the benefit of the nation and its divine imperial family, participation in which was mandatory. For the groups that perceived themselves as religious, and did not want to be incorporated into the state cult, a new category was created: 'Sect Shinto' (*kyōha shintō* or *shūha shintō*).[7]

In addition to these older 'Sect Shinto' organizations, a number of new religions established in the post-war period are also referred to as 'Shinto-derived new religions' (*shintōkei shinshūkyō*) (Inoue 2002: 408). Most of them belong to the 'Ōmoto lineage': the group of religions influenced by the beliefs and practices of Ōmoto. Several of these groups claim to possess secret knowledge going back to ancient times, referred to as *koshintō* ('old Shinto'). They typically combine promises of spiritual salvation and millenarian regeneration with a variety of praying and healing practices, as well as social activism, organic agriculture, investment in 'traditional' Japanese arts and outspoken opposition to organ transplantation. Examples include Sekai Kyūseikyō, Seichō no Ie, Ananaikyō, Worldmate and Sūkyō Mahikari. Whether or not all these movements should be categorized as 'Shinto' may be subject to debate. Considering the difficulty of establishing an authoritative definition of 'Shinto' and the normativity inherent in any such attempt, however, I suggest that the primary criterion for classifying groups should be self-definition. In any case, there is a large, diffuse group of organizations that, while being significantly different from 'standard' shrines (but then, who decides the standard), lay claim to the 'true' Shinto tradition as much as Jinja Honchō does. Thus, the boundaries of the category Shinto are as unclear and contested as ever.[8]

It is precisely in these 'borderlands' of Shinto, among these religious movements, that the universal paradigm is at its most pronounced. Already in the pre-war period, some of them established overseas mission activities and constructed shrines abroad. Izumo Ōyashirokyō, for instance, founded a shrine and mission organization in Hawaii in 1906. Religions such as Tenrikyō, Konkōkyō, Ōmoto, Seichō no Ie and Sekai Kyūseikyō have all employed foreign mission activities. The last two groups are well-known for having attracted significant numbers of followers in Brazil; others have been active in Europe, the US, Australia, Southeast Asia and Africa, with varying degrees of success. The international orientation of these religions does not make them disregard their Japanese cultural identity, however. On the contrary, some of them are known for their conservative-nationalist stances, their interest in preserving and revitalizing 'traditional Japanese culture' such as *ikebana* and tea ceremony, and their strong support for the imperial family.[9] Yet, unlike proponents of the ethnic paradigm who assert that Shinto is something intrinsically Japanese that cannot be fully grasped by foreigners, they maintain that this ancient Japanese tradition – or, more precisely, their interpretation of it – has global significance. Accordingly, they believe that it is their task to share this tradition, and its soteriological potential, with the world.

Thus, 'Sect Shinto' organizations and 'Shinto-derived new religions' not only proselytize, they are also active in a variety of charity activities and set up development programs abroad. To name but one example: Ananaikyō, an Ōmoto-derived religion founded in 1949, has set up an international development NGO called Organization for Industrial, Spiritual and Cultural Advancement (OISCA). It currently has projects in around thirty countries focusing on topics such as (organic) agricultural development, reforestation and environmental education.[10] Organizations such as OISCA are strongly aware of their Japanese heritage and believe that Japan has a special mission to fulfil in bringing peace and prosperity to other nations of the world. Thus, universalistic though its agenda is, the movement is also strikingly nationalistic: the supposedly unique Japanese spirit of human-nature coexistence (*kyōsei*), and the ancient Shinto tradition in which this spirit is rooted, are seen as guiding principles for solving environmental problems and poverty worldwide.

This, indeed, was the message delivered by president Nakano Yoshiko during her presentation at a symposium on Shinto and the environment, organized by Shintō Kokusai Gakkai in 2009 (Nakano 2010). Nakano's participation in this event is significant: founded in 1994, Shintō Kokusai Gakkai has constituted a prominent alternative Shinto voice, which has actively supported research on and dissemination of knowledge about Shinto abroad.[11] It has funded chairs at universities in the US and UK, organized conferences abroad and regularly invites foreign scholars to symposia in Japan. Its main sponsor, Fukami Tōshū (1951–), is also the founder and leader of Worldmate, one of the 'Shinto-derived' new religions.[12] Thus, like organizations such as Sekai Kyūseikyō and OISCA, Shintō Kokusai Gakkai has a strong international orientation and agenda, representing a contemporary version of the universalist paradigm. As we shall see in Chapter 4, it has also been active in the development of the Shinto environmentalist paradigm.

Finally, there is a fifth approach to Shinto, which I refer to as the spiritual paradigm. It is perhaps not as easily recognizable and clearly demarcated as the other paradigms, as notions of Shinto as a spiritual tradition have been combined with each of the ethnic, local and universal paradigms. Nevertheless, I have decided to classify this as a separate paradigm, as I believe it constitutes a significant, distinctive subcurrent in modern representations of Shinto, which has acquired paradigmatic status within some circles of Shinto scholars and practitioners. This paradigm rests on the assumption that the core essence of Shinto cannot be known through historical inquiry, intellectual reflection or ideological reasoning. According to this view, Shinto is fundamentally a non-rational religion that can only be known experientially – an experience that is pre-reflexive, non-discursive and emotionally moving. For instance, during one of my interviews I talked to a shrine official who confirmed my impression that there are many different definitions of Shinto, but added that, ultimately, these do not matter – for Shinto is an 'intuitive religion' (*chokkan shūkyō*) that can never be truly understood by words alone, but must be grasped intuitively (interview, February 2011; cf. Yamamura 2011: 51).

I refer to this understanding of Shinto as the 'spiritual paradigm'. That does not mean I endorse the term 'spirituality' as an analytical concept, however, for it is employed in many different ways and has an ambiguous character, in English as well as Japanese (where it is referred to as *reisei*, *seishin* or *supirichuariti*). But then, it may be exactly this lack of a clearly defined substance that gives the term its ideological potential – for the term is widely used, but hardly reflected upon, let alone historicized. 'Spirituality' is used to signify a variety of other-world-oriented beliefs and practices, including such things as experiences of the divine, communication with supernatural beings, meditation practices and esoteric ancestry theories. It is sometimes conceptualized as the essence of religion – communication with and experiences of the divine, however shaped – without its institutions, dogmas and, importantly, politics. At other times, however, it is seen as religion's Other and placed in opposition to it. As an 'emic' category employed for purposes of academic and religious identity politics, therefore, the term 'spiritual' is highly relevant.[13]

When the spiritual paradigm is combined with the ethnic paradigm, this often leads to the assumption that foreigners (or 'Westerners') do not understand what Shinto really is about, as they are rational and analytical, whereas Japanese are allegedly intuitive, sensitive and emotional. Thus, a classical Orientalist myth is re-employed, and used as a strategy for asserting Shinto's essential otherness and incomprehensible nature. However, it may also be combined with the universal paradigm: the assumption that 'Westerners' are generally incapable of Shinto-type spiritual experiences then gives way to the argument that they may well (re) learn this, if only they overcome the alienation from nature supposedly resulting from 'their' Christian worldview. Accordingly, one sometimes comes across the argument that Shinto is similar to other worship traditions – in particular, those of the Native Americans and those of the ancient Celts, not surprisingly two traditions that have been reinvented and popularized by contemporary followers of 'neo-paganism' and 'New Age' – or even that each nation has had 'its own version of Shinto'. Yet such statements are often accompanied by the assertion that, in other countries, such 'nature spirituality' has been marginalized, and the nature they (used to) worship destroyed. Japan, it is argued, is the only country where an 'ancient nature religion' has survived as a central part of contemporary society (e.g. Yamamura 2011: 54–55; Yasuda 1990).

Whether the 'Shinto' spiritual experience is seen as uniquely Japanese or potentially universal, the accompanying rhetoric is the same: critique on the ideological aspects of 'Shinto', or on the historical involvement of shrine priests and other Shinto actors in politics, is easily discredited by referring to the critic's lack of understanding, supposedly due to his or her overtly rational approach and lack of spiritual sensitivity. By defining Shinto as spiritual, the tradition is dissociated discursively from 'politics' and 'ideology', which are dismissed as external and peripheral to the spiritual essence. This is a well-established discursive strategy in religion and religious studies, as Robert Sharf (1998) has demonstrated, and Shinto is no exception.

The following argument by Stuart Picken is illustrative for this combination of the universal and spiritual paradigms and shows how easily the notion of Shinto as an ancient spiritual tradition can be used to deny its political aspects:

> Sadly, the first image a Westerner may have of Shinto was shaped by the nationalistic propaganda employed by both sides of the Pacific during World War II. State Shinto, as it is called to differentiate itself from the ancient way, hijacked the *natural religion* of Shinto (…). Close to sixty years after the war, in the new millennium, Shinto has slowly emerged from the gloom of misunderstanding. Apart from a few unenlightened cynics who refuse to believe even the most basic evidence to the contrary, Shinto is returning to its origins and trying again to become what it always was, the spiritual roots of the Japanese people. This is the Shinto I wish you to find – the Shinto whose true characteristics are *caught rather than taught* – for this is the Shinto that can revitalize the natural aspects of human spirituality by teaching us how the world is seen with nature by our guide. (2002: 24–25; my emphasis)

The implications are clear. 'State Shinto' is presented as an evil Trojan horse, which invaded and took over the 'natural', apolitical religion Shinto, seen as a passive victim that was not to blame for any involvement with imperialist ideology. It is the 'true', 'natural' Shinto that constitutes the 'spiritual roots' of the Japanese people. Thus, Shinto is conceived of as a singular spiritual (rather than, say, ritual, cultural or ideological) tradition, while 'the' Japanese people are essentialized and dehistoricized. This familiar historical narrative is coupled with the claim that, Japanese though its origins may be, Shinto provides invaluable spiritual lessons for today's world – yet these have to be *caught* experientially, not *taught* intellectually.

Another important contemporary representative of the spiritual paradigm is Kamata Tōji, a professor at Kyoto University and prolific author of popular religious books, who also defines himself as a 'Shinto songwriter'. Kamata has written a number of books on Shinto, pilgrimage and sacred places (2000, 2008, 2011). According to him, the essence of Shinto lies in the intuitive, pre-discursive awareness of the sacred power present at these places. In order to grasp this essence, one has to go there, feel the energy and take part in ascetic and other devotional practices. Kamata sees modern 'State Shinto' as an invention and a distortion of these spiritual traditions and argues for a revitalization of *shinbutsu shūgō* (Shinto-Buddhist) beliefs and practices (2000: 89–107). His ideas are reflected in the contemporary trend to define shrines as 'powerspots' with strong spiritual energy. Notions of shrines as places with some sort of 'cosmic power' providing all sorts of benefits to visitors are ubiquitous in today's 'powerspot' discourse and greatly contribute to the popularity of certain shrines, especially those associated with *en-musubi*: success in love (Rots 2014b: 42–45; N. Suga 2010).

We will encounter Kamata Tōji again in later chapters, as his ideas have exercised influence upon the discourse on Shinto as an ancient tradition of nature worship. Indeed, Kamata is one of those who suggest that Shinto can provide valuable, even crucial resources for overcoming the global environmental crisis. This is one of the core tenets of the 'Shinto environmentalist paradigm', which I will discuss in later chapters. First, however, let us have a closer look at notions of 'nature' in modern Japanese ideology and social practices, as this is crucial for contextualizing contemporary Shinto discourse.

Chapter 3

LOVE OF NATURE

The Green Orient

In the introduction, I discussed the case of an international interfaith conference on religion and environmental issues, co-organized by Jinja Honchō and the Alliance of Religions and Conservation, which took place in Ise in 2014. This conference, I argued, is a clear illustration of the popular view that religions have an important role to play in promoting environmental sustainability, which has been embraced by scholars and religious leaders alike, to the point that it has led to significant transformations in religious self-understandings and practices. This development has not remained unchallenged, however. As Poul Pedersen summarized:

> The religious environmentalist paradigm is based on two claims. The first is that traditional religious ideas and values play a decisive – or even determining – role in human environmental behaviour. The second is that traditional religious ideas and values express an authentic ecological awareness and a strong conservationist commitment which are similar to those of modern environmentalist concerns. (...) However, there are two good reasons to reject the claims of the religious environmentalist paradigm. Firstly, they rest on a simplistic and untenable idea of how values and behaviour are related, and secondly, they are anachronistic projections of modern phenomena onto the screen of tradition. (1995: 264)

Contemporary understandings of the environment rest on a particular imagination of nature on a 'global' (or transnational) scale, which is a by-product of modernization processes. Accordingly, Pedersen writes, 'We should not reject the idea that traditional religious values may reflect conceptualizations of the environment, but these are not identical to our modern ecological and conservationist understanding of nature' (1995: 267). According to him, environmentalist readings of ancient sacred texts are anachronistic projections: 'ecological representations of nature belong to a conceptual framework of globality and are therefore fundamentally different from traditional representations of nature with their predominant localized focus' (Pedersen 1995: 269; cf. Tsing 2005: 1–18). Arguably, what is at stake in much religious environmentalist discourse is not only a concern for environmental problems but also identity politics. By reinventing their own tradition as, say, ancient ecological wisdom, a variety of actors (religious, academic and/or political) dissociate themselves from the powerful but exploitative and morally corrupted 'West', as well as its dominant religious tradition, Christianity (Pedersen 1995: 272).

However, just because environmentalist re-readings of 'sacred' texts are anachronistic, that does not mean they are invalid. Any scripture considered to be of ongoing relevance for people's lives is constantly reinterpreted according to changing social and historical contexts, and interpretation is necessarily subject to transformation. Sacred texts have always been interpreted anachronistically, as exegesis is contingent upon historical change: this applies to environmentalist interpretations as much as it does to nationalist, feminist or fundamentalist ones. Moreover, religious actors expressing a concern for environmental issues may have various reasons for doing so – including, possibly, the sincere belief that 'nature' (or 'Creation') is in urgent need of human protection, and that doing so constitutes a religious obligation. Yet one thing does not exclude the other: a genuine concern for environmental degradation may well go hand in hand with other motivations and interests. Thus, Pedersen's thesis is relevant, as it rightly points to the identity politics involved in many environmentalist redefinitions of 'religious' (or cultural, for that matter) traditions.

Arne Kalland (2008) has elaborated further upon Pedersen's thesis. As he pointed out, in religious environmentalist discourse, there are two binary oppositions that often reoccur. Both are based on an essentialist understanding of 'Western' culture and the Judeo-Christian tradition supposedly underlying it. In the first dichotomy, 'the West' is positioned vis-à-vis the 'ecological noble savage': the 'indigenous peoples' supposedly living in harmony with nature and in possession of 'traditional ecological knowledge' (2008: 95).[1] In the second dichotomy, 'the West' (or its variant, the 'monotheistic' or 'Abrahamic' religious tradition) is placed in opposition to 'the East' and its traditions, such as Hinduism, Buddhism, Daoism and Confucianism. The latter are conceptualized as holistic and non-dualistic, whereas the 'Abrahamic' religions are seen as fundamentally dualistic (Kalland 2008: 99).[2] As I will show in the following chapters, one of the defining characteristics of the 'Shinto environmentalist paradigm' is that it combines these two different binary oppositions. That is, Shinto is reimagined as, essentially, *both*: a primitive indigenous tradition of ancient ecological knowledge, akin to Native American or Aboriginal traditions, *and* a sophisticated holistic Asian wisdom tradition, diametrically opposed to 'Western' Christianity.

As mentioned in the introduction, one of the foundational texts underlying present-day religious-environmentalist discourse is Lynn White's article 'The Historical Roots of Our Ecologic Crisis', which was published in *Science* (White 1967). White famously alleged that the contemporary global environmental crisis was partly due to Judeo-Christian (i.e. 'Western') notions of man's divinely ordained domination over nature. In this article, Christianity is contrasted with 'paganism' and 'animism' on the one hand, and with Asian religions on the other. If the Christian view of nature as subordinate to humans has caused environmental destruction, as White argues, by implication Eastern views of nature and human culture as interdependent and mutually constitutive should have given way to some sort of ecological equilibrium and prevented environmental destruction. Indeed, White considered the possibility of adopting alternative, 'holistic' Eastern worldviews such as Zen as a means to overcome Western anthropocentrism, asserting that Zen Buddhism conceives of 'the man-nature relationship as very nearly the mirror image of the Christian view' (1967: 1206).[3] In the end, however, he did not believe such worldviews would be able to achieve widespread acceptance in 'the West' due to their cultural deviance. Instead, he proposed a re-evaluation of Franciscan thought as some sort of proto-environmentalism, which could acquire new significance in the present age. Others, however, took White's arguments one step further; they argued that 'the West' should learn from and incorporate 'Eastern worldviews', which were presented as antidotes to environmental problems (e.g. Watanabe 1974; Murota 1985; Yasuda 1990).

White's argument has not remained unchallenged. Soon after the publication of his article, Yi-Fu Tuan rightly pointed out that there are significant discrepancies between attitudes towards nature, as formulated in classical texts, and actual behaviour – not only in Europe but also in China, where Daoist and 'animistic' understandings of nature could not prevent massive deforestation long before the advent of 'Western' technology and science (Tuan 1968). Nevertheless, White's article has exercised significant influence on subsequent discourse on culture, religion and environmental issues (Pedersen 1995: 260). Significantly, they have also had a profound impact in Japan, where they affected popular understandings of both 'Eastern' and 'Western' religious attitudes to nature (Fujimura 2010).

The association of religion with environmental sustainability has been particularly strong in the case of Asian religions. Daoism, Buddhism, Hinduism and Confucianism have all been described as ecological traditions grounded in a deep awareness of the interdependence of all beings, as opposed to the anthropocentrism supposedly characteristic of the Abrahamic religions. This is particularly clear in the case of Daoism: in the early 1970s, Huston Smith wrote that Daoism provides invaluable ecological wisdom for our age, establishing the explicit association between 'Tao' and ecology that would influence Anglophone discourse on Daoism for decades to come (Smith 1972; cf. Snyder 2006). As a result, there has long been a firm connection between Daoism and environmentalism, especially in American academic and popular discourse (e.g. Girardot, Miller & Liu 2001).

In recent years, the association of religion with environmental advocacy and ecological thought has also become well-established in China itself, affecting Daoism as well as other worship traditions (Duara 2015: 35–40; Miller 2013; Miller, Yu & Van der Veer 2014; Snyder 2006). Not coincidentally, the leader of the Alliance of Religions and Conservation, which co-organized the conference in Ise in 2014, is Martin Palmer, a well-known scholar of Daoism. In cooperation with the ARC, the Chinese Daoist Association has set up several projects for the purpose of environmental protection. For instance, they have established a 'Daoist Ecology Temple' on the sacred mountain Taibaishan, as well as a 'China Daoist Ecology Protection Eight Year Plan' (ARC n.d.-b; n.d.-c). These activities are supported by the Chinese national government, which has come to see Daoism as 'national heritage' rather than backward superstition, as it did previously. As James Miller writes, 'The Chinese Daoist Association has embarked upon an ambitious agenda to promote Daoism as China's "green religion". (...) In promoting Daoism as a green religion, the Chinese Daoist Association is not aiming to restore some mythical utopia of humans living in harmony with nature, but instead to support a nationalist agenda of patriotism and scientific development' (2013: 249). As a matter of fact, there are some significant similarities between Jinja Honchō and the Chinese Daoist Association, no doubt partly due to the fact that both actively cooperate with and are influenced by ARC. In both cases, institutional authorities have eventually embraced a 'green' narrative initially developed by (foreign) academics, while simultaneously pursuing a nationalist agenda.

Similar developments can be observed in other Asian worship traditions. There is a large body of texts on Buddhism and ecology, and Buddhist leaders worldwide have expressed their concern about environmental problems (e.g. Buddhist Climate Change Collective 2015; Thich Nhat Hanh 2008). Tibetan Buddhism in particular has been reframed as a 'green' religion, which has provided new international legitimacy to the tradition and has helped gain international support for struggles against Chinese oppression (Huber 1997). The modern Thai Buddhist practice of 'ordaining' trees as a tactic to prevent deforestation has also drawn significant international attention and contributed to the spread of notions of Buddhism as a green religion (Darlington 2012). Likewise, there is a sizeable discourse on 'Zen' thought in relation to environmental ethics (e.g. James 2004; Parkes 1997). In Japan, several Buddhist temples have been involved with environmental activism, nature education and the development of various ecological practices.[4]

Similar developments can be observed in India, where Hindu temples have been actively involved with different types of environmental activism (Karlsson [2000] 2013; Kent 2013). Although many of these initiatives have a predominantly local character, some types of religious environmentalism in India have been advocated by Hindu nationalists, who associate 'ecology with the social body, and a common distaste for Westernization and globalization. (...) Their rhetoric connects the pollution of the land and waters with the pollution of the Hindu nation by the presence of "aliens", particularly Muslims' (Duara 2015: 47; cf. Sharma 2012). This is a relevant observation, which draws attention to the fact that environmentalism not always goes together with a concern for minority rights, a cosmopolitan worldview or a progressive agenda with respect to social issues. Some types of environmental activism and conservation may in fact serve nationalist projects and encourage xenophobia, not only in India and China but also in Europe (Duara 2015: 48–49). This observation is important for understanding the intertwinement of environmentalism and nationalism in contemporary Shinto ideology, especially when it comes to Jinja Honchō's position.

Figure 3.1 Shinto is not the only East Asian tradition that has been reinterpreted in the light of the religious environmentalist paradigm. Here, Daoist priests visit Ise Jingū, together with representatives of other religions, during the interreligious conference 'Tradition for the Future' in June 2014. Photo: ARC / Alexander Mercer (Valley Foundation).

The Problem of 'Nature'

As mentioned, one of the main assumptions underlying the religious environmentalist paradigm is that Asian religions such as Buddhism, Daoism, Hinduism and Shinto relate to nature in fundamentally different ways from Abrahamic religions, especially Christianity, which makes them more environmentally sustainable. Authors making such assertions do not usually define what they mean by the term 'nature', however, despite the fact that the term carries a number of different meanings and connotations. Nature is often perceived as a universal given, an existential *a priori* which sets the conditions for human culture and society but is not part of it. As Kate Soper has summarized, the term historically refers to 'those material structures and processes that are independent of human activity (in the sense that they are not a humanly created product), and whose forces and causal powers are the necessary condition of every human practice' (1995: 132–133). Thus, in conventional discourse, there is a binary opposition between the realm of phenomena that are created by humans and subject to historical change ('culture', 'society', 'politics' etc.) and the realm of the physical phenomena providing the conditions for those creations (i.e. 'nature'). Indeed, one could argue that the nature-culture dichotomy is one of the most influential and powerful myths of modernity, as it has exercised profound influence on contemporary understandings of the world, shaping many of the social and educational structures associated with modernity (Ingold 2000: 1; cf. Soper 1995).

One core characteristic of this conceptualization of nature as a universal given, ontologically opposed to the realm of human history, culture and politics, is that it denies its own historicity. Like any concept, 'nature' is itself a historical construction, established and reified in the course of the European history of thought. However, as the construction of 'nature' as a universal and non-discursive given became successful, this historicity has come to be concealed. Thus, Anna Tsing argues that 'nature' is one of the 'most historically successful universal claims' (2005: 88). Yet, notions of universality are themselves the product of a particular imagination; as such, they are necessarily locally embedded and historically contingent. Tsing convincingly shows how notions of nature as universal go back to the project of developing a system for mapping all 'the world's' species (botany and Linnaean taxonomy). This project, she argues, was developed by means of the integration of non-European knowledge of plants and their properties, a process that was later concealed. 'Nature' became universalized, while knowledge of 'nature' was claimed by European 'scientists' who denied colonial contributors access to this knowledge and removed any internal reference to the historical knowledge production process that had led to the system's establishment. In other words, 'nature' and 'science' were dehistoricized (Tsing 2005: 90–95).

In reality, then, conceptualizations of nature are culturally contingent and subject to historical change. In the words of Roy Ellen, 'How people conceptualise nature depends on how they use it, how they transform it, and how, in so doing, they invest knowledge in different parts of it. (…) [Nature] means different – often contradictory – things in different contexts. It is constantly reworked as people respond to new social and environmental situations' (2008: 326–327). Likewise, in the formulation of Macnaghten and Urry, 'there is no singular "nature" as such, only a diversity of contested natures; and (…) each such nature is constituted through a variety of socio-cultural processes from which such natures cannot be plausibly separated' (1998: 1). Accordingly, in recent decades, scholars have become increasingly aware of the historical and cultural embeddedness of the concept 'nature' and displayed an interest in perceptions and constructions of nature beyond the West. For instance, several scholars have written about the historical configuration of the category 'nature', and conceptualizations of nature and the environment, in Japan (Asquith & Kalland 1997; Berque 1986, 1992, [1986] 1997; Eisenstadt 1995; Kalland 1995, 2002; Kirby 2011: 69–84; Martinez 2005; Morris-Suzuki 1998: 35–59; Rots 2013b; Tellenbach & Kimura 1989; Thomas 2001).

As in other countries, 'nature' has featured prominently in the modern Japanese imagination. As Morris-Suzuki has written, 'In Japan, images of nature have played a particularly central role in molding the imagery of nationhood' (1998: 35). That is, 'different ways of understanding the natural environment evolved over time and created a store of vocabulary and imagery which have been central to modern constructions of what it means to "be Japanese"' (1998: 38). Likewise,

Julia Thomas has shown that 'nature' was one of the core concepts of modern
Japanese ideology; she describes it as 'the changing, contested matrix within which
the political possibilities of modernity were explored' (2001: 3). Thus, conceptions
and representations of nature were central to the construction and reification of
the Japanese nation. Notions of nature carry great ideological significance exactly
because they are not usually recognized as the historical and political constructs
they are; they conceal their own historicity, and are therefore easily employed as
discursive tools for depoliticization (cf. Barthes 1957). This makes them particularly
useful for nation-building projects, as nations are naturalized historical constructs.
In other words, images of nature are often connected to images of the nation, to the
point that 'whoever can define nature for a nation defines that nation's polity on
a fundamental level' (Thomas 2001: 2). Not surprisingly, then, images of natural
symbols and landscapes often feature prominently in nationalist imaginations (e.g.
Schama 1995; Schwartz 2006; Witoszek 1998).

Thus, universal though they may seem, notions of 'nature' are culturally
dependent and subject to historical change. The image of nature as the realm
of physical things not made by humans, diametrically opposed to 'culture' and
'society', is not shared universally. Most cultures in the world have concepts
denoting aspects of the physical environment, partially corresponding to the
category 'nature' as it developed in the European history of thought, but these
concepts do not cover the exact same meanings as 'nature'. Importantly, they
are not necessarily opposed to 'culture' either. In modern Japan, there are two
words that may be translated as 'nature': *shizen* and *tennen*. These terms overlap,
but they have slightly different nuances: *shizen* tends to be more abstract and
general than *tennen*, which has more concrete and material connotations
(Kirby 2011: 72).[5] Although already used in classical Chinese sources, in their
contemporary meaning these terms are Meiji-period products. At the time, a
large number of European scientific and political concepts were incorporated
into the Japanese language. Initially, a variety of existing philosophical concepts
(most of them Confucian) were used to translate 'nature', until eventually *shizen*
became the term of choice in the 1890s (Thomas 2001: 7, 32–34). In this sense,
shizen is similar to *shūkyō*: both were pre-existing Chinese concepts, which were
rediscovered and re-employed as a translation of a modern epistemic category
in Meiji-period Japan, in the process acquiring profoundly new meanings
(cf. Josephson 2012).

In popular and scholarly discourse (primarily but not only in Japan), it has
often been suggested that 'the' Japanese have a unique way of relating to nature,
diametrically opposed to the 'Western' tendency to control and exploit nature.
Japanese culture is supposedly characterized by a profound love of nature, an
intuitive appreciation of nature's beauty and a harmonious coexistence between
humans and their natural surroundings. Notions of the Japanese love of nature

were implicit in the Japanese nation-building project and figure prominently in
post-war *nihonjinron* discourse. As several scholars have argued, this imagery is
idealized, essentialist and at odds with reality (Kalland 1995; Kirby 2011: 69–84;
Martinez 2005; Morris-Suzuki 1998: 35–59). However, as these images continue to

be reproduced in popular texts, mass media and advertisements, they have been naturalized and become part of the mainstream national *doxa*.

Thus, in everyday conversation as well as popular publications, one regularly comes across the claim that, unlike 'Westerners', 'the Japanese' have a unique love of nature. This is supposedly evidenced by such quintessentially Japanese art forms as haiku poetry, garden architecture, the tea ceremony and even martial arts. It is also associated with the simplicity of Zen religious practice and, as we shall see later, the 'animistic' orientation of Shinto. Japanese people are believed to live in harmony with nature and fully appreciate its beauty, especially when it comes to the specific characteristics of the four seasons – cherry blossoms in spring, chirping cicadas in summer, red maple leaves in autumn and snow-covered landscapes in winter. They are also said to have a strong awareness of the passing of these seasons and a high sensitivity towards the impermanence of natural beauty (Shirane 2012).

Japanese culture is formed by this awareness of the natural world, the story goes; the experience of living in harmony with nature is reflected in the importance of harmony (*chōwa*) in Japanese society, and has given this society its unique character. Thus, the myth of the holistic love of nature and its beauty is one of the main markers of Japanese identity and a central and recurring theme in many popular and scholarly texts that deal with Japan. It is perceived as a timeless feature of an essentialized and dehistoricized 'Japanese culture', which is identified with the nation-state and its allegedly homogeneous society.[6] In reality, however, the 'love of nature' myth is a modern construct, grounded largely in imported notions of 'nature' and its relation to 'national culture'. As it is one of the main pillars on which the Shinto environmentalist paradigm stands, a brief discussion of its genealogy is in order.

The Love of Nature: A Brief Genealogy

It has been suggested that the myth of the Japanese love of nature goes back to Orientalist representations of Japanese culture as characterized by sensitivity and refinement, such as the writings of Lafcadio Hearn (1850–1904) and the imagination of Japanese aesthetics by European artists and authors taking part in the *Japonisme* movement (Kalland 2008: 96; cf. Cox 2003: 14–47). Although nineteenth-century Orientalist imagination undoubtedly contributed to the development of the myth, it is important to bear in mind that modern Japanese notions of nature and nation were also influenced by Edo-period ideology. In the pre-modern period, several Confucian and *kokugaku* scholars reflected upon 'nature', variously conceptualized.[7] Of particular relevance for this study is the work of Motoori Norinaga (1730–1801), which may be considered the first systematic indigenous attempt to conceptualize 'Japan' as a nation akin to its modern-day meaning; that is, a primordial entity, representing a unique culture, strictly demarcated and fundamentally different from other countries (Morris-Suzuki 1998; cf. Anderson [1983] 1991). Norinaga's work focuses on the study of ancient chronicles, in particular the *Kojiki* and its cosmogony, as well as literary classics such as the *Man'yōshū* and *Genji Monogatari*. He was highly critical of what he considered the poor state of Japanese culture, society and politics at the time, which he contributed to the corruptive influence of Chinese ideas, in particular Confucianism. The solution to this deterioration was, according to Norinaga, a return to the ancient Way of Japan. As Japan was the place where the gods had created the world, the Japanese people were potentially superior to the other peoples of the world; they would not need any imposed morality if only they were to return to this ancient Way, since living according to the Way would automatically make them behave respectfully. This ancient Way was referred to by Norinaga as 'the natural Way of the Gods' (*shizen no shintō*) (Morris-Suzuki 1998: 48). These ideas exercised considerable influence on the discursive construction of 'Shinto' as a primordial, divinely ordained and uniquely Japanese tradition, as discussed in the previous chapter.

Modern notions of the harmony between humans, nature and deities are often attributed to Norinaga. It should be noted that he did not use the category *shizen* in the modern sense (i.e. as a particular ontological realm opposed to 'culture'), but rather used the term in the meaning of 'spontaneous', 'natural' or 'things as they are'. Thus, he argued, Japan's 'Way of the Gods' was more 'natural' than Chinese notions, as it was in accordance with the will of the gods (Thomas 2001: 44–45). Importantly, however, Norinaga also addressed ways in which people relate to the physical environment. In particular, phenomena we now refer to as natural elements were said to have the power to evoke feelings of beauty and melancholy, a sense of *mono no aware* ('the pathos of things') – most powerfully expressed in poetry – leading to 'an acute sensitivity of the affective and emotional qualities of life' (Nosco 1990: 178; cf. Motoori [1763] 2011). The concept of *mono no aware* refers to an intuitive awareness of the finitude and fragility of all beauty, leading to feelings of melancholy. It is often associated with cherry blossoms (*sakura*), whose beauty is short-lived. This has become a powerful cultural trope, which was employed during the Pacific War to describe and legitimize the fate of suicide pilots (Ohnuki-Tierney 2002).

Thus, in the work of Norinaga, we find for the first time the association of an appreciation of nature's beauty and harmony with nationalist assertions of Japanese divine superiority. As Morris-Suzuki summarizes, his writings 'established a connection between Shinto mythology, Japanese nationalism, a belief in spontaneous human virtue, and a profound sense of the natural environment as the chief stimulus to that virtue' (1998: 49). His myths were to be re-employed in the early twentieth century, when Japanese authors struggled to define their national identity vis-à-vis Western nations. The Japanese love of nature (as exemplified by the feeling of *mono no aware*) would become a central aspect of the discourse on the Japanese uniqueness and Japan's alleged spiritual and aesthetic superiority to the West. One of the authors who developed these ideas further was Haga Yaichi (1867–1927), a *kokugaku*-influenced scholar of Japanese literature and nationalist theoretician who argued that the unique Japanese national culture was 'directly connected to nature' (Rambelli 2007: 139). Likewise, early twentieth-century writings on Japanese art actively contributed to the imagining of the nation in

relation to an idealized 'love of nature'. Two examples of influential works on
Japanese aesthetics in which the myth of the harmony of the Japanese people with
nature was told are *The Book of Tea*, written by Okakura Kakuzō (1863–1913) and
first published in 1906 (Okakura [1906] 1956), and *Art, Life, and Nature in Japan*,
written by Anesaki Masaharu (1873–1949) and published in 1932. The following
excerpt of Anesaki's work is illustrative of this discourse and foreshadows post-war
cultural-nationalist narratives on environmental issues:

> In many countries nature is thought of as necessarily wild and bold, in
> contrast to human refinement. According to that conception, life consists in
> the combat against nature, or in the conquest of it. But the Japanese lives too
> close to nature to antagonize her, the benignant mother of mankind. Just as art
> has permeated every corner of life in Japan, so Japanese art always derives its
> model and inspiration from nature. (…) Although the land is sometimes visited
> by earthquakes, hurricanes, and volcanic eruptions, the people have adapted
> themselves to such conditions, and live in amicable intimacy with nature. They
> enjoy the delights of the seasons ([1932] 1973: 6–8).

Anesaki draws a reassuring picture of a gentle, artistic, peace-loving people,
living in harmony with each other and their natural surroundings. The reality,
of course, was quite different: this work was written in the early 1930s, when
the Japanese imperialist project was in full swing, and the country was heavily
militarized. Moreover, Meiji-period industrialization had already caused large-
scale environmental pollution at the time (Murota 1985: 107), raising questions
about the concrete application of the alleged 'love of nature'. Thus, the discrepancies
between Anesaki's narrative and the historical reality are striking. Importantly,
mythical images of the Japanese people and their love of nature not only contribute
to a sense of national belonging and to notions of otherness; they can also be read
as attempts to conceal political and social realities that do not fit the ideal.

In any case, Anesaki's text was part of a larger project to naturalize the
Japanese nation-state – quite literally. In his work, human qualities are projected
onto the natural landscape of the Japanese archipelago, and assertions about the
character of the Japanese people are justified by referring to the allegedly mild
climate and gentle geographical features. The implication, of course, is that there
is an existential correlation, going back to primordial times, between the Japanese
nation/race (*minzoku*) and the physical landscape of the Japanese territories.
Significantly, such an association between a national community and a particular
physical territory is a central aspect of much nationalist myth-making. Anthony
D. Smith uses the term 'ethnoscape' to refer to this perceived correlation between
nation and landscape. He defines it as 'the idea of an historic and poetic landscape,
one imbued with the culture and history of a group, and vice versa, a group part of
whose character is felt by themselves and outsiders to derive from the particular
landscape they inhabit' (1999: 150).

Although Anesaki gained some fame internationally as a scholar of Japanese
art and religion, the most influential academic theory of the Japanese 'ethnoscape'

was developed by philosopher Watsuji Tetsurō (1889–1960). Most important, it was Watsuji who introduced the concept *fūdo* and gave it its academic credibility. First published in 1935, Watsuji's classic *Fūdo* constitutes one of the main intellectual foundations for the post-war *nihonjinron* discourse (Befu 1997). It has had profound influence, laying the foundation for a large body of post-war scholarship on Japanese culture. This includes contemporary Shinto scholars such as Sonoda Minoru, who, as we shall see, uses Watsuji's terminology to explain the fundamental interconnectedness between the Japanese natural environment and 'ancient Shinto' (e.g. Sonoda 2010). Considering the significance of the notion of *fūdo* for the Shinto environmentalist paradigm, a brief discussion of Watsuji's theory is necessary.

With Anesaki, Watsuji argued that there is a fundamental interrelatedness between a natural landscape, including its geographical and climatological features, and the culture and society of the people who live there.[8] The term *fūdo* is made up of the characters 'wind' and 'land'. It is often translated as 'climate', but this translation is too narrow. Watsuji opens his work by explaining that he uses it 'as a general term for the natural environment of a given land, its climate, its weather, the geological and productive nature of the soil, its topographic and scenic features' ([1935] 1961: 1). Berque's translation of the concept as 'milieu' (1992: 94), then, does more justice to Watsuji's original meaning.

According to Watsuji, a milieu consists of more than just physical phenomena; not only does it influence the ways in which individuals experience their existence (for instance, someone who lives in a tropical climate will experience life differently from someone who lives in an arctic climate), it also has profound implications for the development of human culture and society. Thus, people who live in tropical climates are said to have a different culture and worldview from those who live in arctic climates, which is caused by the differences in weather, landscape, vegetation and so on. There is certainly some validity to this assumption; in Watsuji's work, however, it quickly turns into environmental determinism and cultural essentialism. Historically constructed discourses of differentiation are naturalized by referring to the fundamentally different milieus in which the 'nations' of the world live – and have lived, since primordial times, as migration is hardly taken into account.

Watsuji divides the world into three different types of milieus: monsoon, desert and meadow. Each of these milieus has its regional differences and subtypes – the monsoon climate in Japan is different from that in India, for example. In his work, Watsuji gives elaborate descriptions of the different milieus, the way the climate has shaped the landscape, the corresponding features of agricultural systems and food culture and, accordingly, people's mentality, material culture and social structures. His narrative begins by asserting the inferiority of the other people of Asia vis-à-vis the Japanese, reproducing European stereotypes that were employed to justify colonial rule. For instance, about Southeast Asia, Watsuji writes:

The climate of the South Seas affords man a rich supply of food; hence his attitude is that all is well as long as he is blessed with nature's generosity. But, here, the relationship between man and nature contains no variety and, as a result, man is moulded to a passive and resignatory pattern. (…) So they became easy prey for and ready lackeys of the Europeans after the Renaissance. ([1935] 1961: 22–23)

Significantly, at the time of writing, Japan was preparing its own imperialist actions in the region; accounts such as this were welcome ideological justifications for the 'liberation' of the 'passive' Southeast Asians from European powers.

His description of people in the Middle East as naturally aggressive, however, is even more remarkable: 'The most striking example of desert's man struggle with the desert is his mode of production; in other words, desert nomadism. Man does not wait passively for nature's blessings; he makes active incursions into nature's domain and succeeds in snatching a meagre prey from her. This fight to nature leads directly to a fight with the other man' ([1935] 1961: 49). As the Jews always 'continued to retain their desert character', a justification for anti-Semitic persecutions, in full swing in Germany at the time, is easily made: 'it was the Jews themselves, who invited such persecution' ([1935] 1961: 51). Thus Watsuji contributed to a sizeable anti-Semitic discourse in Japan, which continues to influence popular understandings of Judaism today (Goodman & Miyazawa [1995] 2000).

By contrast, European culture is presented as rational and scientific, features that were supposedly shaped in interaction with the natural environment. As nature in Europe (in particular in Greece and Italy, where European culture originated, according to Watsuji) is 'docile, bright and rational' ([1935] 1961: 79), and as the meadows throughout the continent were easily cultivated, the rationality that supposedly characterizes the European mentality is quickly explained:

There is a link between the lenience and the rationality of nature, for where she is lenient man readily discovers order in nature. And if in his approaches to nature he takes due account of such order, nature herself becomes even more lenient, and man, in turn, is led further to search for the order in nature. Thus, Europe's natural science was clearly the true product of Europe's 'meadow climate'. ([1935] 1961: 74)

As may be expected, this European rationalism is contrasted with the Japanese emotional receptivity for nature, in particular the seasonal changes and dramatic contrasts, which are supposedly due to the typical type of monsoon milieu that is found only in Japan. This 'had created a distinctive and complex sensitivity to nature, vividly represented in Japanese art, architecture, and literature' (Morris-Suzuki 1998: 57).

Apart from the aesthetic implications, according to Watsuji, the Japanese *fūdo* has also had profound social implications. For instance, the heat and humidity of the Japanese monsoon summer caused the Japanese people to build open houses, which, together with the importance of cooperation in the cultivation of rice (likewise conditioned by the climate and geography of the Japanese isles),[9] has contributed to the 'unique collectivism' of the Japanese people and the strength of their social ties. In fact, according to Watsuji, it is this notion of the 'house' or 'household' (*ie*) as central social unit that constitutes the main characteristic of Japanese society, going back to ancient times; it is here that one finds such typically Japanese features as filial piety and self-sacrificing love. Watsuji's naturalization of the *ie* as an essential, primordial feature of the Japanese nation is a clear example of myth-making; as several authors have pointed out, the *ie* system was largely a Meiji invention, which became part of the state ideology and was actively promoted by the government (Morris-Suzuki 1998: 114–115; Ueno 2009). Not only did this ideology contribute to gender inequality, it also actively propagated uncritical love of the nation and its regime through the extrapolation of the notion of *ie* to the nation. That is, the nation was presented as one big family, of which the emperor was the head. Although Watsuji did not uncritically accept this aspect of Meiji ideology ([1935] 1961: 148), his essentialism and environmental determinism did provide an important intellectual justification for this type of ideology.

Post-war Appropriation and Critique

In post-war Japan, expressions of the 'love of nature' myth and *fūdo*-type explanations of the Japanese 'natural character' have been manifold, in academia as well as beyond, and I do not have the space to give a comprehensive overview of this discourse. It is important to note, however, that in the post-war period, pre-existing notions of Japanese ways of interacting with nature were combined with environmentalist rhetoric, giving rise to a type of cultural-nationalist argumentation that seeks the solution to environmental problems in 'Japanese tradition'. Such views were expressed by Japanese as well as Anglo-American scholars. They were informed by Whitean notions of environmental destruction as a moral crisis rooted in cultural and religious values, rather than, say, technology or capitalist ideology. In many of these texts, 'Japanese culture' was placed in binary opposition to 'Western culture'. This idealized Japanese culture was often equated with 'Zen', which acquired significant popularity in the United States in the 1960s, largely thanks to the work of D. T. Suzuki. Indeed, drawing on the ideas of people like Haga, Anesaki and Watsuji, Suzuki also dwelled upon the topic of the Japanese perception of nature:

> In these prosaic days of ours, there is a craze among the young men of Japan for climbing high mountains just for the sake of climbing; and they call this 'conquering the mountains'. What a desecration! This is a fashion no doubt imported from the West along with many others not always worthwhile learning. The idea of the so-called 'conquest of nature' comes from Hellenism, I imagine, in which the earth is made to be man's servant, and the winds and the sea are to obey him. Hebraism concurs with this view, too. In the East, however, this idea of subjecting Nature to the commands or service of man according to his selfish desires has never been cherished. For Nature to us has never been uncharitable, it is not a kind of enemy to be brought under man's power. We

of the Orient have never conceived Nature in the form of an opposing power. On the contrary, Nature has been our constant friend and companion, who is to be absolutely trusted in spite of the frequent earthquakes assailing this land of ours. (1959: 334)

In this excerpt, which was published in 1959 but goes back to lectures given in 1935, 'Nature' becomes a rhetoric device allowing the author to condemn 'Hellenistic' and 'Hebraic' worldviews (i.e. the two pillars of 'Western' civilization), while romanticizing the 'East'. It also allows him to lament the moral and cultural degradation of modern Japan supposedly caused by the 'import' of many Western ideas. This has become a recurring trope: authors who argue that Japanese tradition offers a solution to environmental problems, and who are confronted with the reality of environmental destruction brought about by the Japanese state as well as private enterprises, often retort by stating that this is the unfortunate result of modernization and Westernization; a return to 'tradition', it is argued, would solve such problems (e.g. Sonoda & Tabuchi 2006; Umehara 2009). In any case, Suzuki's argument is illustrative of scholarly accounts of the importance of the unique Japanese 'sense of nature' (*shizensei*) for the development of national culture. Other examples of prominent scholars in Japan who addressed this topic are anthropologist Ishida Eiichirō (1903–1968) and Buddhist scholar Nakamura Hajime (1912–1999).[10]

Given the paradigmatic status of the Japanese 'love of nature' myth and the international impact of the Lynn White thesis, it comes as no surprise that a large number of authors – both inside and outside Japan – have suggested that Japanese culture and religion can provide alternative models for approaching and coexisting with the environment. Most of these arguments are characterized by cultural essentialism – that is, 'the' Japanese are treated as a transhistorical, uniform entity, and the nation's historical construction process is not questioned. Furthermore, although there is ample reference to artistic practices, poetry and Japanese (Zen) Buddhism, there is an overall lack of practical suggestions as to what such alternative models might actually look like, and how they can concretely contribute to overcoming environmental problems. A well-known example is Watanabe Masao's article, published in *Science*, which repeats the now-familiar myth that Japan has 'a love of nature which has existed from very early days. (…) For the Japanese and for other Oriental peoples, man was considered a part of nature, and the art of living in harmony with nature was their wisdom of life' (1974: 279). Following White, Watanabe suggests that, perhaps, Japanese cultural values may help to conceive of new ways to conceptualize our attitude towards the environment, yet he does not offer much in terms of concrete suggestions.

This point has been made more explicitly by others. Murota Yasuhiro, for instance, has argued that 'we need to return to the Japanese way of thought to find a direction for the future' (1985: 110). David Shaner likewise stated that 'much of the Japanese tradition is in concert with [an] ecocentric and communitarian perspective', so we should 'consider aspects of the Japanese experience of nature as a possible conceptual resource for environmental philosophy' (1989). The well-known geographer Yasuda Yoshinori described Europe as the 'civilization of deforestation', responsible for destroying 'the world of animism', 'the peaceful relationship between man and nature in Asia, Africa and South America' and, correspondingly, their natural environments (1990: 3). Japan, according to him, represents 'the forest civilization': it escaped the 'invasion of the "civilization of deforestation"' (1990: 4) and has preserved an ancient animistic worldview, which must be revitalized in order to counter environmental destruction.[11] And the argument continues to be repeated today. For instance, architect-designer Azby Brown recently published a book in which he argued that we could learn many practical lessons for living sustainably from Edo-period Japanese society (2009).[12] Midori Kagawa-Fox has published an article on Japanese 'environmental ethics' that claims to offer new ethical perspectives yet is grounded in a rigid East-West dichotomy and reproduces familiar *nihonjinron* stereotypes (2010). Romano Vulpitta similarly argues that in this time of egotism, in which traditional social structures are disappearing, 'the West' would do well to learn from the Japanese people's sense of nature, their tolerance towards others, and their unselfish worship of the emperor (2011).[13] The list could go on and on.

These claims have not remained unchallenged. As mentioned, several scholars have scrutinized Japanese conceptions of nature, including the 'love of nature' myth (Asquith & Kalland 1997; Kalland 1995, 2002; Kirby 2011; Martinez 2005; Morris-Suzuki 1998; Thomas 2001). By showing how such notions have developed historically, their works constitute an important counterbalance to the ever-expanding body of texts that uncritically assume that 'the Japanese love of nature' is a natural given and to texts suggesting that all it takes to overcome contemporary environmental problems is a return to 'traditional (Japanese) values'. Some scholars have also explicitly targeted those who suggest Japanese worldviews are superior to and more sustainable than 'Western' ones. For instance, Ian Reader has responded to Yasuda Yoshinori's naive plea for an 'animism renaissance' (1990) by pointing out that every culture, including those in Africa and Asia, 'has devised its own ways of manipulating and exploiting its environment for its own benefit, generally with little regard for the overall and long term needs of future generations' (Reader 1990: 15). Moreover, he has rightly drawn attention to the fact that the alleged 'forest civilization' Japan at the time 'consume[d] 40% of the world's trade in tropical timber each year, and it is logging for the Japanese trade that has denuded many of the forests of the Philippines and Thailand, and is about to do the same for Sarawak [Borneo]' (1990: 15). Likewise, several authors have lamented the environmental destruction of Japan itself, criticizing modern Japanese policymakers and politicians for not practising what they preach and destroying traditional landscapes (Kerr 2001; McCormack [1996] 2001).

When confronted with this type of critique, proponents of the view that traditional Japanese values should be revitalized in order to deal with environmental problems do not usually disagree; on the contrary, they tend to concur. Their point is, however, that the environmental problems of modern Japan are the consequence of the Meiji-period modernization project, and the incorporation of

'Western' technology and thought, as a result of which the Japanese people have lost their traditional values and ways of life (e.g. Yasuda 1990: 4). Or, as Watanabe wrote, 'Still immersed in nature itself, the Japanese people do not quite realize what is happening to nature and to themselves, and are thus exposed more directly to, and are more helpless in, the current environmental crisis' (1974: 282).

It is ironic, to put it mildly, that the country that has played a central part in the large-scale deforestation of great parts of Southeast Asia (Dauvergne 1997; Tsing 2005) – a development that had already started in the 1970s, when Watanabe wrote his article – is portrayed as a nation of victims, 'helpless in the current environmental crisis'. Nevertheless, the notion that Japanese environmental destruction is the result of 'modernization' and 'Westernization', sometimes seen as imposed by 'Western' imperial powers, is widespread – as is the related notion that prior to the Meiji period the Japanese lived in harmony with nature and did not experience any environmental problems. This is not historically accurate; as environmental historian Conrad Totman has shown (1989), there have been different periods in pre-Meiji Japanese history when there was large-scale deforestation, as well as the depletion of other natural resources. The notion of perpetual ecological harmony may well reflect artistic celebrations and representations of nature but does not correspond to actual reality. There is a significant discrepancy between ideal and reality, historically as well as in contemporary society.[14]

A similar point has been made by Arne Kalland. Drawing on the work of Totman, he has argued that 'there have been many serious cases of environmental destruction in premodern Japan. (...) We have overlooked the fact that for millennia the Japanese have tried to conquer nature as much as westerners have done' (1995: 245). Kalland points out that the 'nature' that is traditionally appreciated in Japan is not at all similar to modern American notions of nature as 'wild' and 'untouched' (cf. Cronon 1996). Using Lévi-Strauss' classical distinction between the raw and the cooked as an underlying structure of myths (1964), Kalland argues that

> The Japanese have, like most other people, an ambivalent attitude toward nature. (...) Many Japanese seem to feel an abhorrence toward 'nature in the raw' (*nama no shizen*), and only by idealization or 'taming' (*narasu*) – e.g., 'cooking', through literature and fine arts, for example – does nature become palatable and even lovable. In other words, nature can be both raw and cooked, wild and tamed. Torn by destructive and creative forces, nature oscillates between its raw and cooked forms, and in its cooked form nature and culture merge. It is in this latter state, as idealized nature, that nature is loved by most Japanese. (Kalland 1995: 246; cf. Kalland 2002: 147–150)

Thus, 'nature' as it is appreciated in Japanese culture is highly cultivated indeed. According to Kalland, the significance of nature for Japanese culture lies in the fact that it functions as 'a repertoire for metaphors' (1995: 251). That is, natural elements do not acquire significance until they are culturally mediated. Accordingly, there is a striking difference between established Japanese conceptions of 'nature' and contemporary notions of the environment: the former are concerned with particular symbolic images and places, while the latter are based on an imagination of nature as a single, global realm, visible in yet transcending particular localities. Hence, Kalland continues,

> the quantity of nature, if I can put it that way, is of no great importance, and nature invisible to an actor – as one located in faraway places – is of little general interest. (…) Only when nature is brought into the realm of the known, e.g. tamed, and there are some immediate personal gains, do most Japanese become interested in protecting nature. (1995: 255)

In other words, environmental advocacy in Japan is often concerned with particular locales, and immediate threats to public health (Kirby 2011) or nearby landscapes of interest, rather than more abstract issues. As I will show in this study, the same applies to shrine-related environmental advocacy: while priests and parishioners may be mobilized to protest against the demolition of shrine forests, that does not mean they will protest against the overseas logging activities of companies purchasing shrine rituals. And although shrine actors throughout the country have been active in preserving local *chinju no mori*, this has not translated into engagement with large-scale environmental problems such as climate change. Of course, Japan is by no means unique in this respect – anywhere in the world, it is usually easier to mobilize people over local concerns than abstract issues. It does mean, however, that there is little or no empirical evidence supporting the claim that Japanese worldviews and values lead to a more general concern for the environment than 'Western' ones.

As this chapter has demonstrated, the notion that there is a particular, uniquely Japanese way of coexisting with nature, determined by the particular geographical and climatological conditions of the Japanese isles, was and remains central to discursive constructions of Japanese national identity. Drawing on this discourse, in recent decades a large number of authors have argued that Japanese cultural and religious traditions provide valuable ideological resources for overcoming today's environmental problems. Such arguments are legitimized by the ideas of foreign scholars such as Lynn White and his followers. They are grounded in essentialist notions of 'East' and 'West', which are placed in binary opposition, and figure prominently in contemporary identity politics. As illustrated by various cases of environmental destruction caused by Japanese actors, such idealized notions of nature by no means automatically lead to environmentally friendly behaviour; on the contrary, as Arne Kalland has argued (2002), they may even have an opposite effect. Nevertheless, they remain central to present-day formulations of national identity, to policymaking and to various social practices – including those associated with Shinto, as the following chapters will show.

Chapter 4

THE SHINTO ENVIRONMENTALIST PARADIGM

Living with Nature

In recent years, the assumption that Shinto has an intimate connection to nature has become commonplace. The association between Shinto and environmental issues has achieved mainstream acceptance as well. Today, even the president of the generally conservative Jinja Honchō, Tanaka Tsunekiyo, asserts that Shinto is of great significance for overcoming environmental problems. For instance, at the 2014 ARC conference in Ise, Tanaka declared that Shinto perceives humans and nature as 'one body' (*dōtai*), since humans are 'part of nature' (*shizen no ichibu*). Shinto, according to him, 'originates in reverence for nature: from the time of its inception until today, "nature" has remained its foundation' (2014: 157). Shinto is deeply concerned with the natural environment, Tanaka argues, as illustrated by its involvement with tree-planting – a core element of Japanese culture, according to him – and forest conservation (2014: 182–186). Shinto, therefore, has a 'message to the world': humankind must return to its 'original values' and relearn how to 'live together with nature' (*shizen to tomo ni ikiru*) (2014: 188). Tanaka does not specify what exactly 'living in nature' entails in a modern consumption society, nor does he give any concrete suggestions as to how Shinto (or other religions) can contribute to solving contemporary problems. Yet, the rhetoric is characteristic of contemporary Shinto discourse and illustrative of the fact that the Shinto environmentalist paradigm has been adopted even by the conservative shrine establishment.

Similarly, in a recent book discussing contemporary issues and challenges in shrine Shinto, research journalist Yamamura Akiyoshi writes as follows: 'Environmental destruction continues worldwide. The Shinto notion of *kami* residing in nature, and of "coexistence and co-prosperity" between humans and nature, is now beginning to be understood internationally. The clue to solving environmental problems lies in Japan's sacred forests (*chinju no mori*)' (2011: 39). This statement is typical for the contemporary understanding of Shinto as a tradition with great potential for solving environmental problems, not only in Japan, but globally. As Yamamura argues, Shinto is based on the belief that nature is the dwelling place of deities, and, therefore, has sacred properties. Humans and nature are said to be interconnected, existing in a state of mutual dependence and coexistence (*kyōsei* or *kyōzon*) – a worldview often juxtaposed with 'Western', 'monotheistic' anthropocentrism, which is seen as the root cause of global environmental destruction. In the aforementioned quotation as well as in similar expressions of the Shinto environmentalist paradigm, such worldviews are presented as an antidote to environmental problems all over the world.

The association of shrine worship with 'nature', however conceptualized, is not particularly recent. The idea that Shinto is concerned with deities residing or manifesting themselves in natural elements such as trees, mountains, rivers and celestial bodies can be found in works that predate the explicit association of religion with environmental studies inaugurated by the Lynn White thesis. Ono Sokyō, for instance, noted that shrines are often characterized by beautiful natural surroundings and stated that 'natural objects' and 'natural phenomena' have been worshipped as *kami* since ancient times (1962: 7). Later, Joseph Kitagawa wrote that 'the early Japanese are believed to have found *kami* everywhere: (...) they took for granted the common *kami* (sacred) nature of all beings within the world of nature' (1988: 233). However, although the notion that there is some sort of connection between *kami* and natural phenomena (mountains, rivers, rocks and trees) has long been taken for granted in descriptions of Shinto, not until recently has the relation between 'nature', *kami* and 'Shinto' been subject to more serious theoretical and ideological reflection. In particular, the extension of 'nature' to 'the environment', and the explicit association of Shinto with environmental issues, is of fairly recent date. Although such ideas were first expressed in the 1970s, they did not gain much attention and popularity until well into the 1990s.

Today, by contrast, 'nature' and 'environmental issues' have become standard tropes in written introductions to Shinto – books, websites, tourist pamphlets and so on – and become a core component of many contemporary Shinto self-definitions. Reflecting the spread of the religious environmentalist paradigm worldwide, Shinto has been redefined as an ancient tradition of nature worship that contains valuable cultural and ideological resources for establishing sustainable relationships between humans and nature. This understanding of Shinto has now become so firmly established that it may be considered a new paradigm in its own right, which combines elements from the five earlier paradigms discussed in Chapter 2. In particular, contemporary discourse on Shinto and the environment contains many ideas that are typical of the local paradigm. It is no coincidence that Yanagita Kunio is quoted repeatedly by representatives of the Shinto environmentalist paradigm: contemporary advocates of the notion of Shinto as a nature religion typically focus on the importance of shrines and their forests for empowering local communities, regularly using concepts such as *furusato* and *satoyama* and attributing ancient ecological knowledge to 'local' people (*jimoto no hitotachi*), who are romanticized and seen as keepers of tradition. Correspondingly, as we shall see in later chapters, most Shinto-related environmental activism has a predominantly local character, typically focusing on the preservation of particular shrine forests rather than issues of nationwide (let alone global) significance.

Importantly, however, the Shinto environmentalist paradigm has strong national and international components as well. Accordingly, it has also incorporated elements from the imperial, ethnic and spiritual paradigms: an awareness of the emperor as the symbolic head of the Japanese national community, who engages in tree-planting and rice cultivation, expressing a strong affinity with nature; a notion of Shinto as intimately connected with Japanese national culture and the *fūdo* by which it is shaped; and the assumption that the divine character of *kami* in nature can only be experienced intuitively, not grasped intellectually. Most significantly, the Shinto environmentalist paradigm has contributed to a revitalization of the international pretensions characteristic of the universal paradigm: although it developed in Japan, Shinto is once again seen as a tradition with global significance or even salvific potential, not only by members of so-called Shinto-derived new religions but also by senior shrine priests and increasing numbers of non-Japanese followers and sympathizers (Rots 2015c). By creatively combining pre-existing elements in the light of recent developments, the Shinto environmentalist paradigm has succeeded in gaining significant popularity in Japan as well as abroad.

When using the term 'Shinto environmentalist paradigm', I do not mean to suggest that environmental problems constitute the main concern of most contemporary Shinto actors. To many of them, other issues (shrine income, local community well-being and the survival of the imperial institution, to name but a few) are of more immediate relevance. Rather, I use the term to refer to the trend to conceptualize Shinto as a worship tradition intimately connected with 'nature', and the explicit discursive association with 'the environment', 'nature conservation' and 'ecology'. As we have seen, 'nature' is a powerful yet fuzzy concept that carries a number of different meanings and possesses significant ideological potential. The concept 'environment' is hardly less complicated. As Macnaghten and Urry have pointed out, 'nature' and 'the environment' do not mean the same: nature may be imagined as 'pure', 'wild' or 'pristine', whereas 'the environment' is usually associated with problems, distorted balance and destruction (1998: 19–21). It is a recent category that has quickly assumed global significance – not least because it serves to explain changes in physical landscapes and to conceptualize the global interconnectedness of nature, climate and local livelihoods. When using the term 'environment', therefore, I use it as a generic term covering a variety of concepts and assumptions that have developed in the last fifty years or so – including notions such as ecology, pollution, conservation and climate change. In contemporary discourse on 'Shinto and the environment', these different notions are all present, either implicit or explicit.

Consequently, in my use of the term, 'environmentalism' does not refer to one single current of thought, but rather to a variety of ideological positions, all of which assert the importance of environmental issues without necessarily agreeing on other topics. Expressions of environmentalism may differ significantly, not only in their conceptualization of 'the environment' and in the issues considered most urgent and relevant but also in their historical narratives and in the solutions offered for overcoming problems. 'Environmentalism' may be associated with left-wing activism; however, it can also go hand in hand with religious conservatism or with popular nationalist discourse, as long as environmental issues take centre stage in discursive practices. Environmental issues may provide different actors with valuable symbolic capital, which can serve to establish social networks. Indeed, it has been argued that it is precisely with regard to the issue of environmental advocacy that temporary alliances can be made between groups and institutions that are in opposition when it comes to other issues: environmental issues such as whaling or tropical deforestation have provided important areas for cooperation, facilitating relations between actors with profoundly different agendas (Kalland 2009; Tsing 2005).

The same, arguably, applies to contemporary Shinto environmentalism. In an online comment to a blog post written by me on this topic, the American Shinto priest Patricia Ormsby made the insightful remark that Shinto 'as it is currently practiced (...) fosters a respectful dialogue between conservative and progressive elements of society, bringing them together in an era of intense polarization, when cooperation is becoming more and more critical' (Ormsby 2012). While there is undeniably a number of issues that are contested and divide the shrine world (e.g. Breen 2010b), I would argue that it is precisely on the topic of 'the environment' (and, in particular, the importance of *chinju no mori*) that different actors, representing various political and ideological positions, can come together and strengthen ties. 'Nature' and 'the environment' are discursively depoliticized, apparently 'neutral' topics that provide a common ground on which various Shinto institutions, clergy, scholars and laypeople can find each other – at least on an abstract level. Although it may be questioned to what extent environmental problems constitute a top priority for most Shinto leaders and shrine priests, few would deny the value and importance of the natural environment (*shizen kankyō*), whether acting upon it or not. In sum, one of the reasons for the increasing popularity of the Shinto environmentalist paradigm may well be its capacity to unite a diversity of actors – priests, ideologues and practitioners – around the shared symbolic capital of 'nature', 'the environment' and, most of all, 'sacred forests'.

Two Academic Trends

One of the main characteristics of the Shinto environmentalist paradigm is the fact that it denies its own historicity. According to its advocates, there is nothing new or inventive about the association of Shinto with environmental issues, even if some of the terminology has changed; as they argue, 'Shinto' appreciations of nature's sacred character have contributed to nature conservation since prehistoric times. It is only natural, they suggest, that Shinto actors speak out on behalf of the natural environment today. It is questionable, however, to what extent premodern forest preservation practices can be attributed to Shinto (or Buddhist) worldviews, and to what extent such practices indicate the presence of concerns about the environment akin to present-day ones (Domenig 1997; Rambelli 2001, 2007; Totman 1989).

As mentioned, the conceptualization of 'the environment' as a universal category, associated with various crises that are characterized by their global interconnectedness and political urgency, dates from the second half of the twentieth century (Macnaghten & Urry 1998). This conceptualization rests on notions of 'wilderness conservation' that go back to the nineteenth century and have spread globally in the context of modern imperialism (Cronon 1996; Neumann 1998; Tsing 2005). While I do not deny the historical existence of 'sustainable' premodern agricultural, forestry and hunting practices in different parts of the world, it is important to keep in mind that such practices were developed in order to sustain human livelihoods and had a predominantly local character. Unlike present-day environmentalism, they did not rest on notions of global ecological interconnectedness, or on formulations of a differentiated 'natural environment' in need of protection. As we have seen in the previous chapter, the explicit association of religious texts, beliefs and practices with 'environmental issues' did not emerge until the late 1960s, whereupon it rapidly acquired popularity and led to the transformation of existing traditions (Kalland 2008; Pedersen 1995; Taylor 2010). In sum, assertions that Shinto has 'always' been concerned with the natural environment are arguably anachronistic. The Shinto environmentalist paradigm emerged in the late 1970s, after which it spread gradually – first among scientists and non-Japanese interpreters, then among organizations associated with so-called Shinto-derived new religions and a handful of proactive shrine priests, and finally, in the 2000s, among the shrine establishment.[1]

The development of the Shinto environmentalist paradigm in Japanese academic discourse can be attributed to two concurrent scholarly trends. The first of these is represented by a group of scholars known for their popular writings, who combine an interest in various spiritual matters with *nihonjinron*-type theories on the unique features of 'Japanese culture', often combined with a Watsujiesque environmental determinism. Although representing different academic disciplines, these scholars have been grouped together and labelled collectively as 'spiritual intellectuals' (Prohl 2000; Shimazono 2004: 275–292).[2] However, rather than 'spirituality' *per se*, it is the essence and origins of the Japanese nation that constitute their main research interest; their descriptions of Japanese spirituality and sacred places are embedded within a larger ideological discourse that is primarily concerned with the question of what it means to be Japanese. Many of their works have clear romantic-nationalist subtexts and are characterized by a nostalgic lamentation of lost values and traditions not unlike that found in Yanagita Kunio's work.

Some of the best-known scholars in this group are Iwata Keiji (1993), Kamata Tōji (2000, 2008, 2011), Nakazawa Shin'ichi (2006), Umehara Takeshi (1989, [1991] 1995, 2009), Yamaori Tetsuo (2001) and Yasuda Yoshinori (1990, 1995, 2006). These scholars typically subscribe to the view that Meiji-period Shinto was an unfortunate aberration, and that the essence of Shinto can be found in supposedly ancient local traditions of nature worship, as well as in beliefs concerning nature's divine character, which are also said to have influenced Japanese Buddhism. Not all of these authors would personally identify with Shinto (Nakazawa and Umehara, for instance, have also written extensively about Buddhism); some write about Japanese culture and religion in general, rather than Shinto *per se*. However, they all share an interest in nature worship, environmental issues (however vaguely defined), (sacred) forests, spirituality and Japanese national identity.

The second scholarly trend behind the redefinition of Shinto as a nature religion is more closely connected with Shinto institutions, as illustrated by the fact that some of the representatives are active as shrine priests. It is not limited to Shinto circles, however, but also includes a number of scientists not directly affiliated with shrines. This trend consists of the close association of Shinto with the study of sacred shrine forests (*chinju no mori*) and corresponding attempts at nature conservation. Since the early 1980s, several prominent scholars and scientists have pointed out the ecological and cultural significance of these forests, which have since become one of the core symbols of contemporary Shinto and attracted the interest of various urban environmentalist groups. Scholars, scientists and priests interested in the topic of shrine forest conservation have joined forces and set up academic organizations for this purpose. Using their core concept, I will refer to them collectively as the *chinju no mori* movement.

From the initial period, the *chinju no mori* movement has had an interdisciplinary character, bringing together scholars and scientists from a variety of disciplines. One of the most prominent representatives is the architect and urban planner Ueda Atsushi (1930–) (A. Ueda [1984] 2007, 2001, 2003, 2004a,b). Ueda's 1984 work *Chinju no mori* (a revised version of which was published in 2007) is one of the movement's foundational texts. In this book, Ueda introduced the topic of *chinju no mori* to a general audience, arguing for the preservation of these small urban forests. His approach was primarily geographical, mapping various *chinju no mori* still existing at the time (with a strong focus on the situation in Shiga Prefecture, where he began his research), but he also made reference to history, spirituality and ecology – topics that would be discussed more elaborately by other representatives of the movement in later years. Ueda's description of *chinju no mori* as 'broccoli-shaped' broad-leaved forests, which are 'natural' in the sense that they have not experienced much human intervention, remains paradigmatic today, despite the fact that in reality many shrine forests are planted and (partly) composed of coniferous trees.

Ueda's geographical study of existing shrine forests was complemented by the work of the internationally famous ecologist Miyawaki Akira (1928–), who has devoted his long career to forest ecology and, in particular, reforestation projects (Miyawaki 2000, 2013). In 1982, Miyawaki published a long essay in the weekly shrine newspaper *Jinja Shinpō*,[3] in which he urged shrine priests to take the initiative in preserving and replanting shrine forests, and instructed them on the best ways to do so (Miyawaki 1982). According to Miyawaki, a healthy ecosystem is best achieved by planting native tree species, which he refers to as *furusato* trees; in most of Japan, these indigenous trees are broad-leaved evergreens. Miyawaki's organization has set up tree-planting projects at sites throughout the world, including some Japanese shrines (e.g. Yaegaki Jinja in Yamamoto, Miyagi Prefecture, discussed in Chapter 8).

Soon after Miyawaki's article, the shrine newspaper published a series of reports on a symposium on the topic of 'shrines and green' (*jinja to midori*)

('"Jinja to midori" zadankai' 1982). At this symposium, in which a number of well-known scholars and scientists participated, several issues were addressed that would later become core topics and tropes in Shinto environmentalist discourse. Among the participants were Ueda Kenji, one of the most prominent post-war Shinto intellectuals; Shirai Eiji and Fukushima Hiroyuki, at the time head priests of, respectively, Tsurugaoka Hachimangū in Kamakura and Meiji Jingū in Tokyo; and two scientists who have published widely on environmental issues and forest preservation, Tomiyama Kazuko and Tsutsui Michio. Thus, the symposium established an important trend: discourse on Shinto and the environment generally has a multidisciplinary character, at least with respect to the background of the contributors. Conferences, symposia and workshops on Shinto, religion, environmental issues and sacred forests often bring together scholars and scientists from a variety of disciplines (including history, religious studies, archaeology, urban planning, forestry and environmental sciences), as well as religious actors (Shinto priests, representatives of 'new religions' and sometimes Buddhist or Christian priests), artists and even, occasionally, 'green' entrepreneurs.

It is worth having a look at the summary of the symposium published by *Jinja Shinpō*, as this constitutes one of the first accounts of a growing awareness of environmental issues on the part of Shinto actors. The report describes Shinto's relation to the environment as follows:

> In this world filled with beautiful forests, our country was the country blessed by the purest environment. The people lived together with nature, loved it, worshipped and lived in harmony with it; for thousands of years, they grew forests and lived in forests, in an ideal environment. From this environment, Shinto, the faith of the Japanese, emerged spontaneously. However, recently, because of rapid modernization, forests have been destroyed (...). Forests have been turned into roads, power plants and houses (...). As so much of Japan's green is disappearing, people are now once again becoming aware of the importance of shrine forests (*chinju no mori*) all over the country. The awareness that with these forests, the only remaining green places in Japan's cities, the Japanese people's living environment must be protected is now spreading – not only among shrine people, policy makers and nature conservation organizations, but also among ordinary citizens. ('"Jinja to midori" zadankai' 1982)

In the early 1980s, the *chinju no mori* conservation movement was gradually spreading and gaining attention. Importantly, as this symposium indicates, it was not only advocated by scientists such as Ueda Atsushi and Miyawaki Akira but also embraced by some Shinto priests and scholars. The collaboration between scientists, conservationists and Shinto priests was taken further in subsequent years. As *chinju no mori* gradually took on more significance, ecologically as well as symbolically, several Shinto scholars joined forces with Ueda Atsushi and Miyawaki Akira. Two of the most prominent ones are Ueda Masaaki (1927–2016) and Sonoda Minoru (1936–). The former was a historian specializing in prehistoric East Asia, head priest of Obata Jinja in the city of Kameoka (Kyoto

Prefecture); the latter is a scholar of religion specializing in *matsuri* traditions, head priest of Chichibu Jinja in Saitama Prefecture. Both scholars have published extensively on topics related to Shinto and nature, in particular *chinju no mori*, which they see not only as important ecological resources but also as invaluable remnants of an ancient Japanese culture that needs to be revitalized in order to overcome the challenges of today (Sonoda 1997, 1998, 2000, 2006a,b, 2007, 2009, 2010; M. Ueda 2001, 2003, 2004a,b, 2010, 2011, 2013). What is more, both Ueda and Sonoda have made active attempts to bridge the gaps between scholarship, Shinto theology, public outreach and shrine-based activism – in particular through their work for Shasō Gakkai (Sacred Forest Research Association), a non-profit organization founded in 2002. Through its annual conferences, regular symposia, annual journal (*Shasōgaku kenkyū*: 'research in sacred forest studies') and book publications (M. Ueda & A. Ueda 2001; M. Ueda 2004c; M. Ueda et al. 2003), Shasō Gakkai has done much to facilitate the interdisciplinary – ecological, historical, archaeological and geographical – study of shrine forests. While it has been criticized by some local activists for being too abstract and academically oriented (fieldwork data, November 2011), it also seeks to educate shrine priests in forest management by offering courses on the topic and disseminate knowledge about various local shrine initiatives.

The Spread of a Paradigm

As illustrated by the case of Shasō Gakkai, the Shinto environmentalist paradigm is not merely an academic construct. It has also been adopted and advocated by various individuals and organizations that self-identify as 'Shinto'. As with other instances where religious texts and practices have been reinterpreted in the light of environmental issues, the boundaries between scholarship and religious activism are often fluid and unclear. It is also important to point out that the development and popularization of this paradigm has taken place in a transnational context. Although the two academic trends discussed above were predominantly Japan-oriented, notions about Shinto as a 'nature religion' with environmental significance have developed in interaction with global trends – especially Anglophone scholarship – and acquired legitimacy through purportedly 'international' activities and support.[4] In this section, I will discuss the contributions of two Japan-based religious-academic organizations: the International Shinto Foundation and the Shintō Bunka Kai (Shinto Culture Society). In the next section, then, I will address some of the ways in which scholars and academic organizations outside Japan have contributed to the discourse.

The International Shinto Foundation is devoted to the dual purpose of facilitating the academic study of Shinto and spreading a positive image of the tradition both in Japan and abroad. As mentioned in Chapter 2 (see footnote 11), the US-based ISF and the Japan-based Shintō Kokusai Gakkai are semi-independent; the latter has now adopted International Shinto Studies Association as its new English name. Until recently, however, it was a single organization. Its hybrid character is reflected in its activities, where religious leaders and priests would sit on panels together with renowned scholars of Japanese religion. The format is not uncontroversial: some other scholars have expressed scepticism concerning ISF's academic character and accused those who participate in their events of downplaying Shinto's political role.[5] Such accusations notwithstanding, the organizations facilitate the research of Shinto in history without interfering with the contents of this research. Academic freedom is guaranteed, it appears, and some of the regular speakers at ISF (and ISSA) conferences have a historical-constructivist approach to Shinto that is significantly different from the essentialist narratives typical of 'emic' Shinto discourse.

That said, the organizations do have an agenda that goes beyond mere academic activities. In particular, they have contributed to spreading the image of Shinto as a nature religion with relevance for environmental issues, in Japan as well as abroad, by organizing a number of symposia on this topic. Most significantly, in 1998, the ISF organized a bilingual symposium titled 'The Kyoto Protocol, The Environment and Shinto' at the Church Center for the United Nations in New York (International Shinto Foundation 2000). Later, in 2009, Shintō Kokusai Gakkai held a symposium in Japanese on 'the world environment seen from the perspective of Shinto' in Chichibu, Saitama Prefecture (Shintō Kokusai Gakkai ed. 2010). In 2011, the United Nations International Year of Forests, it organized another bilingual symposium on the topic of 'the forest culture of *shinbutsu*' (i.e. *kami* and Buddhas) in Kumano, Wakayama Prefecture (Shintō Kokusai Gakkai ed. 2012).[6]

The symposium on the Kyoto Protocol and Shinto clearly illustrates the International Shinto Foundation's multifaceted character. Among the speakers brought together for this event were a UN representative, a diplomat who had been involved in negotiations for the Kyoto Protocol, an American climate change specialist, a scholar of religion active in interreligious initiatives and Worldmate founder Fukami Tōshū himself. While such a multidisciplinary encounter can be fruitful, the conference proceedings give the impression of a symposium in which each speaker talked about their own topic of expertise, without engaging in serious cross-disciplinary dialogue. In particular, the interesting but difficult question as to how exactly Shinto might contribute to the success of the Kyoto Protocol – what can shrines do to promote the use of alternative energy and contribute to the fight against climate change; what is the significance of climate change when perceived from a Shinto perspective; what might a Shinto-based, philosophically sound environmental ethics look like, and what possible consequences could this have for policymaking – was not really addressed. The first three speakers mainly talked about the politics of climate change and the Kyoto protocol but did not have anything to say about the possible role Shinto, or religion in general, might play in this respect. The other two speakers, by contrast, talked about religion but did not seriously address the topic of climate change. Fukami was one of them: he did express some ideas about 'Shinto' and 'animism', but he did not make any concrete suggestions as to how this Shinto could contribute to solving environmental problems (Fukami 2000).

Eleven years after the New York symposium, Shintō Kokusai Gakkai organized another symposium devoted to the question of Shinto and the environment (Shintō Kokusai Gakkai 2010). Although the conference addressed 'global' issues, it was conducted in Japanese only, and the number of foreign participants was limited to a handful of Japan-based scholars. By now, Sonoda Minoru had become head of the organization, pointing to a more direct connection with the *chinju no mori* movement. The symposium took place at the shrine where he is head priest, Chichibu Jinja in Saitama Prefecture, and he was also one of the speakers. As mentioned, Sonoda is one of the leading contemporary representatives of the Shinto environmentalist paradigm, actively spreading the interpretation of Shinto as an ancient, collective worship tradition based on an intimate connection between human communities and their *fūdo*. He is one of today's most vocal Shinto ideologues, who has not only written a significant number of books and articles but also given many speeches, presentations and interviews. In addition, he has great missionary zeal and is actively trying to promote the image of Shinto as an ecological tradition with an important message for today's world. According to Sonoda, Shinto is defined by the Japanese *fūdo* in which it took shape, but its contemporary environmental relevance extends far beyond the borders of Japan. Hence the title of his lecture, '*chinju no mori* to the world' (Sonoda 2010).

This international agenda was also represented by some of the other speakers at the symposium. One of them was the Korean scholar Lee Choon Ja (known in Japan as Lee Haruko), who presented a paper that compared *chinju no mori* to sacred forests elsewhere in East Asia (Lee 2010). Lee is a professor at Kobe Women's University and long-term resident of Japan, who has done comparative research on the topic of sacred forests in East Asia (Lee 2009, 2011). Although *chinju no mori* are usually associated with Shinto and, by extension, Japanese culture and history, Lee also applies the term to sacred trees and green temple surroundings in Korea and Taiwan. Her work constitutes an interesting exception to the overall discourse on this topic. In a field where the term 'international' is applied often but usually serves as a rhetoric device to provide extra legitimacy for academic activities or assert the uniqueness of the Japanese nation, Lee's comparative research in various East Asian countries constitutes an unusual but interesting attempt to transcend the exceptionalism and Japanocentrism typical of most Shinto environmentalist discourse. In various publications, she has rightly drawn attention to the fact that Shinto shrines are hardly unique, showing that countries such as Korea and Taiwan have sacred groves not unlike Japanese *chinju no mori*, and that people there worship sacred trees that are similar to Japanese *shinboku* (Lee 2009, 2010, 2011).[7]

By contrast, the presentation by Nakano Yoshiko, president of the Ananaikyō-affiliated development organization OISCA, was characterized by a *nihonjinron*-type idealization of the 'Japanese harmony with nature', which according to the speaker should serve to teach people in developing countries how to live sustainably (Nakano 2010). As mentioned in Chapter 2, OISCA is active in reforestation projects, organic farming and environmental education abroad (Watanabe 2015). There are some interesting similarities between Ananaikyō and Worldmate, in terms of institutional practices as well as ideology, due to the fact that they both belong to the Ōmoto lineage. Today, several of the religious movements that belong to this lineage self-identify as 'Shinto' – or, at least, claim to have inherited knowledge of a pure, esoteric 'ancient Shinto' (*koshintō*). Interestingly, perhaps the most vocal advocates of religious environmentalism and sustainable practices today are not shrine priests but representatives of some of these Ōmoto-derived 'Shinto' movements.

Seichō no Ie, for instance, places great emphasis on environmental issues. It has recently constructed completely new, carbon-neutral and sustainable headquarters, the 'office in the forest' (*mori no naka no ofisu*) in mountainous Yamanashi Prefecture, a new base from where it wants to contribute to building a society in which humans and nature live in balance.[8] Contrary to mainstream Shinto, the organization also advocates vegetarianism as a way to reduce global warming (Dessì 2013: 133). Another large Ōmoto-derived religion, Sekai Kyūseikyō Izunome Kyōdan, likewise expresses an interest in nature and environmental issues. It is especially known for its emphasis on organic farming as well as for its utopian sacred gardens, which are said to 'purify the spirit'.[9] Fascinating though these developments are, I do not have the space to discuss them extensively in this study, which is primarily concerned with shrine-related ideas and practices. Suffice to say that developments and attitudes towards nature and the environment within these movements, and the wider subculture to which they belong (which has taken on transnational shapes, judging from the various activities undertaken in South America, Southeast Asia and Africa), would constitute interesting and potentially relevant topics for future research.

The activities organized by the International Shinto Foundation and Shintō Kokusai Gakkai are not endorsed by the Jinja Honchō leadership, even if they occasionally involve priests and take place at shrines that are members of Jinja Honchō. However, there are some other organizations that have organized seminars and conferences on the topic of Shinto and ecology in recent years, thus contributing to the popularization of the Shinto environmentalist paradigm in the shrine world. Particularly relevant in this context is the Shintō Bunka Kai, or Shinto Culture Society, a Jinja Honchō-affiliated academic organization devoted to research on Shinto-related topics. Between 1999 and 2007, the Shintō Bunka Kai brought together a number of scholars, representing different academic disciplines, to discuss the topic of 'nature and Shinto culture' (*shizen to shintō bunka*) at a series of conferences. There were conferences on Shinto culture in relation to the sea, mountains, rivers, trees, fire, soil, water, the wind and iron. The proceedings of these were published in three volumes (Shintō Bunka Kai 2009a,b, 2010). The conferences are exemplary of one of the defining characteristics of the Shinto environmentalist paradigm: its capacity to bring together scholars and scientists from a variety of disciplines, together with shrine priests and religious leaders. There were papers presented by, among others, archaeologists, Shinto scholars, ethnologists, religious studies scholars, environmental and forest scientists, and popular authors writing about 'spirituality'. At times, this situation may have provided participants and audiences with new perspectives and created opportunities for cross-disciplinary dialogue – especially since every conference included a lengthy panel discussion. At other times, however, the papers appear more or less isolated. Some of them seriously address the question as to what relationship there might be between 'Shinto culture' and 'nature', while others are limited to the description of disparate topics such as archaeological findings, contemporary *matsuri* and environmental history.

Different though the various contributions were, the underlying assumption of the conferences was clear: Shinto is intimately connected with the Japanese natural environment and with the Japanese people's alleged ancient spirit of gratitude for nature's bounty. This tradition has been disturbed, it is suggested, by modernization and the import of 'Western' technology; the solution to environmental problems, therefore, lies in the rediscovery of ancient Shinto values. The preface formulates some of the core assumptions and tropes characterizing the Shinto environmentalist paradigm and is therefore worth quoting at length:

> Our country Japan is an island country surrounded by sea, and approximately 73% of the land is mountainous, while 66% is covered by forests. Because of these special geographical characteristics, we were given abundant nature, as well as our four seasons. While living in coexistence (*kyōsei*) with nature, we Japanese have come to be grateful for receiving the various blessings of the sea and the mountains in our daily lives. The evidence for that certainly lies in the fact that natural phenomena [literally: mountains, rivers, grass and trees] are worshipped and venerated one-by-one as the myriad deities (*yaoyorozu no kamigami*), displayed in the country's 80,000 shrines and their *matsuri*. (…) A special traditional folk culture has developed, which is devoted to this mind of gratitude for nature's grace. However, in modern times, the influx of the Western scientific and technological civilization has led to the all-too-sudden industrialization of the last 150 years. As a result, today, in this so-called advanced information society, our lives are full of convenience and affluence. However, the other side of the story is that humans have attacked nature, and it is a fact that the Western value system and thought that conceives of nature as a mere possession has influenced our society as a whole, as well as the minds (*kokoro*) of the people. (Matsuyama 2009: 1–2)

The author continues by making the familiar claim that Western values are responsible not only for the erosion of the traditional Japanese spirit of gratitude and love of nature but also for the destruction of the environment. Not surprisingly, the solution for today's problems is to be found in 'the Shinto value system and sense of nature that has been raised as intellectual thought, which has been the traditional culture of our country since ancient times' (Matsuyama 2009: 2). This excerpt sums up nicely the main axioms underlying the Shinto environmentalist paradigm: first, there is an intimate connection between Shinto and nature, going back to ancient times; second, 'the' Japanese have a long history of nature-loving and ecologically sustainable behaviour, much of which has sadly been lost due to the twin evils of 'modernization' and 'Westernization'; and third, the Japanese 'forest civilization' – of which *chinju no mori* are said to be the main remnant – is diametrically opposed to 'Western' civilization and its Judeo-Christian heritage, which supposedly stipulates that nature is subordinate to man. The echoes of Lynn White are obvious, which is no coincidence: the White thesis has had profound influence on Japanese religious and academic thought (Fujimura 2010). The irony is that, despite the ubiquitous critique of 'Westernization' as a root cause of Japan's moral and environmental degradation, the Shinto environmentalist paradigm is itself shaped in close interaction with ideas that developed in 'the West', especially in the US and UK.

A Transnational Trend

Thus far, I have focused primarily on the development of the Shinto environmentalist paradigm in Japanese academic discourse. It is important to emphasize, however, that Shinto is not an isolated phenomenon, and that ideas take shape within a transnational context.[10] Conceptualizations of 'Shinto', 'nature' or even of the Japanese nation itself may have taken shape in Japan, but they have done so in constant interaction with 'foreign' ideas and developments, language differences notwithstanding. The same is true for the Shinto environmentalist paradigm.

The explicit association between Japanese religion and the global environmental crisis was first made in the United States in the 1960s and 1970s. As we have seen, Lynn White himself wrote that Zen 'conceives of the man-nature relationship as very nearly the mirror image of the Christian view' (1967: 1206). At the time, 'Zen' was very popular in the US, not only because it attracted followers interested in meditation practices but also because it lent itself to a variety of artistic and commercial purposes, ranging from beatnik literature to garden design (see Borup 2004). This Zen was largely based on the writings of D. T. Suzuki and was far removed from the historical reality of Japanese temple practices. Suzuki attributed the supposedly unique Japanese experience of nature, and its aesthetic expressions, to 'Zen' – which he reimagined as the essence of Japanese culture (Suzuki 1959). Shinto, on the other hand, was not (yet) widely perceived as a tradition with potentially universal features – which is not entirely surprising, as Shinto's involvement with Japanese imperialism and wartime aggression was probably still fresh in many people's memories. Thus, scholar of religion H. Byron Earhart suggested that 'Japanese religion' might become a valuable ideological resource for overcoming the consumerism apparently responsible for environmental problems (1970),[11] yet as he did not believe Shinto could attract non-Japanese followers he placed his hopes on Zen. Drawing upon his classroom experiences, he suggested that

American students studying Japanese religion are drawn especially to those features which deal with man's relationship to nature. In the creation story of Japanese mythology many gods participate in the emergence of the cosmos, and the gods remain intimately connected with all phases of life. Almost any

dimension of nature – rocks, streams, mountains, thunder – may be or become
sacred or kami. The kami, one might say, are a part of nature – but that would be
an unfortunate Western way of putting it. It would be more true to the Japanese
experience to say that nature itself intrinsically manifests the sacred or is kami.
A general principle of Shinto is that man basically is one with nature, and
American undergraduates find this side of Shinto fascinating. (…) But of course
Shinto is too closely tied to Japanese national history to gain many Occidental
'converts'. Those Westerners who try to adopt some of the Japanese worldview
usually do so through the popularized versions of Zen, and its thesis that one
must become awakened to his oneness with nature. (1970: 2–3)

Although Earhart dismissed the idea that Shinto might have applicability in
'the West', the association between Shinto and environmental ethics had been
made, and it was only a matter of time before it would be taken further by others.
I have already mentioned the 'Religions of the World and Ecology' conference
series, organized by Harvard University between 1996 and 1998. The third of these
was devoted to the topic of 'Shinto and Ecology' and took place in March 1997. It
was convened by Rosemarie Bernard, who would later summarize the conference's
main conclusions as follows:

Japanese indigenous religion and its orientation to the world, which are
interconnected with nature and aesthetics, have a great deal to offer in the
struggle to conserve the environment. (…) At present, the only significant
green spaces in crowded Japanese urban centers are the groves that surround
Shinto shrines. Even the simple preservation of those shrine groves is a difficult
task to achieve given the onslaught of pollution as well as pressures to make
spatial concessions to further urban growth. The Shinto community is aware
of the importance of its special position as guarantor of groves of urban and
outlying greenery. Moreover, they are aware of the crucial challenges of
translating tradition into modern relevance, so as to transform belief systems
into environmental practice. (Bernard n.d.)

The conference took place in March 1997 and brought together Japanese
Shinto leaders as well as foreign scholars. Among the participants were shrine
priests and representatives of the emerging *chinju no mori* movement, such as
Miyawaki Akira, Sakurai Takashi, Sonoda Minoru and Tanaka Tsunekiyo, who
would later become president of Jinja Honchō. They met with well-known scholars
such as Carmen Blacker, Allan Grapard, Norman Havens, Miyake Hitoshi and
Emiko Ohnuki-Tierney. Unfortunately, of the ten conferences addressing the
relationship between ecology and particular religious traditions – ranging
from Christianity, Islam and Buddhism to Jainism, Daoism and Indigenous
Traditions – the conference on Shinto was the only one that never made it into
a book. Jinja Honchō has published a report containing summaries in Japanese
of the conference papers and discussions (Jinja Honchō 2000), but it was not
distributed widely and is not endorsed by the conference organizers. Despite

the fact that the proceedings were never published officially, the conference did constitute an important justification for interpretations of Shinto as a nature- and environment-oriented tradition and gave new impetus to existing conceptualizations of Shinto. At the very least, it showed Japanese Shinto actors that the topic of religion and the environment had attracted international academic attention, and that redefining Shinto in such terms could be a way to acquire more positive publicity.

In the 1990s and 2000s, the idea of Shinto as a nature religion with significance for environmental issues gradually spread among the Anglophone academic community. For instance, in a lecture given on the occasion of the inaugural symposium of the International Shinto Foundation in 1994, the late Carmen Blacker, well known for her work on Japanese shamanism (Blacker [1975] 1986), gave a speech titled 'Shinto and the Sacred Dimension of Nature'. In this speech, she said: 'From 30 years of study of Shinto and of respect for its divinities I am convinced that it can guide us to a new way of looking at the world around us. It can remind us that there is a holy dimension in natural objects' (Blacker [1994] 2003). This new perspective was not to be found in 'State Shinto' – 'a recent and disastrous aberration of the traditional beliefs' – but in something 'older and more universal', 'which has always been part of Japanese culture, but which can be understood elsewhere'. That is, 'Shinto can remind us that the natural world is not a machine put there for our sole enjoyment' ([1994] 2003). Likewise, sociologist John Clammer has advocated the Shinto environmentalist paradigm, arguing (in reference to Sonoda 2000) that the 'self-conscious positioning of Shinto as an ecologically sensitive religion does indeed have its basis in the characteristics of the religion' (2010: 99). According to him, Shinto has the potential to address environmental issues, as it 'lies at the basis of much of Japanese culture and potentially provides a means by which the life-affirming and eco-centric nature of that culture might creatively address the current global crisis, and especially its environmental aspects' (2010: 100).

Bernard, Blacker and Clammer are examples of scholars who have argued that Shinto contains some relevant clues for addressing today's environmental problems and endorsed notions of Shinto as an ancient religion grounded in an awareness of the interdependence of humans, nature and deities. Although their conclusions may be challenged, they are made in an academic context, based on long-time scholarly engagement with Japanese society and religion. In addition, however, there is a growing body of pseudo-academic literature that takes the argument a step further. In these texts, Shinto is described as the quintessential Japanese 'nature spirituality', and it is assumed uncritically that 'Shinto' views of nature provide ways of relating to the environment that may help 'us Westerners' overcome 'our alienation from nature'. For instance, such ideas are expressed in a book chapter on Shinto and ecology written by Daniel Shaw, who wants to 'convince the reader that the beliefs and values exhibited in Shinto spirituality can play a fundamental role in developing a post-modern Japanese ecological attitude fit for the needs of twenty-first century Japan' (2009: 311). He does not succeed – not only because the article is poorly structured but also because it is grounded in a problematic cultural-essentialist understanding of Shinto (the concept itself is neither defined nor historicized), a lack of reference to any primary sources and the absence of any historical perspective. His arguments, however, are illustrative of popular discourse on the significance of 'Shinto spirituality' for developing environmentally sustainable societies today.

Scholars such as Thomas Kasulis and Stuart Picken have likewise contributed to the understanding of Shinto as Japan's 'nature spirituality'. Kasulis has written a book in which he identifies Shinto as the basic substratum of Japanese culture, characterized by 'naturalness' and 'simplicity'. Naturalness, he argues, 'is a prominent theme in almost every serious discussion of Shinto – and rightly so. (...) [The term] has two senses for the Japanese: either a close connection between humans and nature or the cultivated ability to *make* things natural' (2004: 42–43; emphasis in original). Simplicity, then, 'follows from Shinto's emphasis on naturalness. (...) The natural surroundings of the shrine may be groomed, but the landscaping usually does not have the planned design associated with "Japanese gardens". (...) The best way to make something natural is to keep it simple' (2004: 44). This is a puzzling statement, not only because those well-designed Japanese gardens are often praised for the very same qualities but also because it may be argued that nature is not simple at all. The artificially simplified 'nature' appreciated in Japanese aesthetics is highly cultivated indeed – 'cooked' as Kalland and Asquith would say (1997) – while unmediated nature is chaotic, complex and diverse. Yet, the argument is typical of the Shinto environmentalist paradigm: Ueda Masaaki, for instance, likewise argues that Shinto shrine groves are 'natural', as opposed to 'artificial' gardens, parks or plantation forests (e.g. Ueda 2011).

Kasulis' conceptualization of Shinto has received some serious criticism (e.g. Thal 2006), but it remains within the limits of scholarly interpretation. That is arguably not the case for some of the works by Stuart Picken. His book *Shinto Meditations for Revering the Earth* (2002), for instance, contains a number of English-language 'Shinto' prayers for nature worship, written by himself. It constitutes one of the most outspoken examples of the reinterpretation of Shinto as an ancient tradition of nature spirituality, the purpose of which is made clear in the preface:

> I would like to help awaken you to what religion began as, when nature was the spirit's only guide. Before prophets and gurus, priests and preachers, human beings followed their own inner stirrings, and their religion was natural religion. It was not manmade, artificial, or invented. Its sentiments, beliefs, and responses were drawn from direct communion with the natural. (...) This religion really was in every sense of the term 'pre-historic'. *It emerged before history was invented* to tell us who we are, where we came from, and what we should do with ourselves. It predates the great religions of history. (...). This simple approach to religion that listens to nature, that enriches spirituality, and that restores purity does exist. It has survived in only one modern technological society. It is called *Shinto*, and it lives in modern Japan. (2002: 9–10; first emphasis mine)

Shinto is here presented as the archetypal *Ur*-religion. It is defined as the very remnant of the pure, spontaneous religious spirit of our ancient ancestors, which supposedly existed before the advent of man-made dogmatic religion. It was not constructed, but emerged spontaneously, as 'the communal response of the ancient immigrant dwellers of Japan to the stunning natural environment in which they found themselves' (2002: 16). Any historical connection to politics or ideology is denied, or downplayed as an unfortunate aberration, as 'real' Shinto supposedly transcends both history and politics (2002: 24–25). 'Nature' itself is presented as the ultimate cause. Thus, in works such as this one, Shinto is mythologized in the Barthesian sense of the world: it is quite literally naturalized, and thus depoliticized. Contrary to what Picken suggests, the ahistorical, depoliticized understanding of Shinto as a 'nature religion' is inherently ideological. It can be employed to serve various agendas, nationalist as well as environmentalist.

A Note on Miyazaki

Although the Shinto environmentalist paradigm undeniably has a strong academic component, it is not solely a theoretical affair. In the following chapters, I will examine shrine-based practices in relation to ideological developments and look more closely at the various ways in which shrine priests and other local actors have contributed to the development of the Shinto environmentalist paradigm. First, however, I will briefly discuss the possible influence of popular culture in this respect – in particular, the oeuvre of Miyazaki Hayao (1941–). It is beyond the scope of this book to provide an in-depth analysis of his work, and I should emphasize that I have not engaged in research on the reception of Miyazaki's films. Nevertheless, they were repeatedly mentioned in the conversations I had with people at shrines and related non-profit organizations, as well as colleagues and students, who often associate my research with some of the works by Miyazaki.

'Popular culture' is a somewhat diffuse generic category that includes manga comic books and anime films as well as other mass media texts and consumer goods. Contemporary understandings of Shinto, shrines and deities are partly influenced by some of these popular culture texts. Some of the most popular shrines today are those visited by fans, who go there as part of a 'pilgrimage' to the sites shown in their favourite manga or anime. For instance, shrines such as Kanda Myōjin and Hikawa Jinja in Tokyo are associated with anime (*Love Life!* and *Sailor Moon*, respectively) and visited by large group of fans. Although shrines are not usually involved in the production of anime or manga, they do capitalize on these trends by selling *ema* (votive tablets), *o-mamori* (protective amulets) and other objects that have images of the main characters. Today, there are even special guidebooks that list the shrines featuring in popular manga or anime (e.g. Okamoto 2014).

In recent years, there has been a remarkable rise in the number of manga and anime creatively reimagining themes and characters derived from so-called religious traditions (as well as inventing new ones), some of which have gained significant popularity. Examples include such diverse works as *Seinto Oniisan* (*Saint Young Men*) by Nakamura Hikaru, which depicts Jesus and Gautama Buddha in twenty-first-century Tokyo; *Onmyōji* by Okano Reiko, about a medieval Yin-Yang ritualist; *Kannagi* by Takenashi Eri, which tells the story of a goddess who has become homeless after her *shinboku* (sacred tree) was cut down; and even the work of the historical revisionist Kobayashi Yoshinori, who employs mythological imagery to emphasize the divine nature of the imperial family. Not all of these texts have contributed to the Shinto environmentalist paradigm, and not all of them are 'religious' in the narrow sense of the word – some of them may even be considered blasphemous by religious actors. Nevertheless, these manga and anime (and many others) draw upon religious traditions, as well as a variety of popular myths and beliefs. Even the usually conservative shrine establishment seems to have realized the effect of popular imaginations of *kami* and related topics, a genre which is now referred to by the term 'Shinto anime' (Ishihara 2009).

I do not have the space here to discuss the topic of 'Shinto anime' at length; nor will I try to answer the question whether or not these texts should be categorized as 'Shinto' and/or 'religion'. Jolyon Thomas has proposed the term *shūkyō asobi* (which may be translated as 'religion play' or perhaps 'playful religion') to refer to these practices and texts, which creatively blur the boundaries between religion and entertainment (2007, 2012: 16–17). It is important to bear in mind, however, the crucial distinction between, on the one hand, manga and anime *produced by* religious institutions in order to communicate mythological and theological narratives to young audiences (e.g. Christian publications of the Bible in manga version, or Jinja Honchō's publication of a manga version of the *Kojiki*), and on the other, the work of individual, independent artists reinterpreting and appropriating elements from existing traditions. While the former are adaptations of established sacred texts, the latter are contemporary fictional creations. While undeniably drawing upon religion, we should be careful not to *equate* apparently religious imagery in popular culture with the worship traditions from which they borrow.

This may seem obvious, but when reading interpretations of and commentaries upon anime and manga – in scholarly books and articles, online reviews, Internet forums and so on – one often comes across simplistic assumptions regarding the 'religious' character of these texts. The term 'religious', however, is not usually defined. Moreover, many authors have noted the phonetic similarity between 'anime' and 'animism' and have drawn the unsubstantiated conclusion that the two must be interrelated, claiming that anime exhibit the animism supposedly characteristic of Japanese culture and religion (e.g. Buljan & Cusack 2015). This is especially the case for films made by the world-famous director Miyazaki Hayao, several of which are seen as 'religious' and said to contain elements of 'Shinto', 'animism' or 'folk religion' (e.g. Boyd & Nishimura 2004; Wright 2005). Miyazaki himself, by contrast, has always been reluctant to see his own works as 'religious' and has never claimed that they represent 'Shinto' as such.[12] Nevertheless, the association between Miyazaki's films, Shinto (or Japanese 'folk religion') and ecology is made often. Considering his great popularity, his oeuvre has undoubtedly contributed to understandings of Shinto and nature, in Japan as well as abroad. Indeed, some of these films are so influential and well-known that scholars now refer to them to explain particular worship traditions and Japanese attitudes vis-à-vis nature (e.g. Nakamura 2009: 30).

Miyazaki himself has criticized the utopian and nationalistic tendencies inherent in some recent interpretations of Japanese animism, in particular the works of Umehara Takeshi (Inaga 1999: 125). Nonetheless, there are some significant, undeniable similarities between his films on the one hand, and the recent discourse on Shinto, nature and Japanese identity, on the other. Not only are his films appropriated by contemporary scholars reemploying mythical notions of 'the Japanese view of nature' (e.g. Hori 2008); they also seem to influence understandings of Shinto abroad, as many authors commenting on Miyazaki films uncritically assume that the spirit worlds portrayed in them correspond to Shinto worldviews. For instance, as one of them wrote, 'Miyazaki is cinematically practicing the ancient form of Shinto, which emphasised an intuitive continuity with the natural world' (Wright 2005: abstract). Such ahistorical, romantic images of a singular, nature-oriented ancient Shinto are surprisingly common, not only in popular but also in academic discourse. Considering the ubiquity of these ideas, the hypothesis that Miyazaki's films have significantly influenced popular understandings of Shinto, in particular with regard to its supposed relationship with 'nature', seems justified.

Rather than 'practising the ancient form of Shinto' or simply being influenced by Shinto worldviews, therefore, it may be argued that the exact opposite has been the case: by creatively reimagining spirits and deities as well as traditional landscapes, Miyazaki has actively contributed to the discursive construction of Shinto as an ancient tradition of nature worship, and to the association between *kami* and environmental issues. This is clearly visible in his masterpiece *Princess Mononoke* (*Mononoke Hime*, 1997), which tells the story of deities and spirits living in deep primeval forests, who turn into violent demons as a result of the destruction of their dwelling places. Criticizing ideas of 'progress' and the exploitation of natural resources that have come with modern industrialization, the film can be interpreted as a story about an existential battle between human society, which has embraced modern technology and become alienated from the nature it exploits, and the animal deities who live in and are dependent upon the forest for their survival.

Of particular relevance in this context is also *My Neighbor Totoro* (*Tonari no Totoro*, 1988), which tells a more optimistic story of two young girls who move with their father to an old farmhouse in the Japanese countryside. They live next to a small sacred grove, surrounded by ancient trees and inhabited by a large teddy-bearish deity named Totoro, as well as some smaller spirits. Loved by children and adults alike, *My Neighbor Totoro* is probably one of the most popular and well-known Japanese films today, to the point that the film has achieved paradigmatic status – and not only because Totoro itself has become an iconic figure, present in every kindergarten or souvenir shop, that has come to represent innocence, benevolence and social harmony. Japanese landscape planners today use the term 'Totoro' to refer to 'traditional Japanese' landscapes, in which humans actively interact with and give shape to their natural surroundings through agriculture and other practices. As mentioned previously, this model is referred to as *satoyama* by today's ecologists and used to challenge traditional conservationist notions of pure nature as 'wild' and untouched by humans. Totoro is now employed as a mascot for conservation projects, such as the Totoro no Furusato Foundation, which seeks to restore *satoyama* landscapes in the Sayama Hills, west of Tokyo (Totoro no Furusato Kikin n.d.).

My Neighbor Totoro corresponds to and revitalizes popular notions of uniquely Japanese ways of coexisting with nature, as well as a correlated nostalgic longing for a 'lost past', where people live in harmony with their human and non-human neighbours (Yoshioka 2010). Thus, the film has come to represent a particular view on human-nature relationships and authentic Japanese landscapes that has gained great popularity in recent years. Moreover, it visualizes a notion that has taken centre stage in contemporary Shinto discourse: the *chinju no mori*, or sacred grove. *Chinju no mori* are discursively associated with *satoyama*, representing the same idealized traditional values and alleged ecological significance (e.g. Iwatsuki 2008). They are generally conceptualized as small, old forests, with a strong local character. *Chinju no mori* are seen as the dwelling places of deities, who are strongly connected to (and, for that matter, dependent on) their particular locales. If treated well, these deities are generally benevolent and protect nearby communities. Similarly, Totoro lives in a small grove, surrounded by high, old trees, and his dwelling place is recognizable as a Shinto shrine because of its *shimenawa* rope and small *torii* gate. Totoro is a protective creature, who rescues little Mei when she is lost; moreover, he is life-giving, performing a ritual dance that makes the acorns planted by the girls grow into trees. In sum, *My Neighbor Totoro* has popularized several of the notions associated with *chinju no mori*, even though the term itself is not used in the film. In the next chapter, I will discuss this concept in more detail.

Chapter 5

CHINJU NO MORI

Multiple Meanings

In recent decades, *chinju no mori* has become one of Shinto's core concepts. In principle, it refers to the groves surrounding Shinto shrines, which may be anything from a handful of isolated trees to a sizeable forest. As will become clear in this chapter, however, the term carries a number of different meanings, and there is some variety as to how exactly it is used. Nevertheless, in contemporary discourse on *chinju no mori*, there are a number of recurring themes. The following definition, published in a popular-scientific glossy magazine devoted to the topic of shrine forests, is illustrative:

> [Chinju no mori are] forests that have remained from the ancient age of myths until the present time. These are forests where old trees grow in abundance; where high trees, brushwood and plants growing under the trees are in balance. Many birds, insects and micro-organisms have the space to live here. These are forests with rich ecosystems. Inside, one can find pure gardens (*kiyorakana niwa*), where annual festivals (*matsuri*) are organised. These are places that remind one of distant, ancient times. This is where the voices of the gods (*kamigami*) sound in your ears. This is where our ancestors lived, humbly and diligently, in harmony with nature. (Motegi 2010: 111)

Although perhaps not a scientific definition, this description is representative as it contains several core elements that often appear in writings on *chinju no mori*. First of all, there is the notion that *chinju no mori* are primordial worship places, located in old primeval forests, which 'have remained from the ancient age of myths until the present time'. The notion of continuity between the ancient past, the present and the future is a common feature of most descriptions of shrine forests, those that focus on the ecological aspects as well as those that are mainly concerned with worship traditions. Second, *chinju no mori* are often described as places with high biodiversity, characterized by ecological balance between plants, trees, birds, insects and micro-organisms. In reality, this is not always the case: in some cases at least, shrine forests have less species diversity than surrounding areas (e.g. Nakayama et al. 1996), and many shrine forests face environmental threats (e.g. Sagai 2013). Yet, the ideal of *chinju no mori* as places of great ecological significance has been influential: it has been one of the reasons why scientists such as Ueda Atsushi and Miyawaki Akira have actively tried to protect remaining shrine groves, and it has no doubt motivated people to take part in tree-planting, cleaning litter and other forest conservation activities. Third, the definition is typical as it describes *chinju no mori* not just as ecologically important but also as sites characterized by ritual purity, where one can hear the 'voices of the gods' and take part in worship ceremonies. In other words, *chinju no mori* are sites that have been subject to sacralization: they are set apart from the ordinary, physically, discursively and by means of ritual practices, and they are perceived – by some, at least – as locations where divine beings reside. In sum, in the popular imagination, *chinju no mori* are sacred sites with ecological significance, representing ancestral worship traditions and a corresponding 'harmony with nature'.

Despite these commonalities, different actors in the shrine world and academia use the term differently, according to personal preference, institutional politics or disciplinary orientation. In scholarly and religious discourse on *chinju no mori*, we can distinguish at least four different meanings. They overlap partially but differ with regard to how broadly the term is used and what is included or excluded. All four meanings continue to coexist and be used alongside each other, which sometimes causes conceptual confusion. The four meanings I distinguish are as follows:

1. *Chinju no mori* are the remnants of primeval forests, which have remained more or less untouched since prehistoric times, thus constituting ecological as well as historical continuity. Alternatively, they may be the remnants of secondary forests, which are not primeval as they have experienced disruption at some point of history (e.g. fire or logging) but which have regrown and become self-sustaining (i.e. 'natural'). They are usually small and clearly demarcated, surrounded by rice paddies or (especially in modern times, as a result of urbanization) houses and other buildings. They are considered 'sacred' and have been the location of worship practices and *matsuri* since ancient times. Inside, there is a shrine where people come to worship a protective deity, believed to be intimately connected with that particular locality and its community. They are typically made up of indigenous broad-leaved trees; seen from a distance, they resemble a big head of broccoli. This definition of *chinju no mori* allocates more or less equal importance to ecological and cultural-symbolic aspects of the forest. It has come to constitute the ideal type and may now be considered the 'classical' description. Scientists who have described *chinju no mori* in these terms include Suganuma Takayuki (2001, 2004) and Ueda Atsushi (2001, 2004a,b, [1984] 2007).

2. In its second meaning, the term *chinju no mori* is still limited to remaining areas of primeval or secondary forest (as above) but not necessarily only those associated with shrines. While it is recognized that many of these remaining forests are indeed shrine forests, it is not their 'sacred' character that makes

Figure 5.1 A typical broad-leaved *chinju no mori*. Tokiwa Jinja, Mito, Ibaraki Prefecture.

them significant but rather their ecological composition. *Chinju no mori* are often shrine-related, but this is not necessarily always the case: they may also surround Buddhist temples or private residences. What matters, therefore, is not the presence of a shrine but biodiversity and ecological continuity. *Chinju no mori* are said to be among the few remaining areas of 'indigenous' forest, made up of various 'indigenous' tree species, in Japan. They are contrasted to plantation forests, which are said to be ecologically unsustainable and largely made up of 'foreign' trees. The main representative of this view is the ecologist Miyawaki Akira, well known for his various reforestation projects in Japan and abroad. In his terminology, *chinju no mori* are '*furusato* forests' composed of '*furusato* trees'. According to this view, at places where the indigenous trees have been cut down or given way to invader species, forest maintenance and reforestation projects should be set up in order to re-establish forests in their 'original' shape (Miyawaki 1982, 2000; Nanami 2010).

3. As the concept gained popularity, it came to be dissociated from biology and ecology proper and was extended to other types of shrine forests. In the third meaning, then, *chinju no mori* becomes a generic term used for various shrine forests and groves. It includes the above-described ideal type but is not limited to it: the term may refer to any type of 'forest' or woodland surrounding a shrine. In contrast to the second meaning, therefore, what matters here is the 'sacred' (and, indeed, 'Shinto') character of the forest, not its ecology. This may include modern planted forests, the most famous of which is the forest surrounding Meiji Jingū in Tokyo. Meiji Jingū's forest has now become the archetypal 'man-made *chinju no mori*' (Aomame 2010) – a notion that would be considered a contradiction in terms by those who subscribe to ecological definitions of the term, but not by those who use it more generically. Furthermore, depending on the speaker, the term *chinju no mori* may also be used to refer to forested 'sacred' mountains associated with shrines, such as the *shintaizan* of Mount Miwa (discussed in more detail in the next chapter); to small patches of woodland that are so small they hardly qualify for the label 'forest', often consisting of little more than a few old *shinboku* trees adjacent to (urban) shrines; and even to large areas of plantation and/or mixed forest, such as those owned by Ise Jingū – as long as they are shrine-owned. Thus, the meaning of the term *chinju no mori* has come to be extended to any type of 'forest' as long as it is somehow associated with a shrine, and, hence, considered to have certain 'sacred' properties. Although not endorsed by forest scientists, this is how the term is often used in common parlance.

4. In recent years, the term *chinju no mori* is increasingly used to refer to shrines as a whole, not only their forests, especially by Shinto actors themselves. That is, the term has come to include the entire precincts of a shrine: not only its forested area, but also the shrine buildings, the *sandō* (the path or road approaching the main buildings), isolated *shinboku* trees and so on. In this use of the term, ecological or landscape characteristics are no longer relevant: *chinju no mori* is here used to distinguish shrine space from the outside world. Put in Durkheimian terms, *chinju no mori* have come to equal a 'sacred space' as a whole, set apart from the 'profane' outside. More prosaically, the term may simply correspond to shrine property: land owned by the shrine (possibly extending to such 'liminal' space as a parking area) is called *chinju no mori*, and the *chinju no mori* ends where the property ends. In fact, however, in recent years the term has come to be extended beyond the *physical space* of the shrine and shrine precincts; it now also includes the *imagined social space* of

a 'local community' centred around, and regularly congregating at, the shrine and its forest. Since the early 2000s, there has been a significant increase in the number of times the term is used in *Jinja Shinpō* articles; in many of these articles, however, the term no longer exclusively refers to actual forests. It is increasingly used as an abstract denominator encompassing the shrine's entire physical space as well as the community (*kyōdōtai*) to which it is said to belong (cf. Rots 2017).

As the aforementioned list makes clear, the term *chinju no mori* is used for different purposes, ranging from environmental advocacy to community empowerment and from landscape design to shrine politics. While the concept's vagueness may have contributed to its adaptability and popularity, the lack of conceptual clarity sometimes causes confusion. Even within one shrine, different actors may have different understandings of the term – and, correspondingly, different priorities and agendas, as the following examples will illustrate.

In 2011, I had the opportunity to interview two people working for Ise Jingū, both of whom conceived of the shrine forests in quite different terms. The first interviewee, a shrine official working for the publicity department (interviewed twice, in February and December 2011), stressed the intimate historical relationship between the shrine, the river, the rice paddies and the forested mountains. The forests, the water cycle and the rice cultivation, he suggested, constitute a single symbiotic system going back to ancient times, of which the shrine and its lands have always constituted an integral part. According to him, an intuitive appreciation of the intrinsic sacred qualities of the natural landscape is central to Shinto – as illustrated by his statement that Shinto is essentially an 'intuitive religion' (*chokkan shūkyō*). Although used for growing timber, he considered the shrine forests as an important[1] aspect of the religious landscape (*shūkyō fūdo*) of the Ise region.[1] As the timber is produced sustainably and not for economic purposes, the forests are said to be part of the local ecological equilibrium that was achieved in prehistoric times, which purportedly has been maintained for centuries. Constituting an essential part of this holistic ecological-religious system, Ise's forests are inherently sacred. Hence, the shrine official argued, it is perfectly fine to refer to them as *chinju no mori*.

The second interviewee was also employed by Ise Jingū. A forest specialist, he works for the department responsible for forest maintenance. He was so kind as to show me around the shrine forests and explain about the various aspects of forestry and timber production; during this visit, I had the opportunity to ask questions (December 2011). One of the things I asked was whether it would be possible to refer to these forests as *chinju no mori*. In contrast to his colleague at the publicity department, he answered that it was not. *Chinju no mori* are small, old shrine forests, where no logging takes place; hence, he argued, they are substantially different from the forest of Ise. Ise's forest is called *kyūikirin*; it is made up of both a production forest and a 'natural' part that is left untouched (see Chapter 9), but it is not an isolated, clearly demarcated shrine grove. While he did not deny the sacred character of Ise Jingū's forests *per se* (in particular the 'natural' parts, which are not used for the production of timber), he objected to using the word *chinju no mori* in this context, as to him this term refers to a fundamentally different category of forests.

In sum, even at a single shrine, different actors may use the term *chinju no mori* differently. The first interviewee's use of the term corresponds to what I have distinguished as the third meaning: *chinju no mori* has come to be used to refer to any kind of forest, as long as it is deemed 'sacred' and associated with (or owned by) a Shinto shrine. By contrast, the second interviewee understood the term more narrowly, as referring to a small and 'natural' forest; his understanding of the term therefore corresponds to the first meaning.

Another interesting example comes from the island of Awaji, located between Shikoku and the Kansai region. According to local mythology, it was here that Izanagi dipped his spear into the sea (as narrated in the *Kojiki*) and created the islands of Japan, of which Awaji was the first. According to a museum of natural history in Kobe I had visited previously, Awaji still contains some 'original' *chinju no mori* going back many centuries, which were described as remaining areas of primeval forests. I therefore decided to visit the island, together with a colleague working on the same topic. The first forest we visited did indeed look like the archetypal, 'broccoli-shaped' *chinju no mori* described above; it was fenced off, consisted of different broad-leaved tree species and was surrounded by rice paddies. However, there was no shrine. Instead, there was a *torii*, a small pebbled square with a basic stone altar, a donation box, an information board, a hedge and a large fence. This was one of the ancient imperial tombs that are scattered around the Kansai region. While they may be described as 'Shinto' depending on one's use of that term, they are not typically classified as shrines (*jinja* or *jingū*) as they are not religious institutions (*shūkyō hōjin*) where people come together to worship *kami*; they have neither permanent priests nor shrine buildings. It is usually forbidden to enter these small forests, so they may well have ecological value, but the forests do not necessarily go back to ancient times; many of these tombs were 'rediscovered', and their trees (re)planted, during the Meiji period. Thus, whether or not they are categorized as *chinju no mori* depends largely on what definition is used: a forest scientist describing to the second of the four meanings above might use the term *chinju no mori* in this context, because of the forest's ecological composition, while Shinto scholars may be reluctant to do so, because of the absence of a shrine community (*ujiko*) for whom the forest is a historical meeting place.[2]

Next, we visited one of the island's best-known shrines, Izanagi Jingū. The shrine consists of a typical post-Meiji concrete *torii*, a straight *sandō* lined with trees and stone lanterns, fairly large shrine grounds with a picturesque pond and garden, shrine buildings, an impressive old *shinboku* and a few other trees behind the shrine buildings. While aesthetically pleasing, it was not exactly what one would consider a 'forest'. Wondering whether there might be another forested area elsewhere, we approached one of the priests, asking where the *chinju no mori* was. He looked at us in a surprised way, apparently not understanding the question, so we asked again. He then responded by saying that, of course, the *chinju no mori* was right where we were – at the open space in the middle of the shrine grounds, in front of the main building. The *chinju no mori* was everywhere around us, he said. Thus, according to him, the entire shrine precincts constituted the *chinju no mori*, and there was no difference between the 'forested' and the 'non-forested' parts. This response clearly corresponds to what I have distinguished as the fourth meaning of *chinju no mori*: in recent years, the term no longer refers to physical forests only. It has also come to be used for the space of the shrine as a whole, its entire physical territory, as well as, possibly, the community to which the shrine is said to belong. In the understanding of this priest, the entire shrine grounds constituted the *chinju no mori*.

Chinju no mori: *Concept and Connotations*

In the above section, I have given some examples of the different ways in which the concept *chinju no mori* is currently employed. In order to better understand the various connotations carried by the concept, however, it is necessary to have a closer look at its history. The term *chinju no mori* is made up of three words: *chinju*, which refers to a local protective deity (also called *chinjugami*); the genitive particle *no*; and *mori*, which is commonly translated as forest. The word *chinju* is made up of two Chinese characters, meaning 'to pacify' (*shizumeru*) and 'to protect' (*mamoru*). In classical Chinese, the term was used to refer to military checkpoints and border defence, already appearing in *The Records of the Three Kingdoms* (third century CE) (M. Ueda 2013: 18); likewise, in Nara-period Japan, it was used in a military context (M. Ueda 2004a: 20). It was then incorporated into medieval Buddhist discourse, where it came to signify guardian deities protecting the Dharma.[3] Accordingly, in premodern Japanese Buddhism, the term *chinjugami* was typically used to refer to the local, place-based deities believed to dwell around and protect temples; they were (and are) worshipped by Buddhist monks at small shrines belonging to temple complexes. Over time, the word also came to be used for local deities, who were associated with particular village communities. It overlapped with the term *ujigami* – a concept historically used for ancestral spirits that had become protective *kami*, which later was extended to include local deities in general (M. Ueda 2004a: 21). As Sonoda writes,

> Until the mediaeval period, in fact, *chinju* meant the *kami* protecting the precincts of a Buddhist temple, but from the late Heian period onwards, as influential temples expanded their provincial landholdings and enshrined their ancestral clan *kami* and the guardian *kami* of their temples, *chinju* shrines came to be widely distributed throughout the provinces, and these became the tutelary shrines of the local agricultural communities. (2006b: 9)

In Meiji- and Taishō-period Japan, the term *chinju* was typically associated with village deities, as in the popular expression *mura no chinju* ('the god of the village') (Azegami 2009). They were usually worshipped at local shrines, constituting a focal point of village communities. In post-*shinbutsu-bunri* Japan, they came to be dissociated from Buddhism altogether and were reclassified as Shinto. In contrast to newly established imperial shrines, however, they were not usually associated with the national ritual-ideological system that would later become known as 'State Shinto'. On the contrary, they were often the subject of state-imposed limitations, such as the shrine merger movement and the prohibition on shrine priests to engage in so-called religious activities (Azegami 2009; Azegami & Teeuwen 2012; Breen 2000). Nevertheless, *chinju* had been established as a term primarily associated with Shinto rather than Buddhism, and this continues to be the case today.

Although the term *chinju* goes back to ancient China, the combination *chinju no mori* is of much more recent date. While the shrine forests to which the term refers are often said – either correctly or not – to have remained since ancient times, the concept itself was not introduced until the late nineteenth century. According to Ono Ryōhei, it was coined by novelist Tayama Katai (1872–1930) in 1892 to describe the defining features of Japanese countryside landscapes (Ono 2010). It subsequently appeared in dictionaries published in 1894 and 1898, but at the turn of the century it was not yet widely used.[4] In the late Meiji, Taishō and early Shōwa periods, however, the term gradually spread and came to be used for local shrine forests in general, acquiring the meaning of 'sacred place' (Ono 2010). The term was popularized through a well-known children's song, *Mura matsuri* ('village *matsuri*'), which includes the lines 'Today is the happy day of the *matsuri* | Of the village's guardian deity' (*Mura no chinju no kamigami no | Kyō wa medetai o-matsuri no hi*) (A. Ueda [1984] 2007: 7). Today, this song evokes nostalgia for Shōwa-period rural traditions, especially among elderly people; it is often mentioned by authors who want to stress the cultural significance of *chinju no mori* (e.g. Miyawaki 2000: 17; Sonoda 1998: 40; M. Ueda 2004a: 21).

In the early post-war period, the term *chinju no mori* fell into disuse – as did associated notions of protective deities, sacred space and ancestral villages. Between 1946 and 1978, it was not used much, as illustrated by the fact that in *Jinja Shinpō* articles from this period it shows up only very sporadically. It was not until the late 1970s and early 1980s, when people such as Miyawaki Akira and Ueda Atsushi started doing research on the topic, that the term came to be used more regularly. Likewise, the association of *chinju no mori* with ecology and nature conservation dates from this period. Since the 1990s, the concept has been used increasingly regularly, often appearing in the titles of books and articles on various topics – including but not limited to shrines, forest management, landscape conservation, spirituality and Japanese national identity (e.g. Makino 1994; Miyawaki 2000; Sōyō 2001; A. Ueda 2003; [1984] 2007; M. Ueda 2004c; M. Ueda & A. Ueda 2001; Yamada 1995; Yamaori 2001).

In sum, the meanings attributed to the term *chinju* have changed significantly in the course of history, ranging from military uses to Buddhist theology to contemporary Shinto practices. The term *mori*, it seems, is no less ambiguous. Several scholars have stated that there is an essential difference between *hayashi*, which supposedly originally referred to man-made (i.e. planted) forests, and *mori*, said to refer to natural forests. Ueda Masaaki in particular has repeatedly asserted the fundamental difference between *mori* and *hayashi*. For instance,

> In English, *mori* is called 'forest', and *hayashi* 'wood'. Similarly, in the ancient Japanese language (*Nihon no yamatokotoba*), the word *mori* refers to things in their natural state (*shizen no mama no mono*), whereas *hayashi* refers to nature that has been changed by human action. (…) In the ancient Japanese language, *mori* and *hayashi* were clearly distinguished, but afterwards the terms were mixed up in daily life. (2011: 4)[5]

Ueda Atsushi has expressed himself in similar terms, saying there is a fundamental difference between *mori* on the one hand, and *hayashi* and parks (*kōen*) on the other – in terms of physical shape as well as atmosphere and history (2004a: 165–166; [1984] 2007: 16–17). Likewise, well-known forest ecologist Shidei Tsunahide has written that *mori* refers to 'deep forests', in contrast to *hayashi* (1993: 7). He explains:

> In my understanding, the reason that deep forests have remained for such a long time is because these forests were cherished as dwelling places of gods. (…) I do not think I am wrong in saying that *mori* was a mountain covered with a deep forest, a forest rising up; a natural forest thought of as important, as it was seen as the home of the gods. By contrast, *hayashi* refers to the forests stretching from the foot of the mountain to the plains of the *satoyama*, which have been considerably changed by human activity. Forests made up of *sugi* [*Cryptomeria japonica*; Japanese cedar], *hinoki* [*Chamaecyparis obtusa*; Japanese cypress] or *kunugi* [*Quercus acutissima*; sawtooth oak] are *hayashi*, not *mori*. But the sacred forests (*chinju no mori* and *miya no mori*) surrounding shrines are *mori*, not *hayashi*. (Shidei 1993: 9–10)

Ueda Masaaki, Ueda Atsushi and Shidei Tsunahide all assert that sacred forests are *mori* (i.e. 'deep' and 'natural') rather than *hayashi* (i.e. 'artificial'). There is an obvious problem with Shidei's distinction, however. *Sugi* and *hinoki* are usually planted; historically, they have been used widely for timber production. Thus, they are said to be typical of *hayashi*, and not of *mori*. Nevertheless, they can often be found in shrine forests, despite the fact that the latter are classified as *mori*. Clearly, most shrine forests were planted at some point in (pre)modern history, rather than being fully 'natural' or primeval (cf. Komatsu 2012: 288–290). *Hinoki* and *sugi* in particular are high, coniferous trees, and forests made up of these trees tend to have a somewhat dark, mysterious atmosphere – ironically, precisely those qualities that Shidei attributes to *mori*. Accordingly, until recently, these trees were often used for newly (re)planted shrine forests. It is no coincidence that many *shinboku* are *sugi* or *hinoki*. Only in the last few decades, as Miyawaki's mantra '*furusato* trees for a *furusato* forest' gained prominence, has replanting 'original' tree species and returning forests to their 'original' shape become the standard at shrines throughout the country. This is a fairly recent development, however;

previously, sacred qualities were more commonly attributed to coniferous than to broad-leaved trees, judging from the fact that the former were often turned into *shinboku* and planted along shrine *sandō*.

Moreover, Ueda Masaaki's claim that in classical Japanese a clear conceptual distinction existed between man-made forests, referred to as *hayashi*, and natural forests, referred to as *mori*, is questionable. Arguably, such a distinction is a product of modernity, in which the realm of 'nature' is discursively differentiated from the realm of human constructs. Interestingly, Ueda's conceptualization of ideal forests as 'untouched' by humans, and his association of 'untouched' with 'natural', is more in accordance with modern European and American notions of 'wilderness' as constituting 'pure nature' (Cronon 1996; Tsing 2005: 95–101) than with 'traditional Japanese' notions of nature as best preserved when cultivated (Kalland 1995). As a matter of fact, the discussion about whether *chinju no mori* should be maintained carefully by humans or, on the contrary, are better left untouched, has been going on since the early 1980s.[6] The dispute continues to be unresolved. As we shall see, however, most *chinju no mori*-related organizations today undertake activities that, if we were to apply Ueda's dichotomy strictly, would come down to the transformation of *mori* into *hayashi* (or even, in some cases, into parks): tree-planting, collecting acorns, weeding, pruning and so on. Nevertheless, the shrine forests where these activities take place are never defined as *hayashi* but usually as *chinju no mori* (or, alternatively, as *shasō* – a concept I will discuss later in the text).

In reality, then, the distinction between *mori* and *hayashi* has probably never been as clear-cut as Ueda suggests. As other members of the *chinju no mori* movement have rightly pointed out, it is often impossible to differentiate between the two, as most forests are both natural *and* partly shaped by human activities (Watanabe Hiroyuki, personal communication, June 2013).[7] Arguably, then, the difference between *mori* and *hayashi* primarily lies in the symbolic connotations and cultural meanings attributed to the forests, rather than their physical properties. The term *mori* carries profound symbolic capital: it is discursively associated with notions of a spirited, non-human 'other world', ancestral traditions and memories, and an idealized 'original' Japanese society, as well as corresponding constructions of national identity. It has a certain numinous, transcendent quality, which also applies to *chinju no mori*. Through the ideal typical distinction between *mori* – human society's Other – and *hayashi* – human-made, hence profane – certain types of forests are discursively sacralized, while others are left to the realm of human culture and society.

To Shinto scholars such as Ueda Masaaki and Sonoda Minoru, worship in forests – *mori*, that is, not *hayashi* – constitutes the original shape of Shinto. As they often point out, before there were any shrine buildings, people would come together and conduct ceremonies in sacred groves, referred to as *yashiro*. A widely used argument for the identification of forests with primordial shrine worship is the fact that the character that would later come to be used for writing *yashiro* (社) is pronounced as *mori* in some classical texts, such as the *Man'yōshū* (Sonoda 1998: 42–43; Ueda 2004b: 11–12). This is presented as etymological evidence for

the theory that, originally, forests and worship places were one and the same thing, and there was no conceptual distinction between the two. These sacred groves, it is argued, represent the origin of shrine worship; accordingly, *jinja* 神社 (usually translated as 'shrine') literally means the *yashiro/mori* 社 (dwelling place/forest) of the *kami* 神 (deity). As Sonoda concludes, 'In sum, Japanese *jinja* were originally nothing but the sacred forest (*shinsei na mori*) where the *kami* resided' (1998: 43).

Furthermore, Ueda and Sonoda have argued, these sacred groves not only constitute the origins of Shinto but also of Japanese society as a whole: the first communities took shape around these worship places, which became the sacred centres near which towns (*machi*) were established. According to Sonoda, since ancient times the sacred forest has been at the centre of what is now called 'town-making' (*machi-zukuri*) or 'community-making' (*komyuniti-zukuri*) (Sonoda 1997: 22–25): the establishment of social and economic bonds between residents of a given locality. Hence, it is here that society originated. This is supposedly evidenced by the Japanese word for society, *shakai*: composed of the characters *mori/yashiro* 社 and 'meeting' or 'congregation' 会, it literally means 'meeting in the forest' or 'meeting at the shrine' (M. Ueda 2004b: 15).[8] Thus, Shinto is seen by these scholars as a 'community religion' that is an intrinsic part of Japan's 'religious culture' (*shūkyō bunka*); in contrast to so-called world religions like Buddhism or Christianity, it is intimately connected with the landscape or *fūdo* of a particular place and co-constitutive of its culture and local society (Sonoda 1998: 10–13).

As the character for shrine (or society) can be read as *mori*, the term *chinju no mori* is sometimes written with this character, instead of the common character meaning 'forest' (i.e. 鎮守の社 instead of 鎮守の森). When written in this way, the emphasis is on the sacred character and social significance of the place, rather than the physical shape. I have not come across any texts by forest scientists in which *chinju no mori* was written with this character; it is mainly used by Shinto actors and scholars of religion. In recent years, however, a third, slightly different way of writing the concept has gained popularity. Instead of the common character for 'shrine', *chinju no mori* is now often written with an old character that means 'forest' or 'grove', yet is similar in shape to 'shrine' (杜 instead of 社). This character is now used widely in Jinja Honchō publications, such as the *Jinja Shinpō* newspaper, and is favoured by its president (Tanaka 2011: 9). As a result, it has spread rapidly throughout the shrine world.

By adopting this little-used yet ancient character (found in classical sources such as the *Man'yōshū*), the shrine establishment is doing three things. First, it discursively establishes *chinju no mori* as something that goes back to the ancient period, giving it a 'classical' status (whereas in fact, as we have seen, the term is a late nineteenth-century invention that has little to do with ancient *kami* worship). Second, it suggests that shrine forests resemble, yet are ultimately different from 'ordinary' forests, as indicated by the fact that it is written differently. And third, by using a character that is very similar in shape to the character meaning 'shrine', the suggestion is made that these forests constitute sacred space and are closely connected to Shinto as a whole. Significantly, those using this character tend to use the term *chinju no mori* in either the third or the last of the four meanings outlined in the beginning of this chapter. To them, it is not the ecological composition of the forest that defines the *chinju no mori* – and perhaps not even the existence of a forest *per se*. The main significance of *chinju no mori* lies in the fact that they symbolize a connection between the present and the ancient past, and between the shrine grounds and the community to which they are said to belong; not in their physical and biological features.[9]

Chinju no mori *and Nationalist Ideology*

Applying Lefebvre's terminology, we may say that *chinju no mori* are not merely relevant as clearly demarcated physical spaces that stand out in human-made urban or agricultural landscapes. They are also relevant as *mental* and *social* spaces. That is, the ways in which they are imagined influence the ways in which they take shape physically, and vice versa. Meanwhile, the meanings attributed to their physical characteristics are discursively embedded, drawing upon existing symbols and norms. As they acquire meanings in this discursive context, *chinju no mori* clearly constitute mental space as much as they are physical. And as these various norms inevitably concern relationships – between humans and nature, between various organisms in an ecosystem, between people today and their ancestors (and, possibly, their descendants), between priests and their *ujiko* (shrine parish), and between different members of an (imagined) community (be it the village, the neighbourhood or the nation) – they also constitute a social space. They are shaped by spatial practices that are embedded within large social structures; as such, they are inevitably contingent upon power relations. Like other sacred sites, *chinju no mori* are by no means neutral: they represent a particular social, political and economic value and may be subject to competing claims. Thus, they are of ideological significance.

As suggested, in recent years, the *chinju no mori* trope has gained widespread popularity in Shinto circles. We have already seen that the concept is employed differently by different actors: Miyawaki Akira sees them as remaining areas of primeval or similar 'natural' forest (so-called climax forest) that need to be preserved for ecological reasons; Ueda Atsushi stresses their ecological as well as their cultural relevance and sees them as an integral part of traditional Japanese landscapes; Ueda Masaaki and Sonoda Minoru are active in the preservation movement and recognize the ecological significance of shrine forests, yet also conceive of them as ancient sacred places that are central to local community building and social cohesion. Recently, however, the concept is also increasingly used by scholars and institutions that adhere to what I have distinguished as the 'ethnic' or 'imperial' paradigms – notions of Shinto as the singular, primordial, underlying substratum of Japanese culture, intimately intertwined with the spirit of the nation. Thus, the term now appears regularly in publications by Jinja Honchō (for instance, its weekly newspaper *Jinja Shinpō*), as well as scholars directly related to this organization. Its president, Tanaka Tsunekiyo, follows Sonoda when he writes that *chinju no mori* constitute the origins of Japanese society, as these were the places where people sensed the presence of the sacred and came together to perform worship ceremonies (*matsuri*) (Tanaka 2011: 10–13). According to him, local communities originated in the collective worship practices taking place at *chinju no mori* in ancient times.

Significantly, Tanaka has argued that the role of Shinto priests is fundamentally different from priests in other religions; while the latter are preachers who mediate between this world and the divine, Shinto priests merely conduct rituals *for the benefit of the community*, he asserts. Thus,

> When seen from our perspective as shrine priests, shrine ritual worship and governance (*jinja no 'matsurigoto'*) is always 'public.'[10] Private affairs do not take place at all. Put simply, all we do is pray for the peace and safety of the nation and the community (*kyōdōtai*) where we live. These are, so to speak, public prayers (*paburikku na inori*). (Tanaka 2011: 7)

Tanaka's claim that shrine practices are intrinsically public is problematic. Not only is there a wide diversity of ritual and devotional practices taking place at shrines, shrines also earn most of their money by performing rituals on behalf of private companies and individuals. Although they constitute the focal points of *matsuri* and other 'public' events, the reality is that shrines are actors that operate within the post-war Japanese 'religious market', competing with other religious and commercial institutions for the patronage of individual and corporate sponsors (cf. Reader & Tanabe 1998). In fact, if it were not for the financial support from companies, many shrines would have even greater difficulty paying their employees and maintaining their buildings. Tanaka does not deny this reality. However, he does not see companies as private actors but describes them as collective entities akin to local communities, both of which constitute the building blocks of Japanese society.

Central to Tanaka's argument is the notion of *kyōdōtai*, which refers to a community, but which literally means 'collective body'. As he argues, most Japanese are part of such a local 'collective body', which can be experienced most directly during a *matsuri*, when people of all ages 'become one body' by carrying a portable shrine (*mikoshi*) together. Ultimately, these local communities together constitute the 'collective body' of the Japanese nation: the *ujiko* to which 'all Japanese belong'. This collective body is symbolically united by the imperial family, which constitutes its head (Tanaka 2011: 19). Although the political consequences are not necessarily the same, the similarity of these ideas to pre-war *kokutai* ('national body') ideology is significant; they point to an organicist understanding of nationhood that denies internal diversity and downplays historical contingencies. Moreover, they naturalize the imperial institution, by suggesting that the emperor is the head of the 'body' that constitutes the Japanese nation. Clearly, such views are of an inherently ideological nature and have potential political significance.

As mentioned, *chinju no mori* are conceptualized as the dwelling places of deities. Representing a symbolic connection between this world and 'the other world', they are often presented as places capable of evoking numinous experiences.

Figure 5.2 Associated with the mythical first emperor Jinmu, Kashihara Jingū in Nara Prefecture is closely intertwined with modern imperial Shinto. It is also famous for its forest, however, showing that nationalism and nature conservation are not necessarily at odds.

Representatives of the 'spiritual paradigm' in particular have described sacred forests as mystical, other-worldly places, allowing visitors to directly experience the divine (e.g. Kamata 2008; Nakazawa [1992] 2006; Yamada 1995). Not surprisingly, then, in popular-scientific magazines and books, the association between *chinju no mori* and spiritual power is made regularly (e.g. Ōmori 2010). This discursive sacralization of *chinju no mori* is not limited to the genre of 'spiritual' books and magazines, however; similar arguments can be found in the writings of more 'mainstream' Shinto scholars, as well as authors associated with the *chinju no mori* movement (e.g. Ueda 2011: 4–5). They are related to notions of *chinju no mori* as primordial sacred places that represent a connection not only between humans, nature and gods but also between contemporary society and the ancestral past. The symbolic significance of *chinju no mori* lies partly in the fact that they exist as *actual physical localities* that can be visited and experienced, and to which various sacred, cultural and moral qualities can be attributed. As forests, *chinju no mori* are 'real' physical places. Indeed, they are part of the physical landscape of Japan; they belong to the *country*, physically as well as symbolically.

Sacred forests, then, have become intertwined with notions of the country Japan as sacred. In contemporary nationalist discourse, the sacredness of forests extends beyond the possible presence of deities: forests are sacred because they are seen as vestiges of an imaginary golden age, characterized by purity and harmony, and as the original essence of the nation. This original essence, however, is nearly forgotten as a result of 'modernization', which is said to have brought about moral decline, environmental problems and the decline of traditional faith. Such, at least, is the historical narrative often presented in works on sacred forests – as well as, in my experience, in ordinary conversation with shrine priests and other officials. Calls for the preservation of *chinju no mori* often go together with nostalgic lamentations on the state of Japanese society and culture. Scholar of religion Yamaori Tetsuo, for instance, has used the metaphor of the 'crying *chinju no mori*' to describe today's Japanese people's loss of 'their' traditional faith (2001). Likewise, Sonoda Minoru has explicitly associated the degradation of the environment with individualization, the erosion of family life and even increasing crime rates, claiming that

> The period of rapid economic growth from the 1960s to the 1980s has done particularly severe damage to the country's natural environment through overdevelopment and frequent pollution. The price of consumerism and material wealth has been paid in the form of the disintegration of 'hometown communities' and spiritual confusion, and in the 1990s this has undoubtedly been one of the reasons for the frequent occurrence throughout Japanese society of events that border on the pathological. (Sonoda 2000: 44)

Thus, the decline in the number of *chinju no mori*, and the overall deterioration of the natural environment, are seen as symptomatic for the current state of Japanese society as a whole. Technological and economical 'progress' is criticized by Sonoda for bringing about both environmental destruction and moral decline (Sonoda 1998: 166–167; 191–192; Sonoda & Tabuchi 2006). Similarly, Ueda Masaaki and Umehara Takeshi have repeatedly condemned the materialism and egoism supposedly characteristic of the post-war bubble economy and advocated a return to 'traditional' values – those associated with 'original Shinto', the 'religion of the forest' – as a prerequisite for overcoming the contemporary crisis. The solution, it is suggested, lies in the revitalization of Japan's 'original' civilization, which is built on the notion of forests as sacred; and, subsequently, on its spread internationally (e.g. M. Ueda 2004b: 16–17; Umehara 2009: 53–54). Thus, in the narratives of Sonoda, Ueda, Umehara and like-minded authors, the mythical ancient history is presented as an ecological golden age and juxtaposed with the current age of decay and destruction. The only solution for overcoming the present crisis and (re)establishing an ecologically and ethically sustainable society is a return to (or, at least, a revitalization of) ancient values and practices pertaining to sacred forests.

Thus, the Shinto environmentalist paradigm is embedded within wider nationalist discourse, taking the shape of moral and cultural pessimism and even, in some cases, millenarianism. That does not mean that the environmental concerns expressed by its advocates are not sincere, nor does it tell us anything about the ecological importance of shrine forest preservation *per se*. Indeed, environmental advocacy may very well be compatible with moral conservatism and cultural nationalism. It does mean, however, that Shinto-related environmental ideas and practices are influenced by, and take shape in the context of, ongoing debates on Japanese national identity and society. Levinger and Lytle (2001) have demonstrated convincingly that myths of a past golden age (whether ecological, cultural, social, linguistic, racial, moral or spiritual) can have significant mobilizing potential. If one accepts the preposition that once upon a time the situation was much better than today, it also follows that, provided that the causes of decline are known and removed, this situation can be recovered.

Such beliefs, of course, can give way to violence – say, if the presence of a different ethnic or religious community is seen as the cause of decline. But this is not necessarily the case: they can also motivate people to become active in more constructive ways. For instance, if the generally deplorable state of sacred forests is seen as symptomatic of the state of Japanese society as a whole, then the preservation of *chinju no mori* symbolizes the preservation of traditional Japanese culture and morality. Thus, Sonoda applauds the fact that

> local groups throughout Japan are making persistent efforts to construct, restore or maintain old and new 'hometown communities'. (…) The shrine groves that more than eighty thousand shrines in Japan have preserved from the countless pressures of centuries, and the religious symbolism of shrine fields and kami mountains are being rediscovered and revalued as expressions of Japan's ancient animistic view of life. This suggests new possibilities for shrine life in the future. (2000: 45)

The efforts referred to by Sonoda include various local projects designed to revitalize local communities by organizing social and cultural events, restoring traditional village- or cityscapes, planting trees and so on. Called *komyuniti-zukuri* (community-making), in the past two decades or so these projects have been set up all over the country, usually run by volunteers (Marmignon 2012; Sorensen & Funck 2007). They also include so-called *mori-zukuri* (forest-making) projects set up for the restoration and maintenance of both *chinju no mori* and *satoyama* – again, usually run by local volunteers, although shrines and shrine priests may be involved in their organization. These are often combined with educational activities, designed to teach people (in particular children) about both nature and 'traditional culture' (*dentō bunka*) – two categories that are usually seen as fully compatible, since 'love of nature' is widely considered to be an integral part of traditional Japanese culture. Children, after all, are the next generation, so they have to be taught the significance of *chinju no mori*.

Hence, many shrine-based projects today involve educational events, ranging from scouting groups to tree-planting, and from guided shrine forest walks to courses in making 'traditional' Japanese food. Again, we see that the significance of *chinju no mori* extends well beyond environmental education proper: shrine forests, it is often argued, should play a central part in teaching children not only the importance of protecting nature but also of preserving traditional culture and maintaining good relations with neighbours. As vestiges of Japanese tradition, they are seen as places where children can be socialized as members of their community – and, ultimately, as patriotic and morally responsible citizens (Jinja Honchō 1999; 'Jinja to "midori" zadankai' 1982; Sonoda & Tabuchi 2006).

Shasō Gakkai

As mentioned previously, one of the organizations that have contributed to the growing interest in shrine forest preservation, by scientists and environmentalists as well as shrine priests, is Shasō Gakkai. Founded in 2002, Shasō Gakkai has actively contributed to the spread of the Shinto environmentalist paradigm. It has drawn attention to the topics of nature conservation and other environmental issues in relation to Shinto shrines, and established these as legitimate concerns both from an academic and a shrine-institutional perspective. It has also been fairly successful in establishing 'sacred forest studies' as a serious, inherently interdisciplinary field of study. Perhaps most important, it has facilitated interaction between scientists, scholars, Shinto priests and laypeople. This has been achieved by means of academic conferences and symposia, as well as the publication of various books and journals that have contributed to an increasing knowledge of shrines and shrine forests. For instance, Shasō Gakkai has been responsible for sharing information about existing projects (e.g. the Tadasu no Mori conservation project in Kyoto, discussed in the next chapter), inspiring others to set up their own projects as well. It has also organized 'forest instructor courses' for the purpose of educating shrine priests and volunteers in the practicalities of forest ecology and preservation.

The main purpose of Shasō Gakkai, then, is to facilitate the study of sacred forests and to contribute to forest conservation. On its website, it is described as a non-profit organization 'devoted to removing the fences between different scientific disciplines related to "forests of the gods" (kamigami no mori) in order to promote research on them. It aims at the creation of new scholarship with a strong local focus, as well as the conservation and development (kaihatsu) of sacred forests (shasō)' (Shasō Gakkai n.d.-b). As this description makes clear, Shasō Gakkai is a research organization with an academic character, but it also wants to contribute to the application of scientific knowledge to actual forest conservation practices. It has an explicitly interdisciplinary orientation, combining insights and involving representatives from various academic disciplines.[1] As stated previously, 'nature' and 'the environment' tend to bring together actors with diverse agendas and allow for unusual coalitions, precisely because they carry significant symbolic capital while leaving space for multiple interpretations and appropriations. This certainly applies to shrine forests as well.

As a non-profit organization (NPO hōjin), Shasō Gakkai has a limited budget. The organization is based in Kyoto, where it has a small office. Most of its academic events (symposia, seminars and so on) take place at shrine buildings or, occasionally, universities, throughout the country but mostly in the Kansai and Kantō regions. In contrast to other shrine forest conservation organizations, Shasō Gakkai is not connected to one particular shrine. Nor, for that matter, is it affiliated with a university or another research institute. Nevertheless, several well-known scholars, scientists and shrine head priests are involved with its activities. Most members are individual citizens, but there are also many shrines affiliated with Shasō Gakkai, as well as a few Buddhist temples.[12] In sum, modest though its budget and organization may be, the activities of Shasō Gakkai are supported by a wide range of prominent intellectuals and shrine officials, at least nominally.

The name Shasō Gakkai has been translated as 'shrine forest society' (Breen & Teeuwen 2010: 209); in my opinion, however, 'sacred forest research association' would be more accurate. The main reason for this is that the organization explicitly states that it is concerned with all types of sacred forests, not only those belonging to shrines. As illustrated by the membership of several Buddhist temples, Shasō Gakkai is not solely concerned with shrine forests; it does not define itself as a 'Shinto' organization but wants to have a transdenominational character. That is also the main reason why, when the organization was founded, it was not called 'Chinju no Mori Gakkai' – which would have been more logical, perhaps, considering the fact that *chinju no mori* had already become a popular concept, whereas *shasō* was a fairly unknown term used by hardly anyone. But *chinju no mori* was generally associated with Shinto shrines only, while *shasō* could be used in a more inclusive sense, also including other types of 'sacred forest' in Japan. Ueda Atsushi has described it as follows:

> The term *shasō* is made up of two characters. *Sha* 社 refers to 'the god of the land (*tsuchi no kami*)' or 'the gathering of people with the god of the land as its centre = community'.[13] *Sō* 叢 means 'gathering of plants and trees (*sōmoku no atsumari*)', so the compound word '*shasō*' may be understood as 'the forest of the god of the land' or 'the forest of the community'. (2004a: 189)

He then proceeds by saying that there are four types of *shasō*. The first of these are shrine forests, or *chinju no mori*; Ueda's description of these corresponds to the first of the four meanings I have distinguished in the beginning of this chapter. The second are the sacred groves of Okinawa, *utaki*, which he defines as 'similar to the *chinju no mori* of mainland Japan, or perhaps it would be good to call them their original shape' (A. Ueda 2004a: 189; cf. M. Ueda 2004b: 12–15).[14] The third are 'other shrine and temple forests' that are not considered as *chinju no mori*, for instance because they have been planted and used for wood production. And the fourth are the ancient mounds containing (imperial) tombs (*kofun*, *go-ryō* or *tsuka*), which today are often covered by trees (A. Ueda 2004a: 189).

In theory, then, *shasō* relates to *chinju no mori* as 'furniture' relates to 'chair': all *chinju no mori* are *shasō*, but not all *shasō* are *chinju no mori*, as the category also includes other types of forests deemed sacred. In reality, however, the terms are often used interchangeably, even by the scholars who have come up with this distinction. For instance, in an article titled 'What is a *shasō*?' (A. Ueda 2001), Ueda

Atsushi describes all aspects of an ideal shrine forest – including a *torii* (gate), a *sandō* (main road leading to the shrine), *shinboku* (sacred trees), shrine buildings (such as *shinden* and *haiden*), a shrine office, *matsuri* and so on. On the other hand, confusingly, the definition of '*shasō*' quoted above is given in an article titled 'What is a *chinju no mori*?' (A. Ueda 2004a). In actual discourse, therefore, both terms by and large mean the same thing – the only difference is perhaps that, thanks to the activities of Shasō Gakkai, the term '*shasō*' today has slightly more 'scientific' connotations (being associated with forest ecology and landscape design) than '*chinju no mori*', which may have more cultural and literary associations. Yet both concepts usually refer to shrine forests.

If not a Shinto organization *de jure*, it is clear that Shasō Gakkai's activities are almost completely limited to shrine forests. More than 90 per cent of all articles, conference presentations and research activities address shrine forests, if not more. Likewise, its seminars and symposia normally take place at Shinto shrines. That does not mean, however, that all those involved in the organization are personally affiliated with Shinto institutions. Among the active participants are many scientists and other people interested in forest conservation, for whom 'Shinto' beliefs and ritual practices may not be personally relevant. Nevertheless, the forests that constitute the objects of research are shrine forests, a few exceptions notwithstanding.

Shasō Gakkai organizes a number of activities, some of them of an academic nature, others more practically oriented. In the past fifteen years or so, Shasō Gakkai has been responsible for an impressive number of publications on shrines, forest conservation and related topics. Its foundational work is the book *Chinju no mori wa yomigaeru: Shasōgaku koto hajime* ('Restoring *chinju no mori*: the beginning of *shasōgaku* [sacred forest studies]') (Ueda & Ueda 2001), in which the purposes of Shasō Gakkai were explained and 'sacred forest studies' (*shasōgaku*) was established as a legitimate field of study. This was followed by a second edited volume, published a few years later, titled *Tankyū 'chinju no mori': Shasōgaku e no shōtai* ('Research on "chinju no mori": An invitation to *shasōgaku*') (M. Ueda 2004c). In between these two books, both of which are anthologies of academic papers, a guidebook was published, which was more practically oriented (Ueda et al. 2003). This book does not only contain information about the spatial configuration and architecture of shrines but also about tree species, birds and insects. Soon thereafter, in 2005, Shasō Gakkai took part in the Aichi World Expo, where it presented Japan's 'sacred forests' to a general audience. In the context of this event, the documentary series *Nihon wa mori no kuni* ('Japan is a land of forests') was produced (Sonoda & Mogi 2006). In sum, in the first years after its establishment, the scholars and scientists running Shasō Gakkai were highly productive.

In addition to these publications, every year Shasō Gakkai organizes a two-day symposium, the results of which are published in its journal, *Shasōgaku kenkyū* ('research in sacred forest studies'). Each time, this conference takes place at a different location. For instance, in June 2013, it took place at Ise Jingū and the nearby Shinto university, Kōgakkan University. Previous locations include

Shimogamo Jinja, Fushimi Inari Taisha and Tsurugaoka Hachimangū (Kamakura). There are also shorter seminars, which typically last half a day and consist of a few public lectures. In addition to its annual journal, six times per year Shasō Gakkai publishes a newspaper with information, which is circulated among its members and available online. It also publishes occasional research reports; for instance, Shasō Gakkai members have been active in monitoring the state of shrines and shrine forests in the area of Tohoku that was hit by the tsunami of 11 March 2011. Finally, there are the 'sacred forest instructor courses', in which participants learn forestry theory from prominent scientists in a series of workshops. Those who finish the course and pass the exam are given a certificate as well as a symbolic gift, the 'Shasō Gakkai helmet'.

In 2013, I attended Shasō Gakkai's annual symposium in Ise. It lasted two days: the first day started with a short visit to Gekū, the Outer Shrine, followed by a tour of the Sengūkan, the recently built *shikinen sengū* museum. In the afternoon, we went on an excursion to the shrine forest, where the head of the *eirinbu* (forest department) showed us around. He explained us about the history of the forest and about current production processes (see Chapter 9). The second day started with an official visit (including ritual purification) to Naikū, the Inner Shrine, followed by lectures and paper sections at Kōgakkan University. In total, there were about sixty to seventy participants. I was told that this number is higher than normal – usually, the annual conferences attract approximately thirty to forty people – which may have been due to the fact that it took place in Ise. Among the participants were scientists and scholars, but most of the people I talked to were involved with local shrine forest projects as volunteers and took part in Shasō Gakkai activities to learn more about Shinto culture and forest preservation. By contrast, there were not many shrine priests. Despite the fact that Shasō Gakkai has a strong 'Shinto' identity – most of its publications are primarily concerned with shrines and shrine forests, which is also where its seminars and symposia take place – the number of shrine priests actively involved in the organization seems limited.

Whether this is because of a lack of time or a lack of interest remains to be found out. Some local activists to whom I talked accused the organization of being too abstract and academic. Because of this, they argue, it is incapable of really appealing to the 'local communities' whose histories and identities are said to be closely intertwined with 'their' *chinju no mori*, and whose involvement is necessary for the shrine (forest)'s preservation (interview data, November 2011). Indeed, it is true that Shasō Gakkai has an academic character – as illustrated by the high number of scholars and scientists active in the organization – but that is not all there is to it. Among the people taking the 'forest instructor' course, for example, are many 'laypeople' who are neither academically nor religiously affiliated, but who are simply interested in becoming active in forest conservation and want to learn the basics of forest ecology and maintenance. Moreover, among the activities organized by Shasō Gakkai are excursions and field research trips. Thus, academic though the organization's focus may be, it is not merely theoretical; attempts are made to apply scientific knowledge to concrete conservation practices, and to educate those involved in these practices. That said, at the activities where I was present, I did not get the impression there were many shrine priests involved; most participants were either scholars or non-clergy volunteers active in local forest conservation projects. So perhaps there is some truth to the argument that Shasō Gakkai's activities are fairly academic and have limited appeal to local shrine priests and communities.

Chapter 6

LANDSCAPES OF THE PAST

The God's Body

Landscapes are imbued with memory. As anthropologist Tim Ingold has argued, a landscape is 'an enduring record of – and testimony to – the lives and works of past generations who have dwelt within it, and in so doing, have left there something of themselves (…). To perceive the landscape is therefore to carry out an act of remembrance' (2000: 189). Landscapes embody stories; walking in them can become an act of remembering akin to story-telling (De Certeau 1984). These stories are not univocal: landscapes are heterogeneous, as are the stories and memories associated with them. Space may be contested, and landscapes are often subject to competing claims and narratives, embodying multiple and at times conflicting memories. Various historical narratives are projected upon and engraved in landscapes, which come to represent national origin myths, memories of past glory or suffering, divine presence and more (Schama 1995). Thus, landscapes are closely connected with collective identities and nationhood (Smith 1999). Japan is no exception: notions of a primordial forest landscape figure prominently in the nationalist imagination, and the perceived physical remnants of this primordial landscape are subject to attempts at conservation, sacralization, heritagization and other place-making activities.

One example of a place that is believed to embody ancient Japanese culture is Mount Miwa, a well-known forested mountain in Nara Prefecture, located near the city of Sakurai. Often referred to as a 'sacred mountain', it attracts a steady flow of visitors. At the foot of the mountain lies the shrine Ōmiwa Jinja, which is widely regarded as one of the oldest shrines in Japan. The area around the mountain is dotted with burial mounds (*kofun*), which are associated with early Yamato emperors, and other sites identified with myths, poems and historical events mentioned in ancient texts such as the *Man'yōshū* and *Nihon Shoki*. Thus, the region is regarded as an important centre of ancient Japanese civilization. It is not only associated with Kofun-period traditions, however, but also with the earlier Jōmon period. Several contemporary Shinto authors have argued that Jōmon-period Japan was characterized by nature worship, which according to them constitutes Shinto's 'original shape'. Such notions are often projected upon

Mount Miwa and Ōmiwa Jinja. They are mentioned repeatedly in texts on *chinju no mori* and constitute a recurring theme in Shinto environmentalist discourse.

The worship practices and beliefs associated with this shrine are often described as remnants of ancient nature worship. This is supposedly evidenced by the absence of a *honden* (main hall). In many shrines, the *honden* is considered the most sacred place. It is usually out of bounds to visitors and houses the sacred object (e.g. a mirror) that constitutes the *shintai*: the material symbol or body of the deity. In the case of Mount Miwa, however, the mountain itself is seen as the *shintai*; hence, it is also called *shintaizan* (*shintai* mountain). Accordingly, it is suggested, the mountain as a whole is worshipped as a deity. Miyake Hitoshi, an expert on Japanese mountain worship traditions, describes it as follows: 'At Mount Miwa, behind the worship hall of the shrine is the Miwa *torii*; behind there is the sacred forbidden area (*kinsokuchi*). (…) Mount Miwa as a whole is seen as the place where the deity resides. (…) The mountain as such has become the object of worship' (2009: 121).

The fact that a mountain is perceived as the physical embodiment of a particular deity or spirit is hardly unique, neither in Japan nor elsewhere. What makes Mount Miwa special, however, is the role it has come to play in justifying notions of Shinto as an ancient 'nature religion', and the association with environmental

Figure 6.1 Worship hall (*haiden*) of Ōmiwa Jinja in Nara Prefecture. Famously, Ōmiwa Jinja has no main hall (*honden*): the mountain behind it, Mount Miwa, is said to constitute the body of the deity. In recent years, Ōmiwa Jinja and Mount Miwa have become some of the main symbols of Shinto environmentalism.

issues, which as we have seen has acquired paradigmatic status in recent years. Redefined as the quintessential example of ancient Shinto nature worship, Mount Miwa has become one of the Shinto environmentalist paradigm's main symbols. It is often presented as a potential cultural and philosophical resource for the establishment of a new environmental ethics. For instance, at a symposium held at the shrine in 2001, Nomura Shigeo, one of the contributors, argued that

Especially in recent years, environmental problems receive much attention, and the twenty-first century is called the age of the environment. Since ancient times, no *honden* has been constructed at the shrine, so the worship of the god Ōmononushi-no-ōkami residing on Mount Miwa has continued in its original shape uninterruptedly until the twenty-first century. And so in each and every tree and blade of grass (*ichiboku issō*) the deity is believed to be present, and trees are treated with great care. I think that when it comes to the environmental problems that have become so prominent these days, only Shinto can instil reasonableness into people's minds. (Ōmiwa Jinja 2002: 52)

Thus, Mount Miwa has come to be closely associated with notions of primordial nature worship in 'ancient Shinto' and has become a core symbol for the Shinto environmentalist movement. Shrine actors have been actively involved in framing the shrine in such terms, and their narrative has been endorsed by a number of Japanese and non-Japanese scholars (e.g. Kamata 2008, 108–139; Watt 2014). Kamata Tōji, for instance, argues that Ōmiwa Jinja is one of the three shrines that can serve as models for the establishment of a new, universally and ecologically oriented Shinto (Kamata 2011: 22; cf. Kamata 2008).[1] Significantly, it was also one of the shrine forests visited by forestry experts from ARC and WWF in 2005 (together with nearby Kashihara Jingū and Ise Jingū), when they were in the process of developing an international 'Religious Forestry Standard' in cooperation with Jinja Honchō (ARC n.d.-e). In sum, the discursive association between Mount Miwa, 'ancient Shinto' nature worship and environmental issues has become firmly established, through various institutional and academic practices.

However, while the association is understandable, it does rest on some questionable assumptions. In fact, even though the shrine is one of the oldest in the country, the interpretation of Mount Miwa as the place where ancient Shinto is best preserved is historically problematic. Rather than representing some sort of 'pure Shinto' going back to ancient times, worship practices on Mount Miwa have developed, and been transformed, in the context of medieval Buddhist and *shinbutsu shūgō* practices. In the medieval period, Mount Miwa constituted one of the main centres for the development of 'Buddhist Shinto': *kami* worship embedded within in a Buddhist institutional and theological context, which came to be referred to as *ryōbu shintō* ('Shinto of Two Parts') (Andreeva 2010). The institutional and ideological separation of 'Buddhism' and 'Shinto' in the early Meiji period was artificial and unprecedented and came about as the result of government coercion. It led to the dismantling of Buddhist buildings and the reconstruction of the shrine as an important Shinto centre (Antoni 1995).

Thus, Nomura's claim that worship practices at Mount Miwa have continued 'uninterruptedly' in their 'original shape' since ancient times until today must be discarded, if only because of the significant transformations they have gone through in the course of history. Yet even if the claim were true, the question would still remain: how exactly can an ancient worship tradition contribute to the development of a more environmentally sustainable society and economy in the twenty-first century? Despite the fact that Mount Miwa is mentioned repeatedly in texts asserting the importance of Shinto for environmental issues, few authors succeed in specifying the potential relevance of this tradition today.

Furthermore, the often-made claims that the belief in Mount Miwa as a *shintaizan* – a mountain believed to be the deity's physical body – is a remnant of Jōmon-period mountain worship, and that the mountain has been set apart as a sacred forbidden area since ancient times, have been challenged. As Gaudenz Domenig has pointed out, 'the earliest document of the shrine that calls Mount Miwa as a whole a *shintaizan* dates only from 1871' (Domenig 1997: 100). Rather than setting part of the mountain apart as sacred and taboo out of reverence for nature, as many contemporary Shinto scholars claim, the reasons for doing so may have been more prosaic:

> The reason was, in short, that the sacred mountain land of the shrine had come to be repeatedly misused by gatherers of firewood, stones, or mushrooms, and by people cutting trees or even making fields for agriculture.[2] (…) It was this continued exploitation for economic reasons that eventually called for a new way of protecting the shrine's forest and its purity as a sacred ground. After the traditional means of declaring the shrine forest a forbidden zone had failed to improve the situation, was finally a more effective solution found by calling the whole mountain a *shintaizan*. This stratagem worked. (Domenig 1997: 101)

As the quotation implies, the redefinition of Mount Miwa as a 'sacred' mountain, entrance to which was restricted, was not based on some sort of ancient 'animistic' reverence, at least not primarily. Rather, it was the result of considerations of a more economic nature: the shrine authorities wanted to restrict access to the mountain's natural resources. The very fact that the ban had to be reinforced by means of a theological invention shows that, to foraging peasants at least, the 'sacred' character of the mountain was not a self-evident given; or, if it was, at least that did not prevent them from getting wood and other forest resources. Similar examples of forest and mountains that were sacralized and declared taboo – complete with promises of divine retributions that would cause misfortune among those violating the taboo – in order to prevent peasants from appropriating shrine and temple lands can be found elsewhere in Japan (Rambelli 2001: 75–80).

This brings us back to one of this study's core theoretical concerns: processes by which sacred space is produced. The sacralization of a place – in this case, the redefinition of a mountain as the physical body of a deity, which comes to be seen as the object of veneration and taboo – is not necessarily rooted in the experience of the 'numinous' character of a given place, as scholars such as Mircea Eliade and Kamata Tōji would have us believe (e.g. Kamata 2008). Sacralization processes are intimately intertwined with political and economic realities and may be employed as strategies to lay claim to particular land areas, while excluding other actors from the land (or even displacing them). Of course, the fact that a certain place has a particular economic value and political significance does not mean it cannot be experienced as 'divine' and 'sacred', and become subject to devotion. Quite the contrary: attributions of sacredness add to the symbolic and ideological value of a place and therefore to its political and economic importance, just as much as political and economic factors may serve as incentives for sacralization. The point here is simply that land sacralization processes are inherently political and economically embedded – irrespective of the 'truth' of the numinous qualities attributed to a given place – and, therefore, are often subject to contestation by competing actors. Moreover, the meanings attributed to a particular place are never fixed, despite the fact that they may be perceived as age-old. The association of Mount Miwa with environmental issues is quite recent indeed, yet it has achieved the status of a self-evident truth, in contemporary Shinto ideology if not beyond.

A Forest Civilization?

Japan is one of the countries with the highest percentage of forest cover in the world, a fact which is often mentioned in texts on Shinto and the environment (e.g. Matsuyama 2009: 1; Nakamura 2009: 22; Shintō Kokusai Gakkai 2012: 3). In 2015, it had a total forest area of 68.5 per cent.[3] There are clear spatial divisions between the forested mountains, where few people live and work, and the densely populated lowlands, which have little forest cover. Considering the omnipresence of forested mountains, it should come as no surprise that Japan has been defined as a 'country of forests' (Sonoda & Mogi 2006) that has given birth to a unique 'forest civilization' (Nakamura 2009; Umehara [1991] 1995). The notion that forests are the birthplace of Japanese 'religion' (and, by extension, of Japanese culture and society) is one of the axioms underlying the Shinto environmentalist paradigm and has been advocated by a number of influential Japanese scholars (e.g. Nakazawa [1992] 2006; Sonoda 1997, 2000; M. Ueda 2001, 2004a,b, 2013; Umehara 1989, [1991] 1995; Yamaori 2001). While the historical accuracy of such claims may be debated, it is probably safe to say that forests and mountains – in Japan, the two categories often overlap – have long played a central part in the Japanese imagination, representing an 'other' world associated with deities, ancestral spirits and death (e.g. Blacker [1975] 1986: 69–85; Miyake 2009: 109–110; Sonoda 1998: 46–51).

Thus, forests and mountains may have symbolized, and evoked memories of, ancestral pasts, inducing feelings of nostalgia and longing as well as mystery and fear. Incidentally, this is not a uniquely Japanese phenomenon: as Robert Harrison has pointed out, forests have also featured prominently in the 'Western' cultural imagination. According to him, 'forests have the psychological effect of evoking memories of the past' and may even 'become figures for memory itself' (1992: 156; cf. Schama 1995). This statement is of particular relevance for Japan as well, as forests have long constituted a powerful literary trope, associated with the afterlife, the ancestral past, and (lost) cultural and spiritual traditions (Abe Auestad 2014). Forests are associated with the (idealized) past and figure prominently in nostalgic narratives lamenting a supposed loss of traditional worldviews and practices, for instance in the oeuvre of Yanagita Kunio (Hamashita 2004; cf. Ivy 1995).

Not surprisingly, then, in modern times, forests have come to be associated with the Japanese nation itself, constituting an important aspect of the national 'ethnoscape' (Smith 1999: 150). We have already seen how the narrative of the Japanese love of nature was developed and appropriated in the context of the Japanese nation-building project; not surprisingly, the forest trope has become a prominent aspect of this. 'The Japanese' are said to have an intimate connection with forests, which not only evoke gratitude, creativity and fear, but which are also imagined as the primordial space where the nation originated. The fact that many forested areas today consist of dilapidated *sugi* monocultures, planted in the post-war period for timber production yet mostly left to grow wild (Kerr 2001: 52–56; Knight 1997), has not undermined such imagery. Rather, the sad state of most contemporary Japanese forests has given rise to a new type of nostalgia for Japan's 'original' broad-leaved evergreen forests on the part of scientists, local residents and romantic nationalists alike. As Augustin Berque has written,

> In Japan, as in Europe, there is a myth about the primordial forest, the haunt of ancestral fears, but there is also nostalgia for a nature which is disappearing. Unlike Europe, however, and for obvious reasons, this forest has joined the mythological constellation of things essentially Japanese; in effect, in the mind of the Japanese of today, it plays the role of the original matrix in which national authenticity is rooted. This forest has a name: the glossy-leaved forest that once covered the plains of most of the larger islands (*shōyōjurin*). (…) The underlying concept is that this forest milieu, that of Jōmon prehistoric culture, was the crucible from which Shintoism was born. ([1986] 1997: 88–89)

The notion of Japan as a 'forest civilization' has been advocated by, among others, the environmental scientist and botanist Nakamura Yōichi (1957–). According to him, 'Japan is the only country where there has been a long connection between forests and civilization. It is a fact that there are no other such countries in the history of the world; it seems like a miracle' (Nakamura 2009: 9). When looking at the world's history, he argues, we can say that 'the history of civilization is surely the history of forest destruction' (2009: 10). In particular, 'Western civilization' is built upon massive deforestation; the nature-loving traditions of northern Europe (i.e. Germanic and Celtic tribes) were supposedly suppressed by the Christian missionaries, who brought with them the spirit of deforestation, destroyed animism and felled trees (2009: 13–15). Not surprisingly, Japan is presented as diametrically opposed to 'Western civilization' in its relationship to forests, as evidenced by its high forest cover (2009: 22). The reason for this, Nakamura emphasizes, is *not* that the Japanese refrained from logging trees: they have always used a lot of wood for construction purposes. Nevertheless, Nakamura asserts, Japan has never experienced large-scale deforestation. One of the reasons for this, he states,

> is Japan's traditional religion Shinto, and its belief that gods live in nature. Forests were seen as places where gods reside, and have become the object of worship itself. In Japan's rural villages, there are shrines and shrine forests (*chinju no mori*) where the gods that protect those areas are worshipped, and these have come to be venerated as sacred places. To Japanese, the sight of a shrine forest with a shrine in its middle is very common, but in the rest of the world it is very uncommon to have a religious institution in the middle of a forest. (2009: 23)

As a matter of fact, as the environmental historian Conrad Totman has pointed out, there have been periods of far-reaching deforestation in Japanese history. He characterizes 'Japan's forest history prior to the seventeenth area as a stereotypical era of exploitation forestry, in which woodland users generally showed little concern for preservation of site or restoration of yield' (1989: 4). Totman's argument is partly acknowledged by Nakamura, who distinguishes three periods of deforestation in Japanese history: the Nara and early Heian periods, when large wooden Buddhist temples were built; the late medieval and early Edo periods, when the population increased rapidly; and the modern period (2009: 24–25). However, Nakamura emphasizes the Japanese capacity to overcome these challenges, even referring to the Shōwa emperor (Hirohito)'s practice of planting trees (2009: 25) – a symbolic annual event that was established in the post-war period (Knight 1997: 715) – as well as to Ise Jingū's timber production, used for rebuilding its shrine buildings every twenty years and said to be sustainable (2009: 26–29; see Chapter 9).

In contrast to Totman, then, Nakamura does not devote much attention to the question as to how it was possible that the 'forest-loving' Japanese people caused deforestation – not only in the modern period, when 'Western technology' had invaded the country, but also in two earlier periods. As Totman makes clear, periods of deforestation were followed by periods of reforestation (the most extensive of these was in the Edo period, when it was the result of an ambitious project designed by the authorities). However, the incentives for this reforestation were economic and pragmatic, rather than based on any kind of 'Shinto' appreciation of nature as sacred. As Totman writes,

> Just as we do not find woodland regulators and tree growers justifying their own actions, or urging action by others, in the name of 'nature', so we do not find any themes of Buddhist reverence for 'sentient beings' showing up as reason or rationale in forest policy. (…) Nor do other religious doctrines, such as Shintō or Shugendō, show up as motivators in the actions of forest preservers. Doubtless, a few gnarly old trees were left standing near shrines or other sacred places out of an aesthetic-religious sensibility, but such occurrences were local in application and severely limited in their environmental impact. (1989: 179)

Thus, in contrast to Nakamura, Totman does not see Shinto as a factor of importance in Japan's history of de- and reforestation (nor, for that matter, Buddhism). Likewise, he challenges the notion that there is some sort of unique appreciation of nature intrinsic to Japanese culture. Nevertheless, Nakamura's views are widespread and can be considered representative for contemporary views on Shinto and the environment. Moreover, although those 'gnarly old trees' near shrines may historically have been 'severely limited in their environmental impact', in the past three decades or so they have become an important symbol of the intertwinement between ecology, nature conservation, sacred space, local community cohesion and Japanese national heritage. Hence, their impact today may be very different from earlier times. Likewise, the relationship between Shinto and the natural environment has undergone significant change, not only because of ongoing discursive associations but also because of the various grass-roots organizations trying to give shape to this ideal.

Nakamura's paper echoes the ideas of his predecessor, the well-known geographer Yasuda Yoshinori (1995, 2006). Yasuda first presented his ideas to an Anglophone audience in a short yet provocative essay in which he contrasted 'Western' and 'Japanese' forest history, then argued that a revival of the 'traditional' Japanese forest civilization and corresponding religious worldviews is needed in order to overcome the global environmental crisis – a process he referred to by the concept 'animism renaissance' (Yasuda 1990). More specifically, Yasuda distinguishes between two types of civilization, the 'civilization of deforestation' and the 'forest civilization'. The former, he argues, spread from ancient Mesopotamia to the Mediterranean area, after which it was 'inherited by the people of Europe' and fused with Christianity (1990: 2–3). Yasuda idealizes so-called primitive civilizations in pre-Christian Europe, Africa, Asia and the Americas, calling them 'golden', 'peaceful' and based on 'harmony between man and nature'. This is a clear example of the appropriation of the 'noble savage' stereotype by representatives of the religious environmentalist paradigm, discussed earlier (Kalland 2008): 'primitive' people are believed to live in harmony with nature, and, accordingly, to possess ancient ecological knowledge that has profound relevance for today's world. Sadly, however, the 'civilization of deforestation' has 'destroyed the American Indian civilization and eventually laid waste to the seven continents of the world'; it 'destroyed nature and the spiritual richness of the people who lived in harmony with nature', Yasuda laments (1990: 3). As their cultures and environments were destroyed, he suggests, the ecological knowledge of 'primitive' people has virtually disappeared.

Nevertheless, 'There is another genealogy of civilization which can be called the "forest civilization" and which still survives today in Japan' (1990: 3). According to Yasuda,

> Fortunately, due to the isolation policy of the Tokugawa Shogunate, Japan escaped the invasion of the 'civilization of deforestation'. Animism survived until recent decades, maintaining the traditions begun in Jomon culture. Shinto played an important role in preserving Animism as the trees sacred to the gods

survived in the consecrated precincts of Shinto shrines. (...) Although we can no longer return to the primitive world of Jomon or other early civilizations, we need to remember and recognize the sacredness of the forests which bring forth and nurture all of mankind. (1990: 4)

Thus, Japan is presented as the sole country in the world that has not succumbed to the destructive 'civilization of deforestation', and where, accordingly, the ancient spirit of 'animism' – here presented as the underlying foundation of Shinto – has been preserved. In addition, Yasuda suggests that the spirit of animism characteristic of the 'forest civilization', which is said to have been preserved in Shinto, may serve to re-establish a global environmental awareness.

Animism Politics

Texts that frame Japan as a 'forest civilization' have exercised considerable influence upon contemporary Shinto thought and practices, despite the fact that they were originally developed in a 'secular' (i.e. not religiously affiliated) Japanese academic context. The idealization of Jōmon-period forest culture characteristic of the work of Yasuda (and Umehara, who is discussed in more detail shortly) is particularly evident in the work of Ueda Atsushi and Ueda Masaaki, two of the leading scholars behind the establishment of Shasō Gakkai, together with Sonoda. Ueda Atsushi, for instance, has argued that Jōmon people perceived of the forest as a divine mother, and worshipped the forest's 'mysterious power', which laid the foundation for later developments: 'This kind of forest-centred faith, and the belief in a return to the forest [after death], was not only strong among the "people of the forest" [i.e. Jōmon-period people], but has also remained strongly in the consciousness and behaviour of later Japanese people' (A. Ueda 2004b: 135). Likewise, Ueda Masaaki conceives of *chinju no mori* as remnants of Jōmon-period worship places and traces several elements of *kami* worship to this period – in particular, the worship of sacred mountains (*shintaizan*) such as Mount Miwa and the demarcation of certain areas as 'taboo' and 'forbidden forest' (M. Ueda 2004a: 37; 2013: 95–114).[4]

Central to these narratives on the ancient Japanese 'forest civilization' is the notion of 'animism'. 'Animism' is a European term, derived from the Latin *anima*, which means 'soul', 'spirit' or 'breath'. It was coined by the British cultural anthropologist Edward Tylor (1832–1917), who defined it as 'the belief in spiritual beings' that is the foundation of all religious systems. In his evolutionist model, 'animism' was considered to be the first, most primitive stage of religious and cultural development (Morris 1987: 100). As such, it served the same purpose as Frazer's stage of 'magic' and Durkheim's 'totemism'. Similarly, Sigmund Freud (1856–1939) used the term 'animism' to refer to the first stage of mankind's cultural development. Unlike his British predecessor, however, for Freud the term did not merely refer to a particular period in history but also to a psychological condition. According to him, 'animism' is characterized by the 'over-estimation of psychic processes', in which emotional impulses are followed directly (Morris 1987: 158). Thus, in the work of Tylor as well as that of Freud, 'animism' is not merely a neutral category employed to describe a particular type of 'religious' belief; it is a pejorative term, associated with primitiveness, simplicity, impulsivity, emotionality and underdevelopment (sociocultural as well as psychological).

Later generations of anthropologists explicitly distanced themselves from both the social-evolutionist and the Freudian interpretations of culture. In particular, the notion of 'primitive' cultures, and the identification of European prehistorical societies with present-day 'isolated' communities, was criticized. Accordingly, associated notions such as 'animism' and 'totemism' fell into disuse and disappeared from the academic vocabulary of anthropologists and scholars of religion. Not until the turn of the twenty-first century was the concept rediscovered and applied seriously by European anthropologists, who used it to refer to alternative modes of relating to and representing elements of nature (Descola 2005; Ingold 2000).[5] Before that time, however, the term remained popular among Japanese authors – along with other classical European anthropological categories, such as 'totemism' (e.g. Nakazawa 2006) and 'shamanism' (e.g. Kamata 2008), which were (and are) used widely.[6]

Significantly, in today's Japan as well as in nineteenth-century Europe, 'animism' is not merely a social-scientific category used to denote a particular belief system. The term is also used for academic identity politics, to differentiate between nations or societies, and carries normative connotations. The crucial difference is that in Japan, the term has been reappropriated and reversed; 'primitiveness' and 'backwardness' have come to be perceived as positive features, as these are associated with the social and ecological harmony supposedly characteristic of primordial, Jōmon-period Japanese society. At times, this reversal is explicit, as in the case of Umehara Takeshi's claim that the overcoming of modernity's problems lies in the revival of a prehistoric animistic worldview, which he labels 'ancient postmodernism' (Umehara 2009). At other times, the superiority of animistic modes of relating to the environment is asserted more implicitly. Significantly, in Japanese literature as well as scholarship, the term 'animism' represents not only an evolutionary stage or a particular epistemological attitude; it also has come to constitute a marker of national identity, serving as a rhetoric device to set Japan apart from the West. This is clearly visible in the work of anthropologist Iwata Keiji, who has described animism as a particular mode of relating to the world, characterized by the experience of a spiritual presence rather than intellectual reasoning. Japanese culture, according to Iwata, is grounded in such an 'animistic' experience of reality, not unlike some Southeast Asian worldviews but opposed to 'Western' ones (Iwata 1993; cf. Clammer 2004). Similarly, the term 'animism' has been used to explain certain supposedly unique features in Japanese literature (Gebhardt 1996).

One of the most prominent Japanese authors who has advocated the return of 'animism', which is identified with an idealized 'ancient Japanese' forest culture, is Umehara Takeshi (1925–). Schooled as a philosopher, Umehara is one of the most prominent Japanese public intellectuals. According to him, the essence of

Japanese culture can be found in the 'forest culture' developed in the Jōmon period and in the 'animism' by which this culture was characterized. As he has repeatedly stated, in order to overcome today's challenges, humanity has to embrace the spirit of animism developed in the Jōmon period (Umehara 1989; [1991] 1995; 2009). Although a scholar of Buddhism himself, to Umehara Japanese Buddhism does not constitute the essence of Japanese religion. Nor, for that matter, does Shinto. Shinto, he argues, has in the course of history gone through two major transformations and has become very different from its original shape. The second of these transformations took place in the Meiji period, when Shinto was appropriated and abused by the state for political purposes. Like other representatives of the Shinto environmentalist paradigm (e.g. Sonoda 1998: 9; M. Ueda 2001: 61–65), Umehara is critical of 'State Shinto' imperialism, arguing that it led to the distortion and even, partially, destruction of Shinto as it had existed previously. He does, however, suggest that this was the consequence of the import of destructive 'Western' ideas, rather than any intrinsic 'Japanese' causes ([1991] 1995: 15–16).

More important, the first transformation of Shinto, according to Umehara, took place at the time of the Ritsuryō system, the Chinese-style legislative and political system implemented in the seventh and eighth century. In fact, the ritual state cult and imperial mythology that were developed during this period have long been considered the original shape of Shinto, a view challenged by historians only in recent decades.[7] However, Umehara argues that the imperial cult of the Ritsuryō period does *not* constitute Shinto's original shape. He describes it as the first 'State Shinto' period, in which a previously existing 'Shinto' was appropriated and drastically reformed by the political authorities. Umehara argues that well-known Shinto texts (the *Kojiki*, *norito* prayers and so on) and ritual purification practices (*misogi* and *harae*) were invented during this period, modelled after Daoism ([1991] 1995: 17–20). Unlike historical-constructivist scholars such as Kuroda, however, Umehara does subscribe to the view that Shinto has a unique, transhistorical essence. In order to recover this original essence, the 'underlying Japanese spirit', we have to disregard the 'inventions' made during the Ritsuryō and Meiji periods and study the religious practices that existed prior to the introduction of continental culture and ideology – using archaeology, anthropology, ethnology and comparative religion ([1991] 1995: 20–22).

This essence, according to Umehara, is animism. The animistic worldview goes back to the Jōmon period, when the hunter-gatherers dwelling in Japan's forests developed a sophisticated spiritual culture, as 'evidenced' by wooden ritual objects from this period ([1991] 1995: 28). Animism, then, is defined as 'the thought that says animals, plants and even inorganic things have a spirit that is connected to humans; and that, through this spirit, all living things can live. (...) [It is] the thought that sees spirits living in places in nature' (Umehara 1989: 13). Thus, animism is not only the belief that certain natural elements and non-human organisms are spirited but also that their spirit constitutes a *continuity with* human spirits, despite differences in outward appearances.

The initial shape of animism, Umehara suggests, is the worship of spirits in trees (1989: 13–14). In prehistoric Japan, he argues, trees came to be worshipped as divine bodies, symbols of fertility and/or places where deities resided. As archaeological findings suggest, in the course of the centuries, the worship of trees came to be extended to logs and wooden pillars, which took centre stage in worship practices ([1991] 1995: 49). According to Umehara, this worship of pillars constitutes the 'origins of Shinto' ([1991] 1995: 51). He is not the only one who has made this point: for instance, in the documentary *Nihon wa mori no kuni* ('Japan is a land of forests'), co-produced by Shasō Gakkai, the association between trees, pillars and ancient Shinto beliefs is made explicitly (Sonoda & Mogi 2006). In particular, reference is made to the Onbashira Matsuri held every six years at Suwa Taisha in Nagano Prefecture, where high trees are chopped down, carried or pushed down the hills, and raised during a shrine ceremony. Likewise, Ueda Masaaki has advocated the notion that the worship of trees and pillars is central to Shinto in its 'original', Jōmon-period shape (2001: 43–45; 2004b: 6–8). In addition to Suwa Taisha's Onbashira Matsuri, traces of this tree-/pillar worship are said to have remained at the shrines of Ise, which are built above wooden pillars buried in the ground; and, of course, in the 'sacred trees' (*shinboku*) found at shrines throughout the country.[8]

According to Umehara, 'animism' in its original, 'pure' shape has disappeared, but some animistic elements have remained. These, he suggests, have influenced later Japanese beliefs and ritual practices, such as the association of deities with particular animals often found at shrines (e.g. the god Inari is commonly associated with foxes) (1989: 16). Animism is also considered to have influenced some Japanese Buddhist doctrines. For instance, Umehara attributes the Tendai doctrine that grasses and trees possess Buddhahood to the ancient Japanese animistic worldview (1989: 19). This traditional 'animistic' view has great salvific potential, Umehara argues, and it must be revitalized in order for humankind to overcome its many problems – especially those pertaining to the environment (Umehara 2009). As asserted by both Umehara and Yasuda, Japan is one of the few places in the world where traces of the original 'animistic' worldview have remained, incorporated into later Buddhist and Shinto beliefs. According to Yasuda, one of the main reasons for this was that, in contrast to other parts of Asia, Africa and the Americas, Japan escaped colonization by Western powers. Yet, given that in mainland Japan 'animism' has been transformed and incorporated into other traditions, the question remains as to how the 'original shape' of Japanese religion can be reconstructed.

According to Umehara, this can be done by 'studying the religions of the Ainu and Okinawa' (1989: 15). His suggestion is that in Japan's periphery, ancient traditions have been preserved best – an argument that goes back to the works of Yanagita Kunio, which has continued to influence Japanese ethnology (*minzokugaku*) and religious studies since. As Morris-Suzuki writes, in the work of Yanagita and his followers, 'Okinawan culture could be represented as an anthropological treasure house whose contents revealed "the shape of things as they were in the beginning" and as they had once been throughout the entire Japanese archipelago' (1998: 31).

These ideas have strongly influenced Umehara, who devotes much space in his work to discussions of Ainu and Ryukyu beliefs and practices (1989: 16–18; [1991] 1995: 36–43).

The association of Ainu and Ryukyu worship practices with 'ancient Shinto' remains remarkably common, not only in contemporary Shinto discourse but also in Japanese academia. Many Japanese scholars consider worship practices and beliefs from Okinawa Prefecture, as well as Ainu traditions, to be the remnants of a primordial nature religion that has not been preserved in mainland Japan but only in the periphery. Ueda Masaaki, for instance, has argued that *utaki* – Okinawan sacred groves – are similar in shape and purpose to Japan's primordial *chinju no mori* and, hence, represent the original shape of Shinto shrines (2004b: 13). Accordingly, as we have seen, *utaki* and *chinju no mori* are today often grouped together under the common denominator *shasō*, especially by scholars who are affiliated with Shasō Gakkai (Suganuma 2004: 87–89; A. Ueda 2001: 8, 26; M. Ueda 2004b: 12–14).

Needless to say, the suggestion made by Umehara, Ueda and like-minded scholars, that Okinawa's *utaki* have remained unchanged since ancient times and constitute the original shape of Japan's sacred shrine forests, is historically problematic. In fact, *utaki* were not conceptualized as Shinto until they were annexed by the imperial regime and redefined as shrines in the national Shinto cult, in a process referred to as *utaki saihen* ('reorganization of the *utaki*') in 1940.[9] The association of Ainu beliefs and practices with ancient proto-Shinto Japanese traditions, as suggested by Umehara, is likewise questionable – as is his statement that 'Okinawan culture and Ainu culture are very similar' ([1991] 1995: 37). The best-known worship practice historically conducted by Ainu is the *iomante* ceremony, a famous annual ceremony that includes the ritual sacrifice of a bear. Indeed, much of Umehara's discussion concerns this particular ceremony, as well as some apparent similarities between certain Ainu and Japanese words. It remains unclear, however, why the *iomante* tradition should be seen as a remnant of 'ancient Japanese' worship traditions. Similarly, Miyake's inclusion of this ceremony into his list of Japanese mountain worship traditions (2009: 120) is puzzling, as it implies that this is just another example of the local diversity existing within the generic category 'Shinto culture', rather than an altogether different cultural practice performed by a non-Japanese people, who were forcibly assimilated into the Japanese nation-state in the modern period.

The tendency to perceive aspects of Ryukyu and Ainu traditions as remnants of ancient Shinto practices is not only problematic because it denies the many differences between these traditions and those of mainland Japan (as well as, significantly, the historical diversity among various Ainu and Ryukyuan communities) but also because of the political implications. Perhaps more than anything else does this approach illustrate the social-evolutionist assumptions underlying contemporary discourse on (the origins of) 'Japanese religion', showing that many Japanese scholars still have not overcome colonial models of cultural classification. According to nineteenth-century European social-evolutionist worldviews, 'Western civilization' had once passed through primitive stages of development (associated with 'animism' and 'totemism'), but made significant progress since. However, these 'primitive' stages of development were then associated with the various 'underdeveloped' cultures 'discovered' (and reified as 'tribes') by European scholars. Thus, these societies were denied any precolonial history of their own. Significantly, they also became colonial subjects of the empires of which these social-evolutionist scholars were citizens, such as the UK and France. It has been argued, therefore, that the theories that constructed these 'tribes' as 'primitive' and 'undeveloped' served to legitimize colonial exploitation (e.g. Lewis 1973).

Likewise, the Ainu and the Ryukyu people were subject to Japanese colonial oppression, exploitation, cultural annihilation and forced assimilation by the state (Morris-Suzuki 1998: 9–34). Arguably, they continue to be Japan's colonial subjects today, framed as Japan's very own exotic, primitive Others. Certainly, attitudes vis-à-vis cultural diversity within Japan have changed in recent years (Sugimoto 2009), and both Ainu and Ryukyu cultural traditions have seen somewhat of a revival (Hein & Selden 2003; lewallen 2016). Nevertheless, in conservative scholarship and ideology, the cultural practices of these minorities continue to be dehistoricized and conceptualized as remnants of Japan's ancient 'Shinto' tradition. Indeed, it may be argued that a revival of cultural practices contributes to the reclassification of Ainu and Ryukyu practices as 'ancient Japanese' traditions – different from mainland culture, yet included within the parameters of a depoliticized cultural 'regional diversity' (expressed in food culture, traditional performing arts and local *matsuri*), which paradoxically serves to strengthen the single-nation narrative. The association with Shinto is all the more ironic, of course, considering Shinto's historical involvement (if only as ideological justification) with Japanese imperialism. After all, the annexation of the Ryukyu Islands, and the near-complete annihilation of Ainu culture, were very much part of the imperial project.

Tadasu no Mori

Notions of 'original Shinto' are not merely ideological constructs projected upon existing shrines such as Ōmiwa Jinja. They also serve as inspiration for contemporary place-making practices. This is clearly visible at Shimogamo Jinja, where one of the first systematic modern attempts at shrine forest conservation – or, some might argue, shrine forest construction – took place. Located in Kyoto, at the place where the Kamogawa and Takanogawa Rivers converge, Shimogamo Jinja is one of Japan's most famous shrines. Officially known as Kamo Mioya Jinja, it is regarded as one of Kyoto's oldest shrines. According to shrine mythology, it was founded in the first century BCE, but in reality it probably dates from the sixth or seventh century CE. In any case, the first shrine buildings are said to have been constructed during the reign of Emperor Tenmu (675–686); whether or not worship practices were conducted at the location of the shrine during the

Figure 6.2 Tadasu no Mori, Shimogamo Jinja, Kyoto.

prehistoric period is subject to speculation. Both Shimogamo Jinja and its sister shrine Kamigamo Jinja (Kamo Wakeikazuchi Jinja) are historically connected with the Kamo lineage, one of the most powerful lineages in Kyoto; their deities are related and may have originally been Kamo ancestral deities (*ujigami*) that later came to be associated with episodes and deities from the official imperial mythology.

In the Heian period, the Kamo shrines were among the most powerful shrines in the country, intimately connected with the imperial cult. Shimogamo Jinja's main festival, Aoi Matsuri (co-organized with Kamigamo Jinja) is also said to go back to the Heian period, or even predate it; references to the shrine and its *matsuri* can be found in eighth-century texts (M. Ueda 2003: 12). The festival continues to be conducted annually and is now considered one of Kyoto's three great *matsuri* (together with the Gion Matsuri and Jidai Matsuri). Because of its long history and the various cultural traditions it has preserved, Shimogamo Jinja was inscribed on the UNESCO World Heritage List in 1994. Today, it attracts significant numbers of tourists, both domestic and foreign. Recently, Shimogamo Jinja has also become a popular *powerspot*: in particular, two romantically intertwined *shinboku* trees (located on the left side of the *sandō*, right before the gate to the main shrine buildings) are often visited by young people praying for *en-musubi* (i.e. success in love).

In addition to its shrine history, *matsuri* and spiritual power, Shimogamo Jinja is well known for its forest, Tadasu no Mori. The following text from a tourist pamphlet illustrates the various qualities attributed to this small forest:

> In the middle of Japan's ancient capital, Kyoto, at the convergence of the Takano and Kamo rivers, lies a plot of old forest. A World Heritage [Site], this forest – Tadasu no Mori – harbors a vivid wild life. Chinese nettle trees, zelkova trees, cherries, maples, willows, some over 600 years old, provide sanctuary for many rare species of birds, bugs and butterflies. Artists pause by the shaded river bed to sketch a rare mushroom just unfurling, or paint the autumn colors. Young mothers stroll their toddlers through the quiet woods. (…) The visitor walking along the [shrine] approach (*sandō*) through the trees is invited to sense the mystic depth of nature, filled with a myriad *kami* (gods, or life spirits). (Shimogamo Jinja n.d.-b)

Written with the character meaning 'to investigate' or 'to verify', the origins and original meaning of the forest name are unclear. *Tadasu no Mori* is said to mean 'forest of truth', 'forest of justice', or 'forest of the delta'; alternatively, the term may refer to the 'clear water' flowing through the forest, or it may be derived from the *tade* (water pepper) growing there in the past (Cali & Dougill 2013: 119–122; Kyōjō 2010: 3; M. Ueda 2003: 22). Thus, nobody knows for sure what the name originally meant, and how it was assigned. Today, the forest has a size of approximately 12.4 ha – described as 'three times the size of [baseball stadium] Tokyo Dome' in most Japanese sources (e.g. M. Ueda 2003: 20) – which is much smaller than it was in the past. According to Ueda, in ancient times, the forest had a size of 4.95 km^2 (2003: 20).[10] Whether or not that number is correct, it is clear that even in the early Shōwa period the forest was much bigger than today: the area south of Mikage Street, for instance, used to belong to Tadasu no Mori but is now the location of the Kyoto Family Court (Shidei 1993: 16–18).

In any case, Tadasu no Mori is undoubtedly one of Japan's most famous shrine forests. It is said to have been preserved since ancient times, mentioned in Heian-period sources and drawn on medieval maps (Araki 2003: 44–47). Representing such historical continuity, it is perhaps not surprising that Tadasu no Mori is often referred to as a 'primeval forest' (*genseirin*). It has been described as a place that has retained aspects of Kyoto's *genfūkei* ('primeval landscape' or 'primal scene'),[11] which 'has remained as a primeval forest in the middle of Kyoto until the present age' (Inamori 2003: 6–7). Likewise, Ueda Masaaki has referred to Tadasu no Mori as 'a primeval forest' and stated that 'this is truly a forest in the original meaning of the word *mori*' (M. Ueda 2003: 20) – that is, 'natural', deep, mysterious and *not* human-made (cf. Shidei 1993). The term 'primeval forest' is also used widely on signs, in pamphlets and in guidebooks.

It comes as no surprise, then, that Tadasu no Mori is often seen as the prototype of a *chinju no mori*: it has been at its current location for many centuries, representing ecological as well as cultural continuity with the (ancient) past; it is a 'sacred' place, intimately connected with the shrine, where worship practices are said to have been conducted incessantly since early history; and it is a *mori*, composed of autochthonous broad-leaved trees, rather than an artificial *hayashi* or a Meiji-period shrine forest largely made up of 'foreign' coniferous trees. Moreover, the forest is seen as a reminder of the 'traditional Japanese gratitude to nature', which 'people today have forgotten', causing widespread environmental destruction; the return to this spirit of gratitude (as symbolized by the continuous presence of Tadasu no Mori, and the sacred qualities attributed to it) is seen as 'the first step towards environmental conservation' (Sen 2003).

Be that as it may, the often-heard claim that Tadasu no Mori is a primeval forest is incorrect. As any visitor can see, the forest is full of recently planted, young trees, neatly provided with a sign mentioning the species and sometimes the name of its sponsor. The forest is not 'kept wild', but maintained by trained foresters; as in other shrines, the main path is swept, and some trees are covered with plastic to protect them against parasites. In addition to recent tree-planting activities and maintenance work, it is clear that the forest has experienced major disturbances at different periods in history and has been influenced profoundly by human activities. There is some historical evidence of typhoons and battles in the medieval period, which have caused the destruction of parts of the forest (Kyōjō 2010: 3–4). Most noteworthy, during the Ōnin War (1467–1477), the forest was almost completely burnt down, together with the shrine itself (Kyōjō 2010: 4). The newly replanted forest was probably made up of coniferous trees, at least partly, as suggested by late-medieval and premodern illustrations of the shrine forest showing pine trees (Shidei 1993: 25–26). Thus, Tadasu no Mori has not always been the broad-leaved forest it is today: it was a pine forest for at least some periods in history.

Today, there are few coniferous trees left; the broad-leaved *keyaki* (*Zelkova serrate*; Japanese zelkova), *mukunoki* (*Aphanante aspera*; muku tree) and *enoki* (*Celtis sinensis*; Chinese hackberry) that make up most of the forest now are said to be part of the natural vegetation of the area. As such, today's forest is apparently similar to what Shidei has called 'the shape of the original natural forest' (*honrai no shizenrin no sugata*) (1993: 27). However, the *kusunoki* (*Cinnamomum camphora*; camphor tree) that make up more than 25 per cent of all trees in the forest – compared to approximately 20 per cent *enoki*, 19 per cent *mukunoki* and 11.5 per cent *keyaki* (Morimoto 2003: 146) – were planted after the Muroto typhoon and subsequent floods of 1934, which caused serious damage to the forest, uprooting 70 per cent of all trees (Araki 2003: 47–48; Morimoto 2003: 143–147). As Morimoto points out, *kusunoki* are allochthonous to the region, coming from warmer regions further south, and they have changed the forest ecology significantly. In addition, there have been changes in plant composition in recent decades due to desiccation, global warming and ecological isolation (Morimoto 2003: 147–149). One particularly notable ecological change is the fact that the shrine's core symbol, *futaba aoi* (*Asarum caulescens*) has almost completely disappeared from the forest (Morimoto 2003: 147; see Chapter 8).

In sum, Tadasu no Mori is not a primeval forest, but a 'semi-natural forest' (*hanshizenteki na mori*) (Morimoto 2003: 144). Or, as Yoshida writes, it is 'a shrine forest (*shasōrin*), in between a park and a natural forest'; that is, an 'urban forest (*toshirin*)' (2003: 136). Rather than a *mori* in Ueda and Shidei's use of the term (i.e. untouched, mysterious and 'natural'), then, Tadasu no Mori constitutes a city forest, and as such it is intimately intertwined with – and influenced by – the human communities living around it. Indeed, it is an undeniable fact that Tadasu no Mori occupies a prominent position in the (historical) geography of Kyoto. Mentioned in the *Tale of Genji* and classical poems, the forest figures prominently in collective memory, in particular when it comes to imaginations of the Heian period. As the site of one of Kyoto's most-visited shrines and one of its best-known *matsuri*, Tadasu no Mori carries profound symbolic capital. As such, the forest has long been the focal point of various cultural and social activities. Accordingly, forest conservation and maintenance activities have been carried out at Tadasu no Mori for a long time, and several other shrines have tried to follow the example set by Shimogamo Jinja.

Forest preservation activities at Shimogamo Jinja go back to 1887, when an organization was founded for forest maintenance, conducted by ordinary citizens: the Shimogamo Jinja Shin'en Hozonkai ('Shimogamo Jinja shrine garden preservation association') (Araki 2003: 48; Shimogamo Jinja n.d.-a: 8).[12] In the Meiji and Taishō periods, planting and replanting shrine forests came to be seen as ways to express patriotism and to engage citizens with shrines. Paradoxically, this was around the same period that the *jinja gōshi* policy was implemented and many local shrine forests disappeared. This policy, however, primarily affected small rural shrines, whereas tree-planting activities mainly took place at (large) imperial shrines, such as Kashihara Jingū and Meiji Jingū (Araki 2003: 49). In all likelihood, the forest-related activities taking place at Shimogamo Jinja at the time should be interpreted in the context of this development – that is, tree-planting in forests had become a symbolic practice through which citizens could engage with the newly established imperial Shinto – rather than as some sort of early environmentalist project.

In the post-war period, the shrine forest organization was restructured and renamed several times (Kyōjō 2010: 4; Shimogamo Jinja n.d.-a: 8). Today, it is legally registered as a 'public interest incorporated foundation' (*kōeki zaidan hōjin*) named Sekai Isan Kamo Mioya Jinja Keidai Tadasu no Mori Hozonkai ('Association for the conservation of Tadasu no Mori on the precincts of World Heritage Site Kamo Mioya Jinja'), usually abbreviated as Tadasu no Mori Hozonkai ('Tadasu no Mori conservation association') or simply Tadasu no Mori Zaidan ('Tadasu no Mori foundation'). The organization employs various activities. First of all, it is active in forest conservation. This is not limited to maintenance activities such as pruning, weeding and taking measures to protect trees against insects and diseases, as is common at large shrines throughout the country (at least those that can afford to spend money on it). Forest conservation also concerns measures to preserve animal and plant species, and protect the forest environment in general (e.g. keep it clean from litter). Second, the organization actively promotes the conservation of traditional culture; in particular, shrine architecture and *matsuri*. Third, it supports archaeological research in the forest. Fourth, informed by this research, it is active in landscape design. That is, the forest is 'preserved' by 'restoring' it to the shape it supposedly had in ancient times. And fifth, the foundation organizes all sorts of educational and cultural activities, ranging from public lectures and scouting groups to flea markets and open-air concerts.

As a foundation, Tadasu no Mori is institutionally independent from the shrine, which is a *shūkyō hōjin* ('religious juridical person'). This makes it possible to receive support from local authorities, conservation funds and the like, which would not be possible if the activities were employed by the shrine directly, as in that case it would violate the constitutional separation of religion and state (cf. Sagai 2013: 95). In reality, however, the two organizations cooperate closely: unlike some other shrine forest projects elsewhere, which are completely run by non-clergy volunteers, some of Shimogamo Jinja's shrine priests are actively involved in the foundation's work. This includes Sagai Tatsuru, who spends a significant proportion of his working time on activities related to the forest, such as research and dissemination. Sagai has explicitly stated that, in his opinion, environmental issues are one of today's most urgent concerns; in the twenty-first century, they should constitute one of shrine Shinto's top priorities (interview, March 2011). Echoing the ideas of Sonoda Minoru and Ueda Masaaki, Sagai argues that Shinto is a 'primal religion' (*genshi shūkyō*) intimately intertwined with the natural environment; the 'original shape' of this religion has been preserved at Tadasu no Mori, he suggests (Sagai 2013: 90, 97). As 'Shinto is an ethnic religion that was born in the middle of the abundant natural environment' (*yutaka na shizen kankyō no naka kara tanjō shita minzoku shūkyō*) (2013: 97), it has an important responsibility in teaching people today how to relate to the environment.

Today, Tadasu no Mori faces some serious environmental challenges, which the Tadasu no Mori Zaidan is trying to tackle. One of these problems is the high number of trees that have died in recent years. Sagai lists four causes for this: the old age of many of the trees, and the lack of young trees; the dominance of *kusunoki*, at the expense of other broad-leaved trees; the soil getting harder (i.e. less porous) as a result of people and cars treading on it; and the low level of the groundwater. Possible measures to solve these problems are, respectively, tree-planting activities (which take place regularly, and are usually carried out by volunteers);[13] felling *kusunoki* (that, at least, was the opinion of Shidei and his research group; Sagai does not make clear whether or not this has actually been done); demarcating 'human space' and 'sacred space' (i.e. restricting access to certain 'sacred' parts of the forest), and improving the quality of the soil; and re-digging ancient streams, so as to have better water circulation (2013: 95). Another problem he could have mentioned is the death of various broad-leaved trees, which have been eaten by *kashi-no-naga-kikuimushi* (*Platypus quercivorus*; a type of ambrosia beetle). Reportedly, these beetles have caused serious damage in forests in and around Kyoto, and approximately 100 trees in Tadasu no Mori are affected by them; in order to prevent further damage, many trees are now wrapped in plastic ('Nara kare': 2010). Other problems are related to waste, pollution and the ecological impact of climate change (Shimogamo Jinja n.d.-a: 8–9). Needless to say, not all of these problems are easily solved: while litter may be cleaned by helpful volunteers, understanding and dealing with the effects of climate change is significantly more complicated and challenging.

Rebuilding the Forest of the Past

Although the shrine buildings of Shimogamo Jinja were not constructed until the sixth or seventh century, shrine publications assert that its history as a sacred place goes back much further. The argument is that 'nature deities' were already worshipped at this location in the Jōmon period. Strategically located at the confluence of two rivers in the middle of a valley and criss-crossed by small streams providing clear drinking water, it seems likely that this area was already inhabited in prehistoric times. As Sagai argues, given the crucial importance of clean drinking water for survival, places providing such water – streams, sources and waterfalls – were often set apart as sacred and turned into objects of worship (2013: 97). The same, it is argued, applies to Tadasu no Mori, the sacredness of which is said to have been related to the abundance of clear water. Ueda Masaaki likewise suggests that 'water sources or rivers were important in *chinju no mori*, as sacred sites where ceremonies (*matsuri*) took place', and that forests with 'sacred water' became worship sites (M. Ueda 2010: 1; cf. Motozawa 2010).

Claims concerning the sacred status of Tadasu no Mori in the Jōmon period are legitimized by archaeological findings. Since 1990, archaeological excavations have taken place at various locations in the forest. Among the findings were objects from the Jōmon, Yayoi and Kofun periods. These include jars, remnants of statues and pebbles, which are said to have been used in worship ceremonies (perhaps significantly, white pebbles are still used at some other shrines claiming to go back to ancient times, such as Ise Jingū and Atsuta Jingū). There is also the remnant of a structure that looks like a well. Today, some of the archaeological findings – pebbles, in particular – are exhibited at clearly demarcated open parts of the forest, together with information panels stating that these were the sites of prehistoric places of worship. However, even though they constitute evidence of prehistoric habitation, the archaeological findings do not tell us much about the actual ritual practices that were conducted here, let alone about the beliefs held at the time. Those continue to be the subject of speculation.[14]

The significance of these archaeological findings is not limited to claims of historical continuity. Researchers have tried to establish the historical location of streams, sources and worship locations, and the Tadasu no Mori foundation has redesigned the forest accordingly, in order to physically recreate the landscape of the past. One of the reasons for this is nature conservation: as mentioned previously, the forest has suffered seriously from a lack of (ground) water, and it was presumed that rearranging the streams in accordance with the prehistoric layout of the forest would improve the water circulation. Tadasu no Mori has four streams: the Nara-no-ogawa, Semi-no-ogawa, Izumigawa and Mitarashigawa. The former two in particular have been subject to reconstruction work. In 1990, the shrine and its foundation embarked on an ambitious landscape design project, which consisted of the complete re-digging of these streams. Working from south to north, they started with the Semi-no-ogawa, which was completed around 1998. Next, the Nara-no-ogawa was re-dug, in accordance with its presumed former position. This process took place in various stages and was finished in 2009 (Kamo Mioya Jinja 2010: 22–38).

It may well be true that rearranging the water circulation in the forest has positive effects on its ecology. However, I would argue that this is not the only reason why the shrine has embarked on this ambitious landscape design project. The streams flowing through Tadasu no Mori feature prominently in Heian-period literature and poetry (M. Ueda 2003: 21) and, as such, are part of the collective memory of both the city and the nation. In trying to re-establish the 'historical environment' (Sagai 2013: 96) of the forest and its waterways, notions of historical continuity and national heritage are embodied. It is clear that the current physical shape of the forest, in particular its streams, is largely the result of human planning and construction work. Meanwhile, however, Tadasu no Mori is discursively naturalized, as illustrated by the various references describing it as a 'natural' or even 'primeval' forest. The claim made in the English-language tourist brochure that 'Unlike the carefully pruned Buddhist gardens, the Shinto forest is left to grow large and develop its own habitat' (Shimogamo Jinja n.d.-b) is a clear example of this discourse.

Contrary to this assertion, as we have seen, the forest is carefully monitored and managed; for better or worse, its contemporary shape and tree composition are largely the result of human planning, not of a forest left to grow wild. Both as a mental and as a physical space, then, Tadasu no Mori is *produced*, not something that has emerged spontaneously. Indeed, as a physical space, the forest in its contemporary shape is the product of spatial practices such as planting trees, digging streams and keeping pathways free from leaves and weeds. As a mental space, however, it is conceived of as 'natural', and intimately connected with notions of traditional Japanese culture and aesthetics – that is, the beauty of the 'four seasons' and their symbolic significance (e.g. Kamo Mioya Jinja 2003: 113–124; cf. Shirane 2012). Yet, this discrepancy is not commonly recognized.

It may be argued that the symbolic reproduction of an idealized past is an integral part of place-making activities at Tadasu no Mori. Importantly, the forest constitutes an integral of part of Kyoto's 'landscape of nostalgia'. As Jennifer Robertson has demonstrated, in post-war Japan, nostalgic notions of ancestral landscapes are of profound political and economic significance (Robertson 1988: 503–508). This does not only apply to rural landscapes but also to the numerous local cityscape-reconstruction (*machi-zukuri*) and (sub)urban forest-making (*mori-zukuri*) activities taking place in Heisei-period Japan (e.g. Sorensen & Funck 2007). As Lefebvre has written, such nostalgia is 'a manifestation of a major contradiction of modernity': it is an expression of anti-modern sentiments and a longing for an idealized non-modern space (which has both temporal and spatial aspects), yet at the same time the shapes this nostalgia takes – mass tourism, the commodification of rural lifestyles and crafts, the conservation of 'traditional' landscapes – are highly modern, leading to 'space being consumed in both the economic and literal senses of the word' (1991: 122; cf. Ivy 1995). This is exactly the case for Tadasu no Mori: while framed as an ancient natural landscape and a vestige of Kyoto cultural tradition, is it also promoted as a tourist, heritage and recreation site, where ritual and other practices are marketed and commodified.

As the work at Tadasu no Mori is carried out by a foundation, the organizers can apply for financial support from various sources, including those related with heritage conservation. The foundation also has some wealthy individual patrons and is sponsored by a number of enterprises, including the Kyoto-based electronics multinational Kyocera. But forest conservation and landscape design are expensive, so fundraising events and membership recruitment continue to constitute a prominent part of the foundation's work. Hence, various social activities are organized for the purpose of involving Kyotoites in Tadasu no Mori and its conservation work. These include tea ceremonies, firefly-watching, guided forest walks, scouting activities and of course the aforementioned tree-planting ceremonies. In 2011, I attended two such social events: an open-air concert, involving a small student brass band performing at the *kagura* stage of the auxiliary shrine Kawai Jinja, near the entrance of the forest (aptly, their repertoire included music from *My Neighbor Totoro*; perhaps less aptly, it also included *West Side Story*); and a flea market in the forest, where people from the neighbourhood could sell their second-hand things for a small fee (2,000 yen; approximately 20 euros, at the time).

Figure 6.3 Concert organized by Tadasu no Mori Zaidan at Kawai Jinja, Tadasu no Mori, Kyoto.

Organizing a flea market is more than just a fundraising activity, however. Significantly, some Shinto scholars have argued that the first markets were established around *matsuri* sites (i.e. *chinju no mori*), and that this constitutes the origins of the first towns. Sonoda, for instance, suggests that the term *matsuri* is etymologically related to the words for 'town' (*machi*) and 'market' (*ichi*), which according to him shows that the sites of *matsuri* were the focal point around which communities developed – not only through ritual practices but also through trade, as this is how social relations were established (1998: 93–95, 205–206). The organization of a flea market inside Tadasu no Mori, however small, is thus in accordance with theories concerning the social functions of *chinju no mori* in ancient times and therefore not devoid of symbolism. But then, very few of the spatial and social practices carried out in this forest are.

I have had the opportunity to talk to different people involved with the Tadasu no Mori, and it is worth noting the difference in their ways of explaining the value of this type of events. The (non-clergy) PR manager of the foundation told me that the main purpose of these activities is to get people involved with the projects; according to him, community participation is necessary for fundraising, as well as for creating public interest and goodwill. Sagai, on the other hand, saw community involvement as an integral aspect of traditional Shinto worldviews, based on the notion of the existential interdependence of nature, deities and human communities. Reflecting the ideas of Sonoda and Ueda, he stated that the (re) establishment of a strong local community is one of the objectives of the Tadasu no Mori Zaidan (interview, March 2011). After all, *chinju no mori* are conceptualized as sacred places where, in ancient times, people gathered, establishing the first local communities that would become the cornerstone of later Japanese society. Many people involved with shrine forest conservation and education projects state that community building (*komyuniti-zukuri*) is one of their core priorities, so Tadasu no Mori is no exception. Music, dance and theatre performances are seen as an integral part of traditional Japanese culture, so today's open-air concerts are perceived as a continuation of this tradition – even though the musical repertoire may have changed somewhat. Thus, the landscape of the past is recreated not only through forest and river design but also through flea markets and cultural performances – including, of course, the Totoro theme song.

didnt
have
pencil

Chapter 7

FORESTS FOR THE FUTURE

Shrine Activism?

Not everybody takes claims about Shinto's sustainable character and its social and ecological significance at face value. Some scholars have expressed scepticism towards Shinto expressions of environmentalism and questioned the motives behind them, especially with regards to Jinja Honchō (Breen & Teeuwen 2010: 207–209; Kalland 2012; Nelson 2000: 246–247). They have rightly pointed out that Jinja Honchō and related political lobby organizations such as Shintō Seiji Renmei and Nippon Kaigi have actively lobbied for the (re)establishment of imperial symbols and against equal rights for women or immigrants, but have done little or nothing to convince the government to improve its environmental policies (Breen & Teeuwen 2010: 201–202). Accordingly, John Breen has argued that Jinja Honchō's 'real concerns are not nature-oriented at all', as the organization has an 'obsession with prewar, emperor-oriented ethics and rites' (Breen & Teeuwen 2010: 208). Although he acknowledges the work of Shasō Gakkai as a 'serious attempt to give substance to the idea (…) that Shinto is a religion of nature', he adds that their concern for forest conservation is not shared by the shrine establishment, which 'has demonstrated no genuine interest in nature or the environment. (…) We are still a very long way from Shinto acquiring a national, let alone international, voice on the environment' (Breen & Teeuwen 2010: 210).

These words were written in 2010, the year in which Tanaka Tsunekiyo became president of Jinja Honchō, and some things have changed since. Today, Jinja Honchō does express an interest in nature and the environment, not only in English-language texts and at international events but also domestically (e.g. *Kōshitsu* henshūbu 2014). Although the extent to which this interest is 'genuine' may be debated, it has arguably affected Shinto self-definitions and institutional practices, as the following chapters will illustrate. Yet, the question remains: despite the widespread rhetoric on Shinto as a nature religion, *how exactly* can it contribute to overcoming environmental problems such as industrial pollution, climate change and biodiversity loss? How, concretely, can shrines contribute to a reduction in energy consumption and waste production? Few of my interviewees were able to answer such questions, except in very vague terms. When asked for their opinion on these matters, many shrine priests will confirm that Shinto is characterized by a unique appreciation of nature and state that the environment should be a core priority indeed. That does not mean, however, that they think Shinto shrines should engage in environmental activism. As John Nelson wrote in 2000,

> Distracted by particularistic interests, local shrine Shinto has never found a socially active role for itself. (…) The environment could be the issue around which shrines organize and empower local communities. After all, the natural world is considered the realm most obviously identified with kami and their powers. Standing up to golf course developers, demanding more public parks and natural recreation areas, and serving as watchdogs for companies polluting the ecosystem could all be justified as sanctified concerns of a shrine. (2000: 248)

In the seventeen years since these words were published, the environment has indeed become one of the issues around which shrines – some of them, at least – try to organize and empower local communities. There are even a few cases of shrines that have tried to prevent construction projects, with mixed results. Nevertheless, most shrine priests would be reluctant to engage in protests and political activism. Generally speaking, post-war shrine Shinto is characterized by the three Cs: *corporate*, *conservative*, and *community-oriented*. First, Shinto is *corporate*, not only because shrines themselves are competitors in a religious market but also because they often depend on companies for institutional survival. Do not bite the hand that feeds you: few shrine priests will actively oppose projects by important corporate sponsors, even if these have a negative environmental impact. On the other hand, some companies may choose to sponsor projects that are concerned with nature conservation or environmental education: for instance, the Kyoto-based multinational Kyocera has funded the forest preservation project at Tadasu no Mori (Kyocera Corporation 2011: 12; cf. Inamori 2003), whereas other Kyoto-based companies have sponsored activities at Kamigamo Jinja. In these cases, corporate sponsorship can go together with local nature preservation, but this is certainly not always the case.

Second, Shinto is generally *conservative*: shrine priests typically see it as their task to preserve tradition and existing social structures, not to change them. This is not to say that there are no progressive or leftist priests – I have met some – but they are a minority indeed. Most shrine priests are not inclined to challenge the status quo, unless they see no other choice.[1] And third, Shinto is *community-oriented*: maintaining good relations with neighbourhood organizations is essential for institutional continuity, and few priests would engage in acts that may jeopardize relations with the local community upon which they depend. In some cases, this means they have to compromise – for instance, when it comes to protecting local environments.

The following example, discussed by Breen and Teeuwen, illustrates some of the social tensions that may be caused by environmental advocacy. It concerns a shrine priest in Yamaguchi Prefecture, Hayashi Haruhiko (head priest of Shidaishō Hachimangū in the town of Kaminoseki), who opposed plans to use shrine land for the construction of a nuclear power plant. As they write, '[Hayashi] opposed nuclear power on the grounds of its capacity to destroy the environment and human life; it was his responsibility, he maintained, to protect sacred shrine land' (2010: 208). His position met with much opposition within his shrine committee, however, as influential members of the local community (*ujiko*) were in favour of allowing the power plant to be built. Eventually, Jinja Honchō became involved in the conflict and put pressure on the head priest to resign. He was replaced, and soon thereafter, in 2004, the shrine sold its land to the energy company responsible for constructing the plant. Opposition has continued to be fierce, however, especially since the 2011 nuclear crisis in Fukushima. At present, it remains unclear whether and when the power plant will become fully operational.[2]

By getting involved in this local conflict, Jinja Honchō provided the local shrine committee with the opportunity to sell shrine land, which would subsequently be used for a nuclear power plant. Arguably, this is not the kind of approach one would expect from a self-declared nature religion. Part of the discussion concerns the perceived sacredness of the area in question: Hayashi argued that he must protect 'sacred shrine land', while Sonoda Minoru – ironically, one of the leading representatives of the *chinju no mori* movement – reportedly justified the shrine committee and Jinja Honchō's decision on the grounds that this particular area did not constitute a sacred *chinju no mori* and, hence, did not have to be preserved at all costs (Sandvik 2011: 69). Thus, the environmental concerns of Jinja Honchō and Sonoda Minoru apparently do not outweigh concerns of a more economic nature; environmental advocacy, it seems, is only considered appropriate when pertaining to particular, demarcated sacred shrine forests, not to other areas. Most Shinto environmentalism, it appears, is *particularistic* and *situational* rather than holistic, as some interpreters have claimed.[3]

Sonoda himself is all-too-familiar with tensions that can arise as a result of short-term economic incentives, especially when local authorities support construction projects and resource extraction as a means to create jobs and prevent depopulation. Shrine priests may express an interest in ecology and nature conservation and subscribe to the notion that Shinto is an ancient tradition of nature worship that emerged as a part of Japan's 'forest civilization'; that does not mean they will act as environmental advocates. First and foremost, they see it as their responsibility to maintain good relationships between the shrine and members of the local community (*ujiko*) and to correctly perform rituals for the deities. If powerful community members are in favour of selling forest land to, say, project developers, few shrine priests would oppose – even if that leads to the demolition of ecologically valuable forest. This tension between environmental advocacy and economic incentives is well illustrated by the sad fate of the 'sacred' mountain of Chichibu (Saitama Prefecture), the city where Sonoda Minoru works as a head priest.

Chichibu is a small city that is famous for its shrine, Chichibu Jinja, which has elaborate and colourful Edo-period wood carvings and a large annual *matsuri* that attracts many visitors. In addition to the shrine, Chichibu has a number of Buddhist temples, connected by a pilgrimage trail. It is located in a small river basin, next to a mountain, Mount Bukō. This is said to be a 'sacred' mountain, historically associated with the shrine and seen as the dwelling place of its main deity. It also has significant quantities of limestone, however, which is mined and used for the local cement industry. It is quite ironic that one of the main representatives of the Shinto environmentalist paradigm is head priest of a shrine whose sacred mountain is exploited for economic purposes, to the point that its natural environment has been partly destroyed. Indeed, Sonoda has repeatedly expressed a concern for the nature of the mountain and has been active in setting up an organization with the purpose of reforesting the mountain. Yet, his opinion about the mining activities is characterized by ambiguity. When I last spoke to him, he did mention his regret concerning the destruction of the mountain, saying he wished it had never been allowed in the first place (interview, May 2013). Elsewhere, however, he has expressed himself in more apologetic terms (Sonoda 2010). On the one hand, he believes the forest of the mountain should be protected and its sacred character preserved. On the other, the mines apparently have great economic significance for the city.

To Sonoda, Shinto is first and foremost a 'community religion'. This means that the well-being of the human community is considered at least as important as the natural environment. Paradoxically, he has justified this approach by referring to the notion of gross national happiness (GNH) – an alternative to the use of gross national product (GNP) as the main standard for development, taking into consideration various non-economic factors, which is said to have been developed in Bhutan. In Sonoda's interpretation, for a high GNH, four things are important: a rich natural environment, a rich 'traditional culture' (*dentō bunka*), good politics and 'fair' economic development (2010: 22). Thus, in the case of Mount Bukō, a balance must be found between economic activities and a healthy green environment – all for the sake of the (human) community's happiness, rather than the natural environment *per se*. As this case illustrates, associations with 'deep ecology', 'holism' and 'human-nature symbiosis' notwithstanding (e.g. Sonoda 2007; Sonoda & Tabuchi 2006), in its concrete applications shrine Shinto arguably is still primarily concerned with the human community. As such, it is ultimately anthropocentric.

In sum, the reality does not always correspond to the rhetoric. Even a shrine forest such as Tadasu no Mori is not entirely safe from demands for more concrete, despite being a UNESCO World Heritage Site and one of the country's most famous *chinju no mori*. In 2015, the news came out that Shimogamo Jinja had decided to lease a part of the shrine precincts to project developers, who will use it for building luxury apartments. This will reportedly generate eighty million yen annually for a period of fifty years. According to shrine officials, this is necessary to fund the reconstruction of the shrine buildings (Baseel 2015). Local residents and environmental activists have questioned this claim and asked for a disclosure of the shrine's financial situation, which they were not given (Dougill 2015). Although the apartments will not be built inside the forest, but right next to it, protesters are afraid that the construction activities will have a negative impact on the forest ecology and ground water condition – one of the main rationales for the Tadasu no Mori forest design project discussed in the previous chapter. Thus, despite the fact that Shimogamo Jinja has some of the most environmentally oriented shrine priests I have met and developed one of the most ambitious shrine forest preservation projects in the entire country, even here short-term economic incentives outweigh ecological concerns.

Moving Forward

As these examples indicate, Shinto's modern environmental credentials are by no means unambiguous. In many cases, priests have had to accept that shrine land was used for construction, resource extraction or other purposes, because of social pressure or economic concerns. Nevertheless, there are also cases of shrine actors who successfully resisted such plans and succeeded in protecting their *chinju no mori* or nearby sacred mountains from demolition. For instance, Yamamura Akiyoshi tells the story of the head priest of the small Shishigaguchi Suwa Jinja in Yamagata Prefecture (located near the Dewa Sanzan mountains, which are historically associated with *shugendō* and mountain worship). This priest was successful in opposing a construction project that would have led to the destruction of the shrine's sacred forest. In order to prevent this, he cooperated with the communist party, a somewhat unusual (some might say: unholy) alliance, given the latter's secularist ideology and opposition to the imperial institution. Reportedly, however, they were the only politicians interested in helping him, at least initially. Besides, as Yamamura argues, Shinto is ultimately concerned with nature and *matsuri*, and transcends ideology; consequently, it is 'even' compatible with communism. In this case, the alliance between a shrine priest and his supporters on the one hand, and the local branch of the communist party on the other, generated enough critical mass to make the authorities and project developers change their plans. The forest was saved (Yamamura 2011: 61–67).

A second interesting case of shrine-related environmental advocacy took place in the forested western part of Tokyo Prefecture in the early 1990s. Here, the place of concern was a forested local mountain, Mount Konpira, in the vicinity of Mount Takao (Hachiōji City). At the time, there were far-reaching plans to 'develop' this area by blowing up part of the mountain, whereupon the land would be used for a new school building. A group of local activists tried to prevent this, together with a number of foreign expats ('Shizen to kyōzon shitai' 1992). They started restoration work on the dilapidated local shrine, Kotohira Jinja (devoted to the maritime deity Konpira or Kotohira, whose main shrine is located in Shikoku [see Thal 2005]) and recommenced shrine worship. As the shrine did not have a priest, one of the activists, Patricia Ormsby, went to Shikoku to undergo training and become ordained as a shrine priest in the Konpira tradition – the first non-Japanese to do so, reportedly (personal communication, November 2011). The movement received quite a bit of media coverage, and eventually succeeded in protecting the mountain, an achievement that impelled one local newspaper to report on the movement's activities in a series of lengthy articles ('Konpira yama wa nokotta'

1993). The group has also tried to protect other parts of the Mount Takao region, and opposed the construction of a tunnel, but in this case it was not successful. Today, the area attracts many visitors from Tokyo who come to enjoy the natural surroundings and the hiking trails. The shrine is still in use, and some of the members of the original movement reunite at the mountain every month to enjoy a picnic together.

As these two cases illustrate, sacralization can be employed as a tactic for environmental advocacy, and the existence of a shrine may serve as a powerful argument against forest destruction as long as there are people willing to engage in legal and political battles. It may be argued, however, that this type of activism constitutes the exception rather than the rule: many *chinju no mori* have been destroyed without much organized opposition at all, especially when there were significant economic interests at stake. Those shrine priests who do oppose construction projects may end up having conflicts with community members, or even losing their job, as in the case of the priest in Kaminoseki. There are many examples of shrine forests that were sacrificed on the altar of economic growth, and only a few cases of shrine actors successfully opposing construction projects, despite the existence of organizations such as Shasō Gakkai.

On the other hand, not all shrine forests are under immediate threat. Quite the contrary: as they have taken on new symbolic significance, some of them have been subjected to conservation and heritagization initiatives, attracting increasing numbers of visitors. Examples of well-known urban shrines with carefully preserved forested precincts include Fushimi Inari Taisha in Kyoto, Meiji Jingū in Tokyo, Atsuta Jingū in Nagoya and Kasuga Taisha in Nara. Not coincidentally, these are among Japan's most-visited tourist destinations. Meanwhile, priests and volunteers at smaller shrines throughout the country make active attempts to follow in their lead, organizing activities such as cleaning litter, tree-planting, pruning and weeding, guided forest walks, firefly-watching and so on. Central to these activities is the ideal typical notion of *chinju no mori* as sacred sites of great social and cultural significance, characterized by ecological diversity and natural beauty.

Although concerned with shrines and shrine forests, these activities are typically organized by non-profit organizations (*NPO hōjin*) that are *de facto* related to the shrine, but *de jure* independent. The founders and organizers may be shrine priests, but this is not always the case: I have also come across examples of local *chinju no mori* movements that are founded by scientists or non-clergy shrine staff. They usually have limited financial means, so the success of these movements depends on the involvement and engagement of a handful of active volunteers, not all of whom necessarily identify with Shinto. While most shrine initiatives have a strongly local character, and are not necessarily long-lived, there are a few examples of well-organized projects that have been going on for several years and received nationwide attention. I have already discussed the Tadasu no Mori project, which constituted an important source of inspiration for Shasō Gakkai and has long been perceived as a 'best practice' to be followed by other shrines (e.g. Araki 2003). Another early example of a local *chinju no mori* conservation movement is the Sennen no Mori no Kai ('thousand-year forest association'), affiliated with Gosho

Komagataki Jinja, a local shrine near the city of Sakuragawa in Ibaraki Prefecture (Sakurai 1999, 2009; Sakurai & Sakurai 2000). This was one of the first places where the explicit association was made – discursive *as well as* practical – between forest preservation, environmental awareness, moral education, a renewed sense of community and a revitalization of a supposed 'traditional culture' and 'ancient Japanese spirit', which is prominent in many later movements.

The combination of environmental and cultural education can be found in various shrine projects. For instance, Kamigamo Jinja in Kyoto has set up Afuhi Project for the purpose of reintroducing plants with great historical and mythological significance into the local ecosystem, organizing local neighbourhood events and teaching children the basics of Shinto. Similarly, Enju no Kai at Tsurugaoka Hachimangū in Kamakura combines an interest in nature preservation with the organization of various cultural activities and wants to instil patriotic sentiments into participants' minds – as well as, interestingly, contribute to internationalization (Tsurugaoka Hachimangū n.d.). Likewise, Meiji Jingū has set up NPO Hibiki, which organizes guided forest walks, acorn-collecting and tree-planting activities, rice-planting events and nature camps for teenagers, all of which have an environmental as well as an educational component.[4]

In recent years, similar projects have been set up at shrines throughout the country: examples include Shiroyama Hachimangū in Nagoya (Hasegawa & Okamura 2011), Ōmi Jingū in Shiga Prefecture (Morikawa 2006), Mukō Jinja in Kyoto Prefecture (Ueda Masahiro 2006), Hiraoka Jinja in Osaka Prefecture (Hamagami 2006) and Komiya Jinja in Saitama Prefecture (Kokugakuin Daigaku 2014). I have also heard accounts of active shrine-related forest conservation movements in Kumamoto and Gifu prefectures, and I am sure similar initiatives are undertaken at shrines elsewhere, with varying degrees of success. Finally, it is worth noting in this context that throughout the country there are dozens, if not hundreds of 'secular' local non-profit organizations and volunteer groups working to improve local environments, some of which may cooperate with neighbourhood shrines, even though they may not in any way identify with 'Shinto' or be concerned with shrine traditions *per se*. For instance, Hatakeyama Shigeatsu's Mori wa Umi no Koibito ('the forest is the lover of the sea') reforestation project, which aims to reduce pollution and improve the coastal ecosystem at Kesennuma (Miyagi Prefecture), was developed in cooperation with a local shrine (Hatakeyama 2010).

Importantly, the majority of these initiatives not only serve to preserve or improve shrine forests and their ecosystems. The organizers are equally committed to the teaching of 'traditional culture', the reestablishment of a 'community spirit' and, often, a revitalization of supposedly traditional Japanese values (including but not limited to patriotic pride). To what extent they represent cases of genuine environmental advocacy, or merely appropriate natural symbols for ideological purposes, may be subject to debate – and probably differs from project to project, and from person to person. In any case, it is important to bear in mind that different actors within a single movement (priests, organizers, volunteers and participants) may have different motivations and priorities, and that nationalist motives are not *a priori* incompatible with a genuine concern for forest conservation and ecology.

It should be pointed out, however, that the discursive association between Shinto and the natural environment has been intimately connected with the topics of deforestation and forest conservation and with the emerging movement that focused upon the protection and cultivation of *chinju no mori*. Until today, Shinto environmentalist discourse and practices have predominantly focused on the historical and ecological importance of sacred forests, investing in forest conservation and reforestation in Japan. By contrast, other topics – for instance, issues related to (toxic) waste, air and water pollution, and alternative energy – have received comparatively little attention.[5] In particular, until 2011 at least, energy issues received little or no attention in the shrine world – which may be one of the reasons why nuclear power was not seen as a problem by Jinja Honchō.[6] In fact, the only reference made to energy issues in Jinja Honchō's weekly shrine newspaper prior to that year was an article by a climate sceptic who claimed that climate change does not constitute a significant threat and is not even caused by greenhouse gas emissions (Itō 2009) – not the kind of argument one would immediately associate with an 'ecological religion'.

This situation may have changed, however, after the 2011 nuclear crisis and subsequent energy shortage. All of a sudden, electricity became a scarce commodity in Japan, and the reduction of energy consumption was established as an important new national priority. As a result, apparently for the first time, there was some awareness of the issue on the part of Shinto actors. In September 2011, *Jinja Shinpō* reported on a shrine in the city of Shibetsu (Hokkaido) that had installed solar panels. The head priest was quoted saying, 'we would the like the value of the blessing of the sun, of nature's energy, to be reacknowledged' ('Sōshi hyakujūnen kinen jigyō de' 2011) – not a strange thought, considering the fact that the shrine is devoted to Amaterasu, the sun goddess. A similar argument was made by ethnologist Miyake Hitoshi at the Shintō Kokusai Gakkai conference held in the summer of 2011: reinterpreting the *shugendō* worship of the powerful forces of nature in the light of contemporary events, he stated that we ought to turn to these forces again, now as a means to generate energy. Thus, he advocated a nationwide increase in the production of wind, water and solar energy, the argument for which was similar to that of the shrine priest from Hokkaido (Shintō Kokusai Gakkai 2012).[7] One month later, the newspaper published an essay by a professor at Chiba University, who argued that shrines should take the initiative in developing local community projects for generating alternative energy – an argument he has repeated at several other occasions, including Shasō Gakkai symposia (Hiroi 2011, 2012). According to him, it is only natural for these traditional community centres to take the initiative in realizing the transition to renewable energy production nationwide.[8]

Shrine Forest Ecology

Whether or not shrines will play a part in the transition to renewable energy remains to be seen. I have met some young shrine priests who were quite enthusiastic about this idea, but I am not sure how representative they are. Thus far, the ecological significance of Shinto shrines has had a predominantly local character and has been mostly limited to *chinju no mori* conservation. As we have seen, the term *chinju no mori* is used differently by different actors. Few people in the shrine world would deny their importance, however, and many would agree with Ueda Masaaki's statement that

> *Chinju no mori* (= *shasō*) are sacred places where people come together. We think that a renewed appreciation of these places will be highly valuable for the coming age. *Chinju no mori* give life to humans, and they were born out of the interaction with them, so they are the meeting points of nature, gods and people (*shizen to kami to hito to no setten*). In other words, they symbolize the symbiosis (*kyōsei*) between human beings and nature. (2013: 17)

In biology, the term symbiosis (*kyōsei*) refers to the coexistence and co-dependence of two or more different organisms. A well-known example is the clownfish, which lives in a symbiotic relationship with the sea anemone: both species depend on each other for survival. Symbiosis is an important aspect of ecology: the study of the ways in which different organisms in a given area interact. As we have seen, Motegi Sadasumi described *chinju no mori* as forests where high trees, brushwood and plants live in balance, together with birds, insects and micro-organisms (2010: 111). Motegi's claim that in *chinju no mori* different species are 'in balance' reflects classical ecological notions, which conceive of communities of organisms as bounded *systems* characterized by internal equilibrium and interdependence. Environmental problems are attributed to external influences (e.g. human waste and pollution, 'invader' species, climate change) which are said to distort the system's original balance. This notion of *ecosystem* – an originally balanced, organic whole that is vulnerable to distortion – has long held paradigmatic status but has been challenged by ecologists since the mid-1990s. Around the same time, the systems approach was also criticized in other (social) scientific disciplines – influenced by developments in environmental studies as well as transdisciplinary explorations (Scoones 1999). Yet, the notion of ecosystems as balanced and bounded entities has strongly influenced the *chinju no mori* movement. Miyawaki Akira, for instance, conceives of forests as clearly demarcated spaces, and as balanced systems, housing a wide variety of organisms that struggle with each other yet are mutually dependent (2000: 33).

In recent years, the global loss of species diversity has been recognized as one of the greatest environmental crises of our time. It is now seen as an urgent problem that needs to be tackled immediately, by means of conservation practices as well as policy change. Correspondingly, it has become one of the core concerns of environmentalists in Japan, and the 'traditional' Japanese hybrid nature-culture landscapes referred to as *satoyama* (Berglund 2008; Brosseau 2013; Takeuchi et al. 2003) have been promoted as great resources for the protection of biodiversity (Williams 2010). Significantly, the UN now officially supports the so-called Satoyama Initiative, which is concerned with the worldwide conservation of 'socio-ecological production landscapes and seascapes': 'dynamic mosaics of habitats and land uses where the harmonious interaction between people and nature maintains biodiversity while providing humans with the goods and services needed for their livelihoods, survival and well-being in a sustainable manner' (The Satoyama Initiative 2016). The notion of *satoyama* also figured prominently on COP10, the UN's 10th Conference of Parties to the Convention on Biological Diversity (CBD) held in Nagoya in November 2010. It is mentioned explicitly as a valuable template for future conservation initiatives in one of the decisions made at this conference.[9] Given this association of 'traditional' Japanese landscapes with biodiversity and conservation, it comes as no surprise that these claims are extended to *chinju no mori*, which after all are seen as integral features of these traditional landscapes (e.g. Iwatsuki 2008). Thus, in an article published after the implementation of the Nagoya Convention, Ueda Masaaki explicitly made the link between *chinju no mori* conservation and biological diversity (2011: 3).

In reality, however, few shrine forests are as ecologically diverse as some authors suggest. For instance, a study conducted by biologists in Kyoto on the weed *ōbako* (*Plantago asiatica*; Chinese plantain) suggests that shrine forests tend to have *less* ecological diversity than other urban green areas such as river banks (Nakayama et al. 1996). They are characterized by 'relatively nutrient-poor soil, poor light conditions, low species diversity index and daily sweeping of the ground' (1996: 338). The latter practice, sweeping the ground, is common at shrines and temples, but it is said to have a negative impact on soil ecology. In addition, there are two other important reasons for the (generally speaking) comparatively low biodiversity of shrine forests. First, urban shrine forests tend to be ecologically isolated; all-too-often, they are small green islands surrounded by concrete landscapes. These small forests may be neglected and dilapidated, or they may be carefully maintained by enthusiastic volunteers – in either case, if they are not connected with other green areas such as parks, green river banks, temple or castle gardens, suburban fields and mountains, their biodiversity is not likely to be high. As one prominent environmentally oriented shrine priest told me, most non-profit groups focusing on shrine forest conservation make the mistake of solely looking at their small shrine forest, while ignoring the surrounding environment (Sakurai Takashi, interview, May 2013). In order for a local ecosystem to be diverse and sustainable, it needs to be part of a larger ecosystem; that is, it has to be connected with other areas of green space. In contemporary Japanese urban environments, this is not usually the case.

A second reason why shrine forests tend to have limited biodiversity has to do with the tree species found there. Roughly speaking, Japan is divided into two ecological zones: the northern zone, which stretches from the Japan Alps to Hokkaido, is characterized by comparatively cold winters and has summergreen (deciduous) broad-leaved forests; common tree species include *buna* (*Fagus*; beech), *kaede* (*Acer*; maple) and *nara* (some species of *Quercus*; oak). The southern zone is warmer and has evergreen broad-leaved forests (or laurel forests); common tree species here include *kusunoki, yabutsubaki* (*Camellia japonica*; Japanese camellia) and various types of *shii* (*Castanopsis*; chinkapin) and *kashi* (species of *Quercus* that are not deciduous; evergreen oak) (Miyawaki 2000: 67–72; Shidei 1993: 18–24). As mentioned previously, however, many shrine forests today are made up of coniferous trees such as *sugi*, *hinoki* and various kinds of *matsu* (*Pinus*; pine) (Miyawaki 2000: 62). Many of these were planted in the premodern or modern period. Trees planted in the late Edo, Meiji or Taishō periods are now fairly old and have grown high, constituting dark coniferous forests that may evoke feelings of mystery. To many people, visitors and priests alike, these have come to constitute the archetypal shrine forests. However, these coniferous forests let through little sunlight. As a result, they do not usually have many shrubs, weeds and other plants and have comparatively little species diversity. Therefore, ecologists often argue for replacing these coniferous trees by indigenous broad-leaved trees.

This is not always appreciated by shrine priests and parishioners, however. They often associate coniferous trees with shrine worship and sacredness. These different priorities and expectations became clear at a project organized by Miyawaki Akira to replant a shrine forest destroyed by the 2011 tsunami in Miyagi Prefecture. Miyawaki insisted that broad-leaved trees indigenous to the Tohoku region be planted, after which some formerly active members of the *ujiko* decided to withdraw from the project, as they wanted to replant the pine trees and cypresses they had associated with the shrine from the time they were young (interview with the shrine priest, May 2013). Likewise, the expectations of shrine priests are not always compatible with those of environmental activists and volunteers. The former may be more interested in appearance, aesthetics and tidiness, whereas the latter tend to be more interested in preserving trees or animal species and in increasing biodiversity (cf. Hasegawa, Okamura and Kōsaka 2010). This may lead to friction, for example when shrine priests decide to chop down high trees that are considered untidy or annoying for other reasons (falling leaves, insects, too much shade and so on).

In sum, popular myths about the Japanese harmony with nature notwithstanding, in reality different actors have different understandings of what constitutes 'proper' nature. To some, a real shrine forest consists of high coniferous trees; to others, it is made up of 'indigenous' broad-leaved trees. Yet, as one biologist told me, notions of 'indigenous' species and 'original' landscapes are hard to substantiate (Hatakeyama Makoto, interview, November 2015). Ecosystems are never fixed, and there is no way to establish what the 'original' ecosystem of a place was: what moment in history is taken to be the origin? Ecosystems always change, as a result of climate change, natural disasters, invader species, human interference and other types of disturbance; they have taken shape in constant interaction with human and non-human place-making activities. As we live in the Anthropocene, it is an illusion to think that we can re-establish some sort of 'original', 'primeval' landscape. Although they may be more beneficial in terms of biodiversity, Miyawaki's *furusato* tree-planting projects are as much human-made as Meiji-period coniferous shrine forests, post-war *sugi* plantations or contemporary *satoyama* recreations. They likewise reflect normative, ideological notions of the 'proper' Japanese landscape, yet at different moments in history. Nature-making can take multiple shapes.

The Thousand-Year Forest Project

Gosho Komataki Jinja is a small shrine located on the north side of Mount Tsukuba, in the rural town of Makabe in Ibaraki Prefecture. The surrounding landscape is largely made up of fields, rice paddies, forested hills and small town and villages. The area is historically known for its stonecraft, and there are several workshops in the vicinity that make tombstones and stone statues. Although it is only a few hours by car from Tokyo, like other rural parts of Japan Makabe suffers from depopulation, an ageing population and a gradual decline in facilities. The shrine, for instance, cannot be reached by public transport anymore. Unlike the south side of Mount Tsukuba, few tourists or hikers make it here.

In contrast to large shrines such as Shimogamo Jinja, Meiji Jingū and Ise Jingū, which have nationwide (and even international) appeal, Gosho Komataki Jinja is not very well known – even though, in recent years, the shrine has received some media attention. In some ways, it is typical of rural shrines all over Japan: it is historically connected with a particular village community, its *ujiko*; it is a family shrine, run by a single priest, together with his wife; its annual *matsuri* is one of the main cultural events in the area and plays an important part in the cultivation of social relations; it is located at the foot of a mountain, right behind the village, and is flanked by a forest on one side and rice paddies on the other. There are hundreds, if not thousands such local shrines scattered around Japan, historically connected to a particular place; their names and their deities are usually only known to local community members, if at all. Many do not even have a permanent shrine priest.

In some ways, however, Gosho Komataki Jinja is atypical. There is a special quality to its *chinju no mori*. It is bright and cool, and consists of many different trees, mostly broad-leaved. It is mossy, has many fragrant plants, and a stream running through it. Its *sandō* is lined with abstract artworks, and on top of a rock is a small white stone creature that reminds one of a character from a Miyazaki film, which was reportedly donated by a stonemason from the village. Small though it is (approximately 1.5 ha), this is one of the most enchanting and atmospheric shrine forests I have visited. And I am not the only one who appreciates it, judging from the following comments made by visitors:

> Can you hear the sound of water?
> Can you hear the birds chirping?
> When the wind passes through
>> What a good feeling!
> As soon as it is evening
> We can hear the cry of the owl
> I   love   this place
> Sometimes, trying to listen carefully
>> Is a good thing

'Breath' is the blessing of the gods. I feel happiness when I am breathing together with the trees, the breath of a thousand years, while I am embracing a big tree. I receive its energy.

It is the kind of forest in which a Totoro may appear, isn't it?

When I come to this place, it feels as if the cells deep in my lungs get healthy. Like my body is cleaned.

There is a lot to be seen at this place, isn't there? We really have to cherish nature!

('Toikake no mori' 2013)

Gosho Komataki Jinja is not only of interest because of its forest but also because of its long history. It is said to have been founded in 1014. The current shrine buildings are of later date, but still go back more than 300 years. When I visited the shrine, in May 2013, the priest and local volunteers were busy preparing for a special *matsuri* to commemorate the shrine's 1,000th anniversary. This is one of the reasons why the shrine has recently received some media attention and the number of visitors has increased. It is worth noting that Gosho Komataki Jinja has some graves on its precincts, unlike most other shrines. The head priest, Sakurai Takashi, explained this by referring to traditional Japanese beliefs, according to which the spirits of the deceased would 'go to the mountain' and, finally, become *chinjugami*. In modern times, death-related rituals have largely been the domain of Buddhist institutions, but according to Sakurai this was not always the case: shrines

Figure 7.1 Gosho Komataki Jinja, Ibaraki Prefecture.

Figure 7.2 A Miyazakiesque creature in the *chinju no mori* of Gosho Komataki Jinja, Ibaraki Prefecture, donated by a local stonemason.

have historically played an important part in popular beliefs and practices related to the dead. The resurgence of traditional beliefs is an important concern for him, as he considers the decline of faith (*shinkō*) among contemporary Japanese people to be a great problem that has led to various social and environmental problems (interview, May 2013).

The shrine grove has two information panels. The first one says, 'Gosho Komataki Jinja thousand-year forest-making (*sennen mori-zukuri*) | "Living" in the land of nature (*shizen no daichi ni "ikiru"*)', followed by the English sentence 'to return to Nature and to live with it'. The second one has the following text (in Japanese):

> Let us protect nature!
>
> Nowadays, the number of forests where you can still feel nature has become low.
>
> In the forest are various animals and plants, whose lives are interconnected. The air and water that we need to live is made and purified by the forest.
>
> In modern times, because of rapid cultural and industrial development, our irreplaceable nature is being destroyed.
>
> Humans cannot survive independently from nature. Each and every one of us has to learn to understand nature. Starting near ourselves, let us all endeavour to protect nature.

Sakurai is a pioneer in shrine-based environmental activism: he was one of the first shrine priests not only to assert the importance of ecological issues and their intimate connection with Shinto cosmology but also to develop shrine-based projects focused on nature conservation. Sakurai traces his activities to 1971, when he graduated from Kokugakuin University and returned to his native Ibaraki to become priest at Gosho Komataki Jinja. Reportedly, there was a food shortage at the time, and he started growing rice on a small paddy near the shrine (Sakurai 1999: 77). Soon thereafter, however, the pine trees that constituted the shrine forest died one by one, and he became aware of the importance of forest conservation: 'I felt that, without the forest, the god(s) would no longer have their place (*kamisama no basho wa nai*)' (1999: 77). Therefore, in the course of the 1980s, he started carrying out several reforestation and forest conservation activities. In the following years, Sakurai gradually became aware of the ecological interdependence between the mountain, the shrine forest and the rice paddies; he also realized that rural depopulation and environmental conservation are interrelated issues. As he explains, 'the number of people working in the *satoyama* surrounding the shrine was decreasing, and I felt that by only protecting the shrine forest (*jinjarin*), we would not be able to protect the local environment' (Sakurai 2009). Hence, several activities were developed that were related not only to forest conservation but also to rice cultivation, community empowerment and environmental education. His motivation was not solely ecological: community revitalization was considered equally important. In developing these activities, Sakurai received support and assistance from a number of volunteers, as well as from his wife, Sakurai Mayumi. In 1991, the Sennen no Mori no Kai ('thousand-year forest association' or 'millennium forest association') was formally established. As a non-profit organization, it is legally independent from the shrine, although the two are obviously intertwined.

Sakurai's activities did not go unnoticed. In 1997, he and his wife were invited to present their project at the 'Shinto and Ecology' conference at Harvard University (Sakurai & Sakurai 2000). Here, they met with Sonoda Minoru and Tanaka Tsunekiyo, among others. As one of the first local *chinju no mori* conservation movements, Sennen no Mori no Kai has captured the interest of quite a few Shinto scholars and organizations (including Shasō Gakkai and Jinja Honchō), and Sakurai has been invited to give presentations about his activities on various occasions (e.g. Sakurai 1999, 2009). His organization has served as an example for other projects: in the 1980s and 1990s, he addressed topics and organized activities that were not widely considered to be the responsibility of Shinto priests, yet have now become mainstream. As he told me, when he had just started his activities, people 'accused him of being a communist'; today, however, he is acclaimed by many (including Tanaka Tsunekiyo) for his groundbreaking work. Indeed, Sakurai said that in the past twenty years, there has been an important shift in the shrine world: young priests in particular are increasingly aware of environmental issues, and interested not only in forest conservation but also in other topics, such as alternative energy. Needless to say, he applauds this development (interview, May 2013).

Sakurai has listed five main objectives for the Sennen no Mori no Kai. First, it is devoted to the plantation and construction of forests; its aim is to grow a healthy *chinju no mori*, while fostering a spirit of care for all living beings among the participants. Second, it wants to raise awareness of the ecological importance of the local river and contribute to keeping it clean. Third, it wants to teach people the importance of a simple life, without waste or overconsumption. Fourth, it gives people the opportunity to experience rice planting and seeks to 'restore the rice cultivation culture that has been transmitted from ancient Japan'. And fifth, it organizes traditional charcoal-making activities, to make people aware of the intertwinement of the different elements in nature – fire, earth, wood, water and metal, which apparently all play a part in traditional charcoal production (Sakurai 1999: 77–78, 2009). Thus, the purpose of the Sennen no Mori no Kai is not limited to forest conservation and maintenance. The organization has a clear pedagogical purpose, combining environmental education with education in traditional crafts and agricultural practices, in order to teach (young) people the 'ancient Japanese' spirit of respect for nature. Moreover, it has a social agenda: by bringing together local volunteers, Sakurai hopes to create a new sense of community and contribute to social cohesion within the region. For this, regular communication is seen as an important prerequisite: being visible in the neighbourhood, establishing social relations, organizing community events and maintaining a blog on forest-related activities are all part of his project (Sakurai 2009). As a result of these efforts, reportedly more and more people come to visit the shrine – if only just for a stroll.

Sakurai's interest in social cohesion and education is also evidenced by some of his other activities. In addition to his work as a shrine priest and as leader of the Sennen no Mori no Kai, he regularly works in a prison to give pastoral care. As he told me, the prisoners do not usually ask him questions about the gods, and he does not address that topic himself. But they do ask him what the forest looks like, what flowers are in bloom, what birds he has heard, when the rice will be harvested, and what the weather has been like. He always tells them about these things. That, he said, is one of the things the prisoners miss most: being outdoors, in nature, observing the seasonal changes. Nature, here, becomes a symbol of hope and rehabilitation; its sacred qualities can be appreciated by and resonate with anybody, regardless of their particular 'belief'.

Throughout the years, Sakurai has learned a lot about forest ecology; when I visited his shrine, he explained me several things about the forest environment. In contrast to those who suggest that a resurgence of the 'traditional' Shinto 'spirit of gratitude' and an awareness of our 'coexistence with nature' are sufficient, Sakurai suggests that if we really want to solve environmental problems (whether on a local or a global scale), we do need practical and scientific knowledge – for even if we care about nature, we may still do things that are ecologically harmful out of ignorance. As I was told, Ibaraki Prefecture is a very ecologically diverse region; as it constitutes the border area between Japan's two main climate zones, it has species both from northern and from western Japan. But this biodiversity is fragile: as all organisms in an ecosystem are mutually dependent, a small distortion can lead to significant biodiversity loss. Sakurai agrees with many contemporary scientists working on (shrine) forests that broad-leaved trees are more ecologically beneficial than *sugi*, *matsu* or *hinoki*, as the latter species do not let through enough light for a diverse ecosystem to develop. However, based on his own experiences in the field of *mori-zukuri*, he does disagree with them on some other points, suggesting that there are several problems with other *chinju no mori*-based conservation projects.

First, Sakurai is critical of the Miyawaki method of planting *furusato* trees. He is not opposed to planting trees, if necessary; however, he suggests that Miyawaki plants *too many* trees, which may disturb existing ecosystems. The same, *mutatis mutandis*, applies to shrine forest projects that have a strong focus on tree-planting: instead of constantly planting new trees, it is better to let existing forests develop themselves, while doing necessary maintenance work to prevent certain species from getting too dominant.[10] Second, Sakurai does not follow Ueda Masaaki's ideal-typical distinction between *mori* as 'natural' and 'untouched' and *hayashi* as 'artificial'. The term used by Sakurai and others is *mori-zukuri*, 'forest-making'. Rather than setting apart an area of forest as 'forbidden' and staying away from it, as Ueda Masaaki suggests, biodiversity conservation requires more active maintenance, they argue. And third, most important, Sakurai suggests that many other projects have a focus that is *too* local: that is, they are only concerned with a particular *chinju no mori*, but do not consider its immediate environment. However, most animals and plants do not thrive in small, isolated groves. In order for shrine forests to be ecologically diverse, therefore, they need to be connected to other areas of green space. To Sakurai, the shrine forest, the stream and the rice paddy (*shinsenden*; a term used for paddies associated with shrines, where rice is grown that is offered to deities) are all connected and part of a larger ecosystem, which he calls the '*chinju no mori* biotope' (1999: 82–83). Thus, he suggests, conservation activities should not be limited to the shrine precincts but also engage with the surrounding area.

One does not need a shrine in order to set up a project for nature conservation, community cohesion and environmental education. Sakurai's interests extend beyond forest ecology and social activism, however: the activities of Sennen no Mori no Kai are also part of a deliberate attempt at sacralization. The forest's enchanting character – a mossy soil, fragrant plants, Miyazakiesque creatures, old wooden shrine buildings – is no natural occurrence, but the result of years of hard labour. Until three or four decades ago, this was a dark forest, largely made up of pine trees; since then, however, it has been reshaped significantly. In its current shape, the forest is as much the result of place-making activities as it is of 'natural' (i.e. non-human) factors. Put differently, rather than constituting a 'wild' or 'natural' forest, the current shape of the forest is largely the outcome of spatial practices – pruning, planting, weeding and so on – that have contributed to the place acquiring its special (some might say: sacred) character.

During our interview, Sakurai lamented the lack of people who have 'faith' (*shinkō*) in contemporary Japan. He expressed his dissatisfaction with the apparent loss of traditional worldviews and with the social changes that have taken place in recent decades, which according to him are caused by individualization and urbanization. His arguments do not only concern a gradual loss of 'faith' in deities but also the 'desacralization' of nature: the increasing dominance of materialistic and utilitarian perceptions of nature that strip it from its 'sacred' or mysterious qualities. Like his colleagues Sonoda and Ueda, then, Sakurai combines environmental advocacy with moral conservatism and a nostalgic longing for an idealized past. In other words, he is a romantic environmentalist, who is concerned not only with the return of traditional beliefs but also with *re-sacralizing nature*: he wants nature to be conceived of in mystical terms, setting it apart as something that transcends ordinary human society yet simultaneously constitutes its foundation, as the following anecdote illustrates:

> The participants [in the activities of the Sennen no Mori no Kai], myself included, have come to realize that all living creatures take part in the circle of life. As a result, they now understand things about *kami* and Shinto, even if they do not talk about the *kami*. Let me give a concrete example: when these children climb the mountain, even if they do not say anything, they put their hands together in front of the *kami* and pray for not getting hurt. That is the kind of shape in which it appears. In addition, I could see the sprouting of minds touched by the beauty and laws of nature. They became aware of the fact that they themselves are a part of nature, and live because of nature. One by one, the children came to life, and began to shine (…). Networks between people emerged, with nature as their medium. I realized that nature is good for educating children [the importance of] balance. (1999: 80–81)

As this citation makes clear, Sakurai conceives of nature in a holistic way, arguing that all living creatures, including human beings, are part of it. The divine is believed to reside in nature, where it interacts with us. Sakurai attributes several special qualities to nature: it is able to arouse devotion, as well as feelings of reverence and gratitude; it can make people aware of the interdependence of all beings, and teach them how to achieve balance; and, in the end, it fosters social relations. Thus, nature has a sacred character, and we humans have a responsibility to take care of it. In sum, Sakurai is one of very few Shinto priests who not only profess to care about the environment, but who has made active attempts to practice what he preaches.

Owls and Fireflies

Both Tadasu no Mori Zaidan and Sennen no Mori no Kai are legally independent from their respective shrines (they are non-profit organizations, *NPO hōjin*, while the shrines are religious institutions, *shūkyō hōjin*), yet their activities are obviously organized in direct interaction with these shrines. The same applies to NPO Hibiki and Afuhi Project, which will be discussed in the next chapter. When learning about these projects, one might get the impression that shrine priests have become more interested in nature conservation, education and other social and cultural issues. Certainly, there are some indications that young priests are getting more interested in this sort of activities and have become more socially engaged. Still, it is probably safe to say that the majority of shrine priests in the country are busy with ritual ceremonies and administrative duties and are not active in nature conservation or related cultural activities – either because of a lack of time and money, or simply because they do not see it as their main responsibility. Nor, for that matter, do they spend much time working in their shrine forests.

Only the wealthiest shrines in the country, such as Shimogamo Jinja, Meiji Jingū, Atsuta Jingū and Ise Jingū, can afford to permanently hire people for forest maintenance; most other shrines do not have the means to do so, and their forests are by and large ignored. In some cases, this may have led to the preservation of small areas of 'natural' forest; more often, however, the lack of maintenance has contributed to forests growing wild and of invader species taking over. In the case of urban shrines, this has caused discomfort for neighbours, who complain about fallen leaves, insects and untidy appearances, and want the shrine forest removed (Hasegawa, personal communication, May 2013). Such considerations may well have served as an extra incentive for shrines to sell (parts of) their precincts – in addition to the obvious economic incentives for selling land in an urban environment with high real estate prices. In sum, not all shrine priests are equally concerned with preserving *chinju no mori*, especially if there is external pressure to sell some of the land. Despite the emergence of the *chinju no mori* preservation movement, the economic and other incentives that caused shrines to sell parts of their land in the early post-war decades are still there, especially in urban areas.

Thus, when it comes to shrine forest protection, shrine priests are not always the main actors, and their agendas are not necessarily compatible with those of environmental activists. In some cases, *chinju no mori* projects are set up and run completely by volunteers, and the involvement of priests is limited to giving permission (or not) for certain activities to take place. One such example is the non-profit organization Mori-zukuri Kaigi ('forest-making assembly'), established in 2009 for the purpose of nature conservation, forest maintenance work and community development at the Shiroyama Hachimangū shrine in Nagoya. The organization was set up by Hasegawa Yasuhiro, a scientist who at the time was writing his PhD dissertation on shrine forests in Aichi Prefecture (Hasegawa 2012; cf. Hasegawa, Okamura and Kōsaka 2010). Hasegawa has been involved with Shasō Gakkai for several years and presented papers at Shasō Gakkai conferences based on his field research (e.g. Hasegawa & Okamura 2011). He has taken part in Shasō Gakkai's 'sacred forest instructor' course and has applied the skills and knowledge acquired there to his volunteer work at Shiroyama Hachimangū. Rather than 'Shinto', 'sacred space' or 'traditional culture', his main concerns are landscape architecture and environmental conservation. His work thus constitutes an interesting attempt to combine scientific research and analysis with a more practically oriented, activist approach.

Unlike Gosho Komataki Jinja, Shiroyama Hachimangū is an urban shrine, surrounded by houses and other buildings. However, it is not even remotely as wealthy or well known as large urban shrines such as Shimogamo Jinja or Meiji Jingū (or, in Nagoya, Atsuta Jingū). It is not visited by many tourists, but it does have a certain local appeal. When I first visited the shrine, I happened to be there around the time of the *shichi-go-san* festival,[11] and several families with beautifully dressed young children had made it to the shrine in order to attend a ritual ceremony. Like other neighbourhood shrines, Shiroyama Hachimangū is a place where ritual purification ceremonies and weddings are organized, where *o-mamori* and *o-fuda* are sold, and where people come for *hatsumōde* (the first shrine visit of the new year) and other prayers. It is also the locus of the annual neighbourhood *matsuri*. In sum, in several respects, it looks like a 'typical' local urban shrine.

What is special about the shrine, however, is its spatial configuration. As the name suggests (*shiroyama* means 'castle mountain'), Shiroyama Hachimangū is located on the site of a former castle. It was here that Oda Nobuhide (1510–1551), a local ruler and father of the famous warlord Oda Nobunaga (1534–1582), built his Suemori castle in 1547. Nobunaga's younger brother Nobuyuki (1536–1557) is said to have built the first shrine here, devoted to the god of Hakusan (now Shirayama Hime Jinja) in Ishikawa Prefecture (Hasegawa 2012: 139). Before long, however, the Odas were defeated and the castle was abandoned. Today, the only thing that has remained of the castle is the hill on which it was built and the castle moats, which are now dry and have given way to forest. The current shrine was established much later, in 1936 (2012: 139). As it was built on the site of a former castle, it was dedicated to the deity Hachiman, associated with warriors and archery.

The forest of Shiroyama Hachimangū, it follows, is older than its present shrine buildings. Although not a primeval forest, it does go back to the sixteenth century. For a small forest (approximately 2 ha; i.e. a sixth the size of Tadasu no Mori), it can boast a considerable species diversity. The forest predates the time when *sugi* and *hinoki* came in vogue: its main tree species are *konara*, *abemaki* and *arakashi* (*Quercus serrata*, *Q. variabilis* and *Q. glauca*; three types of oak), *kakuremino* (*Dendropanax trifidus*; a type of aralia), *yabutsubaki* and *sakaki* (*Cleyera japonica*).[12] In addition, there are *mukunoki* and *enoki*. Some of these trees are very old, going back to the Edo period. The most famous of these are the shrine's *shinboku*, two entwined *abemaki*: they are a symbol of *en-musubi* and marital love. There are also *kusunoki*, but these were not planted until 1959, after the Isewan typhoon had caused much damage to the forest. Unusually for a shrine forest, there are even some *shuro* (*Trachycarpus*; a type of palm tree) (Hasegawa 2012: 140–141). In addition to trees, the forest houses a variety of other plants and animals – including, reportedly, a rare species of owl. This latter fact, however, is not widely known. I actually asked the volunteers of Mori-zukuri Kaigi why they did not build a campaign around the owl. Thus far, they had had difficulties trying to involve people from the neighbourhood in their activities; an owl-protection campaign might be a good way to raise awareness of shrine forest's importance, and get some positive media attention, or so I thought. That was a bad idea, it turned out: as they explained, it might attract 'collectors' coming to the shrine forest in order to catch the owls. It was better not to advertise the owls' presence too widely, they assured me.[13] Instead, they were developing activities to make

Figure 7.3 Shiroyama Hachimangū, Nagoya.

fireflies come to the shrine forest. That, they believed, would be much better PR, as watching fireflies is a very popular activity in Japan.

Mori-zukuri Kaigi was founded in 2009. Initially, the group consisted of seven people, most of whom did not live in the vicinity of the shrine. In 2012, the organization reportedly had eleven members: six from outside the area and five from within (Hasegawa 2012: 140). In 2013, the number of active members was lower than ten; attempts to permanently involve local community members had not yet been very successful (Hasegawa, personal communication, May 2013). Among the members are some young people, including scientists, as well as a few elderly people who are retired. All of them share an interest in nature and environmental issues; considerations of the shrine as a 'sacred place' or as 'traditional culture' do not seem to play an important part. Revealingly, there are no priests among the group's members. When I first visited the shrine, I was introduced to the head priest, and we had a short conversation. He stated that he was interested in environmental issues and expressed his appreciation for the work done by Hasegawa and the others. It was clear, however, that he was not actively involved in any of the group's activities. As we shall see shortly, there are some small but significant differences in opinion between the shrine management and the NPO.

In an information pamphlet published a year after the foundation of the organization (apparently with the support of Shasō Gakkai), Hasegawa explained its main purposes and activities (Hasegawa 2010). *Chinju no mori*, he writes, are 'places where a culture was created that coexisted with nature' (*shizen to kyōzon shita bunka no sōzō no ba*); they are 'places of faith' (*shinkō no ba*), but their significance extends beyond that. The value of *chinju no mori*, Hasegawa summarizes, is fourfold. First, they have 'natural value' because of their biodiversity and because they are places where old trees have been preserved. Second, they have 'cultural value': they house traditional architecture and cultural treasures, are historical landmarks, and constitute centres of tourism and 'city-making' (*machi-zukuri*; a term that refers to a range of activities employed to improve the living conditions of Japanese urban neighbourhoods). Third, they have 'environmental value', by which he does not refer to their ecology (that would constitute 'natural value') but to their spatial properties: they are 'places where one can experience traditional space' (*dentōteki na kūkan taiken no ba*) because of their spatial configuration (*torii, sandō, temizuya*, shrine buildings and so on).

Fourth, and perhaps most important, they have 'social value' as places where people come to meet, talk, play and worship, and where children can learn about nature; as such, they constitute important community centres (Hasegawa 2010). Most of the regular activities of Mori-zukuri Kaigi in the forest of Shiroyama Hachimangū have a seasonal character. They include cleaning up litter, removing overgrown *kuzu* (*Pueraria lobata*; kudzu) and *sasa* (*Sasa*; a type of bamboo), organizing workshops and guided forest walks by biologists, cultivating mushrooms on the logs of fallen trees, making baskets of dried *kuzu* plants from the forest and more (Hasegawa 2010; cf. Hasegawa 2012: 143–148).

Members of Mori-zukuri Kaigi are only allowed to do forest maintenance work and organize activities in the 'public' part of the shrine forest. As in some other shrines, the area behind the *honden* is fenced off and not open to non-clergy; accordingly, no activities can take place there (Hasegawa 2012: 142). We have seen that scholars involved with Shasō Gakkai such as Ueda Masaaki have applauded the tradition of setting apart a particular part of a shrine forest or mountain as 'sacred' and not allowing laypeople entry to this area. These areas are referred to as *irazu no mori* or *kinsokuchi*, terms that may be translated somewhat loosely as 'forbidden forest'. Because of this tradition, they argued, areas of primeval forest have been preserved until today; accordingly, these areas are said to be of great environmental significance (M. Ueda 2004a: 37–39; Suganuma 2004: 85–94). However, the majority of shrine forests today is *not* primeval, and rapidly growing invader species (such as *sasa* bamboo) are pushing out trees and plants that are less dominant, or so Japanese environmentalists argue.[14] Accordingly, the ideal of the shrine forest that grows naturally and is not controlled or managed is gradually giving way to the realization that in most cases neglect leads to overgrowth and biodiversity decline, and that, in order to protect a shrine forest, human involvement (pruning, cleaning, felling unwanted trees and so on) is necessary.

As this case illustrates, while there is general consensus on the *importance* of shrine forest protection among priests, scientists, environmental activists and urban planners alike, there is plenty of disagreement when it comes to the actual *practice* of forest preservation. Forest conservationists may want to remove *sasa* or *kuzu* from the entire forest and not really care about what parts of the forest are considered 'sacred'; priests, on the other hand, may want to preserve the 'sacred' character of a particular part of the forest, by maintaining its status as a 'forbidden' area and leaving it to 'nature'. But then, there is no clear consensus among shrine priests, either. Before establishing Mori-zukuri Kaigi, Hasegawa conducted a survey among shrine priests in the Nagoya metropolitan area; it turned out that most shrine forests (77–90 per cent, depending on forest size) were 'moderately maintained' (i.e. only basic maintenance activities took place), but that there was considerable variation with regard to forest ideals. While some priests stated that they wanted 'a natural forest' or 'a divine forest with many high trees', others opted for 'a forest where children can play' or 'a forest where seasonal excursions take place' (Hasegawa, Okamura & Kōsaka 2010: 42–43). In other words, some wanted their shrine forest to be primarily a 'natural' or 'sacred' site, while others were more interested in the 'social' and 'educational' properties. The head priest of Shiroyama Hachimangū likewise wants his shrine forest to be primarily an 'urban *shasō*'; that is, a place for recreation and social encounters (Hasegawa 2012: 141). Still, he does want to keep the 'most sacred' part of the forest closed.

In reality, then, there is no consensus on what an ideal shrine forest should look like, and what sort of maintenance activities should or should not take place. Even shrines that have priests who are, in principle, interested in forest preservation, often have difficulties in carrying out maintenance activities. Problems reported include a lack of human resources, a lack of financial means, a lack of practical knowledge and complaints by people living in the vicinity of the forest (Hasegawa, Okamura & Kōsaka 2010: 41–42). The first problem is fairly obvious: most shrines only have a handful of priests, or only one, who is usually busy with his or her various 'priestly' duties (ritual and otherwise) and has limited time available to work in the forest. Second, while activities such as cleaning up litter do not cost money, other forest maintenance activities do; for instance, treating a tree that is suffering from parasitic beetles costs 3,000 yen (approximately 25 euros) per tree per year (Hasegawa 2012: 141). This may not be much if it is only one tree, but these beetles are not known for their moderation; if one broad-leaved tree in a forest is affected, many others are likely to be affected, too.

As for the issue of practical knowledge: few shrine priests are schooled in botany or ecology, so even though they may be willing to do maintenance work, many of them simply do not know what plants they should or should not remove. Hence, weeding activities may end up having a negative ecological impact.[15] As a result of these various constraints, at most shrines forest maintenance activities are kept to a minimum, and shrines often depend on volunteers to do some basic tasks. Not all shrines are successful in engaging volunteers though: prior to the establishment of Mori-zukuri Kaigi in 2009, Shiroyama Hachimangū had not seen any volunteer involvement in forest maintenance (including cleaning up) for fifteen years (Hasegawa 2012: 141).

Having read numerous treatises on the 'Japanese love of nature', and having lived in big cities in which I was longing for green space and clean air myself, one of the things I found most surprising about the Shiroyama Hachimangū project was the problems the organizers had in convincing people who live around the shrine of the forest's importance. One would expect people living in a metropolis like Nagoya to be happy if they have a small forest in their vicinity. Apparently, however, this is not usually the case. Quite the opposite, in fact: many neighbours reportedly perceive the shrine forest as a nuisance and would rather see it disappear. Nagoya is not unique in this respect. Shrine priests in other cities have also told me about the many complaints they have received about their forests, and the difficulties they have experienced in making local communities appreciate the forest's presence. Most of the time, people complain about falling leaves and branches. They also complain about insects coming from the forest and about shade: shrine forests are seen as 'too dark' and block sunlight (Hasegawa, Okamura & Kōsaka 2010: 41).

As a result, neighbourhood committees sometimes put pressure on shrine priests to fell (some of the) large trees – which is exactly what happened at Shiroyama Hachimangū a few years ago, much to the dismay of the volunteers of Mori-zukuri Kaigi, who had lobbied for their preservation. When it comes to low vegetation (i.e. removing *sasa*, *kuzu* and so on), the head priest and volunteers are very much in agreement. The high trees, however, are the main cause of friction. The volunteers want to protect them, because of their ecological significance and old age. The shrine management, however, wants the forest to be a social meeting place, and is not particularly interested in preserving trees that are expensive to maintain (because they require protection from beetles) and cause annoyance to neighbours – who, after all, constitute the shrine's *ujiko*, upon which it depends both financially and practically.

In sum, shrine priests have to take into consideration different factors, and nature conservation is not necessarily always on top of their agendas. In spite of claims made by Jinja Honchō and other organizations concerning Shinto's alleged relevance for overcoming the global environmental crisis, in reality shrines have to deal with competing and at times conflicting interests. For the majority of shrine priests, the most important priorities are correctly performing rituals, so as to maintain good relations with deities and preserve shrine traditions; attracting enough paying worshippers and sponsors, in order to make ends meet financially; and maintaining good relations with the *ujiko*, as they are the shrine's main patrons, and the people who co-organize and finance the annual *matsuri*. Exceptions notwithstanding, for most shrine priests, therefore, environmental issues are of secondary concern at best. Consequently, if environmental activists want to carry out activities in order to preserve the forest, they not only need the support and sympathy of shrine priests but also of the local community.

As we have seen, these days *chinju no mori* are conceptualized not only as community *centres* but even as their very *cradles*: the places around which the community first emerged. Not surprisingly, then, *chinju no mori* are associated with community-building projects, and seen as the focal points – both physically and symbolically – around which new social networks can (and should) develop. This is not limited to social interaction during *matsuri*; in recent years, the notion of *chinju no mori* as community centres has been extended to include educational activities, local markets and, as mentioned, even the development of alternative energy. Accordingly, *chinju no mori* have been described as a form of 'social capital' (Hasegawa 2012: 137). The relationship between shrines and 'local communities' – referred to as *kyōdōtai* ('collective body'), *chiiki shakai* ('local society') or *komyuniti* (the English loanword) – has been described as one characterized by mutual dependence. It may be argued, however, that a 'local community' is largely an imaginary construct, and that in twenty-first-century urban societies few people perceive membership of an *ujiko* as an integral part of their identity. Even if local communities are 'real' in the sense that they represent a loosely defined collective of people living in the same area and coming together twice a year for a festival, that still does not make them a significant reality in the daily lives of their 'members'. Urban society nowadays is characterized by a high degree of anonymity and fluidity; there are few closed communities in which all members know each other. Descriptions of shrines as community centres are therefore prescriptive rather than descriptive: they reflect popular ideals but do not necessarily correspond to social realities.

That does not mean, of course, that activities employed to improve social relations, living conditions and local environments – *machi-zukuri*, *komyuniti-zukuri* or *mori-zukuri* (city-making, community-making or forest-making), as they are called in Japan today – are meaningless. Quite the contrary: in urban societies characterized by a high degree of anonymity (and, perhaps, anomie), such activities can serve to establish social relations and provide people with a sense of security and belonging, even if the 'communities' they are said to help preserve are situational and constantly changing. Forest preservation activities may well serve a similar function. What is crucial, however, is the involvement and support of the people living in the immediate vicinity of the forest – the *ujiko*, so to speak. As the Shiroyama Hachimangū case makes clear, this is not something that is established overnight. Hasegawa and his colleagues are well aware of the importance of community involvement, and they have struggled to engage local residents. While some people have participated in workshops or other events, *permanent* community involvement is difficult to achieve, they have experienced. As they told me, not many Japanese people are really concerned about environmental issues and nature conservation; put bluntly, they only love 'nature' when it has the shape of pretty cherry blossoms, not when it has the shape of fallen leaves or insects from a shrine forest. The absence of a serious Green Party in Japan is symptomatic of this lack of concern, they suggested.

Nevertheless, they are trying to reach out. For this purpose, recently, they have been trying to get fireflies (*hotaru*) to the shrine forest. There are fireflies in some other parts of Nagoya, further away from the city centre, but not yet here. As fireflies are very popular in Japan, the presence of these little insects may well help people in the neighbourhood like the shrine forest better, the volunteers thought. Indeed, throughout Japan there are non-profit organizations active to improve the conditions for both fireflies and dragonflies, in order to protect them or make them return to particular places. These projects have been going on for several decades, as Moon has pointed out: 'From the 1960s, nature protection groups began to draw attention to the diminishing firefly population and launched many anti-pollution campaigns to revive *hotaru*. (…) There are now eighty-five "firefly villages" (*hotaru no sato*) or "firefly towns" (*hotaru no machi*) in Japan, registered at the Ministry of the Environment' (1997: 225). Recently, some of these projects have been carried out in cooperation with shrines (e.g. Abe 2008).

The significance of fireflies is not merely aesthetic; as they are vulnerable creatures, their presence or absence is often seen as indicative of the condition of a local ecosystem. Pollution by pesticides or chemicals, for instance, often leads to their disappearance. In order for fireflies to come back, it is argued, the overall environmental conditions need to be good.[16] Firefly projects are a good example of the tactics employed by Japanese environmental organizations to get local people involved in their projects; even though the importance of fireflies may be symbolic rather than ecological, they do serve to establish coalitions and gain sympathy.

When I last visited the shrine, in 2013, I joined some NPO members on a walk through the forest, together with a firefly expert, who had worked on a similar project elsewhere. He explained us about fireflies' habitats. For instance, he pointed out that old branches and logs should not be removed, but left in the forest, for this is where the larvae of fireflies grow. Whether or not the volunteers of Mori-zukuri Kaigi will be successful in creating their firefly forest, I cannot tell. Nor, for that matter, do I know how long they will continue their activities – the organization is small and highly dependent on the willingness of a few individuals to spend their time and energy on the project. In any case, I do believe it is an interesting case, as it shows us what kind of challenges a newly established *chinju no mori* conservation organization can meet. It also shows that actual attitudes to nature – either of shrine priests or 'ordinary' city dwellers – do not always correspond to what the theory tells us. Fallen cherry blossoms are not the same as fallen oak leaves, and fireflies are not the same as other insects. If environmental activists want to acquire public support, they need to engage not only with the natural environment as a physical reality but also with nature as a 'repertoire for metaphors' (Kalland 1995: 221): they must learn to appropriate natural symbols that can serve to mobilize people in defence of nature, not in opposition to it. Edible mushrooms, fireflies and entwined sacred trees may serve that purpose; high trees, fallen leaves and mosquitoes certainly do not.

Chapter 8

ACORNS FOR TOHOKU

3/11

On 11 March 2011, north-eastern Japan was hit by a large earthquake, nuclear crisis and tsunami that took approximately 20,000 human lives. The disasters sent shockwaves through Japan, and the consequences are still clearly visible today, as over 100,000 people still live as evacuees. Many of these are from the Fukushima region, where the authorities are still struggling to prevent further nuclear contamination, while reliable information is hard to come by. Others are from towns along the Sanriku coast, a beautiful, rugged coastal area in northern Miyagi and Iwate prefectures. In sharp contrast to Sendai and nearby suburban municipalities such as Ishinomaki, Natori and Iwanuma, some of the northern towns have hardly been rebuilt at all. In Rikuzentakata, for instance, the authorities have embarked on an ecologically disastrous project to raise the entire town by pouring layers of concrete all over the land, not allowing its citizens to return.

Meanwhile, however, the disasters have also led to the emergence of new types of community engagement (Marmignon 2012; Tossani 2012), disaster tourism and voluntourism (Avenell 2012), and a veritable memory industry. The amount of books that have been written on the consequences of the disaster is staggering, as illustrated by the fact that the library of the University of Tohoku has an entire section devoted to the topic. The vast majority of these books are in Japanese, but foreign scholars have made contributions as well. In recent years, a number of English-language anthologies have been published on the social, political, cultural and religious effects of the disasters (Kingston 2012; Mullins & Nakano 2016; Starrs 2014). There have been English-language publications on topics as diverse as the role of *matsuri* for community resurrection (Thompson 2014), responses to the nuclear crisis by contemporary artists (Geilhorn & Iwata-Weickgenannt 2017), and the theodicies developed by religious actors in Japan (Fujiwara 2013; Rots 2014a). All these publications make clear one thing: despite all the suffering it caused, the disasters have also given way to a range of cultural and religious initiatives, some of which may have a significant impact on the lives of the survivors. As the consequences of the disasters continue to be experienced by many, the interest in Tohoku on the part of scholars, journalists and artists is not likely to subdue any time soon.

The events of 2011 posed some serious challenges to Shinto organizations. Not only did they cause significant material damage to shrines and shrine forests, they also led to the death, suffering and displacement of many shrine priests and practitioners, thus uprooting local communities. In addition, the disasters constituted challenges of a more theological and ideological nature. That is, they problematized the ideal typical notion of nature as essentially gentle and benign that underlies the popular myth of the harmonious Japanese coexistence with nature, which, as we have seen, has strongly influenced recent reinterpretations of Shinto. Thus, the catastrophes of 2011 quite dramatically put the topic of theodicy onto the agenda of contemporary Shinto thought, leading authors and priests to consider ways to reconcile notions of nature as benevolent and animate with the widespread destruction and suffering brought about by the very forces of nature they had romanticized. There have been various ideological responses to the events, ranging from the rhetoric of 'national resurrection' – a concept that not only refers to the reconstruction of buildings and roads but also to idealized notions of traditional culture, social harmony and morality – to the development of more radically millenarian-environmentalist ideas of destruction and rebirth (Rots 2014a).

Meanwhile, however, the events also seem to have given new impetus to Shinto-related social activism.[1] Local shrine-based volunteer organizations, as well as other Shinto organizations, have set up a variety of activities to support affected shrines and communities. Shrine actors throughout Japan have made efforts to contribute to the rebuilding process by means of fundraising activities, special prayer ceremonies, tree-planting events and other symbolic practices (Kurosaki 2013: 74–76). One example is the head priest of Shitaya Jinja in Tokyo, Abe Akinori, who has been active in fundraising in order to help the reconstruction of shrines in Tohoku; he has repeatedly travelled to the disaster area to bring relief supplies and building materials. Shasō Gakkai has also been involved with reconstruction activities. In 2011, several scholars and scientists related to this organization went to Tohoku in order to monitor the damage done to shrines and shrine forests. Whereas several shrines located on high grounds escaped serious damage, others were severely affected. In some cases, shrine buildings were partly destroyed, and many trees were uprooted. Both Jinja Honshō and Shasō Gakkai have monitored the impact of the disaster, organized symposia, published reports and contributed to reconstruction activities (Kurosaki 2013: 64). Likewise, in the months following the disasters, *Jinja Shinpō* published several articles on the damage done to shrine buildings and reported on the various reconstruction activities conducted by Jinja Honchō and individual shrines. In addition, the newspaper contained accounts of fundraising events organized by shrines throughout the country, as well as other social activities, such as a summer school for children from Fukushima ('Chinju no mori to kodomotachi' 2011) and a special market where farmers from the affected area could sell their products ('Fūhyō higai o tonde ike' 2011).

In the affected area, too, shrine priests have undertaken a variety of activities, as reported in a book by Kawamura Kazuyo (2012). Examples mentioned in this book include shrine priests' involvement in coordinating the work of volunteers coming to Tohoku to assist in cleaning and reconstruction activities; the organization of a variety of special events and festivals (including *matsuri*), serving the dual purpose of providing some joy and distraction for people living in the affected areas, and raising funds for rebuilding activities; and even the construction of a temporary library for children on shrine precincts. This last project is organized at Imaizumi Hachimangū in Rikuzentakata (Iwate Prefecture), a shrine that was almost completely destroyed by the tsunami. The only thing remaining was a high *shinboku*, which reportedly received quite a bit of media attention, as it was one of the trees that survived the tsunami, at least initially (sadly, the tree did die some time later). Here, the non-profit organization Ashita no Hon ('Tomorrow's books') has collected books for children living in areas affected by the tsunami. The shrine priests and their family have set up a temporary library, Niji no Raiburarii ('Rainbow library'), located in a prefab building on the shrine precincts. I twice had the opportunity to talk to one of the organizers, who told me the library serves an important function not only as a place where children can come and play (or read) but also as a place where neighbours can come for a chat – in other words, a community centre. It is important to do these things, she told me, in order to maintain some sort of social cohesion in a community suffering from the death of loved ones, the loss of facilities and ever-increasing depopulation. When I revisited the shrine and its library two years later, however, she was markedly less optimistic: the shrine had not yet been rebuilt (other than a small temporary *honden*); but more important, people from the area were still not allowed to return to their homeland and rebuild their houses – thanks to the local authorities, who have decided to fill the land with concrete in order to raise the entire town by several metres (interviews, May 2013 and November 2015). For the time being, the shrine priests and some of their supporters are still busy trying to raise funds for rebuilding the shrine. However, the longer people live elsewhere, the smaller the chance that the *ujiko* will be reunited – which, after all, is a shrine's main *raison d'être*.

Another shrine that was completely destroyed by the tsunami is Yaegaki Jinja in the town of Yamamoto (Miyagi Prefecture). When I visited the shrine in 2013, it consisted of a small prefab building and a temporary altar; like Imaizumi Hachimangū, it had not yet been rebuilt. The shrine priest – one of the few female Shinto priests whom I have had the opportunity to talk to, incidentally – came across as a remarkably optimistic person, who has a very different understanding of what it entails to be a shrine priest from most of the other priests I have met. Rather than stressing the importance of conducting rituals in order to transmit tradition, or abstract talk on the relationship between the imperial family and the land of Japan, she talked about her experiences in providing pastoral care to *ujiko* members. For instance, she described how many tsunami survivors have reported seeing or hearing the spirits of the deceased, and they often feel the need to talk to somebody about it.

Yaegaki Jinja has received some attention as it was the location of a tree-planting event organized by Jinja Honchō in collaboration with Miyawaki Akira.

In June 2012, approximately 500 people took part in 'everybody's *chinju no mori* tree-planting festival' (*minna no chinju no mori shokujusai*) in order to collectively replant the shrine forest (Kurosaki 2013: 77). In accordance with Miyawaki's principles, only broad-leaved trees were planted. As mentioned previously, some elderly *ujiko* members were not pleased with this decision, as they thought a proper shrine forest should be made up of conifers. On the other hand, the event did attract many local residents, in addition to volunteers from elsewhere. Yaegaki Jinja also constitutes an interesting example of a shrine where, despite the fact that the shrine buildings were destroyed, the annual *matsuri* was conducted as usual. As this *matsuri* is directly related to the sea (and actually involves going into the sea), after the tsunami the shrine priest was not sure whether people would still want to participate; however, most *ujiko* members insisted that it took place (interview, May 2013). The *matsuri* seems to have an important symbolic function as a marker of continuity and community survival, now more than at any time. Indeed, in the areas hit by the tsunami, *matsuri* have been important for re-establishing a sense of community, as others have also observed (Kawamura 2012; Thompson 2014).

Figure 8.1 The site of Yaegaki Jinja in Miyagi Prefecture, June 2013. The wooden shrine buildings were completely destroyed by the tsunami of March 2011. Most of the *chinju no mori* was destroyed, too, with the exception of a handful of pine trees. The young trees in the foreground are broad-leaved trees that were planted in June 2012 by 500 local residents and volunteers, supported by Jinja Honchō and Miyawaki Akira.

Holy 'Hollyhock'

In the year following the disasters, religious and secular organizations nationwide were active in fundraising and volunteer activities in order to support the reconstruction of Tohoku. In October 2011, I visited an *ennichi* (shrine fair) on the grounds of Kamigamo Jinja in Kyoto. The event was organized by a non-profit organization named Afuhi Project (pronounced as 'Aoi Project'). The shrine fair was organized for the purpose of improving the position of the shrine as a place of encounter for members of the local neighbourhood community, although people from other parts of the city were also welcome. Reportedly, the proceeds of this shrine fair were donated to tsunami victims in Tohoku. Several cultural organizations, galleries and shops had stands on the grass field in front of the shrines, where they were selling products (e.g. green tea and art products) and handing out brochures. More interestingly, throughout the day there were various workshops in 'traditional culture', as well as performances and concerts. Not all of these were equally 'traditional' – a manga class and a guitar concert would not usually be classified as such, I think – but they did contribute to bringing together people and increasing the visibility of Kamigamo Jinja not only as a place of worship but also as a centre for local community life. One of the most noteworthy contributions was made by a local children's choir, who performed a number of songs 'for the children in Tohoku'. Some of the songs were quite moving indeed, yet they were performed in Kyoto, at a local shrine fair; presumably, none of the victims of the tsunami or nuclear crisis were present. Nevertheless, performing these songs was a way for the children in the choir to express their sympathy with tsunami victims. Through this symbolic practice, they participated in the nationwide project of 'supporting Tohoku', morally as well as financially, which in the months and years following the disasters gave new impetus to various forms of social activism – not least at Shinto shrines.

Together with Shimogamo Jinja, Kamigamo Jinja – officially called Kamo Wake Ikazuchi Jinja – is considered as one of Kyoto's oldest and most famous shrines. Both shrines are historically associated with the powerful Kamo lineage and were among the highest-ranking imperial shrines in the Heian period. Their deities are believed to be related as well.[2] The two shrines continue to co-organize and co-stage the annual Aoi Matsuri, one of Kyoto's three major festivals, and in 1994 both were enlisted as UNESCO World Heritage Sites. Kamigamo Jinja is located a few kilometres north of Shimogamo Jinja, upstream on the Kamogawa River; hence their respective names (Kamigamo Jinja means 'upper Kamo shrine'; Shimogamo Jinja means 'lower Kamo shrine'). Despite (or, perhaps, because) of these intimate historical, mythological and ritual connections, there seems to be a fair amount of rivalry between the two shrines and their staff. Both shrines, for instance, claim to predate the other, and to be the 'original' shrine of the Kamo lineage; both even claim to be the oldest shrine in all of Kyoto (a claim also made by Matsuo Taisha, which is historically associated with the Hata lineage).

As the origins of neither shrine are clear, their historical narratives are significantly different. John Nelson has pointed out that historical records of the

Figure 8.2 Singing for Tohoku during the *aoi ennichi*, Kamigamo Jinja, Kyoto.

Kamo shrines' early history are extremely scarce, and claims are based on little or no textual evidence (2000: 92). This partly explains Shimogamo Jinja's interest in archaeological research: it is believed to provide 'evidence' of prehistoric worship practices and, therefore, legitimize the shrine's claims to seniority. As they co-organize one of Kyoto's biggest festivals, there are formal relations between the two shrines, and ritual procedures are of course observed. But cooperation does not seem to go much further than the annual *matsuri*. Despite the similarities, when I did my research in 2011, there was no cooperation between both shrines' *chinju no mori* organizations, Tadasu no Mori Zaidan and Afuhi Project.[3]

Kamigamo Jinja is an appealing shrine, with somewhat unusual spatial configurations. It does have a small forest, but it is primarily known for its wide, open grass fields, located in front of the main entrance. These are used for spectacular horse racing and horseback archery (*yabusame*) performances, held several times a year. During Aoi Matsuri, this is where the audience sits to watch the priests and other participants walk in procession to the shrine. Most of the time, however, the fields are empty (except for a few picnickers, if the weather is nice), giving the shrine a park-like appearance. Behind the second *torii* are the main shrine buildings; these are surrounded by a small forested area, and two streams converging in the middle of the shrine grounds. In an English-language shrine pamphlet, this is described as 'an area of thick forest that offers a different enchantment with each season' (Kamigamo Jinja n.d.). While this description is in accordance with the dominant shrine forest ideal, the label 'thick forest' is exaggerated. It is a small, mixed forest; tree species include *ichii* (*Taxus cuspidata*; Japanese yew), *sudajii* (*Castanopsis sieboldii*; a type of chinquapin) and *shidarezakura* (*Prunus subhirtella*; weeping cherry) (Kamigamo Jinja n.d.), most of which appear to have been planted. Like those in Tadasu no Mori, some of Kamigamo Jinja's broad-leaved trees suffer from parasitic beetles, and their stems are covered with plastic in order to protect them.

Unlike some other famous shrines, the *sandō* and shrine buildings at Kamigamo Jinja are not straight. The shrine buildings are asymmetrical, and one has to turn around a corner in order to get to the worship hall, from where the *honden* and *gonden* (the two most sacred places) are only partly visible.[4] In sum, the layout appears somewhat unstructured and chaotic. I was told, however, that this is deliberate, so that visitors will not approach the *kami* in a straight line. According to the priest who showed me around, the spatial organization of Kamigamo Jinja is typical of ancient Shinto – not coincidentally, the shrines of Ise are similar in this respect – while shrines with a straight *sandō* going directly to the shrine buildings (e.g. Shimogamo Jinja) are of a later date. He also explained to me that the actual object of worship is not the *honden*, but the sacred mountain behind it, Mount Kōyama: the original *shintaizan* of Kamigamo Jinja, where the deity was believed to reside. For many centuries, Kamigamo Jinja was one of Kyoto's northernmost human constructions, and the forest of Mount Kōyama began immediately behind the shrine. Unfortunately, in 1948, much of the forest was destroyed and replaced by a golf court. Nevertheless, some hidden shrine ceremonies still take place at the foot of the mountain, near the golf court. For instance, every year on 12 May, the deity is summoned down from the mountain in a famous ceremony called Miare-sai, an important (and secret) preparatory ritual for the Aoi Matsuri (Nelson 2000: 218–220).

The shrine's core symbol is the *aoi* plant. Today, the plant signifies the preservation of heritage, tradition and culture; most of all, it stands for historical continuity. Mentioned in ancient texts and found on old images,[5] it represents the intertwinement of the Kamo shrines with Kyoto as both a physical city and a mental space. Botanically speaking, the name *aoi* refers to a variety of plants, most of them belonging to the genus *Asarum*. The plant that is central to the symbolic and ritual traditions of the Kamo shrines is commonly identified with *futaba aoi* (*Asarum caulescens*; a type of wild ginger). It is often translated into English as 'hollyhock', but this is not botanically correct as hollyhocks are flowering plants that belong to the genus *Alcea*. Confusingly, however, whereas the plant used for the Aoi Matsuri is *futaba aoi*, the plant that appears on shrine amulets is said to be *tachi aoi* (*Alcea rosea*), which *is* a species of hollyhock (Nelson 2000: 266). And to make it even more complicated, the name *futaba aoi* means two-leaved *aoi*; the three-leaved *mitsuba aoi* is another commonly used symbol (it is used for the Tokugawa family crest, for instance), but since *mitsuba aoi* is not a real species, this is actually a three-leaved *futaba aoi*. In any case, the *aoi* that is central to the Kamigamo project that I will describe in more detail shortly is *futaba aoi* (i.e. *Asarum caulescens*), so botanic accuracy arguably matters in this case. As the common translation 'hollyhock' is incorrect, I will refer to the plant by its Japanese name.

Figure 8.3 *Futaba aoi* (*Asarum caulescens*), Kamigamo Jinja, Kyoto.

Nowadays, *futaba aoi* appear frequently as a decorative motif on shrine buildings, traditional clothes and shrine souvenirs (e.g. protective amulets, postcards and biscuits). And, of course, they figure prominently in the Aoi Matsuri. Not just as illustrations, for that matter; during the festival, the actual plant itself is also used. Those participating in the procession decorate their hats with *futaba aoi* leaves – thousands of leaves are used for this purpose every year.[6] Apparently, these leaves have long been used as decorative symbols – according to Nelson, 'the early Kamo people liberally decorated themselves and their horses with it' (2000: 78) – but they have largely disappeared from Kyoto's (sub)urban ecology, and today they are difficult to come by. In modern times, the number of *futaba aoi* growing in the forests in and around Kyoto is said to have decreased significantly (Morimoto 2003: 147) – probably related to the fact that many areas of broad-leaved forest have been replaced by coniferous forest, in which they cannot grow well because of a lack of sunlight, although there may be other causes as well. Presumably, then, the leaves used for today's *matsuri* are cultivated and purchased by (or donated to) the shrines, instead of harvested in the forest, as seems to have been the case in the medieval period. According to the shrine priest I interviewed twice (March and September 2011), there was a time when both the forest surrounding Kamigamo Jinja and the nearby Kamogawa river banks were full of these plants. Until well into the Edo period, he said, they grew there in abundance, but now they have disappeared almost completely. His objective was to reintroduce *futaba aoi* into the local ecosystem, so as to recreate the landscape of the past.

For this purpose, Afuhi Project has been established. It is legally registered as a non-profit organization, and therefore *de jure* independent from the shrine where its activities take place. *De facto*, however, the activities are sanctioned by and organized in cooperation with the shrine. As we have seen, the same applies to many other shrine-related non-profit organizations, such as the Sennen no Mori no Kai discussed in the previous chapter. In a country with a comparatively strict separation of state and religion such as Japan, shrines ('religious juridical persons', *shūkyō hōjin*) have limited leeway when it comes to organizing educational and social activities, or applying for public funding for the conservation of forests and buildings. Establishing non-profit organizations – in cooperation with scientists and scholars, local politicians, entrepreneurs, schools and so on – has become a common tactic for shrines to extend their scope and become active in educational and conservation activities. In other words, establishing this kind of semi-public non-profit organizations in cooperation with non-clergy outsiders allows them to become more active in civil society, while also increasing the possibilities for fundraising. Afuhi Project is no exception.

Afuhi is the same word as *aoi*, transcribed according to classical Japanese *kana* spelling. There are two reasons why the choice to write *aoi* as *afuhi* is significant. First, transcribing the word according to the archaic spelling instead of the modern Japanese pronunciation is a discursive strategy for establishing the connection between today's project and classical Japanese culture. Hence, it gives the project an air of authenticity and tradition.[7] Second, the spelling *afuhi* allows for a double entendre: if written in *kana* instead of the Chinese character (i.e. あ ふ ひ instead of 葵), it may also be read as 'the day of an unexpected encounter' (*meguri au hi*). This may not only refer to a meeting between people but also to an encounter between people and the divine. Thus, the plant *futaba aoi* symbolizes social encounters, as well as the establishment of relationships and mutual dependence: between different people, between humans and nature, and between humans and the divine. As a symbol, then, *aoi* functions similarly as *chinju no mori*, to which the same qualities are attributed. In this project, the *futaba aoi* has come to represent more than only 'traditional culture': it has now been reinterpreted as a symbol for the revitalization of interhuman, human-nature and human-*kami* relations *in today's Japan.* Hence, their reintroduction into the shrine forest and surrounding ecosystem is about more than forest conservation: it is about the reestablishment of social harmony.

I deliberately use the word 'reestablishment' here, for Afuhi Project is similar to other expressions of the Shinto environmentalist paradigm in its understanding of the modern period as a time characterized by social, cultural and ecological decline, which should be overcome by means of a return to 'ancient' values and practices. The disappearance of *futaba aoi* from local ecosystems is seen not just as an environmental problem that must be solved, but as a *symptom* of this general state of decline. Their reintroduction is framed in terms of environmental restoration, but also as a means to revitalize traditional culture. As the current president of the organization, Haga Tōru (a professor in comparative literature from Tokyo University) writes:

> For us Japanese, *aoi* represent the 'homeland of our hearts' (*kokoro no furusato*). In our original landscape (*genfūkei*), these plants were widespread. We are very worried about the fact that the plants have gradually disappeared from Japan's fields as a result of environmental change. Might it be that, together with the *aoi*, we have lost the richness of our heart (*kokoro no uruoi*), the very roots of Japanese culture? By all means, let us once more restore the beauty of the *aoi* throughout the archipelago. (Haga n.d.)

As this quotation illustrates, nostalgia is a core motive behind this and similar projects: environmental and cultural conservation practices are carried out in order to re-establish the social relations, moral values and natural landscapes that are believed to have been (nearly) lost. That, at least, is how those who organize and describe these projects tend to explain their significance, in a veritable 'discourse of the vanishing', to borrow Marilyn Ivy's term (1995). The difference between these practices and the cases discussed by Ivy is that, in the last decade or so, environmental issues have taken centre stage in nostalgic notions of decline and related hopes of resurrection. Nearly all the shrine priests (from Kamigamo Jinja, Shimogamo Jinja, Ise Jingū and various smaller shrines) and Shinto scholars (Kamata Tōji, Sonoda Minoru and Ueda Masaaki) whom I met in the course of my research deplored the condition of the environment, stating that it is our urgent responsibility as humans to solve the current crisis. Although nature conservation is not necessarily their primary objective, they all employ environmentalist rhetoric and express a concern for environmental problems. Yet nearly all of them linked the state of the natural environment to the state of the nation, which, they believed, was characterized by widespread moral and cultural decline. Environmental issues were seen first and foremost as a moral and spiritual problem, rather than a political or technological one. Thus, nostalgic environmentalism is clearly compatible with other types of nostalgia, including nationalism.

Afuhi Project is primarily concerned with education. Its main purpose is to contribute to teaching the next generation 'traditional Japanese culture', of which environmental ethics is believed to be an integral part. The core practice of Afuhi Project consists of giving pots with small *futaba aoi* plants to children of primary school age. These children raise and take care of the plants – supervised by their parents, of course – for one year. Afterwards, they are supposed to return them to the shrine, so that the plants can be planted in the precincts (which the children may do themselves). Thus they contribute to the shrine regaining its alleged former landscape. By taking part in this process, then, the children become symbolically involved with the shrine, and perhaps establish a personal relationship with it. Most plants are distributed by schools cooperating with the project, but it is also possible for individual citizens or families to purchase a plant, raise it, and return it to the shrine. At several Kamigamo Jinja *matsuri* and other events, a small Afuhi Project stand is present, selling pots and trying to raise money by selling souvenirs such as T-shirts and badges.⁸ As a result of these activities, the number of *aoi* plants on the shrine precincts has increased. When I last visited the shrine, in 2013, they mainly grew on the banks of the small stream running through the precincts.

The reintroduction of *futaba aoi* into the local ecosystem does raise a number of questions, however. First, if the ecological conditions that have led to the disappearance of these plants in the first place have not changed, will the plants be able to survive? Is the shrine forest not too dark for them to grow well? That would be an argument for felling some of the existing trees, as doing so would make the forest brighter. Yet, such a policy might not be in accordance with the notion that shrine trees are sacred and should be preserved. When I asked one of the organizers these questions, he responded by saying that he was not quite sure; first, they would have to replant the *aoi* and see if they can last. This raises a more fundamental question, however: what impact would the introduction of a large number of *futaba aoi* have on the local ecosystem? If the plans are indeed successful, and the forest will be planted full of *futaba aoi* as intended, will that make it more ecologically healthy? In other words, one might ask why the establishment of something resembling a plant monoculture should be more desirable than biodiversity. But then, perhaps the ideal of a forest almost completely made up of *futaba aoi* is based on their symbolic rather than ecological significance.

These are complicated questions, to which I have only received partial or vague answers – although this may have been partly due to my own lack of knowledge of local plant ecology. When I interviewed one of the project's organizers (September 2011), he did confirm that, in order for the *aoi* to grow well, different ecological factors must be taken into consideration – according to him, this was very difficult indeed, and it might not be established overnight. He also said that it was important to have ecological balance in the shrine forest – hence, the *aoi* should not become *too* dominant. Right now, however, the first challenge was to reintroduce them and make them grow well, he explained. It remains unclear, however, to what extent these ecological concerns are really taken into consideration. The Afuhi Project's objective to replant *futaba aoi* appears to be based on their symbolic significance and on the desire to recreate the landscape of the past, not on a well-informed vision of the local ecosystem.

Rather than nature conservation, then, Afuhi Project's main objective is something else: educating children in 'traditional culture' (*dentō bunka*), the ultimate purpose of which is to make them identify with Shinto in general, and Kamigamo Jinja in particular. After all, Shinto is not a membership-based religion, and as traditional *ujiko*-based identities and obligations are gradually eroding, shrines have to employ alternative strategies to secure their social status and central place within the local community. Educational activities constitute one such strategy. However, shrines' involvement in public education cannot be far-reaching, for that would violate the constitutional separation of state and religion. Establishing a non-profit organization like Afuhi Project, therefore, is a way for shrine actors to become active in fields that have been differentiated from 'religion', such as education. This is an example of *discursive secularization*, as explained in the introduction: the process by which beliefs, practices and institutions previously classified as 'religion' are redefined in alternative, explicitly non-religious terms.

The focus on educational activities is clearly visible not only in the plant-growing project but also in several of Afuhi Project's other events. I have already mentioned the *aoi ennichi* (shrine fair), which is organized annually for the purpose of improving the position of the shrine as a 'place of encounter' for members of the local neighbourhood community. One noteworthy event I attended when I took part in the 2011 *ennichi* was a workshop in 'traditional food culture', to which children living in the vicinity of the shrine had been invited. One of Kyoto's most famous restaurants had been found willing to send some of its cooks (*pro bono*, I was told) and provide ingredients for this purpose. All food was freshly made by the children, supervised by the cooks. It was absolutely delicious. Each dish was said to be 'traditionally' Japanese: there was no place for 'fusion kitchen' or other recent culinary inventions. Of course, rice was on the menu. The most interesting aspect of the workshop, however, was the ritual aspect. After the food had been prepared, it was offered to the gods of Kamigamo Jinja by one of the shrine priests. Before performing the ritual, the priest told the children about shrine mythology and explained them about the importance of gratitude to the deities. The children were ritually purified and prayed collectively, before they were finally allowed to eat the food they had made. Thus, under the label of 'traditional culture', the shrine actively tried to engage children in shrine mythology, ritual practice and belief. In other words, the event served as some sort of religious socialization in disguise. This illustrates how in contemporary Japan practices may be discursively secularized (i.e. they are reconfigured as 'culture', 'tradition' or 'heritage', not as '*shūkyō*') without losing their devotional aspects. Institutional actors are finding new, alternative ways to secure the continuation of beliefs, ritual practices and sacred places.

Several weeks later, I attended another Afuhi Project event. Unlike the shrine fair, this was not a public event. It was organized in cooperation with schools and took place at a nearby public primary school. The children here were visited by peers from a school in Shizuoka Prefecture, who had come to Kyoto on an excursion. The school from Shizuoka was chosen to take part in Afuhi Project because it is located near a shrine associated with the famous founder of the Tokugawa shogunate, Tokugawa Ieyasu (1543–1616), whose family emblem is also made up of *aoi* leaves. Children from the two different schools were seated at tables and ate lunch together; afterwards, each child gave a brief presentation about a place, festival or historical episode associated with their neighbourhood to the other children sitting at their table (there were about ten to twelve children at each table). Some of them had made big slides with colourful illustrations to support their presentation.

After this social exchange, the students from Shizuoka visited Kamigamo Jinja. It would have been an ordinary school trip, if it were not for the fact that the children did not merely receive a guided tour but were ritually purified, entered the inner precincts of the worship hall and attended a special prayer ceremony. Thus, despite

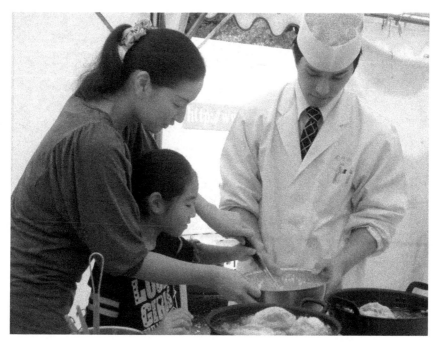

Figure 8.4 Cooking for the gods during the *aoi ennichi*, Kamigamo Jinja, Kyoto.

the fact that some of their teachers complained to me about the strict secularist laws forbidding them to teach children anything about Shinto, their pupils did take part in a ritual ceremony as part of a school trip – after having studied the history, *matsuri* and deities of their local shrine, and given presentations about these topics. Because of their school's involvement in the Afuhi Project, then, these children got to experience a ritual shrine ceremony and learn about Shinto.[9] This is another example of what I referred to above as 'religious socialization in disguise': Afuhi Project provides Kamigamo Jinja with the opportunity to teach the pupils of public schools about shrine beliefs and rituals – and indeed, let them take part in it – in ways that might not be possible otherwise. Although labelled as 'traditional culture' and arranged by a 'non-profit organization', the children did get education in shrine ritual and belief, however briefly.

Thus, under the banner of its non-profit organization, Kamigamo Jinja can offer a range of activities that allow it to engage potential future Shinto practitioners, gain media attention and positive publicity, redefine itself as a site of 'cultural' rather than 'religious' significance, and profile itself as environmentally and internationally oriented, in line with recent Jinja Honchō policies. There have also been 'internationalization' activities as part of the Afuhi Project; for instance, in May 2013, a group of Canadian high school students visited Kamigamo Jinja as part of an exchange program. Shrine priests explained them about *aoi* and 'Japanese culture' in general, after which the students tried their hand at calligraphy and made decorations of *futaba aoi* leaves. Kamigamo Jinja is also

Figure 8.5 Religious socialization during a school excursion, Kamigamo Jinja, Kyoto.

involved with the National Federation of UNESCO Associations in Japan, which has developed the Mirai Isan Undō ('Heritage for the future movement'): an initiative established to spread awareness of a number of different local projects, all of which seek to conserve and re-establish traditional natural landscapes and cultural practices through educational activities (Nihon Yunesuko Kyōkai Rengō n.d.). Not coincidentally, one of the main priorities of this organization is fundraising for the parts of Tohoku hit by the 2011 disasters: it provides financial support for schools, scholarships and social activities.

One of the important characteristics of initiatives such as Afuhi Project, then, is their bridge function: not only do they bring together environmental concerns and practices with education in 'traditional culture' (including Shinto ritual and mythology), they also contribute to the association of local issues (e.g. increasing neighbourhood children's interest and participation in shrine-based social activities) with issues of nationwide significance, such as the conservation of 'Japanese' nature and culture and the reconstruction of areas hit by disaster. By participating in fundraising activities and related practices, children symbolically take part in this reconstruction, and learn to identify not only with their local community but also with that larger imagined community, the nation. Afuhi Project is but one example of an initiative that is established in order to strengthen a sense of Japaneseness through establishing connections with a local community, its shrine and its natural landscape. A similar project has been developed at Meiji Jingū in Tokyo, as the following section will show.

The Emperor's Forest

On a rainy day in November 2011, I joined a group of Tokyoites on a special guided tour of the forest of Meiji Jingū, a well-known modern urban shrine that has become one of the city's most prominent tourist destinations. The event was organized by NPO Hibiki, a non-profit organization affiliated with the shrine, in cooperation with Shibuya University, another urban non-profit organization that offers excursions and workshops by artists, activists and other members of civil society. There were about twenty participants – somewhat lower than expected, but that was probably due to the bad weather. Most of them were in their twenties, with a few exceptions: there was also a middle-aged woman with her son (around eight years old), who had attended similar events previously. The tour was given by one of the leading members of NPO Hibiki, who told us some basic facts about the history and ecology of the forest, as well as the shrine itself. We also visited the shrine buildings, which was a completely new experience for some of the participants. They received a step-by-step instruction on how to wash their hands and rinse their mouth for purification at the *temizuya*, and even on how to pray in front of the *haiden*.

Following the tour of the shrine grounds, we visited a small garden, where dozens of seedlings were standing in pots. We were told that these would be sent to Tohoku, where they would be used for replanting forests. Afterwards, we spent some time collecting acorns in the surrounding forest, which would likewise be planted and sent elsewhere. This way, we were told, we could help 'rebuild' the areas that had been hit by the disasters. Everybody did their best to collect as many good acorns as possible (the acorns had to be whole; otherwise they could not grow into trees). Arguably, the practice had strong symbolic significance: by collecting and planting acorns 'for the people in Tohoku', participants could feel a connection to the victims and the areas in which they live and make a small yet meaningful contribution to their reconstruction. Through this symbolic practice, they became part of a nationwide movement, sharing in a newly imagined collective identity defined by the notions of restoration (*fukkō*) and (national) resurrection (*fukkatsu*).

Contrary to other shrine forests (e.g. Tadasu no Mori), tree-planting at the forest of Meiji Jingū is not common, as the forest was designed to be self-regenerating. Yet, the practice of collecting acorns and planting them in pots has been one of NPO Hibiki's main activities since its establishment in 2001. The seedlings are used for reforestation projects elsewhere, especially those set up by Miyawaki Akira's organization. After the disasters in 2011, many were sent to Tohoku, where they were used to replant *chinju no mori*, such as the one at Yaegaki Jinja. They have also been used for the 'Great Forest Wall': an ambitious project, set up by Miyawaki and his team, to build a 'wall' (or dam) along the coast of Tohoku made of debris on which trees are planted. The original plan was to build a wall of trees with a length of more than 300 kilometres, mainly consisting of 'indigenous' broad-leaved trees, for the purpose of protecting future generations from destructive tsunamis (e.g. Miyawaki 2013).[10] Needless to say, for such an ambitious reforestation project, large numbers of seedlings are needed. The seedlings from broad-leaved trees grown at Meiji Jingū are an important contribution to this project, we were told.[11]

Located behind Harajuku station, and surrounded by the trendy neighbourhoods of Shinjuku, Shibuya and Aoyama, the forest of Meiji Jingū is a unique area of urban woodland. The shrine and its forest have a total area of approximately 70 hectares, more than five times the size of Tadasu no Mori. This is one of Japan's best-known and wealthiest shrines, and one of the most popular places to visit for *hatsumōde*: on the first three days of January alone, more than three million people come here to pray for good luck, safety and prosperity (Cali & Dougill 2013: 80). But the shrine is popular year-round, and in addition to Japanese visitors is also frequented by foreign tourists.[12] Although the shrine and its forest may appear old and 'traditional' to many visitors, they are of relatively young age: construction began in 1915, and the shrine was not officially opened until 1920. Most of the current shrine buildings date from 1958, after the previous buildings had been destroyed in air raids.

The deities enshrined here are Emperor Meiji (1852–1912) and his wife, Empress Shōken (1849–1914). The establishment of the shrine coincided with and arguably played an important part in the popularization of imperial Shinto ideology and ritual in early twentieth century Japan. That does not mean the meanings attributed to it are unequivocal: from the time of its establishment until today, the exact shape and functions of the shrine and its forest have been subject to contestation, debate and alternative interpretations (Fujita et al. 2015; Imaizumi 2013). That was especially the case in the early post-war period, when Shinto had to be dissociated from imperial ideology and reinvented as an 'indigenous religious tradition'. Discussions did not only pertain to the shrine's new legal status but also to its physical shape; for instance, there was a debate about whether the new shrine buildings should be made of wood or concrete, reflecting different notions concerning the ideal shape of shrines (Imaizumi 2013: 242–245).

Despite its historical background, few visitors today associate Meiji Jingū with 'State Shinto' or Japanese imperialism. In sharp contrast to Yasukuni Jinja, Meiji Jingū has been successfully depoliticized and does not attract much controversy.[13] In 2009, it was visited by the US secretary of state Hillary Clinton; in subsequent years, several other foreign politicians followed her example. These visits indicate that the shrine is not widely associated with Japanese imperialism anymore, for if it had been, these foreign ministers would not have paid official visits. Instead, today Meiji Jingū is generally perceived in positive terms, as a vestige of 'traditional Japanese culture' and a 'green oasis' surrounded by concrete jungle. In popular media and on tourist websites, it is praised for its natural beauty, quietness, fresh air and cultural values. In addition, various sacred and spiritual qualities are attributed to the forest, which houses one of Japan's most popular 'powerspots'.[14]

One aspect of Meiji Jingū that has captured the imagination of scholars and visitors alike is its forest. It is sometimes called Yoyogi Forest (Yoyogi no Mori) – not to be confused with Yoyogi Park (Yoyogi Kōen), which lies next to it – but usually it is referred to simply as 'the forest of Meiji Jingū' (Meiji Jingū no Mori). The forest of Meiji Jingū is a mixed forest of approximately 160,000 trees, comprising over

240 species (Meiji Jingū Shamusho 1999: 93, 98), and it constitutes an interesting paradox. On the one hand, it is an artificial forest, completely designed and created by humans. Most specialists will be able to recognize it as such, because the diversity of tree species is much higher than in any 'natural' forest (Meiji Jingū Shamusho 1999: 185). On the other hand, this forest was designed to *become* a 'natural' forest; that is, a forest that is self-regenerating and needs very little maintenance. The website of Meiji Jingū even claims that 'after about 90 years it cannot be distinguished from a natural forest' (Meiji Jingu n.d.). One journalist has described it as follows:

> Meiji Jingū is a 'constructed forest' (*tsukurareta mori*), and many researchers come to have a look at it, even from overseas. Actually, there are other 'constructed forests' elsewhere in Japan, so what is special about this forest? The answer is: this is a *chinju no mori*. It is not a forest made for wood production, but it was made based on the thought 'let's make a natural forest' for the gods to reside (*kamigami no shizumaru 'tennen shizen no mori ni shiyō' to iu mori-zukuri no kangaekata*). That is very different from other forests. (Aomame 2010: 12)

As this citation suggests, Meiji Jingū was designed and constructed by people, but it was designed in such a way that it would become by and large self-regenerating – not temporarily, but permanently. Thus, it has been referred to as a project to 'create an ever-lasting *chinju no mori*' (*eien ni tsuzuku chinju no mori o tsukuru*) (Aomame 2010: 6). In a way, this can be seen as the ultimate naturalization project: a deeply politically embedded historical construction that is the site of (potentially) contested memories, the shrine was quite literally dehistoricized by creating an 'eternal' and 'natural' forest at its site. Arguably, then, Barthes' theory on myth-making – a myth is 'depoliticized speech' employed to naturalize historical constructions (Barthes 1957: 217) – is not only applicable to texts but may also help us explain certain landscape production processes. Places that are associated with collective memory and identity are often naturalized: their own construction processes are concealed, as are the historical and political factors involved in these. This is done not only discursively but also spatially, by means of nature-making activities. Put differently, these places are the outcome of human production processes, yet the circumstances, agendas and contingencies that have shaped these processes are no longer visible, as they have come to be perceived as 'natural' – either in the literal or in the metaphorical sense of the word. This, in my opinion, is an important reason why many Shinto ideologues today insist that shrine forests are *mori*, rather than *hayashi* or *kōen* (parks): by doing so, they are configured as 'natural' (i.e. ahistorical) space, no matter how artificial many of them are.

'Natural' though the forest may seem today, when it was designed, the forest's shape and composition were subject to heated debate. The only part of the shrine forest that already existed at the time was the Edo-period garden now known as the Meiji Jingū *gyoen* (imperial garden), which had been given to the imperial family in the Meiji period (see Meiji Jingū Shamusho 1999: 72–92). Today, this garden is still famous for its irises, as well as for 'powerspot' Kiyomasa's Well.[15] The surrounding area mainly consisted of wasteland and fields, so most of the forest had to be planted anew (Aomame 2010: 12). In the early Taishō period, a committee was established for designing and constructing the shrine and its forest. Several well-known scientists joined this committee. One of them was Honda Seiroku (1866–1952), a forest scientist and landscape architect holding a PhD from the University of Munich, who has designed several of Japan's modern urban parks, including Hibiya Park in Tokyo (Imaizumi 2013: 34; Meiji Jingū Shamusho 1999: 168). Honda developed a plan for a new shrine forest, but it did not go unchallenged. As Imaizumi summarizes, 'The creation of a "sacred" and "solemn" shrine forest was desired by all those involved with planning the shrine and its surroundings. However, exactly what constituted a shrine's forest "sacredness" and "solemnity", and how to differentiate it from the "park", became topics of considerable debate in the planning stage' (2013: 34–35).

Honda wanted the newly planted forest to be an evergreen broad-leaved forest (or laurel forest), with *kashi*, *shii* and *kusunoki* as its main species. These were more suitable to the Tokyo climatological and geographical conditions than coniferous trees, he argued, and would fit well in a naturally regenerating forest (Meiji Jingū Shamusho 1999: 170–175; Ueda 2015: 224–225). This notion has become paradigmatic in recent decades, but in the pre-war period it was by no means self-evident. Honda's plan was opposed by Home Minister Ōkuma Shigenobu (1838–1922),[16] who wanted the new forest to be made up of *sugi*, just as those of Ise Jingū and Nikkō Tōshōgū. 'A mixed forest that looks like a thicket is not suitable for a shrine (*yabu no yō na zōkibayashi de wa jinja rashiku nai*)' (Meiji Jingū Shamasho 1999: 171–172), Ōkuma argued, reflecting the dominant aesthetics at the time. A shrine forest, it was commonly believed, should be made up of old, majestic coniferous trees such as *sugi* or *hinoki*, giving it a dark and mysterious atmosphere. In the end, however, Honda managed to convince Ōkuma and the others by using scientific arguments, and his plan for a self-regenerating mixed forest was accepted (Imaizumi 2013: 38–39).[17]

When it comes to the aesthetics of shrine forests, then, it may be argued that Honda's design constituted the first step towards the post-war paradigm shift: 'native' trees gradually replaced *sugi* and *hinoki* as the trees of choice, and the ideal of a dark coniferous forest gave way to mixed or broad-leaved forests characterized by brightness and species diversity. As such, Honda was one of the intellectual predecessors of Miyawaki Akira, whose ideal *chinju no mori* consists of indigenous *furusato* trees; it is perhaps no coincidence that both are German-educated scientists. As the forest of Meiji Jingū grew older, and its trees more impressive, it has come to receive much attention and is now seen as an example for other human-made *chinju no mori*. Its founder, meanwhile, is praised for his visionary forest design.

The species composition of Meiji Jingū's forest is not the only reason why it is seen as a paradigmatic case of *chinju no mori*-making, however. As we have seen, a core aspect of *chinju no mori*-related discourse and practices is the notion of community. Shrine forests are seen by many as a tool (or even as a prerequisite) for the re-establishment of social relationships among community members and, hence, a sense of collective belonging, either on a local or a national level. Significantly, the construction of the Meiji Jingū forest (i.e. the planting of trees) was not done by professionals but by thousands of volunteers. It was a collective project, in which over 110,000 people are said to have participated (Saigusa 2005). The symbolic significance of this should not be underestimated: instead of being seen as a state-imposed institution, it established Meiji Jingū as a collective memorial site. That is, by involving citizens in the construction process, the forest was symbolically turned into a 'people's forest'; it came to be widely perceived as a 'spontaneous', bottom-up expression of the people's patriotism and love for the deceased emperor, rather than a state-produced sacred space that would become an intrinsic part of the dominant ritual-ideological system. In other words, involving massive numbers of citizens in the forest planting process was an effective political strategy for socializing them into the imperial ritual-ideological system, which ultimately served to legitimize the ruling powers.

Interestingly, Meiji Jingū keeps a record of all its trees. The total number of planted trees in the forest is 122,572, of which 95,559 were donated (Meiji Jingū Shamusho 1999: 98) – an impressive number indeed. The seedlings did not come from a single plantation but were literally shipped from all over the empire. As local communities throughout the country donated young trees or seedlings for the newly planted forest, these communities, too, could symbolically take part in its construction. And as it is made up of trees coming from all over Japan, Meiji Jingū transcends its particular locality; in other words, because of the multi-rootedness (no pun intended) of its thousands of trees, as a symbolic space it encompasses the entire country. Hence, unlike most other shrines, it belongs to the nation as a whole, not to any particular local community. Operating as simultaneously a physical and a mental space – constituting a space that is both material *and* imagined – the forest's physical features (i.e. its pan-Japanese tree composition) have contributed to it being conceived of as a space of nationwide significance. And not just nationwide, for that matter: the forest also has trees from Taiwan, the Korean Peninsula, Manchuria and Sakhalin (Meiji Jingū Shamusho 1999: 177) – Japan's colonial possessions at the time – clearly pointing to its imperial legacy.[18]

Today, there are still people who wish to donate and plant a tree in the Meiji Jingū forest, but their requests are not normally granted. The forest has now reached the stage where it resembles a natural forest; if new trees were planted, the forest's 'natural' conditions might be disturbed (Meiji Jingū Shamusho 1999: 184). Likewise, shrine actors often point out that forest maintenance is kept to an absolute minimum, as the forest should grow 'naturally': reportedly, 'even shrine forest managers are prohibited from picking fruit from the trees or from bringing out even a single dead leaf' (Saigusa 2005). Nevertheless, there are more than twenty people employed by the shrine for doing forest-related maintenance work (Meiji Jingū Shamusho 1999: 159). Some of them (the so-called *hakiyasan*) are responsible for keeping the grounds clean: every day, seven people sweep leaves of the main path, back into the forest (they are not thrown away, as fallen leaves are an integral part of the forest ecosystem). In addition, there are several forest specialists employed by the shrine. They monitor forest growth, remove dead trees, take measures to protect trees from diseases and parasites and so on (Meiji Jingū Shamusho 1999: 159–162). Thus, 'natural' though the forest may be, it is still controlled and 'kept tidy' by people. In sum, rather than a 'wild' forest left to its own devices, the forest of Meiji Jingū is a human-nature co-product, not only because it was designed and constructed by humans but also because it continues to be used and influenced by them. As such, it belongs to the realms of 'culture' and 'politics' as much as it constitutes 'nature'.

This brings us back to the activities of NPO Hibiki. The active participation and dedication of more than 110,000 tree-planting volunteers in 1920 is an important part of Meiji Jingū's foundation narrative. It is not very surprising, therefore, that these volunteers are presented as an example for today's youth. NPO Hibiki was founded in 2001 and was officially registered as a non-profit organization (*NPO hōjin*) in 2003. It organizes a variety of activities, mostly for people in their twenties, although there are also elderly people among the volunteers. These activities take place regularly. They are divided into three categories, called the 'greenery program', the 'rice farming program' and the 'international cultural exchange program'. Each programme has its own group of volunteers, usually referred to as the 'acorn team' (*donguri chiimu*), the 'rice paddy team' (*tanbo*

Figure 8.6 Forest maintenance, Meiji Jingū, Tokyo. The forest of Meiji Jingū is self-regenerating, and fallen leaves are an important part of the ecosystem, so they are swept from the path back into the forest.

chiimu) and the 'international cultural exchange team' (*kokusai bunka kōryū chiimu*). In addition to the 'general activities' employed by these three different teams, there are also a number of *ad hoc* activities. Some of these involve outsiders, such as groups of school children or white-collar workers, who visit the shrine forest and collect acorns as part of school- or company-imposed excursions. There are also special activities for volunteers, such as summer camps or workshops, and of course various promotional activities (fundraising activities, keeping a blog and a Facebook page, running information stands at cultural events and so on). These promotional activities are usually done by people who have been active as volunteers for a long time, as well as by the Hibiki president, who is employed by Meiji Jingū.

As their activities typically take place at the same time (usually on weekend days), there is little interaction between members of the different teams, other than greetings at the beginning and end of the day. I was told that volunteers do not usually take part in more than one program; switching activities is uncommon, and there seems to be quite a bit of competition between the different teams. Hence, if a person wants to become active as a volunteer for NPO Hibiki, they also have to choose which of the three teams they want to belong to. While the total number of people registered as volunteers at any given moment may well be over a hundred, not all of them participate regularly. When I took part in a day of 'general activities' (in May 2013), in which all three teams engaged in their respective practices (simultaneously), there were approximately forty people. They were divided more or less equally among the three teams (the rice paddy team seemed slightly bigger than the other two, but as there was no single collective moment to mark the beginning of the day's activities I did not have the opportunity to actually count the number of people). I was told that the number of participants was a bit higher than usual, which may have been due to the lovely sunny weather.

The first of the three programs is called the 'greenery program', and it is here that the organization's environmental agenda is expressed. In the shrine brochure, an explicit association is made between the construction of Meiji Jingū's forest in the Taishō period on the one hand, and today's environmental problems on the other. At the time of construction,

> About 110,000 young people volunteered to plant trees on the barren ground. Thanks to the dedication and perseverance of the supporters, the grounds turned into a unique man-made forest. [Now,] environmental problems have become serious worldwide, and to combat this, greenery activities are gaining force. In order to create a new forest, we grow new trees from the acorns on the ground. We promote ecological activities and spiritual training through the process. We believe that this program helps to pass down our traditional Japanese value for nature from generation to generation. (NPO Hibiki n.d.)

Today's generation, it is suggested, should learn from the dedication of earlier generations and engage in similar tree-planting activities as expressions of the traditional Japanese appreciation of nature. Thus, the greenery program's core practice consists of collecting acorns (*donguri*), planting them in pots and raising the seedlings. As mentioned, most of the young trees cultivated by volunteers of NPO Hibiki are *not* replanted in the forest of Meiji Jingū, but sent elsewhere – since 2011, many have been used for reforestation initiatives in Tohoku.

The second programme is called the 'rice farming program'. This project is also framed in terms of the preservation of Japanese tradition and presented as a countermeasure against cultural degradation. In typical nostalgic terminology, the brochure describes it as follows:

> Due to the development of technology, our modern lives have become more and more convenient, but at the same time, our tradition, culture and spirit are gradually disappearing. Since the Japanese were an agricultural people, rice farming is influential to our culture and lifestyle. (…) In the rice farming program, we handle all the processes of farming rice by hand, without the use of chemicals or machines. We use the wisdom of our ancestors and draw from their imagination, ideas, and patience. (NPO Hibiki n.d.)

The rice farming activities take place at a tiny rice paddy, in a little-visited part of the forest, north of the shrine. There is nothing particularly noteworthy about a shrine having its own rice paddy: many shrines have (or had) small rice paddies where

Figure 8.7 Seedlings that have grown from acorns collected and planted by NPO Hibiki volunteers. Most of these were sent to Tohoku for reforestation projects, such as the one at Yaegaki Jinja. Meiji Jingū, Tokyo.

ceremonies are conducted, called *shinsenden* ('paddy for rice offerings'). Indeed, even the imperial palace has a small paddy, where the emperor is said to grow rice and perform rituals. What is special, however, is that a modern urban shrine such as Meiji Jingū has a rice paddy, constructed and cultivated by volunteers doing hard manual labour on their free Sundays in order to symbolically take part in the (agri)cultural traditions of their ancestors, while shrine priests show up only for the occasional ceremony. The symbolic significance of having a sacred rice paddy (no matter how small) in downtown Tokyo should not be underestimated: it is a strategy for establishing a symbolic connection between the modern big city society and the imagined ancestral past. Moreover, rice-related rituals are believed to constitute an important part of Shinto ritual practices – and, indeed, are often referred to by representatives of the Shinto environmentalist paradigm in order to illustrate Shinto's alleged intertwinement with nature – so it is not very surprising that Meiji Jingū sanctions this sort of activities.

When I visited the rice paddy in May 2013, there were about fifteen to twenty volunteers, most of them in their late twenties or thirties. They had worked for several hours, and were still busy digging and moving rain water from a temporary basin to the paddy (it was not enough, so they had to add tap water as well). I did not have rubber boots, so I could not participate myself, but I did get the opportunity to talk to some of the volunteers. Their reasons for joining were diverse. Several of the volunteers had office jobs and had to works indoors five days a week; they liked the physical labour, and they liked being able to work outdoors, in nature. Others

Figure 8.8 NPO Hibiki volunteers working on the rice paddy of Meiji Jingū, Tokyo.

mentioned the cultural value of rice cultivation, suggesting that they wanted to contribute to maintaining this aspect of traditional Japanese culture. One young man had a different story. For him, working on a rice paddy associated with a shrine was an active act of worship; he described it as a way not only to stay in touch with nature but also with the divine powers residing in it, and to show them his reverence and gratitude.

Before my brief visit to the rice paddy, I joined members of the 'international cultural exchange team' in their activities. These activities have little to do with 'nature' as such. Their main objective is 'internationalization', that is, teaching foreign tourists about Meiji Jingū and about 'Japanese culture' in general. This is done by means of free guided walks. Starting at the main *torii*, the guided walks include some basic information about the history of the shrine, its garden, the large sake and wine barrels next to the main path (which capture the imagination of many foreign visitors), the *temizuya* (including an instruction on the proper way to wash one's hands and rinse one's mouth), the two *shinboku* trees and the main hall (where Shinto prayer customs are explained, and visitors are invited to say a prayer or make a wish themselves[19]). All volunteers were laypeople, and not all of them were particularly well-schooled in shrine beliefs and practices. Interestingly, the contents of the guided walk were not prescribed very strictly, and I had the impression that there was quite some difference between the volunteers. There also seemed to be considerable variety in English language skills, and communication between volunteers and tourists did not always go very smoothly. That said, NPO Hibiki explicitly tells its volunteers that the guided walks are *not* the same as tours conducted by experts; their main purpose is not education but cultural exchange and social interaction. Hence, volunteers were encouraged not only to tell visitors about Japanese culture but also ask them about their countries of origin.

Although there were a few young people as well, most volunteers in the 'cultural exchange team' were older than those in the other teams: there were several middle-aged and elderly people. In contrast to the volunteers in the 'acorn' and 'rice paddy' teams, they did not seem particularly interested in Shinto, nor in nature or environmental issues. Instead, they had other motivations for joining. One man participated because his company ordered its employees to spend a few hours a week doing 'volunteer' work, and this was one of the more attractive options. Another man said he was doing this because he was retired, enjoyed being active, and liked talking to foreigners. Somebody else wanted to work as a professional tour guide in the future and saw this as a good opportunity to practice. One young woman said that after she had graduated from high school and had not passed the university entrance exam, her parents encouraged her to do something useful, like volunteering work; as she had often visited Meiji Jingū as a child and felt a special connection to this shrine, she wanted to join Hibiki. Some others joined because it gave them the opportunity to practise and improve their English speaking skills.

In sum, NPO Hibiki is a bit of a mixed bag. The 'international cultural exchange program' seems quite different from the other activities, both in terms of volunteers' motivations and contents. Nevertheless, for a religion that continues to be perceived negatively and associated with wartime imperialism (by some, at least), PR activities are of crucial importance. Shinto institutions are actively trying to rebrand their tradition as an ancient, peaceful nature religion, intrinsically Japanese yet tolerant and internationally oriented. Meiji Jingū has been one of the leading shrines in this respect, funding scholarships for foreign graduate students and sending priests abroad in order to study English and give lectures on Shinto. 'International exchange' activities are in full accordance with that trend.

Most interestingly, the practice to collect and plant acorns, raise seedlings, and send them to other parts of the country for reforestation projects mirrors the history of Meiji Jingū's forest, when trees from all over the country were sent to Tokyo for the purpose of constructing a new sacred forest. It creates similar symbolic connections, once again turning Meiji Jingū into a place of nationwide significance that transcends its particular locality, even though the seedlings now travel in the opposite direction. In fact, it may even be seen as a contemporary version of the traditional practice by powerful shrines to establish smaller auxiliary shrines in the province; the main difference being that, in this case, it is not the gods themselves that are replanted in other places, but their trees. Thus, by collecting acorns from Meiji Jingū's sacred shrine forest, we all participated in the reconstruction of Tohoku, one tree at a time – even if that participation was of a highly symbolic nature and limited in impact.

Chapter 9

GOING GREEN, GOING GLOBAL

The Sun Goddess' Forest

In my introduction, I described the recurrent interest in Ise Jingū as the sacred centre of the Japanese nation, a view that is advocated not only by Jinja Honchō but also by Prime Minister Abe and his allies. In this last chapter, I will return to this topic, examining the role of nature symbolism in Ise's most recent resignification: its transformation into a site of 'ancient sustainability' embodying the nation's primordial love of nature.[1] In the years preceding the 2013 *shikinen sengū*, Ise Jingū was framed not only as Japan's *furusato* but also as its foremost *chinju no mori*, symbolically uniting the entire national collective body (*kyōdōtai*) amidst its sacred trees. Correspondingly, the production forest located near the shrine, the *kyūikirin*, has come to signify ancient Japanese ecological wisdom and natural beauty – despite the fact that the forest in its current shape does not date back further than the Taishō period. In this chapter, I will analyse these new representations of Ise and its forest.

The shrines of Ise are without a doubt among the most important, oldest, best-known and most-visited shrines in Japan – especially the two largest, the Inner Shrine (Naikū) and the Outer Shrine (Gekū), which make up Ise Jingū together with approximately 125 smaller shrines. They played a central part in the development of *kami* cults in the medieval period, which preceded and influenced pre-modern conceptualizations of Shinto as the 'indigenous', pre-Buddhist worship tradition of Japan (Breen & Teeuwen 2017; Teeuwen 2007). In the Edo period, Ise was one of the country's most popular pilgrimage destinations, attracting millions of visitors; during this time, it was the centre of numerous popular cults, many of them incorporating elements from Buddhism and other worship traditions (Davis 1992: 45–80). In the Meiji period, the shrines went through some significant transformations. Reconceived as the ancestral shrine of the imperial family, Ise Jingū was incorporated into the modern nation-building project and came to constitute an integral part of the state cult and ideology.

In the post-war period, Ise Jingū has become a 'religious institution' like all other shrines, but it continues to be widely perceived as a place of nationwide significance. It is here that some of Japan's oldest traditions are said to have been preserved. Accordingly, Ise has a special status within Jinja Honchō as the most important shrine complex in the country. It has been redefined as the ancestral homeland not only of the emperor but of the Japanese nation as a whole, not least in PR campaigns – as illustrated by the popular slogan *Nihonjin no kokoro no furusato* (literally: 'ancestral village of the Japanese people's hearts'), used to attract visitors. Ise Jingū is widely considered as the most sacred site in Shinto, and many of Jinja Honchō's policies are geared towards raising money for its rebuilding every twenty years (Breen 2010b). As Breen and Teeuwen have rightly pointed out, in modern Shinto, Ise has a 'central position'; simultaneously, however, it 'is in many senses a very exceptional shrine, and perhaps the least representative of them all' (2010: 22).

In the course of history, the meanings attributed to the shrines of Ise have been subject to continuous change. Considering the proliferation of the Shinto environmentalist paradigm, it should come as no surprise that today Ise is redefined as the quintessential example of the ancient 'Shinto' spirit of harmonious coexistence with nature. This is very clear, for instance, at the Sengūkan: a new museum near the Outer Shrine, opened in 2012, which has impressive exhibitions on various crafts and (agri)cultural traditions associated with Ise and the *shikinen sengū*. As suggested by these exhibitions, Ise's ancient ecological knowledge is preserved in the traditional practices carried out in connection with the shrine, such as ritualized rice cultivation, salt production and traditional building techniques. Similar images have been spread in photo exhibitions elsewhere, in documentaries (Miyazawa 2014; NHK 2013) and in popular books (e.g. Inata 2009). Ise is framed as a site of great natural beauty, ecological diversity and an age-old culture-nature equilibrium supposedly preserved in forestry, rice cultivation and fishery practices. This equilibrium is characterized by the harmonious interaction between the forest, the sea, the rice paddies, the shrine and the human community, which together constitute an integrated whole, representing the ideal symbiosis between *fūdo* and *kyōdōtai*.

As mentioned previously, the *shikinen sengū* is the ritualized reconstruction and replacement of all shrine buildings, which in modern times has taken place every twenty years, and which dates back to the seventh century.[2] In recent years, this practice has come to be redefined as a sustainable tradition that contains important 'hints' for the twenty-first-century world. While it may be argued that completely rebuilding an entire shrine complex every twenty years is a waste of resources and therefore unsustainable,[3] the exact opposite argument is made: in shrine publications, popular books and scholarly texts alike, the *shikinen sengū* is lauded as an environmentally friendly practice that may serve as an example for the rest of the world. In these texts, the *sengū* is described as a process that is imbued with a spirit of gratitude to nature, intimately connected to the shrine's physical environment. The following quotation from an English-language brochure is illustrative of this reinterpretation:

> Since ancient times, people have enjoyed the gifts provided by nature: food, clothing and lodging. Over the centuries, the caretakers of the Grand Shrine of Ise have taken a conservation approach by preserving the natural resources

of the area and planted and maintained the vast forests that surround the sacred landmark. After millennia of use, clean water still flows down from the mountains, replenishing the fields and the crops that are grown there, flowing on to the sea nearby, where it provides the healthy environment from which nourishing plant and animal sea life is harvested. (...) the Grand Shrine has protected to date the benefits of nature through the ceremonies and festivals for the deities. (Public Affairs Headquarters for Shikinen-Sengu 2010: 8)

One of the aspects of the *shikinen sengū* that has drawn the attention of scholars is the craftsmanship and traditional use of materials involved. Not only the shrine buildings are reproduced: every twenty years, new lacquerware, textiles, jewellery, swords and other items are made. Still, it is the architecture that fascinates most – in particular, the use of ancient building techniques believed to predate the introduction of continental architecture (with some adaptations, admittedly) (Adams 1998; Hvass 1999). In construction practices, too, Shinto's respect for and gratitude to nature is recognized. The following description by architect Cassandra Adams is typical of this interpretation:

One group of [construction] rituals marks activities that disturb the natural environment, such as tree harvesting and ground breaking. Consistent with the ancient Shinto understanding of the interdependence of human life and the natural world, these rituals are intended to thank and appease the *kamis* (deities) for the lives that are being extinguished. From the workers' viewpoint, these apologetic actions protect them from heavenly recrimination for the harm they cause by their activities. This group of rituals reveals a major ethical difference between Japanese and western relationships to nature. (...) The core of the difference between these two perspectives is that the ancient Shinto view acknowledged the dependence that humans have on nature for their livelihood, a condition that many westerners (and many modern Japanese) do not appear to understand or act on. (1998: 55–56)

Of course, Adams' interpretation can be challenged. As discussed in Chapter 3, the projection of contemporary notions of 'nature' and 'the environment' onto traditional practices and worldviews is anachronistic. The performance of a certain ritual for a tree that is felled does not tell us anything about ancient attitudes to 'nature', for that tree was not conceptualized as 'nature' (and placed in opposition to 'culture') until the modern period. Even when focusing on the contemporary period, the fact that trees are ritually greeted and thanked when they are felled does not tell us anything about environmental attitudes *per se*; all it shows is that tree-felling is a ritualized practice, which may or may not be traced back to notions of trees as spirited (and, accordingly, in need of ritual pacification), but which is primarily performed because it is part of the prescribed ritual repertoire. And even *if* the labourers felling the trees were filled with a profound sense of reverence and gratitude, that in itself would still not tell us anything about the environmental impact of their activities (or lack thereof), as attitudes do not necessarily correspond to practices. Indeed, as Arne Kalland so compellingly argued (2002), pacification rituals do not guarantee the sustainable use of resources; they can just as easily be used to justify their overexploitation.

Regardless of their validity, however, explanations such as the one above are typical of contemporary interpretations of the *shikinen sengū*. The Ise rebuilding process is regularly described as recycling *avant la lettre*, and therefore seen as a great example of the sustainability and environmental knowledge supposedly present in 'ancient Shinto' (e.g. Satō 2008). This claim is based on the fact that if it has not decayed too much, wood of the former shrine buildings is used for other constructions in the Ise shrine complex, as well as for shrines elsewhere in the country:

> The timbers removed when the Shrine is rebuilt are distributed to shrines throughout Japan, where they are reused, particularly to disaster or earthquake-stricken regions. Some of the sacrificial offerings and other contents of the Shrine are also distributed among other shrines. Following the 61st Shikinen Sengu [in 1993], lumber and contents of the Shrine were distributed among 169 shrines throughout Japan. (Public Affairs Headquarters for Shikinen-Sengu 2010: 14)

Thus, the *shikinen sengū* has come to be redefined as an ecologically sustainable tradition, even though the architectural techniques used are perhaps not so sustainable after all: they lead to the quick decay of building materials, which is why the buildings needed to be replaced regularly in the first place. In any case, it requires a significant amount of timber, which is one of the reasons Ise Jingū has such a sizeable forest – significantly larger than most other shrine forests in Japan. But then, this is not a shrine forest in the ordinary sense of the word. Accordingly, it was not typically referred to as a *chinju no mori*, at least until recently. The shrine management divides the forest into different sections. The first section is similar to shrine forests elsewhere and is referred to by the name *shin'iki*, which may be translated as 'divine area'. These are the areas of forest surrounding the shrines, which more or less correspond to *chinju no mori* elsewhere. As explained in the information brochure published by the shrine forest management department, 'the divine area is strictly protected from cutting to preserve its holiness, and nature has been carefully conserved' (Jingū Shichō Eirinbu n.d.: 3). That does not mean, of course, that these are 'natural' forests not influenced by human activities. They are particularly famous for their old planted *sugi* trees. In fact, the entire spatial configuration of the shrines is the outcome of human planning and has been subject to various historical transformations, not least in the modern period. For instance, the park-like approach to Naikū (between Uji bridge and the *temizuya*) was designed and constructed in the Meiji period as a *shin'en* (divine garden); it differs significantly from the pre-Meiji landscape (Breen 2015: 46–59; Taniguchi 2016). Today, various forest maintenance activities take place here, ranging from sweeping the path to taking protective measures against parasites in order to preserve old trees.

Figure 9.1 For some months prior to the 2013 *shikinen sengū*, old and new shrine buildings could be seen next to each other at Ise Jingū. Built with traditional techniques, the wood of these shrines decays rapidly.

With total areas of, respectively, 93 ha and 90 ha, Naikū and Gekū have comparatively large shrine precincts (the forest of Meiji Jingū has a size of approximately 70 ha; Tadasu no Mori is merely 12 ha).[4] However, this is still very small compared to the main forest, which is referred to by the term *kyūikirin* (translated as 'sanctuary forest'). The *kyūikirin* is divided into two types, which are called *daiichi kyūikirin* ('first sanctuary forest area') and *daini kyūikirin* ('second sanctuary forest area'). They have a size of, respectively, 1,094 ha and 4,352 ha. The former consists primarily of broad-leaved trees (925 ha), with small areas of coniferous forest (*sugi* 87 ha; *hinoki* 75 ha). The latter is a mixed forest: it consists for a large part of planted *hinoki* trees (2,459 ha), which are used as material for shrine buildings, but there is also a significant proportion of broad-leaved trees (1,708 ha), as well as some *sugi*. The main difference between the first and the second *kyūikirin* is that the former is not used for production, and is considered 'natural' and 'sacred', similar to the *shin'iki* areas. The second *kyūikirin*, on the other hand, is used for growing timber and other purposes. It is further divided into so-called special-operation areas – forest areas along rivers and roads, which are not used for timber production, and which are said to be 'academically valuable' (which, I assume, refers to their species diversity, on which scientists do research) – and 'normal-operation areas', mainly made up of *hinoki*, where timber is produced for the *shikinen sengū* (Jingū Shichō Eirinbu n.d.: 2–4).

It should be pointed out that *kyūikirin* is a modern term. In medieval and pre-modern times, the forest was referred to by the term *misomayama* ('timber mountain'), a name that continues to be used today. Until the Kamakura period, wood for the *shikinen sengū* came from this area. But as the forest was also used for other purposes, deforestation and forest degradation gradually increased, and since the fourteenth century the shrines have mostly used timber grown in other parts of the country. In the Edo period, unsustainable forest exploitation continued. Many trees were felled in order to serve as firewood for the millions of pilgrims visiting Ise, which led to erosion, causing the regular flooding of the Isuzugawa River. As a result of this disturbance, in the early twentieth century the forest was largely made up of *akamatsu* pine trees (the roots of which do not go very deep), many of which were younger than fifteen years;[5] as a result, a strong typhoon that hit the area in 1918 caused high floods and significant damage (Kimura 2010: 5–8).

The current forest dates back to 1923 and was designed in accordance with modern European forestry techniques. Thus, the forest of Ise Jingū – in its current shape, that is – is a contemporary of the forest of Meiji Jingū. The main difference, of course, is that the forest of Meiji Jingū was designed to be 'natural' and look 'sacred', whereas the main purpose of the forest of Ise Jingū was the cultivation of *hinoki*, the primary resource for the *shikinen sengū*. The first *hinoki* were planted around ninety years ago; in 2013, some of these Taishō-period trees were used for shrine buildings. For the first time in approximately 700 years, therefore, wood from Ise's own forest was used for rebuilding the shrine, which received quite some media attention ('Boju terasu hikari' 2013; 'Sengū jimae hinoki fukkatsu' 2013). However, for one *sengū*, a significant amount of timber is required (about 10,000 m³, or 14,000 logs), not all of which can be provided by the *kyūikirin*. In fact, only one-fifth of all wood used for the 2013 *sengū* was grown here; the remaining 80 per cent came from production forests in Nagano and Gifu prefectures (Jingū Shichō Eirinbu n.d.; Kimura 2010). At future *sengū*, however, the proportion of timber coming from the *kyūikirin* is expected to increase; the current shrine forest management is working with a 200-year plan, carefully selecting (and marking) the trees that are believed to have the potential to grow high and thick, distinguishing them from those that may be used sooner. As in other shrine forests, Ise organizes tree-planting ceremonies, whereby the *hinoki* of the future are planted by selected volunteers and shrine priests. Likewise, the felling of trees is often accompanied by ritual ceremonies.

As we have seen, however, not the entire *kyūikirin* is used as production forest. In principle, the areas that are designated as 'first sanctuary forest area' as well as the 'special-operation areas' in the 'second sanctuary forest area' are not used for production. Together, these areas make up approximately 40 per cent of the total *kyūikirin*. Even the production forest is not solely made up of *hinoki*: 'some useful trees are left to grow to form a mixed forest with Hinoki cypress and broad-leaved species that is ecologically sound' (Jingū Shichō Eirinbu n.d.: 4).[6] The other areas are mostly made up of mixed or broad-leaved forest and are said to constitute ecologically valuable natural areas. A recent NHK wildlife documentary

(NHK 2013) showed some of the animals living in the forest. According to this documentary, the forest houses 19 mammal species (including sika deer, raccoon dog [*tanuki*] and Japanese macaque), 141 bird species and over 3,000 species of insects. The forest of Ise, it was suggested, constitutes 'the original Japanese forest landscape' (*Nihon no mori no genfūkei*). Among the various animals portrayed were rare species of insects (including swallowtail butterflies, fireflies, cicadas, longhorn beetles and dragonflies), colourful songbirds such as *ōruri* (*Cyanoptila cyanomelana*; blue-and-white flycatcher) and *sankōchō* (*Terpsiphone atrocaudata*; Japanese paradise flycatcher), as well as rare fish, frogs and crustaceans living in the river. In addition, the forest is said to have 120 species of trees and over 600 species of plants (Inata 2009: 92). In sum, the forest of Ise Jingū has come to be seen as a natural area of profound ecological and scientific significance, home to a great diversity of species, some of which are endangered.

Ise, Nature and Jinja Honchō

Although they are different institutions, there is a strong connection between Ise Jingū and Jinja Honchō. Jinja Honchō's core concerns include the continuation of the *shikinen sengū*, the conservation of Ise's status as the most important shrine in Japan and the revitalization of Ise's deep symbolic connection with both the imperial institution and the nation as a whole. Despite the numerous transformations it has gone through in the course of history, Ise is a symbol of continuity – the continuity of ancient building techniques and other crafts, the continuity of the imperial family as a sacred institution and the continuity of worship practices and beliefs. It is a symbol that is carefully protected and reinforced by Jinja Honchō by means of publications, media texts and PR campaigns stressing Ise's 'natural' and 'eternal' character, as well as its strong relationship with both the Japanese people and the life-giving deity that represents the sun and the imperial lineage, Amaterasu.

Jinja Honchō has certainly contributed to the view of Shinto as a tradition with a strong connection to the natural environment, if only because of its green rhetoric. 'Nature', 'sacred forests' and 'the environment' have become central to Jinja Honchō's self-definition, conceptually as well as symbolically. In its newspaper *Jinja Shinpō* as well as books and other publications (e.g. Jinja Honchō 1999; Sōyō 2001), *chinju no mori*, forest conservation and 'coexistence with nature' are recurring topics. As we have seen, shrine forests are not only valued because of their ecological importance or natural beauty but also because of 'their ability to generate, in children especially, love of local community and so patriotic love of Japan' (Breen and Teeuwen 2010: 209). For instance, Jinja Honchō publishes educational texts for children titled *Chinju no Mori Shinbun* (*Chinju no mori* newspaper), which contain a group of cute forest characters[7] – including a red maple leaf, a stag beetle, a cat wearing a watermelon, a tree seedling and a *kappa* (a mythological creature). In these texts, children are taught the importance of rice cultivation, the proper way of praying at a shrine, how to support Japan at international football tournaments, not to bully classmates and a number of other virtues far extending beyond those normally associated with environmental education (Jinja Honchō 2010).

In its English-language publications, Jinja Honchō has repeatedly stressed Shinto's unique appreciation of nature and argued that Shinto may serve as a blueprint for environmental ethics. For instance, in a well-known pamphlet containing a 'message from Shinto' to the world, it explicitly stated that 'the' Shinto view of nature offers solutions to environmental problems that science and technology cannot provide:

> In recent years, so many environmental problems, such as rise of temperature of the earth, destruction of the ozone layer, exhaustion of natural resources, and massive dumping of waste, have become global issues, and it is strongly required to take effective measures against these problems, as well as measure for natural preservation, amenity improvement, and pollution control. (...) As repeatedly mentioned, Shinto regards the land and its environment as children of Kami. In another word, Shinto sees that nature is the divinity itself. (...) So, Shinto suggests to shift a point of view and to look our environment with the spirit of 'reverence and gratitude', that is, with the spirit of parental care for children or with the spirit of brotherhood. And if we could extend this spirit to our neighbors, to our society members, to our country members, to people of the world, and to nature, too, beyond the difference of thoughts, ethics, religions, then this spirit will be the base to foster criteria and morals indispensable for keeping our human life healthy. (Jinja Honchō n.d.-a; see also Palmer & Finlay 2003: 127–129)

In this text, environmental problems are directly attributed to a perceived loss of the 'ancient' spirit of 'reverence and gratitude'. The solution to these problems, it follows, is a restoration of this worldview. Environmental problems are thus reduced to problems of moral and cultural decline, and technological and scientific advancements are dismissed. However, no concrete suggestions are made as to how exactly the 'Shinto view of nature' might contribute to dealing with climate change, resource exhaustion and waste dumping, neither here nor in other Jinja Honchō publications. As I have pointed out, none of the political lobby organizations associated with Jinja Honchō (Shintō Seiji Renmei and Nippon Kaigi) has environmental issues high on its agenda. Nevertheless, it is worth noting that Jinja Honchō is a fairly large and diffuse organization; concerns and agendas of different departments within the organization are not necessarily similar. In particular, members of the international department have recently engaged in several activities oriented towards greater environmental awareness.

For instance, Jinja Honchō has been actively involved in a joint programme (together with the ARC, the WWF and the Lutheran Church in Sweden) to establish a 'Religious Forestry Standard' formulating principles for the management of religious forests worldwide. In 2007, at the inaugural 'Faiths and Forests' meeting in Visby (Gotland, Sweden), a number of religious organizations from a variety of countries agreed to create this standard, with the purpose of formulating criteria for forest management that are 'religiously compatible', 'environmentally appropriate', 'socially beneficial' and 'economically viable' (ARC n.d.-d). This cooperation eventually led to the interreligious conference at Ise Jingū in June 2014, jointly organized by Jinja Honchō and ARC, which culminated in the shrine visit whereby Daoist, Christian, Hindu and other religious leaders collectively worshipped the sun goddess.

Organizing a large interreligious and environment-oriented conference at Shinto's most sacred site has provided international recognition for Jinja Honchō's claims regarding the fundamental interdependence between Shinto, Japan's natural environment and the imperial institution, embodied by the Ise shrines. Simultaneously, it has strengthened Shinto's international profile as a pluralistic, environmentally friendly religion (e.g. Vallely 2014), thus contributing to the dissociation of Shinto from wartime imperialism and nationalist revisionism. In other words, Jinja Honchō's appropriation of the Shinto environmentalist paradigm has contributed to the discursive depoliticization of Shinto, not only domestically but also internationally. This may explain why the activities of Jinja Honchō's international department do not seem to meet with much resistance within the organization. Even though many conservative members of Jinja Honchō are fairly indifferent towards environmental issues, nobody rejects these activities, as I was told multiple times by different people within the organization. Apparently, the stress on nature conservation is not seen as antithetical to imperial agendas, but rather as complementary – or, by some, as peripheral. Reportedly, no people within Jinja Honchō opposed the organization of an interreligious conference at Ise. The only aspect of the conference that met with resistance was the active participation of Daoist priests, who were seen by some as too close to the Chinese state; their presence at Japan's most sacred site therefore was not appreciated.[8] In the end, those in favour of international cooperation managed to convince their anti-Chinese colleagues that the participation of Daoist priests was inevitable, and that refusing them would jeopardize the entire project – not least because ARC has strong connections with Daoist institutions.[9]

It has been suggested that Jinja Honchō's promotion of the Shinto environmentalist paradigm and use of the *chinju no mori* trope amounts to little more than sophisticated greenwashing, used to conceal Jinja Honchō's nationalist agenda (e.g. Breen & Teeuwen 2010: 208–209; Kalland 2012). This criticism is arguably justified, considering Jinja Honchō's support for a government that is in favour of nuclear energy, whaling and widespread construction, and has one of the worst track records in the world when it comes to tackling climate change (Burck, Marten & Bals 2016). It certainly offers a welcome respite from the numerous romantic idealizations of Shinto as a 'green religion' found in cyberspace and popular scholarship. Nevertheless, the question as to what extent Jinja Honchō's commitment to environmental issues is sincere is difficult to answer – not only because Jinja Honchō is an organization with considerable internal diversity in which different opinions and agendas are represented, but also because there is no global standard for environmental activism. All expressions of environmentalism are contingent upon culturally and historically embedded conceptualizations of 'nature' and 'the environment', notions of crisis and possible strategies for improvement. They are intertwined with identity politics, economic issues, competing land claims and cultural values. Jinja Honchō is no exception. Some of the junior members appear genuinely concerned with environmental issues, and see nature preservation as one of Shinto's core priorities in the twenty-first century, together with the preservation of 'traditional culture'. To what extent such ideas can really contribute to a better environment may be (and should be) debated – it ultimately boils down to the fundamental question whether environmental degradation is primarily a matter of values and ethics, or, rather, of economic policies and technologies. It does not mean, however, that Jinja Honchō actors are merely interested in the natural environment as a rhetoric device.

What is clear, however, is that for Jinja Honchō, involvement with ARC is *not only* motivated by a concern for environmental issues. There are also concerns of a more strategic nature. While the commitment of some individual Jinja Honchō members to forest conservation and international cooperation may be sincere, Jinja Honchō's active cooperation with ARC, contribution to the establishment of a 'Religious Forestry Standard' and organization of a large international conference on religion and the environment most certainly also serves PR purposes. Today, Jinja Honchō takes marketing and public outreach very seriously and is willing to invest in professional PR campaigns. Thus, it has hired an advertising company, which has been involved with the preparation of the conference and the production of books and documentaries on Ise's *shikinen sengū* – including those which frame the site and its traditions in terms of ecological harmony and ancient sustainability. In addition, it has organized a high-profile exhibition at the Tokyo National Museum, showing historical treasures from shrines throughout the country.[10] In November 2011, I had the opportunity to talk to some people working for this company, who confirmed my suspicion that cooperation with the ARC was considered important for improving the visibility and general perception of Shinto abroad. It provides Jinja Honchō with an opportunity to redefine and reposition Shinto globally as an internationally oriented, ecological organization that goes back to ancient times yet is of great contemporary relevance.

In sum, the significance of Jinja Honchō's cooperation with ARC is twofold. First, it provides Jinja Honchō and some of its member shrines with the opportunity to learn about nature conservation and sustainable forest management and get support for projects developed to improve shrine forest ecology. Second, it is part of a deliberate PR strategy to rebrand Shinto as a tolerant, open-minded ecological tradition, and contribute to its international dissociation from right-wing nationalism and imperialism – while still maintaining that it is the ancient, indigenous tradition of 'the' Japanese people, closely intertwined with both national culture and its physical landscapes. To the leading actors, this ambivalence is not problematic. As far as I can tell, Jinja Honchō and ARC have a fruitful working relationship, despite their different agendas. They have cooperated for many years: as early as 2000, Jinja Honchō made a pledge 'not only to manage all of their sacred forests in sustainable ways but also only to buy timber from sustainably managed forests on behalf of their 80,000 or more shrines' (ARC n.d.-f).[11]

This is a far-reaching promise, but it is unclear to what extent the promise has been kept; as far as I am aware, no organization has kept track of the type of timber used by shrines nationwide. More fundamentally, Jinja Honchō is not in a position to force its member shrines to use sustainably produced timber only, as shrines are institutionally independent. As a matter of fact, in recent years, the relationship between the umbrella organization and its members has not always been harmonious: there have been a number of conflicts, mainly concerning financial issues, as Jinja Honchō requires small shrines with limited means to contribute financially to the central organization and to the rebuilding of the shrines of Ise (Breen 2010b). Although Jinja Honchō makes continuous attempts to limit the autonomy of local shrines financially, organizationally and doctrinally (Breen & Teeuwen 2010: 202–207), it does not manage the funds and buildings of local shrines. Therefore, if a shrine decides to use inexpensive imported timber for rebuilding a roof, there is very little Jinja Honchō can do about it. Making a promise 'on behalf of 80,000 member shrines' sounds impressive, but Jinja Honchō does not actually have the authority to enforce such a promise.

As we have seen, the continuation of Ise and its *shikinen sengū* is one of Jinja Honchō's core priorities. In the years prior to 2013, raising money for the rebuilding was one of the main purposes of its publicity campaigns. Accordingly, images of Ise featured prominently in these campaigns. Not surprisingly, in these representations of Ise, elements of nature – the forest, river, sea and rice paddies – are displayed prominently, indicating the eternal and uncreated character of the shrine and its *fūdo*.[12] For instance, on posters designed to attract visitors to Ise or sell amulets, Jinja Honchō does not usually show people; rather, the posters show beautiful but generic and ahistorical forests, skies and mountains, sometimes with a simple wooden shrine building. For instance, one such poster shows a picture of a wooden *torii* gate, together with the word 'thank you' (*arigatō*) in large letters and the following text in small print:

> To the sun, to the sunlight, to the warmth of this star,
> Thank you.
> To the rain, to the river, to this clean water,
> Thank you.
> To the earth, to the forest, to my rice,
> Thank you.
> To my ancestors, to my father, to my mother, to my life,
> Thank you.
>
> If we become aware of the things that deserve our gratitude,
> We can protect the things that are important to us.

Behind this *torii* gate,
Prayers expressing gratitude
Have been said continuously
For over two thousand years.[13]

This poster illustrates neatly how natural imagery is employed for ideological purposes. It portrays Shinto as an expression of gratitude for the life-giving forces of nature, as well as for one's parents and ancestors, whose traditions it safeguards. Nature is portrayed as, ultimately, life-giving and benevolent – accordingly, it deserves our reverence and protection. This applies especially to the sun, which is presented as the foundational and primary force of nature, just as the sun goddess is the *prima inter pares* of the myriad deities of Japan – and, accordingly, Ise the most important shrine of the country. As it has provided space for rituals for over 2,000 years, Ise represents a direct continuity between the present and prehistoric past. In addition to the sun, the poster suggests, Shinto is based on gratitude to the earth, water, forests and of course rice – the staple food that has served as a symbolic marker for the unity and continuity of the nation since the Meiji period (Ohnuki-Tierney 1993).

The notion of gratitude towards nature also takes centre stage in a recent commercial, made by Jinja Honchō to advertise Ise talismans (*o-fuda*).[14] Embodying the protective power of the shrines of Ise and the sun goddess, these talismans were produced by Jinja Honchō as a means to raise funds for the 2013 *shikinen sengū*. A young woman is seen walking in a pristine natural landscape with beautiful forests, rivers and rays of sunlight. Her facial expressions and body language suggest feelings of happiness, awe and reverence, and she is wearing a simple white dress that signifies purity and innocence. A female voice-over slowly recites lines similar to the aforementioned poster text. At the end, we see the woman placing a talisman on a *kamidana* ('god-shelf'; a Shinto home altar), putting her hands together and praying to the sun. The advertisement suggests eternal beauty, benevolence and purity, and appears profoundly apolitical. The talisman that is advertised, however, has been the cause of some serious dissatisfaction within the Shinto clergy, as Jinja Honchō put pressure on local shrines to purchase and sell significant amounts of them, at the expense of amulets and talismans benefitting the shrines themselves (Breen 2010b). Thus, it is a contested symbol of Jinja Honchō's attempts to impose its will on member shrines, and therefore highly political indeed.

In addition to museums, documentaries, commercials and other promotion materials, Jinja Honchō has also published some popular books on Ise Jingū and its forest that confirm the image of a site characterized by natural beauty and ecological harmony. One such example is the book *Mizu to mori no seichi, Ise Jingū* ('Ise Jingū, sacred site of water and forest'), written by the photographer Inata Miori and illustrated by many beautiful photographs (Inata 2009). The author describes how, when she first visited Ise, she felt that she became 'part of nature' and was 'purified'; she felt a strong sense of gratitude, as if she was coming home (Inata 2009: 4–5). This, she stresses, is the 'real Japan' (*honmono no Nihon*) (2009: 6). She also describes how she went into the 'natural' area of the *kyūikirin*, where she could feel a divine presence in a special rock, as if she had entered the 'world of myths' (2009: 86). She suggests that it is the forests that 'give people life' and protect them; in mystical vocabulary reminiscent of the work of Kamata Tōji (2008, 2011), she writes how she could feel 'the original energy of life' coming 'directly from the centre of the earth', deep inside this forest (2009: 98). She also expressed her admiration for the large 'natural' *hinoki* that grow in this area. Unlike the *hinoki* planted in other parts of the forests, these are not to be used as building material; they are considered sacred and look quite impressive indeed (2009: 93–98).

In sum, the forest of Ise Jingū and the practices associated with it are described in two ways today. These two descriptions are complementary rather than contradictory, and both of them are expressions of the Shinto environmentalist paradigm, albeit with different nuances. According to the first, Ise is Japan's most sacred and most ancient place of worship. It transcends history and represents nature in its purest, primordial shape. As such, it is the archetypal *chinju no mori*. Inata's book is typical of this approach. As she writes, 'The original natural forests of Japan have been preserved in the various *chinju no mori*, beginning with Ise. (...) *Chinju no mori transcend time*' (2009: 93; my emphasis). Sacredness and naturalness are here two sides of the same coin. Both are conceived of as transhistorical; unlike human society and politics; they are not subject to historical change and contingency. Second, Ise is generally described as a place where humans and nature live in harmony. Traditional practices such as rice cultivation, salt production and shrine architecture are all conceived of in terms of the balance between human culture and the natural environment. Despite the fact that the forests of Ise have long suffered from deforestation and resource depletion, its modern forestry practices are presented as remnants of the Japanese tradition of coexistence with nature. Rather than leaving 'nature' be, this is a narrative of interdependence and balance, not unlike the *satoyama* ideal. In Ise, however, the tradition of interdependence is not only preserved in agricultural practices and traditional arts and crafts but also in its supposedly unchanging ritual traditions – most prominently, the *shikinen sengū*. These traditions, it is argued, 'certainly contain important hints for the world of today. (...) If we want to know how we should live from now on, as part of nature, we should learn from Ise's long history' (Inata 2009: 101–102).

Worldwide Shinto?

The Brooklyn Botanic Garden in New York has a Japanese section. It was designed in 1914 by the Japanese-American landscape architect Takeo Shiota (1881–1943), and it contains different Japanese-style gardens, including a *kare sansui* rock garden modelled after the one at Ryōan-ji in Kyoto. It also has a red floating *torii*, a smaller copy of the famous one at Itsukushima Jinja (Miyajima), and a small shrine, dedicated to Inari (Hinton-Braaten 1983). Until recently, not much happened at this shrine. In April 2016, however, it was visited by the president of Jinja Honchō, Tanaka Tsunekiyo, together with staff from the international department, a shrine priest and two craftsmen. The craftsmen had made a special gift, which was presented to the Brooklyn Botanic Garden: a beautiful *mikoshi* (portable shrine). Reportedly, donating a *mikoshi* was Tanaka's own idea; he was 'inspired to have a *mikoshi* created' for the shrine in the botanic garden during a visit one year earlier (BBG Staff 2016). Clearly, there were some PR considerations as well; the international department had been planning the trip to New York and presentation of the *mikoshi* at the Brooklyn Botanic Garden for months. After all, events such as this serve to increase the visibility of Shinto and gain positive publicity for Jinja Honchō abroad. Incidentally, this was not the first time Tanaka presented Shinto in the US: in 2014, he gave a lecture at Columbia University on the topic 'Shinto and Its Impacts on the Japanese View of Nature and Culture' (Tanaka & Iwahashi 2014).[15]

Until quite recently, Jinja Honchō had little or no interest in such international outreach. Under the presidency of Tanaka, however, this has changed; the cooperation with ARC has probably also played a role. Some people within the organization have now come to realize that international cooperation not only improves knowledge of Shinto outside Japan, but can also be an effective strategy for gaining legitimacy domestically. As Dessì writes,

> the recent attention shown by Shintō institutions to the issue of ecology [is] not only the continuation of a 'traditional' rhetoric but also, and crucially to our discussion, a specific way of adapting to global trends. The response given by Shintō to the growing global awareness of an impending environmental crisis

Figure 9.2 Jinja Honchō president Tanaka Tsunekiyo presents a *mikoshi* to the Brooklyn Botanic Garden, New York, April 2016. Photo: Blanca Begert/Brooklyn Botanic Garden. Courtesy Brooklyn Botanic Garden.

is modulated through a selective approach to the tradition, which emphasizes the allegedly immemorial and respectful attitude of Japanese people towards a 'divine' nature. In this way, by looking to the distant and imagined past, a new identity is shaped that may meet the growing expectations of global society. (2013: 51–52)

In other words, the acceptance and appropriation of the Shinto environmentalist paradigm by Jinja Honchō cannot be seen apart from globalization. Environmental issues have provided Jinja Honchō with a new opportunity to reassert its significance, not only domestically but globally. This is clearly a transnational trend, which, as we have seen, has also affected religious practices and self-definitions elsewhere (e.g. China, India, Thailand and Tibet). When studying contemporary Shinto, this transnational dimension should be taken into consideration, as it has important consequences for shrine practices and ideologies. Jinja Honchō may be nationalistic, but some of its leaders are well aware of global trends. The choice to become more active in international outreach and cooperation, especially in recent years, clearly reflects this awareness.

Thus, it is no longer sufficient to perceive Shinto as an isolated Japanese tradition. Indeed, one of the defining aspects of the Shinto environmentalist paradigm is its international dimension. This takes different shapes, ranging from Jinja Honchō's cooperation with ARC and organization of events abroad to attempts by the International Shinto Foundation to promote the study of Shinto and invite foreign scholars to Japan, and from the construction of new shrines overseas to new types of hybrid 'Shinto' worship gaining popularity among non-Japanese followers. One initiative worth mentioning in this context is San Marino Jinja, which, as the name suggests, is a Shinto shrine built in San Marino. It consists of a small wooden shrine building placed on a large stone, housing a jewel that serves as *shintai*. The shrine is surrounded by a large *torii* gate, stone lanterns and cherry trees, and was inaugurated in the spring of 2014. Like other Shinto shrines, it has a ritual function, reportedly offering Shinto weddings (Antonioli 2014). In addition, it serves as a memorial monument for the victims of the 2011 earthquake and tsunami ('Japan-San Marino friendship society' 2014). San Marino Jinja is served by Francesco Brigante, a former hotel manager who has taken on the role of Shinto priest. Not surprisingly, Brigante describes Shinto as an ecological tradition, 'close to nature', whose way of thinking has to be 'exported' outside Japan ('Fransesco Brigante' 2014).

According to its website, San Marino Jinja is 'the first Shinto shrine in Europe', and it has also been described as such in local media (Antonioli 2014). This is factually incorrect: there has been a shrine in Amsterdam for many years, as I will discuss shortly. Contrary to the Dutch shrine, however, San Marino Jinja is supported by Jinja Honchō. Significantly, one of the main people involved with the project of constructing the shrine is Kase Hideaki, founder of the Japan-San Marino Friendship Society (Associazione di Amicizia Nippo-Sammarinese), which goes back to 2001 and counts over 1,000 members today ('Japan-San Marino friendship society' 2014). The website of San Marino Jinja contains a short essay by Kase, in which he argues that 'Shinto is the world's new religion of ecology' and that 'ecology is becoming a global super religion' (Kase n.d.). Thus, Kase is clearly aware of the legitimacy provided by the Shinto environmentalist paradigm. Meanwhile, however, he is also one of the most outspoken right-wing intellectuals in contemporary Japan: a prominent member of Nippon Kaigi as well as chairman of the 'Society for the Dissemination of Historical Fact', he has spent much of his career denying the historical reality of Japanese war crimes such as the Nanjing Massacre and supporting the production of historical revisionist films.

Apparently, this did not deter the San Marinese authorities from allowing and supporting the construction of a shrine in San Marino by Kase's organization. Quite the contrary: the ambassador of San Marino to Japan, Manlio Cadelo, has long been interested in Japan and its culture and has been one of the driving forces behind the establishment of the shrine. San Marino Jinja has received the support from conservative circles in Japan, as illustrated by the fact that the inauguration ceremony was attended by the mothers of both Prime Minister Abe Shinzō and Jinja Honchō president Tanaka Tsunekiyo, in addition to many members of the Japan-San Marino Friendship Society (Antonioli 2014). Thus, the significance of San Marino Jinja lies not primarily in the fact that it is located outside Japan – there are shrines at other places, including Brazil, Hawaii, the Netherlands and mainland US – but that, to my knowledge, it is the first foreign shrine since 1945 that has received the blessing of the conservative shrine establishment. Until recently, Jinja Honchō was not interested in advocating Shinto internationally, let alone in endorsing the construction of a shrine in Europe. In this respect, it has changed completely.

Jinja Honchō is not the only agent of internationalization within Shinto. Far from it: other groups and individuals made attempts to spread the tradition long before Jinja Honchō became aware of the legitimacy provided by international recognition. In Chapter 2, I discussed the characteristics and background of what I call the universal paradigm: the idea that Shinto, which has emerged and developed in Japan, has worldwide soteriological potential. There are numerous examples of overseas shrines constructed by Japanese missionaries and settlers in the imperial period, most of which were destroyed after the Second World War (see Nakajima 2010). By contrast, some of the shrines founded by Japanese migrants in Hawaii and South America continue to be used today. In addition, there are also a handful of Shinto shrines outside Japan that were established by non-Japanese actors. They are worth mentioning in this context, as they have contributed to the global popularization of the Shinto environmentalist paradigm in recent years. One of them is the Japanese Dutch Shinzen Foundation, a Shinto organization and shrine located in Amsterdam. Founded as early as 1981, the Japanese Dutch Shinzen Foundation defines itself as 'the home of Shinto in Europe', offering 'practical wisdom for the modern world' (Japanese Dutch Shinzen Foundation n.d.). It is run by Paul de Leeuw, a former actor who received his religious training at the Yamakage Shinto centre in Aichi Prefecture, where he was inaugurated as the first non-Japanese Yamakage priest.

Yamakage Shinto has been classified as one of the so-called Shinto-derived new religions (Tsushiro n.d.), but it claims to possess esoteric *koshintō* knowledge said to have been transmitted orally since ancient times. Indeed, as Paul de Leeuw confirmed, Yamakage believes that in medieval times its priests served as secret advisors to the emperor, a position they lost in modern times as a result of the political machinations resulting in the construction of 'State Shinto' (De Leeuw, interview, September 2014). There are no historical sources suggesting that Yamakage priests were indeed imperial advisors – but then, the argument goes, they were 'secret', so no sources could have mentioned them. In any case, small though the group is – it reportedly has a membership of 9,300 (Tsushiro n.d.) – it has gained some wider recognition, mainly because of the work of the former leader, Yamakage Motohisa (1925–2013), who was a prolific writer. Yamakage is also known outside Japan, thanks to the fact that his best-known book, *Shintō no shinpi* ('The mystery of Shinto'), has been adapted and translated into four languages, including English (Yamakage [2000] 2006). The book contains general information on shrine practices and *kami* as well as esoteric spiritual theories and a treatise on spirit healing, which are uncommon for shrine Shinto but typical of religious organizations belonging to the Ōmoto lineage.[16]

Not surprisingly, Yamakage's work also asserts the relevance of Shinto for environmental issues. As he suggests,

> [The] practical task of responding to the ecological crisis is given an ethical underpinning by Shinto, which from ancient times has seen it as the principal duty of human beings to care for and preserve their environment – to live within nature rather than attempting to dominate or destroy it. (…) From earliest times, Japan has endeavoured to preserve and nurture its abundant forests. Yet at times of upheaval and change, the forests have been damaged recklessly. Whenever this has happened, Shinto leaders have been at the forefront of campaigns to restore the forests, recognizing that they are the lungs of the nation and indeed the world. ([2000] 2006: 13–14)

Paul de Leeuw refers to himself as *kannushi*, a Japanese term used for Shinto priests in general. He is regularly hired by Japanese companies and other Japanese organizations in Europe to perform Shinto-style purification ceremonies. For instance, in the autumn of 2014, he officiated in a tree-planting ceremony at a British boarding school, organized by a Japanese former student. Likewise, he takes part in various Japanese cultural events, in the Netherlands as well as elsewhere in Western Europe. In addition, De Leeuw regularly conducts seasonal rituals such as *hatsumōde* (New Year ceremony), spring and summer ceremonies and so on. These take place either at a special location (e.g. the Okura Hotel in Amsterdam) or at his shrine: a *dōjō*-type room with a Shinto altar, located in a house in a residential area in Amsterdam. A significant proportion of the people attending these events are Japanese expats, but there are also some non-Japanese participants. Furthermore, contrary to ordinary Japanese shrine priests, De Leeuw also offers courses on 'Shinto practice': spiritual exercises involving meditation and breathing techniques, which are said to contribute to an 'enhanced awareness of nature' (De Leeuw 2016). These courses mainly attract non-Japanese people.

Thus, De Leeuw is a priest who not only conducts rituals but also sees it as his mission to teach and disseminate spiritual knowledge. Indeed, he expresses a strong interest in spiritual matters. For instance, he told me the story of how he found the location of the *kami* of Holland (apparently, there is only one), something which he could feel intuitively (interview, September 2014). He has asked me not to disclose the location, however, as he does not want too many people to visit the place. Similarly, despite being interested in sharing his ideas on Shinto and attracting more participants, De Leeuw was somewhat reluctant when I asked him whether he would want Shinto to spread widely internationally. The most important thing, according to him, is that people find spiritual harmony within themselves, as well as harmony with nature – more than, say, growing numbers of Shinto believers. Thus, although he wants to share information and spiritual skills, he does not seem very eager to proselytize. As a result, his organization remains small, and he does not have many 'followers' in the conventional sense of the word.

Perhaps the best-known Shinto shrine outside Japan is the Tsubaki Grand Shrine of America, located in Granite Falls, Washington. It is a branch shrine of Tsubaki Ōkami Yashiro in Suzuka (Mie Prefecture) and devoted to the same deities. In addition, several other *kami* are enshrined here, including the protector deity of North America and the founder-turned-*kami* of aikido, Ueshiba Morihei (1883–1969), who was deified and enshrined at Tsubaki Ōkami Yashiro after his death (Tsubaki Grand Shrine of America n.d.-a). Correspondingly, judging from the website and Facebook site, the Tsubaki Grand Shrine of America is particularly popular among aikido practitioners (Tsubaki Grand Shrine of America n.d.-c). The first Tsubaki shrine in the US was built in Stockton, California, in 1986; the shrine in Washington was built in 1992 by the current head priest, Lawrence Koichi Barrish, who called it Kannagara Jinja. Following the donation of a large piece of land, the two shrines reportedly merged in 2001, after which the shrine in Washington came to be known as Tsubaki Grand Shrine of America (Tsubaki Grand Shrine of America n.d.-b). Today, the shrine offers private purification rituals, coming-of-age ceremonies, wedding services and other ceremonies typical of Japanese shrine Shinto. In addition, it also offers various spiritual training programs involving *misogi* (water purification) and aikido.

As with the shrines in San Marino and Amsterdam, nature and ecology play a central part in the self-definition of the Tsubaki Grand Shrine of America, perhaps even more strongly. For instance, the website states that:

> Shinto emerged and developed spontaneously as an expression of the deep intuitive connection with Divine Nature enjoyed by human beings in ancient Japan. Shinto as *natural spirituality* is based on this harmonious primal relationship with the 'infinite restless movement of Great Nature', rather than on the written or revealed teachings of human beings. Realizing that each single component within Nature possesses Divine Spirit giving us joy and benefit, we renew our close ties to Mother Nature and pray for renewal and refreshed life. (…) Shinto is simple, bright and sincere and is the practice of the philosophy of

proceeding in harmony with and gratitude to Divine Nature. (Tsubaki Grand Shrine of America n.d.-a)

Such descriptions of Shinto, as a way to 'renew our close ties to Mother Nature', resemble contemporary neo-pagan ideas, deep ecology and other types of 'dark green religion' (Taylor 2010) more than, say, classical Japanese *kami*-related mythology and ideology. When reading these formulations of Shinto, it is not difficult to see why some non-Japanese are attracted to it, especially those who feel disillusioned with certain aspects of Western culture and are looking for alternative worldviews based on notions of nature as divine and enchanted. It should be pointed out, moreover, that the Tsubaki Grand Shrine is not only a *physical* location, visited by local people who are interested in Shinto and aikido; it also has a significant online presence. In particular, its Facebook group has turned into a prime tool for communication between Koichi Barrish and his followers, in the region as well as elsewhere (at the time of writing, it had as many as 5,230 members). In addition to announcements of ritual ceremonies taking place at the shrine, the Facebook site contains pictures, reflections upon 'Divine Nature' and practical tips for worshipping *kami* at home altars.[17] It has possibly contributed to the spread of Shinto outside Japan, if only because it confirms the recently popular notions that Shinto worship can be carried out anywhere, not only at shrines, and that nature is divine, not only in Japan.

It has been argued that the attempts at international outreach made by organizations such as Jinja Honchō and Shintō Kokusai Gakkai primarily serve to provide them with legitimacy domestically (Isomae & Jang 2012). Much *kokusaika* (internationalization) discourse is concerned with the reification of difference, not with overcoming it (Robertson 1998); to a certain extent, this applies to Shinto as well. But there is more to it. Recent years have seen a remarkable increase in interest in Shinto on the part of non-Japanese actors. This interest is not merely academic: there appears to be a growing number of people outside Japan who feel attracted to, and in some cases take part in, Shinto worship practices. Some of them participate in *shugendō* ascetic practices during a trip to Japan ('Seiyōjin ga misogi' 2011). Others feel attracted to Shinto-type imagery in anime (see Okamoto 2014; Thomas 2012), purchase or create their own *kamidana* and worship selected *kami* at home – for instance, by reciting some of the English-language *norito* written by Ann Llewellyn Evans and Stuart Picken (Evans 2001; Picken 2002). Although most of them do not have shrines nearby (unless, of course, if they live in Japan), some of them are very active on social media. It is too early to say whether this trend will spread, but there is no denying the fact that there are a number of non-Japanese who self-identify as Shinto practitioners. They are actively contributing to Anglophone discourse on Shinto, especially online. For instance, there are a number of Facebook groups where they come together to discuss their interpretations of the *kami* (e.g. Inari) and ask questions on how to worship them at home.[18]

Another initiative that deserves to be mentioned in this context is the blog *Green Shinto*. It is written by John Dougill, a Kyoto-based professor in English literature and author of travel guidebooks and popular-scientific books on a range of topics, including Japanese culture and religion. On *Green Shinto*, he writes on issues related to Shinto, shrine worship and the natural environment. The blog is said to be

> dedicated to the promotion of an open, international and environmental Shinto. It seeks to celebrate the rich heritage of the tradition, from sacred rocks and shamanistic roots to bawdy myths and fertility festivals. It believes Shinto to be essentially diverse, localised and community oriented. It looks to a Shinto free of borders, liberated from its past to meet the demands of a new age. It looks in short to a Shinto that is green in deed as well as in word. (Dougill n.d.)

Dougill is fairly explicit about his agenda and understanding of Shinto, which does not correspond to conservative Japanese conceptualizations of the tradition. In his blog posts, he expresses various opinions – anti-nationalist, anti-nuclear and anti-whaling, for instance – that are not shared by conservative members of the Jinja Honchō establishment, its political lobby organization and the *Jinja Shinpō* editorial board. However, Dougill readily acknowledges the fact that this blog mainly represents his personal opinions and interests and is not necessarily representative of Shinto as a whole (personal communication, September 2011). Rather than idealizing and depoliticizing Shinto by presenting it as, say, peaceful nature worship, as other authors have done (e.g. Picken 2002; Shaw 2009), Dougill does not shy away from controversial political issues, criticizing conservative-nationalist interpretations of the tradition. More important, however, he writes about a range of local *matsuri* and shrine traditions. In addition, he publishes book reviews, interviews with priests and scholars, travel accounts and newspaper articles – as such, his blog is a useful source of information on contemporary Shinto. Significantly, many of his posts explore the alleged 'pagan' character of Shinto, as well as its 'shamanistic' and 'animistic' elements, sometimes in comparison to other (neo)pagan practices. It is this aspect, I believe, that most non-Japanese Shinto aficionados find attractive: its supposed 'pagan' nature spirituality. Jinja Honchō has done little to correct this image: on the contrary, Tanaka has embraced the view that Shinto is a 'primal religion' that has preserved its close connections with nature, similar to Native American, Celtic and other 'pagan' traditions (Nguyen 2014; Tanaka & Iwahashi 2014).

In sum, the Shinto environmentalist paradigm goes hand in hand with globalization; it changes popular perceptions of Shinto outside Japan, to the point that some non-Japanese have started worshipping *kami*, while providing Jinja Honchō and other Japanese religious institutions with new legitimacy domestically. At the same time, however, the Shinto establishment is increasingly nationalistic and influential politically, challenges the post-war separation of religion and state, resists gender equality and pushes for constitutional reform allowing Japan to become more assertive in international politics. Although they may appear at odds, these two trends happen simultaneously, involving some of the same actors. It is this paradox – apparently concerned with the environment and internationally oriented, while increasingly nationalistic and explicitly political – that defines contemporary Shinto.

CONCLUSION

We live in uncertain times. When I was working on the manuscript of this book, multiple reports of unprecedented global warming and species loss were in the news. Scientists have documented that climate change has already transformed life 'across every ecosystem on Earth', affecting 82 per cent of all ecological processes studied (Scheffers et al. 2016). More and more people are aware of the dangers of climate change, which present a significant threat to the world and all its inhabitants. Nevertheless, the United States have elected a president who has argued that climate change is a Chinese hoax and stated that he wants to withdraw from the Paris climate agreement. The extraction of non-renewable resources continues uninterruptedly, subsidized by national governments worldwide, as does global deforestation. Facing such crises, international cooperation is of crucial importance, today perhaps more than at any time in human history. Yet, throughout Europe, Asia and North America, nationalism is on the rise. Parties and politicians who resist international cooperation and have little interest in environmental issues are gaining popularity and have come to power in several countries. Considering these developments, one cannot help but feel that the coming years will be of critical importance.

Can religion play a role in tackling these problems? Until recently, I was sceptical about this: although some individual congregations may have had an impact locally, the appropriation of environmentalist rhetoric by religious scholars and leaders was primarily a matter of identity politics, I thought. However, as mentioned in the introduction, in 2015 religious leaders stepped up: following the lead of Pope Francis (Francis 2015), many of them put pressure on political leaders to take collective action for limiting the impact of climate change. Although this was by no means the only factor that has contributed to the Paris agreement, the fact that these powerful voices joined the chorus of those arguing for far-reaching global action was not without significance. Meanwhile, there are some promising cases of religious-political cooperation that have led to actual change. In Morocco, mosques have been actively involved in the transition to a green economy based on renewable energy (Neslen 2016). In North and South America, native populations have joined forces with environmental activists, resisting the realization of new extractivist projects such as the Dakota Access Pipeline, while referring to indigenous worship traditions. Thus, they give real substance to idealized notions of the 'ecological noble savage' (Kalland 2008; Lohmann 1993), showing that a spiritual connection to the land can go hand in hand with environmental advocacy (cf. Klein 2014: 367–387). In China and India – two of the fastest-growing, largest and most polluting economies in the world – religious actors increasingly play a role in establishing environmental awareness; they have the potential to play a significant role in the 'greening' of these economies, it has been suggested (Duara 2015; Kent 2013; Miller, Yu & Van der Veer 2014).

So what about Japan? Largely devoid of natural resources yet one of the most affluent and technologically advanced countries in the world, one might expect Japan to have taken the initiative in developing technologies for renewable energy, such as solar cells and wind turbines. Puzzlingly, however, it is China that has taken the lead in this respect, while the current Japanese government prefers to devote its energy to subsidizing and exporting nuclear energy (Kingston 2016). According to the Climate Change Performance Index 2017, published by think tank Germanwatch, Japan is the second-worst performer of all fifty-eight countries studied – only Saudi Arabia did worse (Burck, Marten & Bals 2016). Notwithstanding the proliferation of 'sustainability' rhetoric (Kirby 2011: 160–192), Japan's track record in environmental issues remains meagre. While academics, religious leaders, forest-planters and journalists continue to spread the myth of Japan as a nation of 'nature lovers' who can teach the rest of the world how to live in harmony with nature, Japanese state agencies and corporations continue to contribute to widespread construction, (toxic) waste production and large-scale deforestation abroad. Surely, there is work to do.

In 2016, Shinto received significant media attention, not only in Japan but also internationally. It started with the campaign for constitutional change: at the beginning of the New Year, shrine visitors were surprised to come across large posters and banners urging them to sign a petition for a 'proud Japan' with a new Constitution. In May 2016, Prime Minister Abe's choice to invite his fellow G7 leaders to join him on a visit to Ise Jingū and plant trees together led to some critical articles on the new role of Shinto in Japanese politics. Several scholars and journalists have drawn attention to the growing influence of Nippon Kaigi and Shintō Seiji Renmei, pointing out that Jinja Honchō is a key player behind these two lobby organizations (e.g. McCurry 2016; Mizohata 2016; Mullins 2016; Narusawa 2016). In sum, Jinja Honchō has more political influence today than at any time since the end of the Second World War. Considering its self-declared concerns for the environment and its rather far-reaching promise that Shinto's culture of sacred forests will 'save the world' (*Kōshitsu* henshūbu 2014), one would expect Jinja Honchō to use some of its political influence to lobby actively for the transition to a green economy. Thus far, however, this has not happened.

That does not mean some of the actors involved with Jinja Honchō are not genuinely concerned with environmental issues, as I discussed in Chapter 9. Indeed, they may see shrine forest conservation – and, by extension, nature conservation more in general – as an important contemporary responsibility, as it is deemed necessary for preserving the continuity (cultural, ritual and physical) between the ancestral past as the present. Yet the environmental issues the organization chooses to engage with are those that are immediately relevant to some of its core concerns: the preservation of shrines as central institutions in Japanese society, the socialization of children into cultural-nationalist ideology and the (sustainable) cultivation of timber for the rebuilding of Ise Jingū. Meanwhile, more abstract issues that are not immediately related to shrine issues, such as climate change, are by and large ignored.

As this study has demonstrated, shrine-related conservation practices can be meaningful as they may contribute to the preservation of local ecosystems and the creation of a sense of community. It should be pointed out, however, that they nearly always have a small-scale character, focusing on particular demarcated areas rather than large-scale issues such as nationwide pollution problems, climate change or deforestation abroad. This should not be surprising, perhaps; historically, the vast majority of all shrines have had a strong local, place-based character, and this is still the case today. After all, a few noteworthy exceptions notwithstanding, *kami* are generally associated with physical landscapes and localities in *the country Japan* – not with, say, tropical rainforests in Borneo. It does mean, however, that Shinto worldviews can be employed not only to argue for the preservation of particular designated areas but also for legitimizing the exploitation of other, 'non-sacred' areas, and for turning a blind eye to abstract environmental issues that transcend local particularities. *Chinju no mori* have become the focal points of various conservation practices, but they are without exception bounded, demarcated and comparatively small. Sakurai Takashi's statement that most *chinju no mori*-related conservation projects make the mistake of overlooking the surrounding environment and the larger ecosystem of which the shrine forest is a part perfectly illustrates the local particularism characteristic of most Shinto-environmentalist practices (see Chapter 7).

Nevertheless, as several historians have demonstrated, 'Shinto' has carried multiple meanings in the course of history, and shrine actors have successfully adapted to changing circumstances. In the past years, I have met several young priests who expressed a profound interest in international cooperation and environmental activism. They want to contribute to improving the local environment by organizing social and educational activities, maintaining or constructing small *satoyama* areas, cleaning litter, planting broad-leaved trees and so on. They are also interested in meeting non-Japanese peers and sharing their ideas with them. To these young priests, environmentalism and internationalization are not simply PR strategies; they are of crucial importance for reasserting the significance of Shinto in the twenty-first century. To what extent they will succeed in convincing the nationalist hardliners within Jinja Honchō and Shintō Seiji Renmei that these are issues worth taking seriously remains to be seen. However, Jinja Honchō does not represent all its member shrines, no matter how many promises it makes 'on behalf of them'. Throughout history, shrines have negotiated and resisted central authority in numerous ways. There is no reason why local shrine priests cannot take the initiative in establishing alternative energy communities, preserving local ecosystems and protesting destructive construction projects, if they do so in collaboration with grass-roots citizens' groups and non-profit organizations, possibly learning from similar initiatives in other countries. If various such initiatives are successful, they may actually lead to some real changes in Jinja Honchō policy. The seeds have been sown; now we have to wait and see whether a green Shinto will finally emerge.

Aike P. Rots
Oslo, 30 November 2016

NOTES

Chapter 1

1   These were Abe Shinzō (Japan), David Cameron (UK), François Hollande (France), Angela Merkel (Germany), Barack Obama (US), Matteo Renzi (Italy) and Justin Trudeau (Canada). They were accompanied by Jean-Claude Juncker (president of the European Commission) and Donald Tusk (president of the European Council).

2   'Symbolic capital' is a concept developed by Pierre Bourdieu ([1980] 1990: 112–121). It has been defined as 'the accumulated amounts of prestige, celebrity, honour, authority, etc. that is symbolically represented in a cultural product' (Stordalen 2012).

3   Reportedly, all religious functionaries participated in a ritual ceremony for Amaterasu at the Inner Shrine. The only exceptions were the Muslim attendees, who joined in visiting the shrine but refrained from taking part in the ritual itself (interview with Jinja Honchō official, November 2015).

4   For an elaborate discussion of Japanese religious organizations' responses and contributions to globalization, see Dessì (2013, 2016). For a critical analysis of practices concerned with 'internationalization' (*kokusaika*) in Japan, see Robertson (1998).

5   The role of religious organizations and NGOs in UN decision-making processes has not received much scholarly attention. Recently, however, more academic awareness of this topic has emerged. See for instance Stensvold (2017).

6   In 2011, the University of Oxford announced a new research project 'to scientifically measure the coverage of religious and sacred land' and create a database of 'sacred land' worldwide. Sacred land, it was asserted, accounts for 'about 15 per cent of the world's surface'; according to the researchers, 'many of these "religious forests" and sacred sites contain some of the richest biodiversity in the world, including some of the highest numbers of threatened species' (University of Oxford 2011). In the same year, the University of Zürich organized a symposium titled 'Conserving Nature at Sacred Sites: State of Knowledge and Prospects for Research', bringing together academics working on related topics. There are numerous scientific publications on sacred sites in relation to biodiversity and nature conservation; examples include Bhagwat, Dudley & Harrop (2011); Bhagwat & Rutte (2006); Pungetti, Oviedo & Hooke (2012).

7   In this papal letter, which has far-reaching doctrinal authority, Pope Francis argues that global inequality and poverty are closely related to environmental exploitation and degradation. Drawing on the thought of Saint Francis of Assisi (1181–1226), he outlines his theory of 'integral ecology': a holistic worldview that combines environmental, social and spiritual elements (Francis 2015). It is no coincidence that Jorge Bergoglio chose to adopt the name Francis when he was elected pope in 2013 (the first pope ever with that name): Saint Francis of Assisi was declared patron saint of ecology by Pope John Paul II in 1979 and has long been considered an important

role model by environmentalists, both Christian and non-Christian (e.g. Taylor 2010: 27). He is commonly associated not only with Christian devotion but also with modesty, poverty and simplicity, and with a deep appreciation of Creation as a whole, including animals.

8   Inspired by Pope Francis' encyclical, a number of Jewish leaders wrote a Rabbinic Letter on the Climate Crisis, which has been signed by over 400 rabbis (Waskow 2015). Similarly, the Islamic Declaration on Climate Change was issued in August 2015 and endorsed by prominent Muslim scholars and leaders from various countries, including the grand muftis of Lebanon and Uganda and the chairman of the Indonesian Ulema Council (Neslen 2015). Soon thereafter, in October, the 'Buddhist Climate Change Statement to World Leaders 2015' was published. It was signed by a number of well-known Buddhist leaders, including the Dalai Lama and Thích Nhất Hạnh (Global Buddhist Climate Change Collective 2015).

9   These include the 'Statement of Faith and Spiritual Leaders on the upcoming United Nations Climate Change Conference, COP21 in Paris in December 2015', the 'Interfaith Climate Change Statement to World Leaders', and the 'Interfaith Declaration of Climate Change', which was signed by the Dalai Lama and Archbishop Desmond Tutu, among many others (see, respectively, http://actalliance.org/ wp-content/uploads/2015/10/COP21_Statement_englisch2.pdf; http://www .interfaithstatement2016.org/statement; and http://www.interfaithdeclaration.org/ endorsements.html; all accessed 30 June 2016). It should be noted that none of these statements and declarations was signed by Shinto organizations or representatives. For a complete overview of climate change-related interfaith initiatives, see the list provided by the Forum on Religion and Ecology at Yale University (http://fore .yale.edu/climate-change/statements-from-world-religions/interfaith/; accessed 30 June 2016).

10   For critical introductions to Eliade's theory of sacred space, see Cave (2001), Gill (1998). For discussions of the impact of these European theories on Japanese conceptualizations of sacred space, see Prohl (2000), Rots (2014b).

11   In my use of the terms 'strategy' and 'tactic', I follow Michel de Certeau, who used the former term to refer to the acts and machinations of powerful elites and the latter to refer to the practices by which 'the ordinary [hu]man' belonging to the 'marginal majority' negotiates and subverts those strategies. Spatially speaking, the difference between the two is that 'a strategy assumes a place', whereas 'the place of a tactic belongs to the other' (1984: xix). Thus, strategies are involved with the *production* of space (Lefebvre [1974] 1991); tactics *subvert* such produced space (Soja 1996).

12   The distinction between 'physical', 'mental' and 'social' space is one of Lefebvre's many conceptual triads. In addition to this triad, Lefebvre's theory is based on three other core concepts, referred to as 'aspects of space'. These are 'spatial practice', 'representations of space' and 'spaces of representation'. For a more elaborate discussion of these terms, as well as further reflections upon the significance of Lefebvre's theories for the study of contemporary sacralization processes, see Rots (2013a: 69–78). For other interpretations of Lefebvre, see Knott (2005), Soja (1996).

13   This echoes the theory of René Girard, who famously argued that 'the sacred' emerged in human societies in response to the sacrifice of a scapegoat-turned-god, the killing of whom served to prevent the escalation of violence in primordial communities. The sacralization of the scapegoat, and its ritualized worship, thus constitutes one

of the foundations of human society, as it helps preserve a social order that would otherwise collapse into violence (Girard 1990).

14 It is beyond the scope of the present study to give a complete and comprehensive overview of the various academic debates on 'secularization', 'secularism' and 'secularities' (for a useful introduction to earlier secularization debates, see for instance Demerath 2007). Inspired by the works of Talal Asad (2003), José Casanova (1994), Charles Taylor (2007) and others, recent years have seen a renewed interest in these topics (e.g. Calhoun, Juergensmeyer & VanAntwerpen 2011), and the emergence of a 'global comparative perspective' (Casanova 2006) that has led to the publication of a number of studies on secularisms and secularities in Asia and other non-Western contexts (e.g. Bubandt & Van Beek 2012; Burchardt, Wohlrab-Sahr & Middell 2015; Rots & Teeuwen 2017). For a more elaborate discussion of the relevance of Taylor's theory for understanding contemporary Shinto ideology, see Rots (2017).

15 There are various demographic and economic factors that have contributed to institutional decline. Rural depopulation, for instance, is an important reason for the difficulties experienced by numerous local temples and shrines (e.g. Fuyutsuki 2010). Likewise, the decrease in popularity of Buddhist funeral practices cannot be explained solely in terms of a 'decline in belief' but is also related to economic constraints. Some Buddhist temples which have developed alternative, cheaper (but not secular) funeral practices are reporting significant growth, despite their rural locations, as illustrated by Sébastien Boret's ethnographic study of 'ecological' tree burial practices at a Buddhist temple in Tohoku (2014).

16 Both these books were published by the Sacred Forest Research Association, Shasō Gakkai, which will be discussed in more detail in Chapter 5. Shasō Gakkai also publishes the annual journal *Shasōgaku kenkyū* ('research in sacred forest studies'), which likewise has a strong interdisciplinary character. Likewise, the book series *Shizen to shintō bunka* ('nature and Shinto culture'), published by the Shintō Bunka Kai (Shinto Culture Society) based on a series of conferences, contains contributions by scholars and scientists representing a variety of academic disciplines (Shintō Bunka Kai 2009a,b, 2010).

17 Thus, transdisciplinarity is not the same as interdisciplinarity: the latter refers to attempts at establishing dialogues between different academic disciplines, but this may lead to enforcing disciplinary boundaries rather than challenging them (cf. the terms 'interfaith' and 'international', which function in similar ways). Transdisciplinarity, by contrast, refers to attempts (successful or not) to approach a particular topic from different angles, in order to achieve more holistic (i.e. less fragmented) knowledge of that topic.

Chapter 2

1   In addition to *jinja*, Shinto places of worship may be referred to as *gū, jingū, miya, taisha* or *yashiro*; Buddhist ones as *tera, ji* or *in*. In English, these are conventionally translated as, respectively, 'shrines' and 'temples'. There is a certain arbitrariness to this translation: in Vietnam, for instance, *non*-Buddhist worship places are usually referred to as 'temples', whereas Buddhist ones are called 'pagodas' – a term which, when used in the Japanese context, is only used for the multi-tiered towers

functioning as stupas. Moreover, one may question whether 'shrine' is the most suitable term, as the term historically referred to relic boxes, tombs of saints and small chapels, rather than sizeable institutions. As a matter of fact, Jinja Honchō has recently started using the term *jinja* in English-language publications, deliberately leaving it untranslated so as to convey their unique character, which is similar to their use of the term *kami* (e.g. Public Affairs Headquarters for Shikinen-Sengu 2013: 22; cf. Matsutani 2013). For the time being, however, the term 'shrine' continues to be used in virtually all English-language writings on Shinto and Japan, so I will follow the convention.

2   As mentioned in the introduction, I do not assume a rigid distinction between 'primary' and 'secondary' sources; academic texts reflecting upon earlier texts can become 'primary' in the sense that they take on paradigmatic status, influencing later academic discourse as well as religious practices and self-understandings. The boundaries between 'primary' and 'secondary' sources are as fluid and subjective as those between 'emic' and 'etic' – whether a text is defined as 'primary' or 'secondary' (or as 'emic' or 'etic') influences the way it is read and the authority attributed to it. Two examples of articles that can be read either as 'secondary' and 'etic' – that is, scholarly, analytical and reflective – or as 'primary' and 'emic' – that is, an original, 'religious' text reflecting a particular institutional agenda – are Sonoda (2000) and White (1967), both of which were published as academic texts but which can also be read as some of the 'primary sources' of religious environmentalism. I therefore use these categories with caution.

3   For clarity's sake, I do not use the term 'essentialist' as a value judgement. I use it to refer to the notion that a given phenomenon has a particular *core essence* that transcends historical change and contingency, is both foundational and primordial, and is, ultimately, *knowable*. As for the term 'paradigm', I use this to refer to a particular set of correlated, historically established, taken-for-granted assumptions concerning the basic structure and attributes of a certain phenomenon, which shapes and strongly influences interpretations and representations of that phenomenon. It is a foundational, authoritative set of assumptions regarding, first, the basic nature of something, and second, ways in which this basic nature can be known. As such, it is ontological as well as epistemological.

4   There is a large body of academic texts on the development and role of Shinto during the Meiji period, as well as the subsequent Taishō and early Shōwa periods. Murakami Shigeyoshi (1970) and Helen Hardacre (1989) have discussed the relationship between Shinto, *kokutai* ideology and Japanese imperialism, usually referred to as 'State Shinto' (*kokka shintō*). They have influenced later scholars of religion, such as Shimazono Susumu, who has argued that State Shinto has never completely ceased to exist and uses the term to refer to pre-war as well as post-war ideology (2007, 2009). Some Shinto historians, by contrast, have argued that Shinto's responsibility for the development of Japanese imperialism has been exaggerated, instead downplaying its role and pointing to other factors (Nitta 2000; Sakamoto 1994). Others have focused on the histories of particular shrines and priests, showing that local realities were more complicated than suggested by some of the more general accounts, and that shrine priests were not only complicit in but also suffered from state policies, which they had to negotiate (Azegami 2009; Breen 2000; Imaizumi 2013; Sakurai 1992). As war memories remain the subject of much controversy and contestation, and Shinto involvement with politics increases, the debates on the nature and significance of 'State Shinto' are not likely to end any time soon.

5   While it is true that the term *kami* signifies something notably different from the
     omnipotent creator 'God' of Christianity, Judaism or Islam, the generic term 'gods'
     certainly is applicable. While 'God' is, by definition, singular and absolute, 'gods' are
     countable, diverse, culture-specific and not necessarily omnipotent. Accordingly,
     in my opinion, there is no compelling reason not to use the generic terms 'gods' (or
     'deities') to refer to Japanese *kami*; a category which, it should be noted, is diffuse and
     generic itself, and has been subject to significant historical change (Rots 2013a: 20–22;
     Thal 2005: 7–8).

6   For in-depth studies of two of these movements (Kurozumikyō and Ōmoto,
     respectively), see Hardacre (1986) and Stalker (2008).

7   This category included newly developed charismatic movements such as Konkōkyō,
     Kurozumikyō and Tenrikyō (but, until the end of war, not Ōmoto, which was severely
     persecuted by the state). It also included a number of movements associated with
     particular pilgrimage sites and worship traditions, which did not want to become part
     of the newly developed 'Shinto', but chose to become 'religions' in order to maintain
     their distinctive traditions (e.g. Ontakekyō and Izumo Ōyashirokyō). In the pre-war
     period, they were organized in the Sect Shinto League (Kyōha Shintō Rengōkai), an
     umbrella organization that still exists today even though its composition has changed,
     today including Ōmoto but not Tenrikyō (Breen & Teeuwen 2010: 211–212). For a
     discussion of the historical formation of the category 'Sect Shinto', see Inoue (2002).

8   For more in-depth discussions of some of these movements, see Prohl (2006) and
     Staemmler & Dehn (2011).

9   Significantly, some of these movements are actively involved with Nippon Kaigi
     (Guthmann 2017).

10   For an overview of these projects, see the website: http://www.oisca-international
     .org/ (accessed 29 July 2016). For a discussion of OISCA's activities and the ways in
     which the organization relates to Ananaikyō and the category 'religion', see Watanabe
     (2015).

11   Until recently, Shintō Kokusai Gakkai was also known as the International Shinto
     Foundation. It had an office in Tokyo as well as one in New York. Some years ago,
     the US-based International Shinto Foundation became institutionally independent
     from the Japanese organization, Shintō Kokusai Gakkai, which has now adopted
     International Shinto Studies Association as its new English name. Reportedly, the
     separation of the Japanese and the 'international' branch was a tactic for separating
     scholarly activities from more 'religious' PR activities. The two organizations still
     maintain close connections.

12   Fukami was influenced by Sekai Kyūseikyō and Ōmoto, then set up his own religious
     movement. The movement is said to have approximately 30,000 members and has
     a strong proselytizing character (Inoue n.d.; Prohl 2006). Worldmate belongs to the
     Ōmoto lineage, sharing some key characteristics with other religious movements in
     this category: a focus on spiritual healing techniques, involvement in development
     projects (the Worldmate website contains information about a hospital and an
     orphanage set up in Cambodia), and an apparent interest in environmental issues (for
     instance, every month, Worldmate volunteers clean litter on and around Mount Fuji).
     For an overview of these activities, see the website: http://www.worldmate.or.jp/index
     .html (accessed 29 July 2016).

13   For a critical discussion of the formation and historical significance of the category
     'spirituality' in Asia, see Van der Veer (2014). For discussions of the popularity of
     'spirituality' in post-war Japan, see Prohl (2000) and Shimazono (2004).

Chapter 3

1   For a recent example of this approach, which juxtaposes 'indigenous wisdom'
     with 'Western science', see Hendry (2014). For a critical discussion of the category
     'indigenous peoples' in relation to 'sustainability', see Karlsson ([2000] 2013:
     133–143). On the importance of cooperation between indigenous peoples and
     environmental activists, see Klein (2014: 367–387).
2   The arguments of Pedersen and Kalland are similar to those put forward by Garry
     Lohmann in his article on 'Green Orientalism' (1993). 'Seeking an impressive lineage
     for their views somewhere outside their own society, some Western greens treat
     (say) Taoism or Hinduism merely as flavourful ingredients in their own recipe for
     "sustainability" or "biocentrism"', Lohmann argues. By doing so, they

> tacitly assume that it is Westerners alone who have the right to decide what
> a culture is, what is traditional, what is romantic, what is Westernized, what
> must be saved, and what is politically realistic. The only way subordinate
> groups can build alliances with such Orientalists is to act out the parts of
> 'environmentalists', 'traditional peoples' or 'development enthusiasts' to which
> they have been assigned, then twisting and subverting these roles to their own
> advantage.

     He concludes the article by saying that 'telling stories about other people and about
     nature is both unavoidable and productive. But it is also a political act. Being wary
     of Green Orientalism does not mean trying to give up storytelling, but rather
     acknowledging this politics and working to make it less oppressive by not insisting
     on monopoly rights to define others'. In other words, environmental activists need
     to forge alliances with (subaltern) others, and incorporate their narratives, instead
     of projecting their own notions of 'ancient sustainability' or 'ecological wisdom'
     upon them.
3   In the 1960s and 1970s, 'Zen' was perceived as the quintessential Japanese spirituality,
     especially in the US. Shinto, by contrast, was relatively unknown outside Japan.
     American perceptions of Zen were strongly influenced by the work of D. T. Suzuki,
     which had little in common with actual temple Buddhism as it was practised in Japan.
     See for instance Suzuki (1959).
4   One example is the temple Hōnen-in in Kyoto, which organizes guided forest walks
     and other educational and cultural activities, not unlike some of the Shinto shrines
     discussed in this book. Likewise, the abbot of Rinnō-ji temple in Sendai has been
     actively involved with reforestation projects, on the temple grounds as well as in
     the coastal region that was hit by the 2011 tsunami. It is beyond the scope of this
     study to discuss Buddhist environmentalist discourse and practices at length, but
     it is important to point out that Buddhist priests in Japan are not necessarily less
     interested in environmental issues than their Shinto colleagues. For overviews of
     Buddhist environmentalism in contemporary Japan, see Williams (2012) and Dessì
     (2016: 67–71). For a case study of a Buddhist temple that has developed ecological
     practices, see Boret (2014).
5   For instance, *shizen kankyō* refers to the natural environment (in the modern,
     ecological sense of the word), whereas *tennen shigen* refers to natural resources – that
     is, concrete, physical objects. In modern Japanese, *shizen* is the more commonly
     used term of the two. This originally Chinese concept (already used by Laozi),
     alternatively pronounced as *jinen*, was introduced to Japan approximately 1,500

years ago (Tellenbach & Kimura 1989: 153). Throughout history, the term has carried a variety of meanings. Composed of the characters *shi/ji* 自 ('self') and *zen/nen* 然 ('so', 'resembling'), it literally means 'in the way of itself', 'by itself' or 'like itself'. Accordingly, the adverb *shizen ni* does not only mean 'naturally' but also 'spontaneously'. In fact, in the *Man'yōshū*, the characters were pronounced as *onozukara* – a Japanese word referring to something happening spontaneously, 'of/from itself' (Tellenbach & Kimura 1989: 154–155). Thus, some scholars have argued, in pre-modern Japan nature was not conceptualized as something external to human beings: nature and human individuals ('selves') were ontologically and conceptually intertwined, and there was no understanding of nature as something opposed to human society and culture (Eisenstadt 1995; Tellenbach & Kimura 1989). However, Fabio Rambelli has accused these scholars of anachronistically mixing up the ancient adverb *jinen* with the modern neologism *shizen*, arguing that pre-modern understandings of the term should not be confused with modern conceptions of 'nature' (2001: 72–73). See also Kalland (2008: 98–100).

6   On the concept 'culture' in Japan, and the identification of an essentialized 'Japanese culture' with the modern nation-state, see for instance Befu (2009) and Morris-Suzuki (1998: 60–78).

7   For overviews of theories of nature in the Edo period, see Morris-Suzuki (1998: 38–51) and Thomas (2001: 32–59).

8   There are close similarities between Watsuji's theory of *fūdo* and Johann Gottfried von Herder's (1744–1803) idea that the distinctive character of a *Volk* is shaped by its climate and geographical location. Like other Japanese philosophers at the time, Watsuji was well familiar with German philosophy. Indeed, at some point in his book, he mentions Herder, suggesting his influence; however, at the same time he claims to be more scholarly in his approach to the problem than his German predecessor (Watsuji [1935] 1961: 17). He also makes several references to his former teacher Martin Heidegger (1889–1976), suggesting that *Fūdo* is a means to fill a gap in *Sein und Zeit*: the latter's supposed one-sided focus on the relationship between time and existence, and neglect of the way our existence is influenced by space ([1935] 1961: v– vi, 9).

9   On the symbolic importance of rice and wet rice cultivation as markers of Japanese national identity, see Ohnuki-Tierney (1993).

10 On their respective variations on the theme, see Morris-Suzuki (1998: 35) and Kalland & Asquith (1997: 5).

11 These ideas are discussed in more detail in Chapter 6.

12 This lavishly illustrated book is somewhat different in approach from other texts stating that traditional Japan should teach us how to live in harmony with nature. Arguably, it is also more interesting. In contrast to most other authors writing on this topic, Brown does not claim to have written an academic work. Instead, he self-consciously presents his work as a non-academic 'book of stories' (Brown 2009: 7, 11): it is anecdotal and impressionistic rather than abstract and analytical. Moreover, he does not employ the classical tropes of the 'love of nature' myth – references to haiku, the four seasons, *mono no aware*, Mount Fuji and so on – but, rather, looks at actual practices: agriculture, forestry, city planning, dwelling practices, etc. As such, his approach is refreshing. In the end, however, he does end up idealizing Edo-period Japan, overlooking tensions and problems at the time, and overestimating the possible applicability of seventeenth- and eighteenth-century practices for twenty-first-century society.

13   This article was published in the journal of Meiji Jingū, a shrine historically associated
     with emperor worship (see Chapter 8). It was written in Japanese and obviously
     targeted at a Japanese audience.
14   On this topic, see also Thornber (2012). In this book, which looks at cases from Japan,
     China, Korea and Taiwan, Thornber compares idealizations of nature in literary
     texts to actual environmental practices and problems. She likewise suggests that,
     throughout East Asia, there is a significant discrepancy between ideals and reality,
     which she refers to as 'ecoambiguity' (2012).

Chapter 4

1   Several scholars have lauded the work of pre-war Japanese scientist Minakata
     Kumagusu (1867–1941), presenting him as an early environmental activist (e.g.
     Blacker 1983; Katō 1999). Shinto authors arguing for the preservation of shrine forests
     see him as their predecessor (e.g. Sonoda 2006a,b; M. Ueda 2001: 65–67), because
     Minakata vocally opposed the shrine merger policy (*jinja gōshi* or *jinja gappei*) that
     was implemented in 1906 and led to the destruction of a number of shrine forests.
     As I have argued previously (Rots 2013a: 193–196; 2015a: 214), I am not convinced
     that Minakata should be seen as an 'environmentalist' in the modern sense of the
     word. He opposed shrine mergers primarily because of their negative social and
     political consequences, actively speaking out against the corruption involved with the
     process and pointing to the importance of shrines for community cohesion (Minakata
     [1912] 1981). Being a biologist, he did certainly lament the loss of woodland that
     was one of the consequences of this policy, but that was by no means his only reason
     for opposing it. More important, aside from the question of Minakata's purported
     environmentalist credentials, it is problematic to see him as an early example of
     Shinto environmentalism: he was neither a priest nor a Shinto scholar, he did not
     draw on worship traditions to support his arguments, and he did not represent any
     shrine or Sect Shinto organization. For a comprehensive overview and discussion of
     Minakata's work, see Tsurumi (1981); on the effects of the *jinja gōshi* policy on local
     shrines, see Azegami (2009) and Sakurai (1992).
2   The term 'spiritual intellectuals' (*reiseiteki chishikijin*) was coined by scholar of
     religion Shimazono Susumu, and it was he who grouped these different authors
     together, despite their disparate agendas and affiliations. As I have argued elsewhere
     (Rots 2014b: 36–37), 'spiritual intellectuals' is a problematic category: the term
     'spiritual' is a floating signifier that conceals the fact that these authors are engaged
     in ideological projects to assert the uniqueness and essential otherness of an
     essentialized 'Japanese culture'. Moreover, they are not just 'intellectuals', they are
     influential academics who have occupied top positions in leading institutions,
     including Kyoto University and the International Research Center for Japanese
     Studies. On the politics of the category 'spirituality' in modern Asia, see Van der
     Veer (2014).
3   The weekly shrine newspaper *Jinja Shinpō* gives a representative overview of the
     priorities and interests of Jinja Honchō. It is informative as it reports on various
     cultural, educational and academic activities organized by shrines and shrine-related
     organizations. As it gives a clear indication of Jinja Honchō's ideological position(s),
     as well as trends in the shrine world, it constitutes an important source for research

on post-war Shinto. In this newspaper, environmental issues received little or no attention until the early 1980s. From that moment on, however, they were mentioned occasionally – in particular, reference was made to the topics of shrine forest conservation and forest-based (environmental, moral and cultural) education. While arguably not the shrine establishment's main priority, environmental issues, nature conservation and reforestation have become recurring topics, periodically referred to in *Jinja Shinpō* articles on shrine activism, reports of academic events, and even in columns and editorials.

4   On the importance of 'internationalization' for acquiring domestic legitimacy, see Dessì (2013), Gagné (2017), Isomae and Jang (2012) and Robertson (1998).

5   E.g. Isomae & Jang (2012). This is a strange accusation, considering the fact that one of the scholars accused of doing so, John Breen, has written extensively (and critically) on modern Shinto politics and ideology (e.g. Breen 2007; 2010a,b; 2015). For a more nuanced analysis, see Dessì (2013: 96–97).

6   This is a direct translation of the Japanese title of the symposium; the official English title was 'Kami and Hotoke: Spirituality and Forests in Japanese Culture'. The choice to use the term *hotoke* instead of Buddhas is interesting, as it is multi-interpretable: *hotoke* does not only refer to Buddhas but also to ancestral spirits.

7   I have repeatedly been told by shrine priests and laypeople that the Japanese people's unique appreciation of nature is evidenced by their worship of *shinboku*: sacred trees that are believed to embody *kami*. When I replied by saying that *shinboku* are a common sight in countries such as Thailand and Vietnam as well, my conversation partners were often surprised. Few Shinto actors compare their tradition to mainland Asian traditions; it is 'the West' that constitutes their main Other. This, incidentally, constitutes an important area for future research: in-depth comparisons of popular devotional practices throughout North- and Southeast Asia, for instance with regard to tree, animal or spirit worship. Such research would lay bare the various similarities in popular worship practices, across nations and institutionalized religions.

8   During a visit to its worship centre in the town of Uji (near Kyoto), I was told that Seichō no Ie is the world's first truly sustainable religion, but I am not sure to what extent this claim is justified. In any case, several followers of the organization to whom I spoke expressed a concern for environmental issues and were active in the kind of nature-related activities one also comes across at shrines – tree planting, rice cultivation, cleaning litter and so on – as part of their spiritual training. Several volunteers proudly told me about the 'office in the forest' project, which is seen as an important step towards a sustainable future, integrating religion into the natural environment physically as well as symbolically. One does wonder, however, what other reasons there may have been for moving the headquarters from downtown Tokyo to rural Yamanashi. For more background information on this ambitious project, see Taniguchi & Taniguchi (2010).

9   According to the website, there are three such gardens in Japan (in Atami, Hakone and Kyoto), and three abroad (in Thailand, Brazil and, under construction, Angola). In addition to its involvement in organic farming, Sekai Kyūseikyō's interest in environmental issues is illustrated by its contribution to the development of technology for purifying polluted water. See, respectively, http://www.izunome .jp/en/holy_place/ and http://www.izunome.jp/en/action/envi/ (last accessed on 17 October 2016).

10 The same, of course, is true for most contemporary cultural and ideological expressions, which are 'glocal' in the sense that they are the product of an interplay

between local and transnational elements. Nevertheless, most texts produced in the field of 'Japanese studies' continue to have a strongly mononational character, not sufficiently taking into consideration global or transnational developments, nor engaging in cross-border comparative research. Although the present study is primarily concerned with Japanese cases, I do wish to stress that the Shinto environmentalist paradigm cannot be studied in isolation; Japanese ideas and practices are affected by developments elsewhere, and may influence them in turn. I will return to this topic in the last chapter.

11 Contrary to what Earhart suggests, consumerism is by no means alien to Japanese religious institutions and their practices. Shrines and temples are competitors in a religious market that have to attract paying customers in order to survive; as a result, ritual practices and objects are commodified to a large extent. See Reader & Tanabe (1998).

12 For instance, he insisted that originally, he did not want his film *Nausicaä and the Valley of the Wind* to be a religious story: 'I wanted to get rid of any religious undertone. (…) I do like animism. I can understand the idea of ascribing character to stones or wind. But I didn't want to laud it as a religion' (Miyazaki [1996] 2009: 332). On the other hand, he has also stated that 'the role of Nausicaä herself was not to become an actual leader or even a guide for her people. Rather, it was to act as a type of *miko*, a shaman-maiden who works at a Shinto shrine' ([1996] 2009: 407). Thus, Miyazaki refuses to associate his films with any particular religious tradition, yet he does make occasional reference to aspects of these traditions.

Chapter 5

1 The compound word *shūkyō fūdo* was coined by Sonoda Minoru, drawing on the work of Watsuji Tetsurō. According to Sonoda, Shinto (and, by extension, Japanese culture in general) has developed in close interaction with the physical landscape and climate (*fūdo*) of the Japanese archipelago. The Ise shrine official expressed himself in similar terms. See Sonoda (2000, 2010). For a discussion of Sonoda's theory of *shūkyō fūdo*, see Rots (2013a: 236–240).

2 The term *ujiko* refers to a local community that is considered to belong to a particular shrine. In contrast to Christian churches, 'Sect Shinto' organizations or (other) new religious movements, this belonging is not usually based on membership. Rather, it refers to the neighbourhood associated with a shrine by its clergy. Ideally, the people living there are all part of the shrine community and take part in collective rituals such as *matsuri* (which, not unimportantly, they also support financially). In reality, however, not all members of an *ujiko* identify themselves as such, and most neighbourhoods have at least some people who do not feel affiliated with a shrine (for instance, because they belong to another religious organization).

3 A search of the Taishō Canon (a twentieth-century canon of Chinese Buddhist scriptures and their Japanese commentaries) reveals that in Chinese Buddhist texts, the term is often used to refer to the task of Dharma protectors. The term was incorporated in Japan, where it came to be used for guardian deities protecting temples – a meaning which Japanese writers in turn projected onto China (Mark Teeuwen, personal communication, January 2012).

4   For instance, the famous shrine forest activist Minakata Kumagusu never used it. Instead, he used the word *shinrin*: 'the forest (*hayashi*) of the *kami*' (i.e. 神林, not 森林, which is pronounced the same) (Kanasaka 2001: 108–109).

5   As Ueda points out elsewhere, the verb *hayasu* ('to grow') is etymologically related to *hayashi* (2004b: 11). This points to the same difference between *mori* as something that has grown naturally and spontaneously (*shizen ni*) and *hayashi* as something that has been cultivated.

6   For instance, at the 1982 symposium on sacred forests, one of the participants argued:

> There is an idea that it is good not to touch nature; that this is exactly what constitutes nature protection. I think that this is a prejudice that has entered Japan and taken root from the period of rapid economic growth [i.e. the post-war decades] onwards, but this is destroying the Japanese mind. Forests grow exactly *because* people take care of them, cherish them and raise them. ('Jinja to "midori" zadankai' 1982)

The implicit suggestion made here is that the notion that nature is best preserved when left 'wild' and 'untouched' is another unfortunate Western import, along with modern technology and 'individualization'. The comment is relevant, as the question whether nature should be maintained by humans or left untouched continues to be debated fiercely by environmental organizations, policymakers, scientists and 'nature consumers' worldwide – a debate that is by no means limited to Japan. In Japan, however, these arguments have gained significant ground in recent years. These days, 'wild forests' are typically associated with former *Cryptomeria* (*sugi*) plantations: ecologically unbalanced monocultures that in many cases are no longer maintained, encroach upon rural communities and areas formerly used for agricultural purposes, and cause erosion as well as health problems, since many people are allergic to the pollen of these trees. The currently predominant nature conservation ideal is the exact opposite: the hybrid nature-culture landscapes called *satoyama*, which are maintained by humans active in agriculture and foraging practices (lumber and mushrooms, for instance). All over Japan, local volunteer movements are now active in preserving (or recreating) these so-called traditional landscapes.

7   The term often used for forests in scientific discourse is *shinrin* (for instance, *shinrin seitaigaku* means forest ecology), which is made up of both the characters for *hayashi* and *mori* – thus suggesting that the two are interrelated and that their meanings overlap.

8   The word *shakai* goes back to medieval Chinese texts, in which it refers to certain groups or organizations; in Japan, it was first used in the Edo period in order to translate the Dutch term *klooster* ('monastery'). As a common translation of the French concept *société* (of which 'society' is the English equivalent), however, it was not introduced until the Meiji period (Doak 2007: 129–130). Thus, it was introduced around the same time as the functional neologisms *shūkyō* (religion) and *shizen* (nature). Therefore, when used as etymological evidence, the argument that *shakai* points to the sacred forest as the origins of society does not hold. But then, perhaps this statement should be read more metaphorically. Ueda was aware of the fact that *shakai* is a modern neologism (interview, December 2011); he argued that his point is not that the term itself goes back to ancient times, but rather that the modern term reflects the ancient essence.

9   Not everybody agrees with the use of this character for writing *chinju no mori*, though. Ueda Masaaki has pointed out that the character not only means 'forest' but

also has the connotation 'to close' or 'to shut' (e.g. 'closed gate'). Hence, he argues, it does not adequately convey one of *chinju no mori*'s core meanings: a place where humans and nature meet and interact. As such, it cannot be closed off but must have an 'open' (i.e. public) character (M. Ueda 2001: 42; cf. Sonoda 1998: 33–34).

10   The term *matsurigoto* goes back to the Ritsuryō system, the China-influenced system of state administration and ritual ceremonies implemented in the Nara period. Interestingly, it refers to both political administration and ritual ceremonies. The term was reapplied in the Meiji period and used to refer to the role of the emperor.

11   Elsewhere, the relevant academic fields are listed as follows: 'botany, zoology, ecology, archaeology, architecture, landscape gardening, aesthetics/art history, history, ethnology, religious studies, agriculture, forestry, fisheries science, law, sociology, geography, urban planning, civil engineering, environmental science, cultural anthropology etc.' (Shasō Gakkai n.d.-a) – truly a wide variety!

12   In 2011, I was told that the organization had a total of 555 members, including approximately 150 shrines and 10 Buddhist temples (interview, September 2011).

13   For clarity's sake, this is the same character as the one used for 'shrine' (*jinja, yashiro*) and 'society' (*shakai*), also pronounced as *mori* ('forest') in the past.

14   On the appropriation of Ryukyu worship traditions as 'original Shinto' or 'the primordial shape of Japanese religions', see Chapter 6.

Chapter 6

1   The other two are Tenkawa Jinja in Nara Prefecture, a 'spiritual' site popular among New Age adherents, and the shrines of Kumano in Wakayama Prefecture.

2   Ironically, these are the very practices that are considered ecologically beneficial by today's *satoyama* conservationists. Although a number of Shinto scholars have argued that *chinju no mori* are of environmental importance because they have been left relatively untouched for centuries, in reality many 'sacred forests' have less species diversity than surrounding landscapes (e.g. Nakayama et al. 1996). If carried out in moderation, some (agri)cultural practices actually contribute to biodiversity, as scientists of *satoyama* have pointed out (e.g. Takeuchi et al. 2003).

3   Data provided by the World Bank; see http://data.worldbank.org/indicator/AG.LND.FRST.ZS (accessed 31 August 2016).

4   Other scholars have criticized this idealization of the Jōmon period and disputed the view that the worship of natural elements in forests constitutes the origins of Shinto. Rather than the Jōmon period, they consider the subsequent Yayoi period to have been foundational. Those who trace Shinto back to the Yayoi period typically point to its intimate connection with rice cultivation, which is seen as an essential characteristic of Japanese civilization, and with the imperial institution. Not only local *matsuri* but also imperial rituals are said to have been originally connected with rice cultivation and are full of agricultural symbolism (Ohnuki-Tierney 1993: 44–62). For an analysis of the Jōmon versus Yayoi debate, see Rots (2013a: 233–236).

5   As the title of his work (*Par-delà nature et culture*) suggests, Philippe Descola is one of a number of contemporary scholars who have problematized the nature-culture dichotomy; drawing on his field research in the Amazon region, he has argued that this dichotomy is not at all universally shared. Instead, Descola argues that all

belief systems can be categorized into four basic models based on the ways in which humans relate to, and imagine, non-human Others. He refers to these as 'the four ontologies'. The first, 'animism', is characterized by a 'resemblance of interiorities' and a 'difference of physicalities' (e.g. an animal has a different physical shape, yet its 'interiority', or spirit, constitutes continuity with humans). This is contrasted with 'totemism' (resemblance of interiorities and resemblance of physicalities), 'naturalism' (difference of interiorities and resemblance of physicalities) and 'analogism' (difference of interiorities and difference of physicalities). See Descola (2005).

6 These terms are not translated, but transcribed in *katakana*, which indicates that they are foreign loanwords.

7 Kuroda Toshio argued that the ancient imperial cult and mythology were basically a Japanese adaptation of the Chinese system, whereas Shinto is largely a (pre)modern invention (Kuroda 1981). Somewhat differently, Mark Teeuwen has argued that modern Shinto has developed out of medieval Buddhist *shinbutsu* traditions, rather than the ancient imperial cult (2007).

8 However, some have expressed scepticism concerning the supposedly ancient character of *shinboku* worship. Rambelli, for instance, has argued that 'it is essentially a modern phenomenon involving either trees planted by modern emperors (Meiji and Hirohito) or a rediscovery of certain trees that might serve the purpose to represent an "ancestral" Shinto animism centering on tree cults' (2007: 140).

9 Isabelle Prochaska writes that not all *utaki* were turned into shrines: from the more than 900 registered *utaki*, 60 were turned into village shrines, and 150 into smaller shrines. *Torii* gates were placed in front of them, Amaterasu was enshrined as the main deity (alongside the local deities), and new priests were ordained. Thus, the Okinawan *utaki*-turned-shrines were incorporated into the ideological state apparatus. In addition, some new shrines were constructed (or planned) – most notably, a shrine was built in the Shuri castle, the former centre of Ryukyu royal power. Meanwhile, however, *yuta* (Okinawan spirit mediums) were severely persecuted (Prochaska-Meyer 2013: 58–59).

10 I.e. 495 ha: more than 40 times its current size. I am not sure what Ueda's source is. This may have been the total size of the lands belonging to the shrine at some point in history, but in all likelihood that included fields and rice paddies as well as woodland. Incidentally, Ueda speaks of '4,950,000 km^2', but that must be a mistake; I assume he means 4,950,000 m^2, which equals 4.95 km^2.

11 The term *genfūkei* may be translated as 'original landscape'. It does not only apply to the physical landscape but also to mental notions of primordial space. As such, it is similar to the German concept *Urlandschaft* (of which it may have been a translation), which not only has physical connotations but is also associated with early memories, as well as notions of nationhood.

12 Interestingly, Tadasu no Mori was here referred to as a *shin'en*: a shrine garden. The association of shrines with 'natural' forests – as opposed to 'artificial' parks and gardens – typical of contemporary discourse apparently was not yet common. Not coincidentally, at the time the newly designed park-like approach to the Inner Shrine in Ise was also referred to as *shin'en*.

13 On 29 April 2010, the 'Tadasu no Mori citizens tree-planting ceremony' (*Tadasu no Mori shimin shokujusai*) took place for the twentieth time. The trees planted by the volunteers (among whom were many young children and their parents) were *mukunoki*, *enoki* and *keyaki* (which, as we have seen, are common in Tadasu no Mori), as well as the less common *momiji* (*Acer palmatum* or Japanese maple;

well-known for its red leaves in autumn) and *katsura* (*Cercidiphyllum japonicum*);
kusunoki and coniferous trees were absent ('Dai nijū kai': 2010).

14 For a short summary of the archaeological research done in Tadasu no Mori, see
    Suzuki (2010). For a more elaborate discussion of the social and ideological functions
    of archaeology in modern Japan, see Mizoguchi (2011).

Chapter 7

1   The same applies to Buddhist priests, most of whom are conservative, as Duncan
    Williams has pointed out (2012). Nevertheless, some of them have found ways to be
    environmentally active without challenging existing social structures. Williams refers to
    this as 'conservative conservationism' (2012: 391), a term which can also be applied to
    the *chinju no mori* movement.
2   For an in-depth study of the politics behind the nuclear power plant in Kaminoseki,
    strategies for convincing local populations and the establishment of an opposition
    movement, see Dusinberre (2012).
3   Some representatives of the Shinto environmentalist paradigm have stated that Shinto
    is holistic and have associated Shinto with 'deep ecology'. Worldmate leader Fukami
    Tōshū, for instance, argued that 'Shinto belongs to deep ecology' (2000: 35). Similar
    associations have been made by Shinto scholar Kamata Tōji (2000: 128–139), as well
    as by Sonoda himself (2007). The idea that there are some fundamental similarities
    between Shinto and deep ecology is also popular among non-Japanese academics, I
    have experienced: several people have asked me about it, at conferences and on other
    occasions (admittedly, the fact that I am affiliated with a Norwegian university while
    doing research on Shinto environmentalism may have played a part!). 'Deep ecology'
    is a radically environmentalist, non-anthropocentric philosophical movement,
    founded by the Norwegian philosopher Arne Næss (1912–2009). Næss outlined seven
    underlying principles for this movement: (1) a relational understanding of organisms
    (i.e. organisms develop in constant interaction with each other) instead of a model
    that perceives of an individual as being surrounded by an environment; (2) ecological
    egalitarianism (i.e. in principle all beings are of equal value); (3) a recognition of
    the biological importance of diversity and symbiosis (rather than the 'survival of
    the fittest' model); (4) an anti-class attitude and a striving for classless diversity; (5)
    struggles against pollution and resource depletion; (6) a preference for 'complexity',
    not for 'complication'; and (7) a focus on local autonomy and decentralization. While
    some of these principles may be in accordance with contemporary Shinto attitudes,
    others most certainly are not – especially when it comes to deep ecology's more
    politically subversive, egalitarian aspects. See Næss ([1973] 1995).
4   The projects at Kamigamo Jinja and Meiji Jingū are discussed in more detail in the
    next chapter.
5   This argument was also made by the head priest of a shrine devoted to the maritime
    deity Ebisu. He professed a concern for environmental issues, opposed the use of
    nuclear energy and was worried about the perceived alienation of humans from their
    natural surroundings, suggesting that Shinto might have an important part to play
    in supporting sustainable behaviour. However, he was one of the few people I met
    who was downright critical of the *chinju no mori* movement. While not opposed to
    forest conservation *per se*, he was critical of what he considered Shinto organizations'

and priests' one-sided focus on shrine forests. According to him, there was a serious lack of interest in other environmental problems, such as the pollution of the oceans (interview, October 2011).

6   As far as I am aware, contrary to some other religious organizations (Dessì 2016: 74–82), Jinja Honchō has no official position on the issue of nuclear power. Considering its close relations with Prime Minister Abe, who is a staunch advocate of nuclear energy (Kingston 2016), it seems unlikely that Jinja Honchō will publicly oppose it. Indeed, as the case of Kaminoseki illustrates, there are powerful actors within Jinja Honchō who are supportive of the nuclear industry. On the other hand, I have met several shrine priests who mentioned that they were against it. Ueda Masaaki, for instance, has stated that Japan should immediately stop using nuclear power (interview, December 2011). Most priests are aware of the fact that this is a divisive issue, however, so it is not much debated in the shrine world.

7   This part of Miyake's talk is not included in the written proceedings, but it is recorded and can be watched on the symposium DVD that is enclosed with the proceedings (Shintō Kokusai Gakkai 2012).

8   Interestingly, a similar project is under development in Morocco, where 600 mosques are equipped with solar energy systems as a means to increase sustainable energy production and raise environmental awareness in the country (Neslen 2016).

9   COP 10 Decision X/32, 'The sustainable use of biodiversity' (§5–9), states that 'the *Satoyama* Initiative [is recognised] as a potentially useful tool to better understand and support human-influenced natural environments for the benefit of biodiversity and human well-being'. Available online: http://www.cbd.int/decision/cop/?id=12298 (accessed 28 October 2016).

10 Sakurai was not the only person I talked to who expressed this opinion. Miyawaki continues to be one of the most famous Japanese ecologists, but his ideas may not be as widely shared as they were in the 1980s and 1990s; he is criticized for his one-sided focus on tree planting as a symbolic practice and for overlooking other aspects of forest maintenance. That said, I have also talked to shrine volunteers and project leaders elsewhere who cited Miyawaki as their great example. Miyawaki is still very popular in some circles, but the biologists and forest scientists whom I have talked with all disagree with his method.

11 *Shichi-go-san* (literally: seven-five-three) is one of modern Shinto's life-cycle rituals. Every year around 15 November, girls aged three or seven and boys aged five pay official visits to their local shrine, together with their parents and other close relatives. They are dressed in their best clothes, attend a ritual ceremony, and get candy or presents.

12 *Sakaki* is an evergreen broad-leaved tree that has a special meaning in Shinto: its branches are often used for shrine ceremonies and offered to the gods.

13 Although it is not widely advertised, the owls' presence is no complete secret, either. In fact, the shrine website contains some descriptions and pictures of the owls (Shiroyama Hachimangū n.d.).

14 As I have experienced on multiple occasions, one of the main concerns of many *satoyama* and *mori-zukuri* projects is the removal of fast-growing 'invader species' (*gairaishu*) such as *sasa*. While such practices may serve to protect biodiversity, there may be other concerns involved as well. Sébastien Boret has reflected upon this same phenomenon in relation to a local environmental movement in Tohoku, which seeks to keep the *satoyama* free from these species (2014: 136–146). According to Boret, 'the invasion of the land by foreign species has become not only a threat

to biodiversity but also a threat to the ideology of the movement in restoring and protecting the *Japaneseness* of their local "natural" environment' (2014: 142). In other words, notions of 'indigenous' and 'invader' species are embedded within a larger discourse on authentic 'Japanese' (as opposed to 'foreign') nature, which is ultimately nationalistic. The same, arguably, can be said about Miyawaki's '*furusato* forest' ideology.

15   This, incidentally, was one of the reasons why Shasō Gakkai set up its forest instructor course – but the participation of priests in this course depends on, again, human resources and financial means.

16   I am not sure to what extent this is correct. Interestingly, Moon writes:

> It is believed that dragonflies (*tonbo*) or fireflies (*hotaru*) can live, during the caterpillar stage, only in unpolluted water (...). This belief is a myth since it is known that slight pollution is necessary for the survival of caterpillars, especially in the case of fireflies. This means that if the water becomes too pure it might threaten the very survival of fireflies. Nevertheless, the existence of the insect has been widely advertized as a symbol of unpolluted nature, i.e. pure water, and the revival of the firefly through various types of anti-pollution campaigns comprises an essential part of many local tourist development plans. (1997: 224)

Unfortunately, however, Moon does not specify what exactly she means by 'pollution'. The widespread use of pesticides, presumably, does *not* contribute to the survival of fireflies (or dragonflies).

Chapter 8

1   Shinto shrines are by no means the only religious organizations that have been active in disaster relief, fundraising and reconstruction activities. Soon after the disaster, Levi McLaughlin published a useful overview article in which he listed a number of activities undertaken by religious organizations in Japan to provide support for the victims of the disaster. These include temples, shrines and churches providing shelter to people who lost their homes; various religious organizations setting up fundraising events and donating money as well as emergency supplies; Christian churches and Buddhist 'new religions' sending volunteers to the affected area and so on (McLaughlin 2011). His list is by no means exhaustive; others have written more extensively on responses by Buddhist temples and new religions (Graf 2016). The disaster has also served as an incentive for the development of new interreligious initiatives: at Tohoku University, for example, a number of academic and religious actors (including representatives of Buddhist, Shinto, Christian and 'new religious' organizations) have joined forces in setting up a practically oriented, trans-denominational research centre devoted to the topic of post-disaster pastoral and spiritual care (Suzuki Iwayumi, interview, May 2013). For a comprehensive overview of religious responses to the 2011 disasters, see Inaba & Kurosaki (2013).

2   The *kami* enshrined at Kamigamo Jinja – Kamo Wake Ikazuchi no Mikoto, a god associated with thunder – is believed to be the son of Tamayorihime and grandson of Kamo Taketsunumi, enshrined at Shimogamo Jinja.

3   Indeed, when I first interviewed Shimogamo Jinja shrine priests about the conservation of Tadasu no Mori (March 2011), I was surprised to find out that

they were not familiar with Afuhi Project at all. This changed later – not only because I told them about it, but also because representatives of both projects gave presentations at a symposium organized by Kamata Tōji in November 2011 – but as far as I know, they do not work together. That may be surprising, considering the two shrines' close historical intertwinement, but it is illustrative of the rivalry and lack of cooperation between them. There is little or no interaction between priests of the two different shrines, I was told by somebody who knows them quite well; once a priest has worked at and is associated with one of the two shrines, he has little or no chance of being employed by the other. This is perhaps illustrative of the factionalism that characterizes Japanese society – not only religious or political organizations but also academia.

4   While most shrines have a *honden* housing the *shintai* (material embodiment of the deity), a *gonden* is less common. Cali and Dougill explain, 'The shrine maintains that the *gonden* is intended for use in an emergency, if anything should happen to the *honden*. (…) [It] is used every twenty-one years to host the *kami* temporarily while the *honden* is being rebuilt' (2013: 115).

5   The symbolic significance of the *futaba aoi* can be traced back to Kamo foundational mythology. For a discussion of these myths, and the sexual symbolism present in them, see Nelson (2000: 73–84).

6   In addition, the plants are used as decoration during some other ceremonies, such as Shimogamo Jinja's preparatory Mikage-sai ceremony. In 2013, I attended both the Mikage-sai (12 May) and the Aoi Matsuri (15 May). On both occasions, I noticed the *futaba aoi* leaves on the hats of the priests, but I was surprised by how they looked: in the hot weather, they did not last very long, and they had withered completely.

7   It is for similar reasons that Jinja Honchō uses classical *kana* spelling in some of its publications (most notably, the *Jinja Shinpō* newspaper).

8   In 2013, it was also possible to order a pot online and have it delivered to one's home. When ordered online, one pot would cost 2,100 yen (approximately 16 euros at the time), including shipping and VAT. Apparently, however, this was no success: on the redesigned website (http://afuhi.jp/; accessed 2 November 2016), this option no longer exists. Some of the previous texts explaining the project's background have also disappeared: the new website has a more professional appearance but fewer contents.

9   Two of the children did not join the ceremony, which was accepted by their teachers. This may have been because they belonged to a different religious organization, or because their parents did not improve of their involvement for ideological reasons (I asked one boy why he could not join, but he told me that he was not sure why; he simply was 'not allowed'). Whatever the reason, it was clear that the children were not enjoying the situation. As I have written elsewhere, some Christian parents do not allow their children to enter shrines or temples on school trips, which can be a cause for embarrassment (Rots 2012: 333). The same applies to members of some new religions (but certainly not all).

10 This plan has been adapted, apparently because not all coastal municipalities could be convinced to participate. The organizers have come to realize that a single forest wall along the entire coast is not feasible, and now focus on various smaller tree-planting projects. Correspondingly, in July 2016 the name 'Great Forest Wall Project' was discarded; the initiative is now called Chinju no Mori Project (*Chinju no mori no purojekuto*), which points to the rather strong links between Miyawaki's nominally secular organization and Jinja Honchō. One of the municipalities where they have been successful is Iwanuma, south of Sendai: in cooperation with the local authorities,

a number of hills have been constructed and planted with a mixture of broad-leaved trees. These hills are meant to serve as memorial sites, and also as places of refuge in case of a future tsunami. For an English-language summary, see Chinju no Mori no Purojekuto (n.d.).

11   As usual, the reality is a bit more complicated. When I talked to local community leaders in Tohoku who had been involved with this project, they suggested that using the seedlings from Meiji Jingū was not fully in accordance with Miyawaki's principles: due to climatological differences, the species of oak and beech growing in the forest of Meiji Jingū were different from those endemic to the Tohoku region, I was told. Therefore, they were somewhat reluctant to use these seedlings – yet they felt that they could not refuse them, so they did end up using some, while striving to grow as many trees locally as possible.

12   I have got the impression that in recent years, the number of foreign visitors coming to Meiji Jingū has increased significantly; in particular, there are more and more Asian tourists from countries such as China, Thailand and Indonesia. This impression was confirmed by some of the Japanese volunteers to whom I have talked. Meiji Jingū's recent international popularity is also illustrated by its *ema* (wooden plaques on which shrine visitors write their wishes). When I visited the shrine in 2013, I saw *ema* not only in Japanese, but also in English, Chinese, Korean, Thai, French, Portuguese and Indonesian – a linguistic diversity I have not seen at any other shrine.

13   There has been little or no controversy related to Meiji Jingū's historical association with the state and its imperial ideology. Some years ago, however, there was a controversy concerning Meiji Jingū's relationship to Jinja Honchō: there were tensions between the two institutions, and Meiji Jingū even left Jinja Honchō in 2004 (Breen & Teeuwen 2010: 205–207), but the two are now reunited. This conflict seems to have been due to disagreements of a financial nature (as well as, presumably, personal antipathies), not to ideological matters.

14   Since the early 2000s, numerous shrines, temples and other 'sacred places' have been reframed and popularized by mass media as places with significant 'spiritual power' called 'powerspots' (*pawāsupotto*, in Japanese transcription). This so-called powerspot boom corresponds to an increase in media interest in shrines, as illustrated by the large numbers of popular books, magazines, guidebooks, websites and TV programs devoted to the topic. It has also been advocated by local authorities and travel agencies for the purpose of attracting 'pilgrims' or 'spiritual tourists' – at various places (e.g. Izumo and Kumano), they have set up 'powerspot tours' and made powerspot pamphlets and maps listing the sites in their locality considered to possess spiritual power (Rots 2013a: 94–97, 2014b; N. Suga 2010).

15   Meiji Jingū houses one of Japan's most-visited powerspots, Kiyomasa's Well (*Kiyomasa no ido*). This is a well in the middle of a small pond in the shrine garden, which predates the shrine itself by several centuries. It is said to have been dug by Katō Kiyomasa (1561–1611), a general in the army of Toyotomi Hideyoshi (1536–1598) responsible for the conquest of parts of Korea. On 24 December 2009, TV celebrity Shimada Shūhei visited the well and declared it a 'powerspot' giving unique 'profit' (*go-riyaku*); that is, wish-fulfilling capacity. Literally overnight, the well became hugely popular, attracting thousands of visitors lining for hours in order to be able to see the well – and have their picture taken in front of it. The priests at Meiji Jingū were reportedly flabbergasted by the numbers of visitors all of a sudden visiting their shrine garden.

16 Ōkuma Shigenobu was an influential Meiji- and Taishō-period intellectual and politician, who served several terms as home minister, minister of foreign affairs and prime minister. He is also the founder of Waseda University, one of Japan's leading private universities.

17 For a more elaborate discussion of Honda's forest theory and plans, see Meiji Jingū Shamusho (1999: 220–228) and Ueda (2015).

18 The shrine's second *torii* gate, which is the biggest wooden *torii* in the country (approximately 12 metres high), is made of a Taiwanese *hinoki* tree said to have been 1,500 years old, felled for this purpose (Meiji Jingū Shamusho 1999: 29–31).

19 There is of course a semantic difference between 'saying a prayer' and 'making a wish', in Japanese as well as in English. In reality, however, the two often overlap – and not only in Shinto. A typical Shinto prayer consists of a small symbolic financial offering (one or a few coins), followed by two bows, two claps, a silent prayer/wish/request/expression of gratitude, and a final bow. Many shrines have signs prescribing people how to pray – apparently, many Japanese people today are not familiar with the procedure. In fact, as John Nelson has demonstrated (2000: 22–52), there is considerable variety when it comes to praying practices, and shrine visitors are generally free to pray pretty much in whatever way they want. In May 2013, when I visited the shrine as part of the Hibiki guided walk, I was in the company of some Indonesian tourists. Although they were Catholic, they took the prayer very seriously, and stood praying in front of the worship hall for several minutes (usually, shrine prayers only last a couple of seconds). The Japanese volunteer who was guiding them was clearly surprised and uncomfortable with the situation – he had never seen such a display of devotion at a shrine!

Chapter 9

1 On the various transformations of Ise in modern and premodern history, see Breen (2015, 2016), Breen & Teeuwen (2017) and Rambelli (2014).

2 In the first centuries after the establishment of the shrines in Ise, *shikinen sengū* were conducted whenever there was a need for reconstruction, not necessarily after a period of twenty years. Sometimes, the period between different *sengū* was shorter; there has also been a long period in the fifteenth and sixteenth century without *sengū*. In the last four centuries or so, most *sengū* took place after a twenty-year period, although there are some exceptions. There have also been additional smaller *sengū* to repair a particular part of the shrine complex. The last *shikinen sengū*, the 62nd in total, took place in 2013.

3 The 2013 *sengū* took eight years to prepare, cost 57 billion yen (nearly 500 million euros), and involved the felling and processing of 14,000 trees (Breen & Teeuwen 2017: 3–5).

4 The combined size of other, smaller shrines in Ise (referred to as *betsugū*; auxiliary shrines) is another 58 ha; the largest of these is Takihara-no-miya (45 ha). In addition, the precincts of subshrines (*sessha* and *massha*) have a combined size of 26 ha (Jingū Shichō Eirinbu n.d.: 3).

5 Pine trees often grow in areas that have experienced much disturbance as a result of human exploitation, such as Ise's *misomayama*. This has some negative consequences, such as erosion. On the other hand, as Anna Tsing points out, these pine forests were

an important part of Japan's hybrid *satoyama* landscapes and were widely appreciated as places where *matsutake* mushrooms – a popular, nowadays expensive delicacy – used to grow. See Tsing (2015: 151–163, 179–187).

6   There is some disagreement, however, about the extent to which broad-leaved trees should be allowed to 'infiltrate' the *hinoki* plantation area. At the Shasō Gakkai conference in Ise (June 2013), there was a short but interesting discussion between the head of the Ise forest management office and a well-known forest ecologist. The latter suggested that the *hinoki* areas of the *kyūikirin* are too close to being a monoculture and not very ecologically stable; according to him, more species diversity should be allowed. The forest manager did not agree and defended his approach by referring to classical forest theory. Clearly, the two had quite different perspectives and interests.

7   'Cute' (*kawaii*) zoomorphic characters are ubiquitous in Japan, and widely employed for promotion purposes. They promote anything ranging from sports events to tourist destinations and from government policies to all sorts of commodities. Even religious institutions now have their own promotional characters, developed in cooperation with local authorities – as exemplified by the cute yellow cat from Shimane Prefecture, *shimaneko* (a contraction of Shimane and *neko*, cat) who wears a hat shaped like the *honden* (main hall) of Izumo Taisha.

8   The accusation is not entirely unfounded: relations between the Chinese Daoist Association and the Chinese government have improved significantly in recent years, and the two cooperate on a number of issues. As James Miller writes, 'the Chinese Daoist Association has embarked upon an ambitious agenda to promote Daoism as China's "green religion"', by which it aims 'to support a nationalist agenda of patriotism and scientific development' (2013: 249) – not unlike Jinja Honchō's attempts to promote Shinto as a 'green religion' in order to serve conservative-nationalist agendas. There are various reasons why Shinto nationalists dislike China: contested wartime memories, Chinese protests to visits to Yasukuni Jinja by leading Japanese politicians and territorial conflicts. Japanese control over contested islands such as the Diaoyu/Senkaku Islands is high on the priority list of Shintō Seiji Renmei and Nippon Kaigi, and the office of Jinja Honchō in Tokyo is decorated with propaganda posters with pictures of these islands (as well as of the Dokdo/Takeshima Islands, which are controlled by the Republic of Korea), stating that they belong to Japan. It is no coincidence that Yamatani Eriko, an ultra-conservative politician supported by Jinja Honchō and Shintō Seiji Renmei (Mullins 2012: 74), is minister in charge of Ocean Policy and Territorial Issues in the current Abe administration. On the role of China in contemporary Japanese nationalist ideology and politics, see Suzuki (2015).

9   The secretary general of ARC is Martin Palmer, a scholar of Chinese religion who has had long-time connections with both the Chinese Daoist Association and Jinja Honchō, and who is one of the actors involved with the 'greening' of these traditions (see for instance ARC n.d.-b; n.d.-c). It is no coincidence that Daoism and Shinto have developed in similar ways in recent years: they have been subject to the same ideas, and their leaders have interacted on various occasions, mediated by Palmer and his ARC. In fact, had it not been for Chinese financial support, the conference at Ise might not have taken place at all.

10 This 'great shrine exhibition' was held at the Tokyo National Museum in the spring of 2013. It included shrine treasures from all over the country, most of which are not usually on display, such as wooden statues of deities. When I visited the exhibition,

the museum was packed. Reportedly, it was a great success. In 2014, the same exhibition was held at the Kyushu National Museum in Fukuoka.

11 The forest of Ise Jingū was one of the three shrine forests visited and studied in 2005 by ARC members, together with WWF and FSC forestry specialists. The other two were Ōmiwa Jinja – which, as we have seen, has become a core symbol of the Shinto environmentalist paradigm, as the mountain constitutes the body of the deity – and Kashihara Jingū, both in Nara Prefecture (ARC n.d.-e). ARC's international 'Religious Forestry Standard' was developed partly in response to these cases. The purpose of setting up this agreement was that 'millions of hectares of religious forest' worldwide should be managed 'ecologically' by 2014 (ARC n.d.-g). It is unclear to what extent this has been achieved, as there is no comprehensive research project that measures 'religious forestry management' worldwide.

12 Likewise, in Jinja Honchō online media texts, the claim that Shinto is a national, ethnic tradition that belongs to the entire nation (symbolically united under the emperor, the living descendant of the sun goddess herself) is literally naturalized by using symbols of the land, landscapes and natural beauty. The Jinja Honchō website, for instance, juxtaposes instructive texts on shrine rituals, festivals and Shinto's ancient history with generic pictures of sunrise, forests, mountains, animals and the sea, implying that shrine buildings, ceremonies and festivals are as much part of the Japanese landscape as mountains and trees, equally 'natural' and eternal. See http://www.jinjahoncho.or.jp/ (accessed 17 November 2016).

13 Ise Grand Shrine, tourist poster, 2011. My translation.

14 The commercial can be watched on the website of Jinja Honchō: http://www.jinjahoncho.or.jp/ (accessed 17 November 2016).

15 Tanaka gave the lecture in Japanese; it was translated into English by his member of staff Iwahashi Katsuji. Presumably, it was on this occasion that Tanaka first visited the shrine at the Brooklyn Botanic Garden and came up with the plan to donate a *mikoshi*.

16 Arguably more problematic is Yamakage's conviction that there is a large Jewish conspiracy for world domination, as outlined in his anti-Semitic writings (e.g. Yamakage 1985) – perhaps unsurprisingly, those books have not been translated in English. When I asked Paul de Leeuw about this aspect of Yamakage Motohisa's thought, he answered that he did not approve of it, but that this was Yamakage's 'personal opinion', independent from his knowledge on spiritual matters.

17 The Facebook group is called 'SHINTO/Tsubaki America Grand Shrine'. It is a public group, in principle open to anybody.

18 For a discussion of some of these groups, see Rots (2015b: 43–46).

REFERENCES

Abe Auestad, Reiko (2014), 'Between History and Heritage: Forests and Mountains as a Figurative Space for Revitalizing the Past in the Works of Ōe Kenzaburō', in Jianhui Liu and Mayuko Sano (eds), *Rethinking 'Japanese Studies' from Practices in the Nordic Region*, 31–51, Kyoto: International Research Center for Japanese Studies.

Abe Yoshiyuki (2008), 'Chiiki katsudō to chinju no mori: Tonbo no satozukuri', *Jinja Shinpō*, 18 August.

Adams, Cassandra (1998), 'Japan's Ise Shrine and Its Thirteen Hundred-Year-Old Reconstruction Tradition', *Journal of Architectural Education*, 52(1): 49–60.

Ambros, Barbara (2008), *Emplacing a Pilgrimage: The Ōyama Cult and Regional Religion in Early Modern Japan*, Cambridge, MA: Harvard University Press.

Anderson, Benedict ([1983] 1991), *Imagined Communities: Reflections on the Origin and Spread of Nationalism*, revised edition, London: Verso.

Andreeva, Anna (2010), 'The Karmic Origins of the Great Bright Miwa Deity: A Transformation of the Sacred Mountain in Premodern Japan', *Monumenta Nipponica* 65(2): 245–71.

Anesaki, Masaharu ([1932] 1973), *Art, Life and Nature in Japan*, Rutland, VT: Charles E. Tuttle Company.

Antoni, Klaus (1995), 'The "Separation of Gods and Buddhas" at Ōmiwa Jinja in Meiji Japan', *Japanese Journal of Religious Studies*, 22(1–2): 139–59.

Antonioli, Valentina (2014), 'San Marino: Inaugurato il primo tempio shintoista d'Europa', *RTV San Marino*, 22 June. Available online: http://www.smtvsanmarino .sm/attualita/2014/06/22/san-marino-inaugurato-primo-tempio-shintoista-europa (accessed 18 November 2016).

Anttonen, Veikko (2000), 'Sacred', in Willi Braun and Russell T. McCutcheon (eds), *Guide to the Study of Religion*, 271–82, London: Continuum.

Aomame Reiko (2010), 'Meiji Jingū: Eien ni tsuzuku chinju no mori o "tsukuru"', in Ōmori Kōji (ed.), *Voice style plus: Mori no baiburu*, 6–19, Tokyo: Voice.

Araki Naoto (2003), 'Zaidan hōjin Tadasu no Mori kenshōkai no katsudō', *Shasōgaku kenkyū*, 1: 44–52.

ARC (n.d.-a), 'About ARC'. Available online: http://www.arcworld.org/about_ARC.asp (accessed 27 June 2016).

ARC (n.d.-b), 'China Daoist Ecology Protection Eight Year Plan'. Available online: http:// www.arcworld.org/projects.asp?projectID=382 (accessed 2 August 2016).

ARC (n.d.-c), 'Daoist monks and nuns to manage sacred mountains'. Available online: http://www.arcworld.org/projects.asp?projectID=257 (accessed 2 August 2016).

ARC (n.d.-d), 'Initial Agreement on Religious Forestry Standards'. Available online: http:// www.arcworld.org/projects.asp?projectID=335 (accessed 17 November 2016).

ARC (n.d.-e), 'Ise Grand Shrines'. Available online: http://www.arcworld.org/projects .asp?projectID=345 (accessed 31 August 2016).

ARC (n.d.-f), 'Japan: Shintos commit to sustainable management of sacred forests'. Available online: http://www.arcworld.org/projects.asp?projectID=161 (accessed 17 November 2016).

ARC (n.d.-g), 'Millions of hectares of religious forest managed ecologically by 2014'. Available online: http://www.arcworld.org/projects.asp?projectID=529 (accessed 17 November 2016).

Asad, Talal (1993), *Genealogies of Religion: Discipline and Reasons of Power in Christianity and Islam*, Baltimore, MD: The Johns Hopkins University Press.

Asad, Talal (2003), *Formations of the Secular: Christianity, Islam, Modernity*, Stanford, CA: Stanford University Press.

Asquith, Pamela J., and Arne Kalland, eds (1997), *Japanese Images of Nature: Cultural Perspectives*, Richmond, VA: Curzon Press.

Avenell, Simon (2012), 'From Kobe to Tōhoku: The Potential and the Peril of a Volunteer Infrastructure', in Jeff Kingston (ed.), *Natural Disaster and Nuclear Crisis in Japan: Response and Recovery after Japan's 3/11*, 53–77, Abingdon: Routledge.

Azegami Naoki (2009), *'Mura no chinju' to senzen Nihon: 'Kokka shintō' no chiiki shakai shi*, Tokyo: Yūshisha.

Azegami, Naoki, and Mark Teeuwen (2012), 'Local shrines and the creation of "State Shinto"', *Religion*, 42(1): 63–85.

Baffelli, Erica, and Ian Reader (2012), 'Editors' Introduction. Impact and Ramifications: The Aftermath of the Aum Affair in the Japanese Religious Context', *Japanese Journal of Religious Studies*, 39(1): 1–28.

Barthes, Roland (1957), *Mythologies*, Paris: Éditions du Seuil.

Baseel, Casey (2015), '1,400-yr-old Kyoto shrine leasing part of its grounds for condo development', *Japan Today*, 10 March. Available online: https://www.japantoday.com/category/arts-culture/view/strapped-for-cash-1400-year-old-kyoto-shrine-leasing-part-of-its-grounds-for-condo-development (accessed 27 October 2016).

BBG Staff (2016), 'Mikoshi: A Portable Shinto Shrine for BBG', *Garden News Blog, Brooklyn Botanic Garden*, 11 April. Available online: http://www.bbg.org/news/a_mikoshi_a_portable_shinto_shrine (accessed 18 November 2016).

Befu, Harumi (1997), 'Watsuji Tetsurō's Ecological Approach: Its Philosophical Foundation', in Pamela J. Asquith and Arne Kalland (eds), *Japanese Images of Nature: Cultural Perspectives*, 106–20. Surrey: Curzon Press.

Befu, Harumi (2009), 'Concepts of Japan, Japanese culture and the Japanese', in Yoshio Sugimoto (ed.), *The Cambridge Companion to Modern Japanese Culture*, 21–37, Cambridge: Cambridge University Press.

Berglund, Björn E. (2008), 'Satoyama, Traditional Farming Landscape in Japan, Compared to Scandinavia', *Japan Review*, 20: 53–68.

Bernard, Rosemarie (n.d.), 'Shinto and Ecology: Practice and Orientations to Nature', *The Forum on Religion and Ecology at Yale*. Available online: http://fore.yale.edu/religion/shinto/ (accessed 18 October 2016).

Berque, Augustin (1986), *Le sauvage et l'artifice: Les Japonais devant la nature*, Paris: Éditions Gallimard.

Berque, Augustin ([1986] 1997), *Japan: Nature, Artifice and Japanese Culture*, translated by Ros Schwartz, Yelvertoft Manor: Pilkington Press.

Berque, Augustin (1992), 'Identification of the Self in Relation to the Environment', in Nancy R. Rosenberger (ed.), *Japanese Sense of Self*, 93–104, Cambridge: Cambridge University Press.

Bhagwat, Shonil A., and Claudia Rutte (2006), 'Sacred Groves: Potential for Biodiversity Management', *Frontiers in Ecology and the Environment*, 4(10): 519–24.

Bhagwat, Shonil A., Nigel Dudley, and Stuart R. Harrop (2011), 'Religious Following in Biodiversity Hotspots: Challenges and Opportunities for Conservation and Development', *Conservation Letters*, 4(3): 234–40.

Blacker, Carmen (1983), 'Minakata Kumagusu: A Neglected Japanese Genius', *Folklore*, 94(2): 139–52.

Blacker, Carmen ([1975] 1986), *The Catalpa Bow: A Study of Shamanistic Practices in Japan*, second edition, London: Unwin Hyman Limited.

Blacker, Carmen ([1994] 2003), 'Shinto and the Sacred Dimension of Nature'. Paper presented at the symposium 'Shinto and Japanese Culture', International Shinto Foundation, London. Available online: http://www.hartford-hwp.com/archives/55a/558.html (accessed 18 October 2016).

Bocking, Brian (2004), 'The Meanings of Shinto', in Christoph Kleine, Monika Schrimpf and Katja Triplett (eds), *Unterwegs: Neue Pfade in der Religionswissenschaft*, 263–80, Munich: Biblion Verlag.

'Boju terasu hikari: Ise Jingū no kyūikirin' (2013), *Mainichi Shinbun*, 4 May.

Boret, Sébastien Penmellen (2014), *Japanese Tree Burial: Ecology, Kinship and the Culture of Death*, Abingdon: Routledge.

Borup, Jørn (2004), 'Zen and the Art of Inverting Orientalism: Buddhism, Religious Studies and Interrelated Networks', in Peter Antes, Armin W. Geertz and Randi R. Warne (eds), *New Approaches to the Study of Religion. Volume 1: Regional, Critical, and Historical Approaches*, 451–87, Berlin: Walter de Gruyter.

Bourdieu, Pierre ([1980] 1990), *The Logic of Practice*, translated by Richard Nice, Cambridge: Polity Press.

Boyd, James W., and Tetsuya Nishimura (2004), 'Shinto Perspectives in Miyazaki's Anime Film "Spirited Away"', *The Journal of Religion and Film*, 8(2). Available online: https://www.unomaha.edu/jrf/Vol8No2/boydShinto.htm (accessed 18 October 2016).

Breen, John (2000), 'Ideologues, Bureaucrats and Priests: On "Shinto" and "Buddhism" in Early Meiji Japan', in John Breen and Mark Teeuwen (eds), *Shinto in History: Ways of the Kami*, 230–51, Richmond, VA: Curzon Press.

Breen, John, ed. (2007), *Yasukuni, the War Dead and the Struggle for Japan's Past*, London: Hurst & Company.

Breen, John (2010a), '"Conventional Wisdom" and the Politics of Shinto in Postwar Japan', *Politics of Religion*, 4(1): 68–82.

Breen, John (2010b), 'Resurrecting the Sacred Land of Japan: The State of Shinto in the Twenty-First Century', *Japanese Journal of Religious Studies*, 37(2): 295–315.

Breen, John (2015), *Shinto monogatari: Ise Jingū no kingendaishi*, Tokyo: Yoshikawa Kōbunkan.

Breen, John, ed. (2016), *Hen'yō suru seichi: Ise*, Kyoto: Shibunkaku.

Breen, John, and Mark Teeuwen (2000a), 'Introduction: Shinto Past and Present', in John Breen and Mark Teeuwen (eds), *Shinto in History: Ways of the Kami*, 1–12, Richmond, VA: Curzon Press.

Breen, John, and Mark Teeuwen, eds (2000b), *Shinto in History: Ways of the Kami*, Richmond, VA: Curzon Press.

Breen, John, and Mark Teeuwen (2010), *A New History of Shinto*. Chichester: Wiley-Blackwell.

Breen, John, and Mark Teeuwen (2017), *A Social History of the Ise Shrines: Divine Capital*, London: Bloomsbury.

Brosseau, Sylvie (2013), 'Satoyama: Le paysage de la polyculture vivrière', in Philippe Bonnin, Nishida Masatsugu and Inaga Shigemi (eds), *Vocabulaire de la spatialité japonaise*, 402–5, Paris: CNRS Éditions.

Brown, Azby (2009), *Just Enough: Lessons in Living Green from Traditional Japan*, Tokyo: Kodansha International.

Bubandt, Nils, and Martijn van Beek, eds (2012), *Varieties of Secularism in Asia: Anthropological Explorations of Religion, Politics and the Spiritual*, Abingdon: Routledge.

Buljan, Katharine, and Carole M. Cusack (2015), *Anime, Religion and Spirituality: Profane and Sacred Worlds in Contemporary Japan*, Sheffield: Equinox Publishing.

Burchardt, Marian, Monika Wohlrab-Sahr, and Matthias Middell, eds (2015), *Multiple Secularities beyond the West: Religion and Modernity in the Global Age*, Berlin: De Gruyter.

Burck, Jan, Franziska Marten, and Christopher Bals (2016), *Climate Change Performance Index: Results 2017*, Bonn: Germanwatch.

Calhoun, Craig, Mark Juergensmeyer, and Jonathan VanAntwerpen, eds (2011), *Rethinking Secularism*, Oxford: Oxford University Press.

Cali, Joseph, and John Dougill (2013), *Shinto Shrines: A Guide to the Sacred Sites of Japan's Ancient Religion*, Honolulu: University of Hawai'i Press.

Casanova, José (1994), *Public Religions in the Modern World*, Chicago, IL: The University of Chicago Press.

Casanova, José (2006), 'Rethinking Secularization: A Global Comparative Perspective', *The Hedgehog Review*, 8(1–2): 7–22.

Cave, David (2001), 'Eliade's Interpretation of Sacred Space and Its Role toward the Cultivation of Virtue', in Bryan Rennie (ed.), *Changing Religious Worlds: The Meaning and End of Eliade*, 235–48, Albany: State University of New York Press.

Certeau, Michel de (1984), *The Practice of Everyday Life*, translated by Steven Rendall, Berkeley: University of California Press.

Chidester, David, and Edward T. Linenthal, eds (1995a), *American Sacred Space*, Bloomington: Indiana University Press.

Chidester, David, and Edward T. Linenthal (1995b), 'Introduction', in David Chidester and Edward T. Linenthal (eds), *American Sacred Space*, 1–42, Bloomington: Indiana University Press.

Chinju no Mori no Purojekuto (n.d.), 'Project summary'. Available online: http://morinoproject.com/english (accessed 11 November 2016).

'Chinju no mori to kodomotachi: Heisei 23 nen seika' (2011), *Jinja Shinpō*, 5 September.

Clammer, John (2004), 'The Politics of Animism', in John Clammer, Sylvie Poirier, and Eric Schwimmer (eds), *Figured Worlds: Ontological Obstacles in Intercultural Relations*, 83–109, Toronto, ON: University of Toronto Press.

Clammer, John (2010), 'Practical Spirituality and Engaged Shinto: Ecology, Peace and the Critique of Modernity in Reformed Japanese Religion', *3D: IBA Journal of Management & Leadership*, 1(2): 97–105.

Corrigan, John (2009), 'Spatiality and religion', in Barney Warf and Santa Arias (eds), *The Spatial Turn: Interdisciplinary Perspectives*, 157–72, London: Routledge.

Cox, Rupert A. (2003), *The Zen Arts: An Anthropological Study of the Culture of Aesthetic Form in Japan*, London: RoutledgeCurzon.

Cronon, William, ed. (1996), *Uncommon Ground: Rethinking the Human Place in Nature*, New York: W. W. Norton.

'Dai nijū kai: Tadasu no Mori shimin shokujusai' (2010), *Tadasu no Mori*, 2, 1 October.

Darlington, Susan M. (2012), *The Ordination of a Tree: The Thai Buddhist Environmental Movement*, Albany: State University of New York Press.

Dauvergne, Peter (1997), *Shadows in the Forest: Japan and the Politics of Timber in Southeast Asia*, Cambridge, MA: MIT Press.

Davis, Winston (1992), *Japanese Religion and Society: Paradigms of Structure and Change*, Albany: State University of New York Press.

Demerath, N. J. III (2007), 'Secularization and Sacralization Deconstructed and Reconstructed', in James A. Beckford and N. J. Demerath III (eds), *The Sage Handbook of the Sociology of Religion*, 57–80, London: Sage Publications.

Descola, Philippe (2005), *Par-delà nature et culture*, Paris: Gallimard.

Dessì, Ugo (2013), *Japanese Religions and Globalization*, Abingdon: Routledge.

Dessì, Ugo (2016), *The Global Repositioning of Japanese Religions: An Integrated Approach*, Abingdon: Routledge.

Doak, Kevin M. (2007), *A History of Nationalism in Japan: Placing the People*, Leiden: Brill.

Domenig, Gaudenz (1997), 'Sacred Groves in Modern Japan: Notes on the Variety and History of Shintō Shrine Forests', *Asiatische Studien: Zeitschrift der Schweizerischen Asiengesellschaft*, 51: 91–121.

Dougill, John (2014), 'Conservation Conference (2)', *Green Shinto*, 26 June. Available online: http://www.greenshinto.com/wp/2014/06/26/conservation-conference-2/ (accessed 28 June 2016).

Dougill, John (2015), 'Save the Trees (Shimogamo)', *Green Shinto*, 18 November. Available online: http://www.greenshinto.com/wp/2015/11/18/save-the-trees-shimogamo/ (accessed 27 October 2016).

Dougill, John (n.d.), 'About', *Green Shinto*. Available online: http://www.greenshinto.com/wp/about/ (accessed 20 November 2016).

Duara, Prasenjit (2015), *The Crisis of Global Modernity: Asian Traditions and a Sustainable Future*, Cambridge: Cambridge University Press.

Dusinberre, Martin (2012), *Hard Times in the Hometown: A History of Community Survival in Modern Japan*, Honolulu: University of Hawai'i Press.

Earhart, H. Byron (1970), 'The Ideal of Nature in Japanese Religion and Its Possible Significance for Environmental Concerns', *Contemporary Religions in Japan*, 11(1–2): 1–26.

Eisenstadt, S. N. (1995), 'The Japanese Attitude to Nature: A Framework of Basic Ontological Conceptions', in Ole Bruun and Arne Kalland (eds), *Asian Perceptions of Nature: A Critical Approach*, 189–214, Richmond, VA: Curzon Press.

Ellen, Roy (2008), 'Forest Knowledge, Forest Transition: Political Contingency, Historical Ecology, and the Renegotiation of Nature in Central Seram', in Michael R. Dove and Carol Carpenter (eds), *Environmental Anthropology: A Historical Reader*, 321–38, Malden: Blackwell Publishing.

Evans, Ann Llewellyn (2001), *Shinto Norito: A Book of Prayers*, Victoria: Trafford Publishing.

Figal, Gerald (1999), *Civilization and Monsters: Spirits of Modernity in Meiji Japan*, Durham: Duke University Press.

Fitzgerald, Timothy (2003), '"Religion" and "the Secular" in Japan: Problems in history, social anthropology, and the study of religion', *Electronic Journal of Contemporary Japanese Studies*, 10 July. Available online: http://japanesestudies.org.uk/discussionpapers/Fitzgerald.html#1 (accessed 28 July 2016).

'Francesco Brigante, First Shinto Priest in San Marino' (2014), *UBrainTV*, 14 January. Available online: http://www.ubraintv.com/watch.php?id=910 (accessed 18 November 2016).

Francis (2015), *Encyclical Letter* Laudato Si' *of the Holy Father Francis on Care for Our Common Home*, Vatican City: Vatican Press. Available online: http://w2.vatican .va/content/dam/francesco/pdf/encyclicals/documents/papa-francesco_20150524 _enciclica-laudato-si_en.pdf (accessed 30 June 2016).

'Fūhyō higai tonde ike: Chinju no mori de aozora ichiba' (2011), *Jinja Shinpō*, 23 May.

Fujimura Ken'ichi (2010), 'Nihon ni okeru kirisutokyō/bukkyō/shintō no shizenkan no hensen: Gendai no kankyō mondai to no kanren kara', *Rekishi chirigaku*, 52–5(252): 1–23.

Fujita Hiromasa, Aoi Akihito, Azegami Naoki, and Imaizumi Yoshiko, eds (2015), *Meiji Jingū izen/igo: Kindai jinja o meguru kankyō keisei no kōzō tenkan*, Tokyo: Kajima Shuppankai.

Fujiwara, Satoko (2013), 'Reconsidering the Concept of Theodicy in the Context of the Post-2011 Japanese Earthquake and Tsunami', *Religion*, 43(4): 499–518.

Fukami, Tōshū (2000), 'Ecology: A Shinto Perspective', in International Shinto Foundation (ed.), *The Kyoto Protocol, The Environment and Shinto: International Symposium Commemorating the Accreditation as NGO of the United Nations*, 33–5, Tokyo: International Shinto Foundation.

Fuyutsuki Ritsu (2010), 'Kasoka to jinja: Shōdoshima no jirei kara', in Ishii Kenji (ed.), *Shintō wa doko e iku ka*, 160–73, Tokyo: Perikansha.

Gagné, Isaac (2017), 'Religious Globalization and Reflexive Secularization in a Japanese New Religion', *Japan Review*, 30: 153–77.

Gebhardt, Lisette (1996), 'Ein Animist wie Du und Ich: Das Animistische als das Japanische in der Japanischen Literatur', *Japanstudien*, 7: 439–47.

Geilhorn, Barbara, and Kristina Iwata-Weickgenannt, eds (2017), *Fukushima and the Arts: Negotiating Nuclear Disaster*, Abingdon: Routledge.

Gill, Sam (1998), 'Territory', in Mark C. Taylor (ed.), *Critical Terms for Religious Studies*, 298–313, Chicago, IL: The University of Chicago Press.

Girard, René (1990), *La violence et le sacré*, Paris: Éditions Albin Michel.

Girardot, N. J., James Miller, and Liu Xiaogan, eds (2001), *Daoism and Ecology: Ways within a Cosmic Landscape*, Cambridge, MA: Harvard University Press.

Global Buddhist Climate Change Collective (2015), 'Buddhist Climate Change Statement to World Leaders 2015', 29 October. Available online: https://gbccc.org/buddhist -climate-change-statement-to-world-leaders-2015/ (accessed 30 June 2016).

Gluck, Carol (1985), *Japan's Modern Myths: Ideology in the Late Meiji Period*, Princeton, NJ: Princeton University Press.

Goodman, David G., and Miyazawa Masanori ([1995] 2000), *Jews in the Japanese Mind: The History and Uses of a Cultural Stereotype*, expanded edition, Lanham: Lexington Books.

Gottlieb, Roger S. (2006), *A Greener Faith: Nature Environmentalism and Our Planet's Future*, Oxford: Oxford University Press.

Graf, Tim (2016), 'Buddhist Responses to the 3.11 Disasters in Japan', in Mark R. Mullins and Koichi Nakano (eds), *Disasters and Social Crisis in Contemporary Japan: Political, Religious, and Sociocultural Responses*, 156–81, Basingstoke: Palgrave Macmillan.

Grapard, Allan G. (1993), *The Protocol of the Gods: A Study of the Kasuga Cult in Japanese History*, Berkeley: University of California Press.

Guthmann, Thierry (2010), *Shintô et politique dans le Japon contemporain*, Paris: L'Harmattan.

Guthmann, Thierry (2017), 'Nationalist Circles in Japan Today: The Impossibility of Secularization', translated by Aike P. Rots, *Japan Review*, 30: 207-25.

Haga Tōru (n.d.), 'Go-aisatsu', *Afuhi Project*. Available online: http://afuhi.jp/organization/ (accessed 9 November 2016).

Hall, Stuart (2001), 'Foucault: Power, Knowledge and Discourse', in Margaret Wetherell, Stephanie Taylor and Simeon J. Yates (eds), *Discourse Theory and Practice: A Reader*, 72–81, London: Sage Publications.

Hamagami Shinsuke (2006), '"Chinju no mori" katsudō hōkoku: Hiraoka Jinja no mori katsudō hōkoku', *Shasōgaku kenkyū*, 4: 68.

Hamashita, Masahiro (2004), 'La forêt vue par Yanagita Kunio', *Diogène*, 3(207): 15–9.

Hardacre, Helen (1986), *Kurozumikyō and the New Religions of Japan*, Princeton, NJ: Princeton University Press.

Hardacre, Helen (1989), *Shintō and the State, 1868–1988*, Princeton, NJ: Princeton University Press.

Harrison, Robert Pogue (1992), *Forests: The Shadow of Civilization*, Chicago, IL: The University of Chicago Press.

Harvey, David (2000), *Spaces of Hope*, Berkeley: University of California Press.

Hasegawa Yasuhiro (2010), 'Chinju no mori', information brochure.

Hasegawa Yasuhiro (2012), 'Toshi ni okeru jinja keidaichi no shasō no hozen shuhō ni kansuru kenkyū: Riyō shutai oyobi kanri shutai kara no saikō', PhD diss., Nagoya City University.

Hasegawa Yasuhiro, and Okamura Yutaka (2011), 'Toshi ni okeru shasō no NPO ni yoru hozen taisei ni tsuite: Nagoya-shi Chikusa-ku Shiroyama Hachimangū no jirei kara', *Shasōgaku kenkyū*, 9: 49–61.

Hasegawa, Yasuhiro, Yutaka Okamura, and Ryō Kōsaka (2010), 'Assessing the Cultural Services of Sacred Forests in the Nagoya Metropolitan Area', *Journal of Landscape Architecture in Asia*, 5: 39–44.

Hatakeyama Shigeatsu (2010), 'Kaki no mori: Sore wa Murone Jinja kara hajimatta', in Shintō Kokusai Gakkai (ed.), *Shintō no tachiba kara sekai no kankyō o tou: Shintō Kokusai Gakkai setsuritsu jūgo shūnen kinen shinpojiumu*, 30–43, Tokyo: Shintō Kokusai Gakkai.

Havens, Norman (2006), 'Shinto', in Paul L. Swanson and Clark Chilson (eds), *Nanzan Guide to Japanese Religions*, 14–37, Honolulu: University of Hawai'i Press.

Hein, Laura, and Mark Selden, eds (2003), *Islands of Discontent: Okinawan Responses to Japanese and American Power*, Oxford: Rowman & Littlefield.

Hendry, Joy (2014), *Science and Sustainability: Learning from Indigenous Wisdom*, New York: Palgrave Macmillan.

Hinton-Braaten, Kathleen (1983), 'Roses and Bonsai: Brooklyn's Botanic Garden', *The Christian Science Monitor*, 5 April.

Hiroi Yoshinori (2011), 'Chinju no mori/enerugii komyuniti no teian', *Jinja Shinpō*, 24 October.

Hiroi Yoshinori (2012), 'Dai jūichi kai nenji nenkai shinpojiumu "chinju no mori to komyunitii-zukuri": Kichō kōen', *Shasōgaku kenkyū*, 11: 14–22.

Hori Iku (2008), 'Watashitachi wa shizen to kyōsei dekiru no ka? *Mononoke hime* no tetsugakuteki kōsatsu', *Journal of Policy Studies*, 28: 99–107.

Horii, Mitsutoshi (2016), 'Critical Reflections on the Religious-Secular Dichotomy in Japan', in Frans Wijsen and Kocku von Stuckrad (eds), *Making Religion: Theory and Practice in the Discursive Study of Religion*, 260–86, Leiden: Brill.

Hoshino Seiji (2012), *Kindai Nihon no shūkyō gainen: Shūkyōsha no kotoba to kindai*, Tokyo: Yūshisha.

Houtman, Dick, and Birgit Meyer, eds (2012), *Things: Religion and the Question of Materiality*, New York: Fordham University Press.

Huber, Toni (1997), 'Green Tibetans: A Brief Social History', in Frank J. Korom (ed.), *Tibetan Culture in the Diaspora*, 103–19, Vienna: Verlag der österreichischen Akademie der Wissenschaften.

Hvass, Svend M. (1999), *Ise: Japan's Ise Shrines, Ancient Yet New*, Copenhagen: Aristo.

Imaizumi, Yoshiko (2013), *Sacred Space in the Modern City: The Fractured Pasts of Meiji Shrine, 1912–1958*, Leiden: Brill.

Inaba Keishen, and Kurosaki Hiroyuki, eds (2013), *Shinsai fukkō to shūkyō*, Tokyo: Akashi Shoten.

Inaga, Shigemi (1999), 'Miyazaki Hayao's Epic Comic Series: *Nausicaä in the Valley of the Wind*: An Attempt at Interpretation', *Japan Review*, 11: 113–28.

Inamori Kazuo (2003), 'Nihon bunka no genten', in Kamo Mioya Jinja (ed.), *Sekai bunka isan: Shimogamo Jinja to Tadasu no Mori*, 6–7, Kyoto: Tankōsha.

Inata Miori (2009), *Mizu to mori no seichi, Ise Jingū*, Tokyo: Random House Kodansha.

Ingold, Tim (2000), *The Perception of the Environment: Essays on Livelihood, Dwelling and Skill*, London: Routledge.

Inoue, Nobutaka (2002), 'The Formation of Sect Shintō in Modernizing Japan', *Japanese Journal of Religious Studies*, 29(3–4): 405–27.

Inoue, Nobutaka (n.d.), 'Worldmate (formerly Cosmomate)', in *Encyclopedia of Shinto*, Kokugakuin University. Available online: http://k-amc.kokugakuin.ac.jp/DM/detail.do?class_name=col_eos&data_id=22894 (accessed 24 November 2016).

International Shinto Foundation, ed. (2000), *The Kyoto Protocol, The Environment and Shinto: International Symposium Commemorating the Accreditation as NGO of the United Nations*, Tokyo: International Shinto Foundation.

Ishihara Shin'ichirō (2009), '"Shintō anime" no tōjō ni yosete', *Jinja Shinpō*, 22 June.

Ishii Kenji, ed. (2010), *Shintō wa doko e iku ka*, Tokyo: Perikansha.

Isomae Jun'ichi (2003), *Kindai Nihon no shūkyō gensetsu to sono keifu: Shūkyō, kokka, shintō*, Tokyo: Iwanami Shoten.

Isomae, Jun'ichi (2012), 'The Conceptual Formation of the Category "Religion" in Modern Japan: Religion, State, Shinto', translated by Galen Amstutz, *Journal of Religion in Japan*, 1(3): 226–45.

Isomae, Jun'ichi, and Sukman Jang (2012), 'The Recent Tendency to "Internationalize" Shinto: Considering the Future of Shinto Studies', *Asiatische Studien: Zeitschrift der Schweizerischen Asiengesellschaft*, 66(4): 1081–97.

Itō Kiminori (2009), 'Chikyū ondanka ron no nani ga mondai ka: "Nisanka tanso ni yoru kikō hendō" e no gigi', *Jinja Shinpō*, 19 January.

Ivy, Marilyn (1995), *Discourses of the Vanishing: Modernity, Phantasm, Japan*. Chicago, IL: The University of Chicago Press.

Iwata Keiji (1993), *Animizumu jidai*, Tokyo: Hōzōkan.

Iwatsuki, Kunio (2008), 'Harmonious Co-Existence between Nature and Mankind: An Ideal Lifestyle for Sustainability Carried Out in the Traditional Japanese Spirit', *Humans and Nature*, 19: 1–18.

James, Simon P. (2004), *Zen Buddhism and Environmental Ethics*, Aldershot: Ashgate.

'Japan-San Marino friendship society, Associazione di Amicizia Nippo-Sammarinese' (2014), *San Marino Fixing.com*, 3 November. Available online: http://www.sanmarinofixing.com/smfixing/san-marino/15655-japan-san-marino-friendship-society-associazione-di-amicizia-nippo-sammarinese.html (accessed 18 November 2016).

Japanese Dutch Shinzen Foundation (n.d.), 'Shinto: Practical Wisdom for the Modern World'. Available online: http://www.shinto.nl/index.htm (accessed 20 November 2016).

Jingū Shichō Eirinbu (n.d.), 'Jingu Sanctuary Forest', information brochure.

Jinja Honchō (n.d.-a), 'Nature, It Is Divine: Message from Shinto', information brochure. Available online: http://www.jinjahoncho.or.jp/en/publications/nature/index.html (accessed 17 November 2016).

Jinja Honchō (n.d.-b), 'What is Shinto?' Available online: http://www.jinjahoncho.or.jp/en/shinto/index.html (accessed 29 July 2016).

Jinja Honchō, ed. (1999), *Shintō no shizenkan ga kyōiku ni hatasu yakuwari*, Tokyo: Jinja Honchō Kenkyūjo.

Jinja Honchō, ed. (2000), '*Shintō to ekorojii' shinpojiumu hōkokusho: Hābādo daigaku sekai shūkyō kenkyūsho shusai*, Tokyo: Jinja Honchō.

Jinja Honchō (2010), *Chinju no mori shinbun*, children's newspaper, Tokyo: Jinja Honchō.

'Jinja to "midori" zadankai' (1982), *Jinja Shinpō*, three parts, 23 August–6 September.

Josephson, Jason Ānanda (2012), *The Invention of Religion in Japan*, Chicago, IL: The University of Chicago Press.

Kagawa-Fox, Midori (2010), 'Environmental Ethics from the Japanese Perspective', *Ethics, Place and Environment*, 13(1): 57–73.

Kalland, Arne (1995), 'Culture in Japanese Nature', in Ole Bruun and Arne Kalland (eds), *Asian Perceptions of Nature: A Critical Approach*, 243–57, Richmond, VA: Curzon Press.

Kalland, Arne (2002), 'Holism and Sustainability: Lessons from Japan', *Worldviews*, 6(2): 145–58.

Kalland, Arne (2008), 'Det religiøse miljøparadigmet og de Andre', *Norsk Antropologisk Tidsskrift*, 19(2–3): 94–107.

Kalland, Arne (2009), *Unveiling the Whale: Discourses on Whales and Whaling*, New York: Berghahn Books.

Kalland, Arne (2012), 'Comment on "Shinto's Sacred Forests"', *PluRel – en blogg om religion og samfunn*. Available online: http://www.tf.uio.no/english/research/projects/goba/project-hub/blog/plurel/shinto/comment-on-shintos-sacred-forests.html (accessed 27 October 2016).

Kalland, Arne, and Pamela J. Asquith (1997), 'Japanese Perceptions of Nature: Ideals and Illusions', in Pamela J. Asquith and Arne Kalland (eds), *Japanese Images of Nature: Cultural Perspectives*, 1–35, Surrey: Curzon Press.

Kamata Tōji (2000), *Shintō to wa nani ka: Shizen no reisei o kanjite ikiru*, Kyoto: PHP Shinsho.

Kamata Tōji (2008), *Seichi kankaku*, Tokyo: Kadokawa Gakugei.

Kamata Tōji (2011), *Gendai shintō ron: Reisei to seitaichi no tankyū*, Tokyo: Shunjusha.

Kamigamo Jinja (n.-d.), 'The World Cultural Heritage Site Kamo Wake-Ikazuchi Jinja (Kamigamo-Shrine)', tourist brochure.

Kamo Mioya Jinja, ed. (2003), *Sekai bunka isan: Shimogamo Jinja to Tadasu no Mori*, Kyoto: Tankōsha.

Kamo Mioya Jinja (2010), *Tadasu no Mori seibi hōkokusho*, Kyoto: Kamo Mioya Jinja.

Kanasaka Kiyonori (2001), 'Ezu/chizu ni arawareta chinju no mori', in Ueda Masaaki and Ueda Atsushi (eds), *Chinju no mori wa yomigaeru: Shasōgaku koto hajime*, 107–32, Kyoto: Shibunkaku Shuppan.

Karlsson, B. G. ([2000] 2013), *Contested Belonging: An Indigenous People's Struggle for Forest and Identity in Sub-Himalayan Bengal*, Abingdon: Routledge.

Kase, Hideaki (n.d.), 'Shintō is the World's New Religion of Ecology', *San Marino Jinja*. Available online: http://www.sanmarinojinja.com/wp-content/uploads/Shinto-is-the-World%E2%80%99s-New-Religion-of-Ecology.pdf (accessed 18 November 2016).

Kasulis, Thomas P. (2004), *Shinto: The Way Home*, Honolulu: University of Hawai'i Press.

Katō, Sadamichi (1999), 'The Three Ecologies in Minakata Kumagusu's Environmental Movement', *Organization and Environment*, 12(1): 85–98.

Kawamura Kazuyo (2012), *Hikari ni mukatte: 3/11 de kanjita shintō no kokoro*, Tokyo: Shobunsha.

Kent, Eliza F. (2013), *Sacred Groves and Local Gods: Religion and Environmentalism in South India*, Oxford: Oxford University Press.

Kerr, Alex (2001), *Dogs and Demons: The Fall of Modern Japan*, London: Penguin Books.

Kimura Masao (2010), 'Ise no jingū kyūikirin no kanri', *Kankyō kenkyū*, 158: 4–12.

Kingston, Jeff, ed. (2012), *Natural Disaster and Nuclear Crisis in Japan: Response and Recovery after Japan's 3/11*, Abingdon: Routledge.

Kingston, Jeff (2016), 'Downsizing Fukushima and Japan's Nuclear Relaunch', in Mark R. Mullins and Koichi Nakano (eds), *Disasters and Social Crisis in Contemporary Japan: Political, Religious, and Sociocultural Responses*, 59–80, Basingstoke: Palgrave Macmillan.

Kirby, Peter Wynn (2011), *Troubled Natures: Waste, Environment, Japan*, Honolulu: University of Hawai'i Press.

Kitagawa, Joseph M. (1987), *On Understanding Japanese Religion*, Princeton, NJ: Princeton University Press.

Kitagawa, Joseph M. (1988), 'Some Remarks on Shintō', *History of Religions*, 27(3): 227–45.

Kjørven, Olav (2014), 'Can There Be Development Without Spiritual Capital?', *The World Post*, 15 July. Available online: http://www.huffingtonpost.com/olav-kjorven/united-nations-development-spiritual-capital-_b_5588436.html (accessed 28 June 2016).

Klein, Naomi (2014), *This Changes Everything: Capitalism vs. the Climate*, London: Allen Lane.

Kleine, Christoph (2013), 'Religion and the Secular in Premodern Japan from the Viewpoint of Systems Theory', *Journal of Religion in Japan*, 2(1): 1–34.

Knight, John (1997), 'A Tale of Two Forests: Reforestation Discourse in Japan and Beyond', *The Journal of the Royal Anthropological Institute*, 3(4): 711–30.

Knott, Kim (2005), *The Location of Religion: A Spatial Analysis*, London: Equinox Publishing.

Kokugakuin Daigaku (2014), '"Tanbo gakkō" kaisai hōkoku', *Kokugakuin Daigaku: Shintō Bunka Gakubu*. Available online: http://www.kokugakuin.ac.jp/shinto/shin05_h26_057.html (accessed 27 October 2016).

Komatsu Kazuhiko (2012), 'Irazu no yama to chinju no mori: Mō hitotsu no kankyōshisō to shite no minzokuchi', in Akimichi Tomiya (ed.), *Nihon no kankyōshisō no kisō: Jinbunchi kara no toi*, 274–94, Tokyo: Iwanami Shoten.

'Konpira yama wa nokotta' (1993), *Tosei Shinpō*, series of ten newspaper articles, 28 September-29 October.

Kōshitsu henshūbu, ed. (2014), '*Chinju no mori' ga sekai o sukuu*, Tokyo: Fusōsha.

Krämer, Hans-Martin (2015), *Shimaji Mokurai and the Reconception of Religion and the Secular in Modern Japan*, Honolulu: University of Hawai'i Press.

Kuroda, Toshio (1981), 'Shinto in the History of Japanese Religion', translated by James C. Dobbins and Suzanne Gay, *Journal of Japanese Studies*, 7(1): 1–21.

Kurosaki Hiroyuki (2013), 'Jinja shintō no katsudō', in Inaba Keishen and Kurosaki Hiroyuki, (eds), *Shinsai fukkō to shūkyō*, 63–87, Tokyo: Akashi Shoten.

Kyocera Corporation (2011), *Kyocera Group Social Contribution Activities 2011*, Kyoto: Kyocera Corporation. Available online: http://global.kyocera.com/ecology/pamphlet/pamphlet2011.pdf (accessed 27 October 2016).

Kyōjō Hiroki (2010), 'Tadasu no Mori no raireki', *Tadasu no Mori Zaidan kaihō*, 1: 2–4.

Lee Choon Ja (Haruko) (2009), 'Higashi Ajia no chinju no mori to sono jizoku: Kankoku no "Chinsan to Tansan shinkō" to Taiwan no "Daijukō shinkō" o chūshin ni', *Shasōgaku kenkyū* 7: 69–83.

Lee Choon Ja (Haruko) (2010), 'Ajia ni okeru chinju no mori to jizoku hozen: Ima naze, mori ka?' in Shintō Kokusai Gakkai (ed.), *Shintō no tachiba kara sekai no kankyō o tou: Shintō Kokusai Gakkai setsuritsu jūgo shūnen kinen shinpojiumu*, 24–9, Tokyo: Shintō Kokusai Gakkai.

Lee Choon Ja (Haruko) (2011), *Kami no ki: Nichi/kan/tai no kyoboku/rōju shinkō*, Hikone: Sanraizu Shuppan.

Leeuw, Paul de (2016), 'Nieuwsbrief Nazomer 2016/Newsletter September 2016', electronic newsletter, 29 August.

Lefebvre, Henri ([1974] 1991), *The Production of Space*, translated by Donald Nicholson-Smith, Malden: Blackwell Publishing.

Lévi-Strauss, Claude (1964), *Mythologiques: Le cru et le cuit*, Paris: Plon.

Levinger, Matthew, and Paula Franklin Lytle (2001), 'Myth and Mobilisation: The Triadic Structure of Nationalist Rhetoric', *Nations and Nationalism*, 7(2): 175–94.

lewallen, ann-elise (2016), *The Fabric of Indigeneity: Ainu Identity, Gender, and Settler Colonialism in Japan*, Albuquerque: New Mexico University Press.

Lewis, Diane (1973), 'Anthropology and Colonialism', *Current Anthropology*, 14(5): 581–602.

Lohmann, Larry (1993), 'Green Orientalism', *The Ecologist*, 23(6): 202–4.

Lovelock, James ([1979] 2000), *Gaia: A New Look at Life on Earth*, Oxford: Oxford University Press.

Macnaghten, Phil, and John Urry (1998), *Contested Natures*, London: Sage.

Madsen, Richard (2011), 'Secularism, Religious Change, and Social Conflict in Asia', in Craig Calhoun, Mark Juergensmeyer and Jonathan VanAntwerpen (eds), *Rethinking Secularism*, 248–69, Oxford: Oxford University Press.

Makino Kazuharu (1994), *Chinju no mori saikō*, Tokyo: Shunjusha.

Marmignon, Patricia (2012), 'Communautés de quartier et associations: Le retour du local après le 11 mars 2011', *Ebisu*, 47: 215–21.

Martinez, Dolores P. (2005), 'On the "Nature" of Japanese Culture, or, Is There a Japanese Sense of Nature?', in Jennifer Robertson (ed.), *A Companion to the Anthropology of Japan*, 185–200, Malden: Blackwell Publishing.

Massey, Doreen (1994), *Space, Place, and Gender*, Minneapolis: University of Minnesota Press.

Masuzawa, Tomoko (2005), *The Invention of World Religions: Or, How European Universalism Was Preserved in the Language of Pluralism*, Chicago, IL: The University of Chicago Press.

Matsutani, Minoru (2013), 'Shinto's *kami* and *jinja* seeking world acceptance', *The Japan Times*, 3 June. Available online: http://www.japantimes.co.jp/life/2013/06/03/language/shintos-kami-and-jinja-seeking-world-acceptance/#.V5iGx_l95aQ (accessed 27 July 2016).

Matsuyama Fumihiko (2009), 'Hajime ni', in Shintō Bunka Kai (ed.), *Shizen to shintō bunka 1: Umi/yama/kawa*, 1–3. Tokyo: Kōbundō.

Maxey, Trent E. (2014), *The 'Greatest Problem': Religion and State Formation in Meiji Japan*, Cambridge, MA: Harvard University Asia Center.

McCormack, Gavan ([1996] 2001), *The Emptiness of Japanese Affluence*, revised edition, Armonk: M. E. Sharpe.

McCurry, Justin (2016), 'G7 in Japan: Concern over world leaders' tour of nationalistic shrine', *The Guardian*, 25 May. Available online: http://www.theguardian.com/world/2016/may/25/g7-japan-world-leaders-tour-shrine-cameron-obama-abe (accessed 1 June 2016).

McCutcheon, Russell (1997), *Manufacturing Religion: The Discourse on Sui Generis Religion and the Politics of Nostalgia*, Oxford: Oxford University Press.

McLaughlin, Levi (2011), 'In the Wake of the Tsunami: Religious Responses to the Great East Japan Earthquake', *Cross Currents*, 61(3): 290–7.

Meadows, Donella H., Dennis L. Meadows, Jørgen Randers, and William W. Behrens III (1972), *The Limits to Growth: A Report for the Club of Rome's Project on the Predicament of Mankind*, New York: Universe Books.

Meiji Jingu (n.d.), 'Nature at Meiji Jingu'. Available online: http://www.meijijingu.or.jp/english/nature/1.html (accessed 14 November 2016).

Meiji Jingū Shamusho, ed. (1999), *'Meiji Jingū no mori' no himitsu*, Tokyo: Shōgakukan.

Miller, James (2013), 'Is Green the New Red? The Role of Religion in Creating a Sustainable China', *Nature and Culture*, 8(3): 249–64.

Miller, James, Dan Smyer Yu, and Peter van der Veer, eds (2014), *Religion and Ecological Sustainability in China*, Abingdon: Routledge.

Minakata Kumagusu ([1912] 1981), 'Jinja gappei hantai iken', in Tsurumi Kazuko, *Minakata Kumagusu: Chikyū shikō no hikakugaku*, 249–89, Tokyo: Kōdansha.

Ministry of Foreign Affairs of Japan (2016), 'Visit to Ise Jingu by Prime Minister Abe and G7 Leaders', 26 May. Available online: http://www.mofa.go.jp/ms/is_s/page4e_000438.html (accessed 27 June 2016).

Miyake Hitoshi (2009), 'Sangaku shinkō to shintō bunka', in Shintō Bunka Kai (ed.), *Shizen to shintō bunka 1: Umi/yama/kawa*, 105–30, Tokyo: Kōbundō.

Miyawaki Akira (1982), 'Chinju no mori o mamore', *Jinja Shinpō*, 15 March.

Miyawaki Akira (2000), *Chinju no mori*, Tokyo: Shinchōsha.

Miyawaki Akira (2013), *Gareki o ikasu mori no bōchōtei: shokuju ni yoru fukkō puranu ga Nihon o sukuu!* Tokyo: Gakken.

Miyazaki, Hayao ([1996] 2009), *Starting Point: 1979–1996*, translated by Beth Cary and Frederik L. Schodt, San Fransisco: VIZ Media.

Miyazawa Masaaki (2014), *Umi yama aida*, documentary film, Nago: Sustainable Investor.

Mizoguchi, Koji (2011), *Archaeology, Society and Identity in Modern Japan*, Cambridge: Cambridge University Press.

Mizohata, Sachie (2016), 'Nippon Kaigi: Empire, Contradiction, and Japan's Future', *The Asia-Pacific Journal*, 14(21): 2.

Moerman, D. Max (2005), *Localizing Paradise: Kumano Pilgrimage and the Religious Landscape of Premodern Japan*, Cambridge, MA: Harvard University Press.

Moon, Okpyo (1997), 'Marketing Nature in Rural Japan', in Pamela J. Asquith and Arne Kalland (eds), *Japanese Images of Nature: Cultural Perspectives*, 221–35, Surrey: Curzon Press.

Mori, Kōichi (1980), 'Yanagita Kunio: An Interpretive Study', *Japanese Journal of Religious Studies*, 7(2–3): 83–115.

Morikawa Minoru (2006), '"Chinju no mori" katsudō hōkoku: "Ōmi no Mori no Kai" no katsudō kara', *Shasōgaku kenkyū*, 4: 66.

Morimoto Yukihiro (2003), 'Tadasu no Mori no shokubutsu to randosukēpu', in Kamo Mioya Jinja (ed.), *Sekai bunka isan: Shimogamo Jinja to Tadasu no Mori*, 142–52, Kyoto: Tankōsha.

Morris, Brian (1987), *Anthropological Studies of Religion: An Introductory Text*, Cambridge: Cambridge University Press.

Morris-Suzuki, Tessa (1998), *Re-Inventing Japan: Time, Space, Nation*, New York: M. E. Sharpe.

Motegi Sadasumi (2010), 'Chinju no mori', in Ōmori Kōji (ed.), *Voice style plus: Mori no baiburu*, 103–11, Tokyo: Voice.

Motoori Norinaga ([1763] 2011), 'Mono No Aware', in James W. Heisig, Thomas P. Kasulis and John C. Maraldo (eds), *Japanese Philosophy: A Sourcebook*, 1176–7, translated by Michael F. Marra, Honolulu: University of Hawai'i Press.

Motozawa Masafumi (2010), 'Mizu no shinkō to matsuri', in Shintō Bunka Kai (ed.), *Shizen to shintō bunka 3: Mizu/kaze/tetsu*, 35–64, Tokyo: Kōbundō.

Mullins, Mark R. (1998), *Christianity Made in Japan: A Study of Indigenous Movements*, Honolulu: University of Hawai'i Press.

Mullins, Mark R. (2012), 'Secularization, Deprivatization, and the Reappearance of "Public Religion" in Japanese Society', *Journal of Religion in Japan*, 1(1): 61–82.

Mullins, Mark R. (2016), 'Neonationalism, Politics, and Religion in Post-disaster Japan', in Mark R. Mullins and Koichi Nakano (eds), *Disasters and Social Crisis in Contemporary Japan: Political, Religious, and Sociocultural Responses*, 107–31, Basingstoke: Palgrave Macmillan.

Mullins, Mark R., and Koichi Nakano, eds (2016), *Disasters and Social Crisis in Contemporary Japan: Political, Religious, and Sociocultural Responses*, Houndmills: Palgrave Macmillan.

Murakami Shigeyoshi (1970), *Kokka shintō*, Tokyo: Iwanami Shoten.

Murota, Yasuhiro (1985), 'Culture and the Environment in Japan', *Environmental Management* 9(2): 105–12.

Næss, Arne ([1973] 1995), 'The Shallow and the Deep, Long-Range Ecology Movement: A Summary', in Alan Drengson and Yuichi Inoue (eds), *The Deep Ecology Movement: An Introductory Anthology*, 3–9, Berkeley: North Atlantic Books.

Nakajima, Michio (2010), 'Shinto Deities that Crossed the Sea: Japan's "Overseas Shrines", 1868–1945', *Japanese Journal of Religious Studies*, 37(1): 21–46.

Nakamura Yōichi (2009), 'Mori to bunmei o kangaeru', in Shintō Bunka Kai (ed.), *Shizen to shintō bunka 2: Ki/hi/tsuchi*, 9–31, Tokyo: Kōbundō.

Nakano Yoshiko (2010), 'Nihon hasshin no kokusai kankyō kyōryoku', in Shintō Kokusai Gakkai (ed.), *Shintō no tachiba kara sekai no kankyō o tou: Shintō Kokusai Gakkai setsuritsu jūgo shūnen kinen shinpojiumu*, 44–54, Tokyo: Shintō Kokusai Gakkai.

Nakayama Yūichirō, Umemoto Shin'ya, Itō Misako, and Kusanagi Tokuichi (1996), 'Ōbako no shuseitaigakuteki kenkyū: Jinja bukkaku keidai ni mirareru waishōkei ōbako no keitaiteki tokusei', *Zassō kenkyū*, 41(4): 332–8.

Nakazawa Shin'ichi ([1992] 2006), *Mori no barokku*, Tokyo: Kōdansha.

Nanami Kō (2010), 'Inochi no mori o tsukuru: Miyawaki Akira shi', in Ōmori Kōji (ed.), *Voice style plus: Mori no baiburu*, 26–37, Tokyo: Voice.

'"Nara kare" kara Tadasu no Mori o mamore!' (2010), *Tadasu no Mori*, 2, October 1.

Narusawa Muneo, ed. (2016), *Nippon Kaigi to Jinja Honchō*, Tokyo: Shūkan Kin'yōbi.

Nelson, John K. (1996), *A Year in the Life of a Shinto Shrine*, Seattle: University of Washington Press.

Nelson, John K. (2000), *Enduring Identities: The Guise of Shinto in Contemporary Japan*, Honolulu: University of Hawai'i Press.

Nelson, John K. (2012), 'Japanese Secularities and the Decline of Temple Buddhism', *Journal of Religion in Japan*, 1(1): 37–60.

Neslen, Arthur (2015), 'Islamic leaders issue bold call for rapid phase out of fossil fuels', *The Guardian*, 18 August. Available online: https://www.theguardian.com/environment/2015/aug/18/islamic-leaders-issue-bold-call-rapid-phase-out-fossil-fuels (accessed 30 June 2016).

Neslen, Arthur (2016), 'Morocco to give 600 mosques a green makeover', *The Guardian*, 5 September. Available online: https://www.theguardian.com/environment/2016/sep/05/morocco-to-give-600-mosques-a-green-makeover (accessed 27 October 2016).

Neumann, Roderick P. (1998), *Imposing Nature: Struggles over Livelihood and Nature Preservation in Africa*, Berkeley: University of California Press.

Nguyen, J. Tuyet (2014), 'Shinto, American natives find common ground: Nature', *My Blog*, 26 November. Available online: https://thewillingtourist.wordpress.com/2014/11/26/shinto-american-natives-find-common-ground-nature/ (accessed 20 November 2016).

NHK (2013), *Ise Jingū: Hikari furu yūkyū no mori ni inochi ga meguru*, TV documentary, *Wildlife*, 117.

Nihon Yunesuko Kyōkai Rengō (n.d.), 'Mirai isan undō katsudō naiyō: 100 nen go no Nihon ni, nokoshitai shizen ga aru. Tsutaetai bunka ga aru.' Available online: http://www.unesco.or.jp/mirai/activities/ (accessed 3 May 2017).

Nitta, Hitoshi (2000), 'Shinto as a "Non-religion": The Origins and Development of an Idea', in John Breen and Mark Teeuwen (eds), *Shinto in History: Ways of the Kami*, 252–71, Richmond, VA: Curzon Press.

Nosco, Peter (1990), *Remembering Paradise: Nativism and Nostalgia in Eighteenth-Century Japan*, Cambridge, MA: Harvard University Press.

NPO Hibiki (n.d.), 'An introduction to NPO Hibiki', information brochure. Available online: http://www.npohibiki.com/pdf/HIBIKI_Brochure_Eng.pdf (accessed 14 November 2016).

Ohnuki-Tierney, Emiko (1993), *Rice as Self: Japanese Identities through Time*, Princeton, NJ: Princeton University Press.

Ohnuki-Tierney, Emiko (2002), *Kamikaze, Cherry Blossoms, and Nationalisms: The Militarization of Aesthetics in Japanese History*, Chicago, IL: The University of Chicago Press.

Okakura, Kakuzō ([1906] 1956), *The Book of Tea*, Rutland, VT: Charles E. Tuttle Company.

Okamoto Takeshi, ed. (2014), *Jinja junrei: Manga/anime de ninki no 'seichi' o meguru*, Tokyo: X-Knowledge.

Ōmiwa Jinja, ed. (2002), *Nihon bunka no naka no shizen to shinkō: Miwayama kara no messēji*, Sakurai: Miwayama Bunka Kenkyūkai.

Ōmori Kōji, ed. (2010), *Voice style plus: Mori no baiburu*, Tokyo: Voice.

Ono Ryōhei (2010), 'Yōgo "chinju no mori" no kindaiteki seikaku ni kansuru kōsatsu', *Randosukēpu kenkyū*, 73(5): 671–4.

Ono, Sokyo (1962), *Shinto: The Kami Way*, in collaboration with William P. Woodard, Boston, MA: Tuttle Publishing.

Orikuchi, Shinobu ([1949] 2012), 'Shinto's Rebirth as a Religion', in James W. Heisig, Thomas P. Kasulis and John C. Maraldo (eds), *Japanese Philosophy: A Sourcebook*, 539–42, translated by Peter E. Nosco, Honolulu: University of Hawai'i Press.

Ormsby, Patricia (2012), 'Good assessment of Shinto', *PluRel – en blogg om religion og samfunn*. Available online: http://www.tf.uio.no/english/research/projects/goba/project-hub/blog/plurel/shinto/shintos-sacred-forests.html (accessed 27 October 2016).

Palmer, Martin, and Victoria Finlay, eds (2003), *Faith in Conservation: New Approaches to Religion and the Environment*, Washington, DC: The World Bank.

Parkes, Graham (1997), 'Voices of Mountains, Trees, and Rivers: Kūkai, Dōgen, and a Deeper Ecology', in Mary Evelyn Tucker and Duncan Ryūken Williams (eds), *Buddhism and Ecology: The Interconnection of Dharma and Deeds*, 111–28, Cambridge, MA: Harvard University Press.

Pedersen, Poul (1995), 'Nature, Religion and Cultural Identity: The Religious Environmentalist Paradigm', in Ole Bruun and Arne Kalland (eds), *Asian Perceptions of Nature: A Critical Approach*, 258–76, Surrey: Curzon Press.

Picken, Stuart D. B. (2002), *Shinto Meditations for Revering the Earth*, Berkeley: Stone Bridge Press.

Prochaska-Meyer, Isabelle (2013), Kaminchu: *Spirituelle Heilerinnen in Okinawa*, Vienna: Praesens Verlag.

Prohl, Inken (2000), *Die 'spirituellen Intellektuellen' und das New Age in Japan*, Hamburg: Gesellschaft für Natur- und Völkerkunde Ostasiens.

Prohl, Inken (2006), *Religiöse Innovationen: Die Shintō-Organisation World Mate in Japan*, Berlin: Reimer.

Public Affairs Headquarters for Shikinen-Sengu (2010), *Grand Shrine of Ise: Spiritual Home of the Japanese People*, Tokyo: Public Affairs Headquarters for Shikinen-Sengu.

Public Affairs Headquarters for Shikinen-Sengu (2013), *Soul of Japan: An Introduction to Shinto and Ise Jingu*, Tokyo: Public Affairs Headquarters for Shikinen-Sengu.

Pungetti, Gloria, Gonzalo Oviedo, and Della Hooke (2012), *Sacred Species and Sites: Advances in Biocultural Conservation*, Cambridge: Cambridge University Press.

Pye, Michael (1981), 'Diversions in the Interpretation of Shintō', *Religion*, 11(1): 61–74.

Pye, Michael (2003), 'Modern Japan and the Science of Religions', *Method & Theory in the Study of Religion*, 15: 1–27.

Rambelli, Fabio (2001), *Vegetal Buddhas: Ideological Effects of Japanese Buddhist Doctrines on the Salvation of Inanimate Beings*, Kyoto: Italian School of East Asian Studies.

Rambelli, Fabio (2007), *Buddhist Materiality: A Cultural History of Objects in Japanese Buddhism*, Stanford, CA: Stanford University Press.

Rambelli, Fabio (2014), 'Floating Signifiers: The Plural Significance of the Grand Shrine of Ise and the Incessant Re-signification of Shinto', *Japan Review*, 27: 221–42.

Rankin, Aidan (2010), *Shinto: A Celebration of Life*, Ropley: O-Books.

Reader, Ian (1990), 'The Animism Renaissance Reconsidered: An Urgent Response to Dr. Yasuda', *Nichibunken Newsletter*, 6: 14–6.

Reader, Ian (2004), 'Ideology, Academic Inventions and Mystical Anthropology: Responding to Fitzgerald's Errors and Misguided Polemics', *Electronic Journal of Contemporary Japanese Studies*, 3 March. Available online: http://www.japanesestudies. org.uk/discussionpapers/Reader.html (accessed 28 July 2016).

Reader, Ian (2012), 'Secularisation, R.I.P.? Nonsense! The "Rush Hour Away from the Gods" and the Decline of Religion in Contemporary Japan', *Journal of Religion in Japan*, 1(1): 7–36.

Reader, Ian (2016), 'Problematic Conceptions and Critical Developments: The Construction and Relevance of "Religion" and Religious Studies in Japan', *Journal of the Irish Society for the Academic Study of Religions*, 3: 198–218.

Reader, Ian, and George J. Tanabe, Jr. (1998), *Practically Religious: Worldly Benefits and the Common Religion of Japan*, Honolulu: University of Hawai'i Press.

Robertson, Jennifer (1988), '*Furusato Japan*: The Culture and Politics of Nostalgia', *International Journal of Politics, Culture, and Society*, 1(4): 494–518.

Robertson, Jennifer (1998), 'It Takes a Village: Internationalization and Nostalgia in Postwar Japan', in Stephen Vlastos (ed.), *Mirror of Modernity: Invented Traditions in Modern Japan*, 209–39, Berkeley: University of California Press.

Rots, Aike P. (2012), 'Ambigious Identities: Negotiating Christianity and "Japaneseness"', in John K. Nelson and Inken Prohl (eds), *Handbook of Contemporary Japanese Religions*, 309–43, Leiden: Brill.

Rots, Aike P. (2013a), 'Forests of the Gods: Shinto, Nature, and Sacred Space in Contemporary Japan', PhD diss., University of Oslo.

Rots, Aike P. (2013b), 'Shizen: la nature', in Philippe Bonnin, Nishida Masatsugu and Inaga Shigemi (eds), *Vocabulaire de la spatialité japonaise*, 444–7, Paris: CNRS Éditions.

Rots, Aike P. (2014a), 'Nature's Blessing, Nature's Wrath: Shinto Responses to the Disasters of 2011', in Roy Starrs (ed.), *When the Tsunami Came to Shore: Culture and Disaster in Japan*, 23–49, Leiden: Global Oriental.

Rots, Aike P. (2014b), 'The Rediscovery of "Sacred Space" in Contemporary Japan: Intrinsic Quality or Discursive Strategy?', in Jianhui Lui and Mayuko Sano (eds), *Rethinking 'Japanese Studies' from Practices in the Nordic Region*, 31–49, Kyoto: International Research Center for Japanese Studies.

Rots, Aike P. (2015a), 'Sacred Forests, Sacred Nation: The Shinto Environmentalist Paradigm and the Rediscovery of *Chinju no Mori*', *Japanese Journal of Religious Studies*, 42(2): 205–33.

Rots, Aike P. (2015b), 'Shinto's Modern Transformations: From Imperial Cult to Nature Worship', in Bryan S. Turner and Oscar Salemink (eds), *Routledge Handbook of Religions in Asia*, 125–43, Abingdon: Routledge.

Rots, Aike P. (2015c), 'Worldwide *Kami*, Global Shinto: The Invention and Spread of a "Nature Religion"', *Czech and Slovak Journal of Humanities*, 3: 31–48.

Rots, Aike P. (2017), 'Public Shrine Forests? Shinto, Immanence, and Discursive Secularization', *Japan Review*, 30: 179–205.

Rots, Aike P., and Mark Teeuwen, eds (2017), *Formations of the Secular in Japan*, special issue of *Japan Review*, 30.

Sagai Tatsuru (2013), 'Kankyō to shintō: Tadasu no Mori no mono kataru', in Waseda Kankyō Juku and Hara Takeshi (eds), *Kyōto kankyōgaku: Shūkyōsei to ekorojii*, 90–7, Tokyo: Fujiwara Shoten.

Said, Edward (1978), *Orientalism*, New York: Pantheon Books.

Saigusa, Nabuko (2005), 'A 150 Year-Project: Meiji Shrine Forest in Central Toky[o]', *Japan for Sustainability Newsletter*, 39. Available online: http://www.japanfs.org/en/news/archives/news_id027807.html (accessed 14 November 2016).

Sakamoto Koremaru (1994), *Kokka shintō keisei katei no kenkyū*, Tokyo: Iwanami Shoten.

Sakurai Haruo (1992), *Yomigaeru mura no kamigami*, Tokyo: Taimeidō.

Sakurai Haruo (2010), *Chiiki jinja no shūkyōgaku*, Tokyo: Kōbundō.

Sakurai Takashi (1999), 'Jissen hōkoku', in Jinja Honchō (ed.), *Shintō no shizenkan ga kyōiku ni hatasu yakuwari*, 75–83, Tokyo: Jinja Honchō Kenkyūjo.

Sakurai Takashi (2009), 'Chinju no mori o shintō kyōka ni dō ikasu ka', *Jinja Shinpō*, 4 May.

Sakurai Takashi, and Sakurai Mayumi (2000), 'Kenkyū happyō "Chinju no mori: sono jissen kara"', in Jinja Honchō (ed.), *'Shintō to ekorojii' shinpojiumu hōkokusho: Hābādo daigaku sekai shūkyō kenkyūsho shusai*, 249–58, Tokyo: Jinja Honchō.

Sandvik, Leif Petter (2011), 'Showcasing Shinto: The Reinvention of Shinto as an Ecological Religion', MA thesis, University of Oslo.

Satō Yamato (2008), 'Kankyō mondai to jinja no torikumi', *Jinja Shinpō*, 18 August.

Schaaf, Thomas, and Cathy Lee (2006), *Conserving Cultural and Biological Diversity: The Role of Sacred Natural Sites and Cultural Landscapes*, Paris: UNESCO.

Schama, Simon (1995), *Landscape and Memory*, New York: A. A. Knopf.

Scheffer, Brett R. et al. (2016), 'The Broad Footprint of Climate Change from Genes to Biomes to People', *Science*, 354(6313): 719.

Schnell, Scott (1999), *The Rousing Drum: Ritual Practice in a Japanese Community*, Honolulu: University of Hawai'i Press.

Schnell, Scott (2006), 'Conducting Fieldwork on Japanese Religions', in Paul L. Swanson and Clark Chilson (eds), *Nanzan Guide to Japanese Religions*, 381–91, Honolulu: University of Hawai'i Press.

Schnell, Scott, and Hiroyuki Hashimoto (2012), 'Revitalizing Japanese Folklore', in Ronald A. Morse (ed.), *Yanagita Kunio and Japanese Folklore Studies in the 21st Century*, 106–13. Kawaguchi: Japanime.

Schwartz, Katrinia S. Z. (2006), *Nature and National Identity after Communism: Globalizing the Ethnoscape*, Pittsburgh: University of Pittsburgh Press.

Scoones, I. (1999), 'New Ecology and the Social Sciences: What Prospects for a Fruitful Engagement?' *Annual Review of Anthropology*, 28: 479–507.

'Seiyōjin ga misogi: Nihon bunka ni fureru kenshū' (2011), *Jinja Shinpō*, 7 November.

Sen Genshitsu (2003), 'Seisan ryokuzui kore wa ga ya', in Kamo Mioya Jinja (ed.), *Sekai bunka isan: Shimogamo Jinja to Tadasu no Mori*, 4–5, Kyoto: Tankōsha.

'Sengū jimae hinoki fukkatsu: 700 nen buri kyūikirin kara shaden yōzai' (2013), *Chūnichi Shinbun*, 24 April.

Shaner, David Edward (1989), 'The Japanese Experience of Nature', in J. Baird Callicott and Roger T. Ames (eds), *Nature in Asian Traditions of Thought: Essays in Environmental Philosophy*, 163–82, Albany: State University of New York Press.

Sharf, Robert H. (1998), 'Experience', in Mark C. Taylor (ed.), *Critical Terms for Religious Studies*, 94–116, Chicago, IL: The University of Chicago Press.

Sharma, Mukul (2012), *Green and Saffron: Hindu Nationalism and Indian Environmental Politics*, Ranikhet: Permanent Black.

Shasō Gakkai (n.d.-a), 'Shasō Gakkai: Nyūkai no go-annai', information brochure, Kyoto: Shasō Gakkai.

Shasō Gakkai (n.d.-b), 'Yōkoso Shasō Gakkai no hōmupēji e'. Available online: http://www.shasou.org/ (accessed 26 October 2016).

Shaw, Daniel M. P. (2009), 'The Way Forward? Shinto and a Twenty-First Century Japanese Ecological Attitude', in S. Bergmann, P. M. Scott, M. Jansdotter Samuelsson and H. Bedford-Strohm (eds), *Nature, Space and the Sacred: Transdisciplinary Perspectives*, 311–30, Farnham: Ashgate.

Shidei Tsunahide (1993), 'Tadasu no Mori no kotonado', in Shidei Tsunahide (ed.), *Shimogamo Jinja: Tadasu no Mori*, 6–31, Kyoto: Nakanishiya Shuppan.

Shimazono, Susumu (2004), *From Salvation to Spirituality: Popular Religious Movements in Modern Japan*, Melbourne: Trans Pacific Press.

Shimazono, Susumu (2007), 'State Shinto and Religion in Post-War Japan', in James A. Beckford and N. J. Demerath III (eds), *The Sage Handbook of the Sociology of Religion*, 697–709, London: Sage Publications.

Shimazono, Susumu (2009), 'State Shinto in the Lives of the People: The Establishment of Emperor Worship, Modern Nationalism, and Shrine Shinto in Late Meiji', *Japanese Journal of Religious Studies*, 36(1): 93–124.

Shimogamo Jinja (n.d.-a), *Sekai bunka isan: Shiseki Tadasu no Mori*, information booklet, Kyoto: Shimogamo Jinja.

Shimogamo Jinja (n.d.-b), *Shimogamo Shrine & Tadasu no Mori*, tourist brochure, Kyoto: Shimogamo Jinja.

Shintō Bunka Kai, ed. (2009a), *Shizen to shintō bunka 1: Umi/yama/kawa*, Tokyo: Kōbundō.

Shintō Bunka Kai, ed. (2009b), *Shizen to shintō bunka 2: Ki/hi/tsuchi*, Tokyo: Kōbundō.

Shintō Bunka Kai, ed. (2010), *Shizen to shintō bunka 3: Mizu/kaze/tsuchi*, Tokyo: Kōbundō.

Shintō Kokusai Gakkai, ed. (2010), *Shintō no tachiba kara sekai no kankyō o tou: Shintō Kokusai Gakkai setsuritsu jūgo shūnen kinen shinpojiumu*, Tokyo: Shintō Kokusai Gakkai.

Shintō Kokusai Gakkai, ed. (2012), *Shinbutsu no shinrin bunka: Kokusai rengō 'kokusai shinrin nen 2011' kinen kokusai shinpojiumu*, Tokyo: Shintō Kokusai Gakkai.

Shirane, Haruo (2012), *Japan and the Culture of the Four Seasons: Nature, Literature, and the Arts*, New York: Columbia University Press.

Shiroyama Hachimangū (n.d.), 'Chie to kōfuku no shisha/mori no tetsugakusha: Fukurō no mori'. Available online: http://www.shiroyama.or.jp/kisetu_info/fukurou.htm (accessed 28 November 2016).

'Shizen to kyōzon shitai: Takaosan fumoto ni sumu gaikokujin ga Kotohira yama kaihatsu hantai undō o tenkai' (1992), *Asahi Taunzu*, 29 February.

Smith, Anthony D. (1999), *Myths and Memories of the Nation*, Oxford: Oxford University Press.

Smith, Huston (1972), 'Tao Now: An Ecological Testament', in Ian G. Barbour (ed.), *Earth Might Be Fair: Reflections on Ethics, Religion, and Ecology*, 62–82, Englewood Cliffs, NJ: Prentice-Hall.

Smith, Jonathan Z. (1987), *To Take Place: Toward Theory in Ritual*, Chicago, IL: The University of Chicago Press.

Smyers, Karen A. (1999), *The Fox and the Jewel: Shared and Private Meanings in Contemporary Japanese Inari Worship*, Honolulu: University of Hawai'i Press.

Snyder, Louis L. (1978), *Roots of German Nationalism*, Bloomington: Indiana University Press.

Snyder, Samuel (2006), 'Chinese Traditions and Ecology: Survey Article', *Worldviews*, 10(1): 100–34.

Soja, Edward W. (1996), *Thirdspace: Journeys to Los Angeles and Other Real-and-Imagined Places*, Malden, MA: Blackwell Publishing.

Sonoda Minoru (1990), *Matsuri no genshōgaku*, Tokyo: Kōbundō.

Sonoda Minoru (1997), *Shintō no sekai*, Tokyo: Kōbundō.

Sonoda Minoru (1998), *Dare demo no shintō: Shūkyō no Nihonteki kanōsei*, Tokyo: Kōbundō.

Sonoda, Minoru (2000), 'Shinto and the Natural Environment', in John Breen and Mark Teeuwen (eds), *Shinto in History: Ways of the Kami*, 32–46, Richmond, VA: Curzon Press.

Sonoda Minoru (2006a), 'Chinju no mori: Sono genzai to igi o tou', essay enclosed with the DVD *Nihon wa mori no kuni*, produced by Sonoda Minoru and Mogi Sakae, Shizuoka: KUNI Director Office, Nihon Bunka Eizō Kenkyūjo.

Sonoda, Minoru (2006b), 'Japan, land of forests: The shrine grove and its meaning today', translation of the essay enclosed with the DVD *Nihon wa mori no kuni*, produced by Sonoda Minoru and Mogi Sakae, Shizuoka: KUNI Director Office, Nihon Bunka Eizō Kenkyūjo.

Sonoda Minoru (2007), 'Nihon ni okeru Deep Ecology to shūkyō bunka', paper presented at the Ise International Forum for Religions, 18 November.

Sonoda Minoru (2009), 'Chinju no mori', in Ōmori Kōji (ed.), *Voice style plus: Kamigami no kuni, Nihon*, 66–72, Tokyo: Voice.

Sonoda Minoru (2010), 'Chinju no mori o sekai e: Mori to mizu – inochi no kamigami', in Shintō Kokusai Gakkai (ed.), *Shintō no tachiba kara sekai no kankyō o tou: Shintō*

Kokusai Gakkai setsuritsu jūgo shūnen kinen shinpojiumu, 9–23, Tokyo: Shintō Kokusai Gakkai.

Sonoda Minoru, and Mogi Sakae (2006), *Nihon wa mori no kuni*, documentary film (DVD), Shizuoka: KUNI Director Office, Nihon Bunka Eizō Kenkyūjo.

Sonoda, Minoru, and Setsuya Tabuchi (2006), 'Transmitting a Made-in-Japan Philosophy of Peace to the World: A Message of Symbiosis from Shinto Shrine Groves', *SPF Voices: Newsletter of the Sasakawa Peace Foundation*, 50(2): 1–4.

Soper, Kate (1995), *What Is Nature? Culture, Politics and the Non-Human*. Oxford: Blackwell.

Sorensen, André, and Carolin Funck, eds (2007), *Living Cities in Japan: Citizens' Movements, Machizukuri and Local Environments*, Abingdon: Routledge.

'Sōshi hyakujūnen kinen jigyō de: Sōrāpaneru setchi' (2011), *Jinja Shinpō*, 5 September.

Sōyō, ed. (2001), *Shintō o shiru hon: Chinju no mori no kamigami e no shinkō no sho*, Tokyo: Ōfū.

Staemmler, Birgit, and Ulrich Dehn, eds (2011), *Establishing the Revolutionary: An Introduction to New Religions in Japan*, Münster: LIT Verlag.

Stalker, Nancy K. (2008), *Prophet Motive: Deguchi Onisaburō, Oomoto, and the Rise of New Religions in Imperial Japan*, Honolulu: University of Hawai'i Press.

Starrs, Roy, ed. (2014), *When the Tsunami Came to Shore: Culture and Disaster in Japan*, Leiden: Global Oriental.

Stensvold, Anne, ed. (2017), *Religion, State and the United Nations: Value Politics*, Abingdon: Routledge.

Stordalen, Terje (2012), 'Rules, Standards, Classics: Bourdieu and Historical Research on Canonicity', paper presented at the Norwegian Academy for Science and Letters, 19 April.

Stuckrad, Kocku von (2003), 'Discursive Study of Religion: From States of the Mind to Communication and Action', *Method & Theory in the Study of Religion*, 15(3): 255–71.

Stuckrad, Kocku von (2013), 'Discursive Study of Religion: Approaches, Definitions, Implications', *Method & Theory in the Study of Religion*, 25(1): 5–25.

Suga, Kōji (2010), 'A Concept of "Overseas Shinto Shrines": A Pantheistic Attempt by Ogasawara Shōzō and Its Limitations', *Japanese Journal of Religious Studies*, 37(1): 47–74.

Suga Naoko (2010), 'Pawāsupotto to shite no jinja', in Ishii Kenji (ed.), *Shintō wa doko e iku ka*, 232–52, Tokyo: Perikansha.

Suganuma Takayuki (2001), 'Chinju no mori wa midori no shima to naru', in Ueda Masaaki and Ueda Atsushi (eds), *Chinju no mori wa yomigaeru: Shasōgaku koto hajime*, 133–54, Kyoto: Shibunkaku Shuppan.

Suganuma Takayuki (2004), 'Ki no rekishi/mori no rekishi: Shokubutsugaku no shiten kara', in Ueda Masaaki (ed.), *Tankyū 'chinju no mori': Shasōgaku e no shōtai*, 83–104, Tokyo: Heibonsha.

Sugimoto, Yoshio (2009), '"Japanese culture": An Overview', in Yoshio Sugimoto (ed.), *The Cambridge Companion to Modern Japanese Culture*, 1–20, Cambridge: Cambridge University Press.

Suzuki, Daisetz T. (1959), *Zen and Japanese Culture*, Princeton, NJ: Princeton University Press.

Suzuki Hisao (2010), 'Tadasu no Mori ni nemuru saishiseki', *Tadasu no Mori*, 2: 2–3.

Suzuki, Shogo (2015), 'The Rise of the Chinese "Other" in Japan's Construction of Identity: Is China a Focal Point of Japanese Nationalism?' *The Pacific Review*, 28(1): 95–116.

Takeuchi, Kazuhiko, Robert D. Brown, Washitani Izumi, Tsunekawa Atsushi, and Yokohari Makoto, eds (2003), *Satoyama: The Traditional Rural Landscape of Japan*, Tokyo: Springer-Verlag.

Tanaka Tsunekiyo (2011), *Shintō no chikara*, Tokyo: Gakken.

Tanaka Tsunekiyo (2014), 'Nihon de, sekai de, shintō ga hatasu yakuwari to wa', in *Kōshitsu* henshūbu (ed.), *'Chinju no mori' ga sekai o sukuu*, 153–89, Tokyo: Fusōsha.

Tanaka, Tsunekiyo, and Katsuji Iwahashi (2014), 'Shinto and Its Impacts on the Japanese View of Nature and Culture', public lecture, Columbia University, 18 November. Available online: https://academiccommons.columbia.edu/catalog/ac:183631 (accessed 29 November 2016).

Taniguchi Hironobu (2016), 'Shin'enkai no katsudō to meiji no Ujiyamada', in John Breen (ed.), *Hen'yō suru seichi: Ise*, 207–36, Kyoto: Shibunkaku.

Taniguchi Masanobu, and Taniguchi Junko (2010), *'Mori no naka' e iku: Hito to shizen no chōwa no tame ni Seichō no Ie ga kangaeta koto*, Tokyo: Nihon Kyōbunsha.

Taylor, Bron (2010), *Dark Green Religion: Nature Spirituality and the Planetary Future*, Berkeley: University of California Press.

Taylor, Charles (2007), *A Secular Age*, Cambridge, MA: Harvard University Press.

Teeuwen, Mark (2002), 'From *Jindō* to Shinto: A Concept Takes Shape', *Japanese Journal of Religious Studies*, 29(3–4): 233–63.

Teeuwen, Mark (2007), 'Comparative perspectives on the emergence of *jindō* and Shinto', *Bulletin of SOAS*, 70(2): 373–402.

Teeuwen, Mark (2017), 'Clashing Models: Ritual Unity vs. Religious Diversity', *Japan Review*, 30: 39–62.

Teeuwen, Mark, and Bernhard Scheid (2002), 'Tracing Shinto in the History of Kami Worship: Editors' Introduction', *Japanese Journal of Religious Studies*, 29(3–4): 195–207.

Tellenbach, Hubertus, and Kimura Bin (1989), 'The Japanese Concept of "Nature"', in J. Baird Callicott and Roger T. Ames (eds), *Nature in Asian Traditions of Thought: Essays in Environmental Philosophy*, 153–62, Albany: State University of New York Press.

Thal, Sarah (2002), 'A Religion That Was Not a Religion: The Creation of Modern Shinto in Nineteenth-Century Japan', in Derek R. Peterson and Darren R. Walhof (eds), *The Invention of Religion: Rethinking Belief in Politics and History*, 100–14, Piscataway: Rutgers University Press.

Thal, Sarah (2005), *Rearranging the Landscape of the Gods: The Politics of a Pilgrimage Site in Japan, 1573–1912*, Chicago, IL: The University of Chicago Press.

Thal, Sarah (2006), 'Shinto: Beyond "Japan's Indigenous Religion"', *Religious Studies Review*, 32(3): 145–50.

The Satoyama Initiative (2016), 'Concept', *IPSI*. Available online: http://satoyama-initiative .org/en/about/ (accessed 28 October 2016).

Thich Nhat Hanh (2008), *The World We Have: A Buddhist Approach to Peace and Ecology*, Berkeley, CA: Parallax Press.

Thomas, Julia Adeney (2001), *Reconfiguring Modernity: Concepts of Nature in Japanese Political Ideology*, Berkeley: University of California Press.

Thomas, Jolyon Baraka (2007), '*Shūkyō Asobi* and Miyazaki Hayao's *Anime*', *Nova Religio*, 10(3): 73–95.

Thomas, Jolyon Baraka (2012), *Drawing on Tradition: Manga, Anime, and Religion in Contemporary Japan*, Honolulu: University of Hawai'i Press.

Thompson, Christopher (2014), 'Are You Coming to the Matsuri? Tsunami Recovery and Folk Performance Culture on Iwate's Rikuchū Coast', *The Asia-Pacific Journal*, 12(5): 2.

Thornber, Karen Laura (2012), *Ecoambiguity: Environmental Crises and East Asian Literatures*, Ann Arbor: The University of Michigan Press.

'Toikake no mori' (2013), *Komagataki*, 1 January.

Tossani, Riccardo (2012), 'Thousand-Year Event: Towards Reconstructing Communities', in Jeff Kingston (ed.), *Natural Disaster and Nuclear Crisis in Japan: Response and Recovery after Japan's 3/11*, 255–76, Abingdon: Routledge.

Totman, Conrad (1989), *The Green Archipelago: Forestry in Pre-Industrial Japan*, Berkeley: University of California Press.

Totoro no Furusato Kikin (n.d.), 'Totoro no mori no shōkai'. Available online: http://www .totoro.or.jp/intro/totoro_forest/index.html (accessed 25 November 2016).

Tsing, Anna Lowenhaupt (2005), *Friction: An Ethnography of Global Connection*, Princeton, NJ: Princeton University Press.

Tsing, Anna Lowenhaupt (2015), *The Mushroom at the End of the World: On the Possibility of Life in Capitalist Ruins*, Princeton, NJ: Princeton University Press.

Tsubaki Grand Shrine of America (n.d.-a), 'Q & A'. Available online: http://www.tsubakishrine .org/qanda/index.html (accessed 20 November 2016).

Tsubaki Grand Shrine of America (n.d.-b), 'Shrine History'. Available online: http://www .tsubakishrine.org/history/index.html (accessed 20 November 2016).

Tsubaki Grand Shrine of America (n.d.-c), 'Tsubaki Kannagara Aikido'. Available online: http://www.tsubakishrine.org/aikido/index.html (accessed 20 November 2016).

Tsurugaoka Hachimangū (n.d.), 'Enju no Kai: Nihonjin no kokoro no genryū o mirai ni'. Available online: http://news.hachimangu.or.jp/dispdtinfo.asp?M_ID=148&C_ID=3 (accessed 27 October 2016).

Tsurumi Kazuko (1981), *Minakata Kumagusu: Chikyū shikō no hikakugaku*, Tokyo: Kōdansha.

Tsushiro, Hirofumi (n.d.), 'Yamakage Shintō', in *Encyclopedia of Shinto*, Kokugakuin University. Available online: http://k-amc.kokugakuin.ac.jp/DM/detail.do?class _name=col_eos&data_id=22895 (accessed 20 November 2016).

Tuan, Yi-Fu (1968), 'Discrepancies between Environmental Attitude and Behaviour: Examples from Europe and China', *Canadian Geographer*, 12(3): 176–91.

Tucker, Mary Evelyn, and Duncan Ryūken Williams, eds (1997), *Buddhism and Ecology: The Interconnection of Dharma and Deeds*, Cambridge, MA: Harvard University Press.

Tucker, Mary Evelyn, and John H. Berthrong, eds (1998), *Confucianism and Ecology: The Interrelation of Heaven, Earth, and Humans*, Cambridge, MA: Harvard University Press.

Tweed, Thomas A. (2006), *Crossing and Dwelling: A Theory of Religion*, Cambridge, MA: Harvard University Press.

Ueda Atsushi (2001), 'Shasō to wa nani ka', in Ueda Masaaki and Ueda Atsushi (eds), *Chinju no mori wa yomigaeru: Shasōgaku koto hajime*, 3–33, Kyoto: Shibunkaku Shuppan.

Ueda Atsushi (2003), *Chinju no mori no monogatari: Mō hitotsu no toshi no midori*, Kyoto: Shibunkaku Shuppan.

Ueda Atsushi (2004a), 'Chinju no mori tte nan darō', in Ueda Masaaki (ed.), *Tankyū 'chinju no mori': Shasōgaku e no shōtai*, 165–93, Tokyo: Heibonsha.

Ueda Atsushi (2004b), '"Irazu no mori" rekishi o mirai e: Toshi keikakugaku no shiten kara', in Ueda Masaaki (ed.), *Tankyū 'chinju no mori': Shasōgaku e no shōtai*, 129–62, Tokyo: Heibonsha.

Ueda Atsushi ([1984] 2007), *Chinju no mori*, Tokyo: Kajima Shuppankai.

Ueda Hirofumi (2015), 'Shinrin bigaku to Meiji Jingū no rin'en keikaku: Kindai Nihon ni okeru ringaku no icchōryū', in Fujita Hiromasa, Aoi Akihito, Azegami Naoki, and Imaizumi Yoshiko (eds), *Meiji Jingū izen/igo: Kindai jinja o meguru kankyō keisei no kōzō tenkan*, 211–30, Tokyo: Kajima Shuppankai.

Ueda, Kenji (1972), 'Shinto', in Ichirō Hori, Fujio Ikado, Tsuneya Wakimoto and Keiji Yanagawa (eds), *Japanese Religion: A Survey By the Agency for Cultural Affairs*, 29–45, Tokyo: Kodansha International.

Ueda Masaaki (2001), 'Shasō no hensen to kenkyū no shimyaku', in Ueda Masaaki and Ueda Atsushi (eds), *Chinju no mori wa yomigaeru: Shasōgaku koto hajime*, 37–68, Kyoto: Shibunkaku Shuppan.

Ueda Masaaki (2003), 'Shimogamo Jinja to Tadasu no Mori', in Kamo Mioya Jinja (ed.), *Sekai bunka isan: Shimogamo Jinja to Tadasu no Mori*, 10–23, Kyoto: Tankōsha.

Ueda Masaaki (2004a), 'Chinju no kamigami: Rekishigaku no shiten kara', in Ueda Masaaki (ed.), *Tankyū 'chinju no mori': Shasōgaku e no shōtai*, 19–43, Tokyo: Heibonsha.

Ueda Masaaki (2004b), 'Chinju no mori no genzō', in Ueda Masaaki (ed.), *Tankyū 'chinju no mori': Shasōgaku e no shōtai*, 5–17, Tokyo: Heibonsha.

Ueda Masaaki, ed. (2004c), *Tankyū 'chinju no mori': Shasōgaku e no shōtai*, Tokyo: Heibonsha.

Ueda Masaaki (2010), 'Tadasu no Mori seibi ni yosete', in Kamo Mioya Jinja (ed.), *Tadasu no Mori seibi hōkokusho*, 1–2, Kyoto: Kamo Mioya Jinja.

Ueda Masaaki (2011), 'Mori to Nihonjin no kokoro: Shizen to ningen no kyōsei no ba, chinju no mori no saisei e', *Culture, Energy and Life*, 95: 3–8.

Ueda Masaaki (2013), *Mori to kami to Nihonjin*, Tokyo: Fujiwara Shoten.

Ueda Masaaki, and Ueda Atsushi, eds (2001), *Chinju no mori wa yomigaeru: Shasōgaku koto hajime*, Kyoto: Shibunkaku Shuppan.

Ueda Masaaki, Ueda Atsushi, Suganuma Takayuki, and Sonoda Minoru, eds (2003), *Mijikana mori no arukikata: Chinju no mori tanbō gaido*, Tokyo: Bun'eidō.

Ueda Masahiro (2006), '"Chinju no mori" katsudō hōkoku: Mukō Jinja no mori katsudō hōkoku', *Shasōgaku kenkyū*, 4: 67.

Ueno, Chizuko (2009), *The Modern Family in Japan: Its Rise and Fall*, Melbourne: Trans Pacific Press.

Umehara Takeshi (1989), 'Animizumu saikō', *Nihon kenkyū*, 1: 13–23.

Umehara Takeshi ([1991] 1995), *Mori no shisō ga jinrui o sukuu*, Tokyo: Shōgakukan.

Umehara, Takeshi (2009), 'Ancient Postmodernism', *New Perspectives Quarterly*, 26(4): 40–54.

University of Oxford (2011), 'Scientists map religious forests and sacred sites', press release, 1 August. Previously available online: http://www.ox.ac.uk/media/news _stories/2011/110108.html (accessed 31 July 2013).

Vallely, Paul (2014), 'History in the making: An unprecedented visit to Ise Jingu, Japan's holiest shrine, to see it rebuilt under the beliefs of the Shinto religion', *The Independent*, 22 June. Available online: http://www.independent.co.uk/news/world/asia/history -in-the-making-an-unprecedented-visit-to-ise-jingu-japan-s-holiest-shrine-to-see-it -rebuilt-9555482.html (accessed 2 June 2016).

Veer, Peter van der (2014), *The Modern Spirit of Asia: The Spiritual and the Secular in China and India*, Princeton, NJ: Princeton University Press.

Vulpitta, Romano (2011), 'Higashi Nihon daishinsai to Nihonjin no shizenkan', *Kamizono*, 6: 25–36.

Warf, Barney, and Santa Arias (2009), 'Introduction: The Reinsertion of Space into the Social Sciences and Humanities', in Barney Warf and Santa Arias (eds), *The Spatial Turn: Interdisciplinary Perspectives*, 1–10, London: Routledge.

Waskow, Arthur (2015), 'Rabbinic Letter on Climate – Torah, Pope, & Crisis Inspire 425+ Rabbis to Call for Vigorous Climate Action', *The Shalom Center*, 29 October. Available online: https://theshalomcenter.org/RabbinicLetterClimate (accessed 30 June 2016).

Watanabe, Chika (2015), 'The Politics of Nonreligious Aid: A Japanese Environmental Ethic in Myanmar', in Philip Fountain, Robin Bush and R. Michael Feener (eds), *Religion and the Politics of Development*, 225–42, Basingstoke: Palgrave Macmillan.

Watanabe, Masao (1974), 'The Conception of Nature in Japanese Culture', *Science*, 183(4122): 279–82.

Watsuji Tetsurō ([1935] 1961), *A Climate: A Philosophical Study*, translated by Geoffrey Bownas, Tokyo: Printing Bureau, Japanese Government.

Watt, Paul B. (2014), 'Shinto at Mt. Miwa Today', paper presented at the 14th International Conference of the EAJS, Ljubljana, 27–30 August.

White, Lynn, Jr. (1967), 'The Historical Roots of our Ecologic Crisis', *Science*, 155(3767): 1203–7.

Williams, Brian (2010), 'Satoyama: The Ideal and the Real', *Kyoto Journal*, 75: 24–9.

Williams, Duncan Ryūken (2012), 'Buddhist Environmentalism in Contemporary Japan', in John K. Nelson and Inken Prohl (eds), *Handbook of Contemporary Japanese Religions*, 373–92, Leiden: Brill.

Witoszek, Nina (1998), *Norske naturmytologier: Fra Edda til økofilosofi*, Oslo: Pax.

Wright, Lucy (2005), 'Forest Spirits, Giant Insects and World Trees: The Nature Vision of Hayao Miyazaki', *Journal of Religion and Popular Culture*, 10(1). Available online: http://www.utpjournals.press/doi/pdf/10.3138/jrpc.10.1.003 (accessed 18 October 2016).

Yamada Masaharu (1995), *Chinju no mori runesansu*, Tokyo: Jupitā Shuppan.

Yamakage Motohisa (1985), *Yudaya no sekai shihai senryoku: Miezaru sekai seifu no kyōi*, Tokyo: Manejimento Sha.

Yamakage, Motohisa ([2000] 2006), *The Essence of Shinto: Japan's Spiritual Heart*, edited by Paul de Leeuw and Aidan Rankin, translated by Mineko S. Gillespie, Gerald L. Gillespie and Komuro Yoshitsuge, Tokyo: Kodansha International.

Yamamura Akiyoshi (2011), *Shintō to Nihonjin: Tamashii to kokoro no minamoto o sagashite*, Tokyo: Shinchōsha.

Yamaori Tetsuo (2001), *Chinju no mori wa naite iru: Nihonjin no kokoro o 'tsukiugokasu' mono*, Tokyo: PHP Kenkyūsho.

Yanagita, Kunio ([1910] 2008), *The Legends of Tono*, translated by Ronald A. Morse, Lanham: Lexington Books.

Yasuda, Yoshinori (1990), 'Animism Renaissance', *Nichibunken Newsletter*, 5: 2–4.

Yasuda Yoshinori (1995), *Mori to bunmei no monogatari: Kankyō kōkogaku wa kataru*, Tokyo: Chikuma Shinsho.

Yasuda Yoshinori (2006), *Isshinkyō no yami: Animizumu no fukken*, Tokyo: Chikuma Shinsho.

Yoshida Hironobu (2003), 'Toshirin to shite no Tadasu no Mori', in Kamo Mioya Jinja (ed.), *Sekai bunka isan: Shimogamo Jinja to Tadasu no Mori*, 135–41, Kyoto: Tankōsha.

Yoshioka Shirō (2010), '"Tonari no Totoro" ni miru "natsukashisa" to "nosutarujia"', *Nihon shisō shi*, 77: 146–65.

Zhong, Yijiang (2016), *The Origin of Modern Shinto in Japan: The Vanquished Gods of Izumo*, London: Bloomsbury.

INDEX

Note: The letter 'n' following locators refers to notes

CPSIA information can be obtained
at www.ICGtesting.com
Printed in the USA
LVHW021942210721
693291LV00004B/106

9 781350 105911